CREATING THE MODERN ARMY: CITIZEN-SOLDIERS AND
THE AMERICAN WAY OF WAR, 1919–1939

STUDIES IN **CMR**
CIVIL-MILITARY RELATIONS

William A. Taylor, Series Editor

Creating the Modern Army

Citizen-Soldiers and the American Way of War, 1919–1939

William J. Woolley

UNIVERSITY PRESS OF KANSAS

Published by the University Press of Kansas (Lawrence, Kansas 66045), which was organized by the Kansas Board of Regents and is operated and funded by Emporia State University, Fort Hays State University, Kansas State University, Pittsburg State University, the University of Kansas, and Wichita State University.

Names: Woolley, William J., author.
Title: Creating the modern Army : citizen-soldiers and the American way of war, 1919–1939 / William J. Woolley.
Description: Lawrence, Kansas : University Press of Kansas, 2022 | Series: Studies in civil-military relations series | Includes bibliographical references and index.
Identifiers: LCCN 2021043908
ISBN 9780700633029 (cloth)
ISBN 9780700633036 (ebook)
Subjects: LCSH: United States. Army—History—20th century. | United States. Army—Organization. | United States. National Defense Act of 1920. | Civil-military relations—United States—History—20th century.
Classification: LCC UA25 .W627 2022 | DDC 355.00973—dc23/eng/20211012
LC record available at https://lccn.loc.gov/2021043908.
British Library Cataloguing-in-Publication Data is available.
Printed in the United States of America

10 9 8 7 6 5 4 3 2 1

The paper used in this publication is acid free and meets the minimum requirements of the American National Standard for Permanence of Paper for Printed Library Materials Z39.48-1992.

Cover image: ROTC officers in front of a University of Florida building with a plaque reading "Headquarters Training Det." University Archives Photograph Collection, Special and Area Studies Collections, George A. Smathers Libraries, University of Florida, Gainesville.

To My Family

CONTENTS

William A. Taylor

In *Creating the Modern Army: Citizen-Soldiers and the American Way of War, 1919–1939*, William J. Woolley, previous Victor and Carrie Palmer Chair of Leadership Values, Helen Swift Nielson Professor of Cultural Studies, and long-time professor of history at Ripon College, provides a comprehensive institutional history of the U.S. Army from 1919 to 1939 based on decades of extensive and meticulous research. Woolley demonstrates that leaders, both civilian and military, worked in tandem to craft the modern American army during this formative period of U.S. history. He lucidly shows that the central elements of this modern army—citizen-soldiers, professional officers, branch structure, and industrial armaments—first emerged with the National Defense Act of 1920, coalesced in the two decades that followed, and ultimately remained familiar foundations to the present day.

This excellent study is a unique and pivotal addition to our understanding of the distinct origins of the modern U.S. Army—and its vital relationship to American society from its very design—during the interwar years after World War I and before World War II. This significant interval was an especially critical period for the army, which sought to integrate the concept of a citizen army, deployed successfully by the United States in World War I, into peacetime while transforming the small constabulary career-professional force of previous years into a larger modernized and industrialized military. Throughout this meaningful story, Woolley illuminates the centrality of policy, especially the momentous consequence of crafting a national military policy in the decades prior to passage of the National Defense Act in 1920. He reinforces the dynamic linkages between a government, the military that it forms, and the society within which these changes take place. Most important, Woolley shows that such civil-military relations, while absolutely significant, are rarely uniform. To his credit, he reveals both high hopes for the modern army and hefty frustrations with the accompanying results, ambitious yet somewhat naïve plans beset by the harsh realities of budget cuts fueled by political and social apathy about military matters, and the potential benefits of careful preparation offset by glaring shortcomings in the ultimate outcomes. The result is that Woolley elucidates a critical lesson: militaries are rarely organizations unto themselves; instead, leaders—both civilian and military—must forge and hone them within a particular society, even if they are beset by fits and starts and endless challenges in doing so. Such a complicated process also imbues militaries with their own specific institutional culture, as was the case with the modern U.S. Army.

Military organization is a woefully understudied yet enormously consequential aspect of civil-military relations. This thought-provoking history goes a long way toward rectifying this imbalance and shines a critical light on how a nation crafts its military and why that very process informs not only its marshal prowess but also its social fabric. Woolley tells a worthwhile story and conveys it well. He deftly bares the significance of several of the most essential facets of civil-military relations writ large, namely how a nation organizes its military and the many hindrances of achieving effectiveness when military roles are in constant flux due to political, technological, and social upheavals as well as countless vagaries about the future battlefield for which it must prepare. The end result is that Woolley exposes the delicate balance between the military, the government, and the broader society as each partner exerts influence—at times in concert and sometimes in opposition—when crafting military power. The clear message is that civilian and military leaders dictate policies that shape armies within a specific social milieu. Such was the situation with the National Defense Act of 1920 and the subsequent interwar period; it remains the case today. Overall, *Creating the Modern Army* is a valuable contribution to a nuanced understanding of the vast difficulties yet supreme importance of effective organization, not only for the military itself but also for the government and society that the armed forces seek to protect.

PREFACE

The modern American citizen army as we know it was largely created in the years between the two world wars. The foundations for that structure were laid in the three decades before America's participation in World War I. During that time, a new organizational structure based on a general-staff system was created that essentially transformed the army from what had been primarily an administrative organization into a tactical one while endowing it with centralized leadership. In addition, the military created schools providing various levels of professional education, fitting them into a hierarchical structure corresponding to the needs of an officer at various points in his career. More important, a new generation was taking over the army, officers who accepted the idea that successful leadership in war rested on an acquired professional education rather than on mere personal experience. And, finally, officers in leadership positions increasingly accepted the idea that building a new army could not take place as a series of random developments but needed to be an enterprise guided by a distinct military policy that enjoyed the support of the nation. In short, the earlier period provided many of the elements out of which the modern U.S. citizen army would be built.

Yet the modern American citizen army itself was actually assembled in the 1920s and 1930s, known as the interwar period. It began with the legislative ratification of a long-sought military policy in the National Defense Act of 1920. The act established the concept of a three-part military, with the professional Regular Army at its core, joined in times of emergency by one or both of two citizen components, the National Guard and the Organized Reserve Corps, and provided the basic blueprint for constructing that force. It organized the various professional schools into a single progressive system and carefully defined the jurisdiction of each element. The National Defense Act finished the transformation of the U.S. Army itself into a European-style mass army by completing the creation of the combat branches, which not only guided the further development of those parts of the army under their competence but also took over from the regiment the task of socializing new officers into the culture of military service. Finally, the army began the process of adapting itself to the opportunities and challenges associated with the rapid industrialization of societies. In the interwar period this meant initiating the process of mechanizing firepower and movement. All of these—the citizen army with its three components, the progressive system of professional military education, the branch structure, and the creation of mechanized forces—remain the central features of the American army in the twenty-first century, were created between 1920 and 1939.

A modern army, even one that was as small as the U.S. Army in the interwar period, is a highly complex and multifaceted organization composed of a myriad of different units. Any effort to carry out an encyclopedic history that would chronicle the changes experienced in every element of the army, especially in the detail needed to understand how those changes took place, would end up so massively detailed that no common thread could be seen. Hence, I have restricted this study to examining the development of what I consider to have been the four major characteristics of the modern American army:

1. The creation of the citizen components of the new army.
2. The development of the branches as the structural basis for organizing the army as well as the creation of the means to educate new officers and soldiers about their craft and to socialize them into military culture.
3. The creation of a rationalized and progressive system of professional military education.
4. The initial mechanization of the combat branches.

In addition, the army's development in this period was greatly influenced by its interaction with the government and with American society, so this interaction is discussed as well.

Although change is often best understood by means of a chronological narrative, treating developments in each of these areas together in a single narrative proved impossible. Hence, I have broken this study down into four chronological periods. The introduction covers the period from 1878 to 1920, during which time the primary issue was the creation of a nationally accepted military policy upon which a modern army could be built. That policy was finally established by the National Defense Act of 1920.

Part I then covers 1920–25, when the principal focus was on the creation of a new national army based on the defense act and the development of the civilian components of a citizen army that was the centerpiece of the policy established by the act. The army's experience with this effort, along with its interaction with both the American government and with American society in this early period, was discouraging and disillusioning. This, together with the fact that the work of creating the citizen components was largely complete by 1925, meant that during the next four years the army tended to direct its attention and efforts inward to building its own structure and culture. So, Part II, while continuing the story of the development of the citizen components as well as the army's ongoing relationship with the government, is primarily concerned with the development of the army's branch structure during the years and the development of its system of professional education. In doing this, I have focused only on the four main combat branches of the army—the infantry, the cavalry, the field artillery, and the coast artillery—since they best illustrate the changes being made and were the elements most involved with the development of the new citizen army and with mechanization. Chapter 6, devoted to the infantry, also illustrates the principal means by which branch structures as well as their culture and identity were developed in the 1920s. Chapters 7 and 8 then deal with the histories of the field artillery and the coast artillery, respectively, for the entire twenty-year period. While these branches, especially the coast artillery, underwent important changes in this period, neither was significantly involved with mechanization— the focus of the last section—so it seemed best to treat their stories all at once rather than arbitrarily divide them among the sections.

Part III concentrates on the army in the 1930s and its main concern of the interwar period—mechanization. Issues related to the further development of the citizen components are treated in chapter 10. The final two chapters are then devoted to the two branches most involved with mechanization, the infantry and especially the cavalry. Since the cavalry was most involved with mechanization and responded to it within the framework of its own long-term development, its entire story during the period is told in chapter 12.

This approach means that as a history of the army in this period, this work is scarcely encyclopedic. The stories of the development of the air service (later air corps), then part of the army; the development of the many support services such as the quartermaster corps or the transportation corps so vital to the success of any military operation; and the massive efforts behind the development of mobilization plans that consumed enormous blocks of the General Staff's time and effort are not covered. Fortunately, these aspects of the army's history in this period have been examined elsewhere. Also, this story involves only the experience of officers, especially those in top leadership positions. The U.S. Army was a top-down organization, with the basic changes being the result of decisions coming from its senior leadership. Lower-ranking officers then carried out these decisions. The experience of enlisted men and, especially, noncommissioned officers is a story that has not been told and should be, no matter how challenging it would be to construct. But, as important as all these topics are, they had little to do with the four-part development of the army. The aviators in the air service/corps were focused on establishing the autonomy of their arm as a means of carrying on strategic warfare based on long-range bombing rather than acting as tactical air support for other elements of the army, so they rarely interacted with the soldiers in the ground forces. One notices the virtual absence of any discussion of the air service/corps in the branch-oriented professional military journals of that period. The various service bureaus also had their own stories of change, but theirs are not particularly related to the issues that are central here. With those caveats in mind, it is my hope that this volume will provide a look at how the modern American citizen army was created and how it established itself in a period of almost revolutionary proportions in the ways wars would be fought.

Finally, I would like to acknowledge and express my appreciation to those who were helpful to me in this project over the course of many years. These include John Taylor at the National Archives and Richard Sommers at the archives of the U.S. Army Military History Institute as well as the archivists at the Command and General Staff College and the State Historical Society of Wisconsin. I also wish to acknowledge my indebtedness to J. P. Clark, William A. Taylor, David Silbey, Brian North, Lieutenant Colonel Stephen F. Mowe, Richard Scamehorn, Stephen D. Woolley, and Eric P. Black, who read and offered valuable suggestions on all or part of my manuscript. In addition, I want to acknowledge my thanks to Joyce Harrison, Kevin Brock, Lisa Stallings, and the people at the University Press of Kansas who helped this work make its way to final publication, and to Michael Taber for producing the index. Their contributions made the book a better one, any faults in it are my responsibility. Lastly, I wish to express appreciation for their ongoing encouragement and support to my family—Allen, Pamela, Jennifer, Stephen, Maria, Mindy, Eric, Brent, Michelle, and especially to my wife, Jean, who was my chief proofreader, editor, critic, and cheerleader.

CREATING THE MODERN ARMY: CITIZEN-SOLDIERS AND
THE AMERICAN WAY OF WAR, 1919–1939

Introduction

The Quest for a National Military Policy, 1878–1920

I N THE LAST QUARTER of the nineteenth century, a small number of officers became aware of two major developments that would be of concern to the U.S. Army. The first was the disappearance of the frontier and with it the disappearance of one of the military's major missions, serving as the constabulary force controlling relations between white settlers in the West and Native American residents. The other was recent and dramatic changes in warfare that could affect American security. The officers were especially influenced by the wars fought between 1866 and 1871 that led to the unification of Germany. In these wars Prussia, although smaller and far less prosperous than its two major opponents, Austria-Hungary and France, quickly and decisively defeated each of them. For these officers, the Prussian successes stood in dramatic contrast to the prolonged and excessively bloody slugging match that was the American Civil War. Aware also that the new drives to imperialism also left areas outside of Europe vulnerable, including the United States, they sought to reform the U.S. Army by organizing it along European, and especially German, lines. This meant, in particular, creating a centralized control structure such as a general staff, developing an officer corps that would be professionally educated, and creating a trained reserve force that could be quickly called up in the event of a war.

Two major factors, however, made this seem an almost hopeless task. One was that American public opinion was traditionally antipathetic, if not openly hostile, to regular armies organized by central governments. This attitude was inherited from English experience with standing armies in the seventeenth century under both the Stuart kings and Oliver Cromwell, during which the army was seen as an instrument of despotism and threat to liberty. This attitude was then reinforced by Americans' experience with the British Army immediately before and during the American Revolution. Hence, while those who framed the Constitution accepted the need for a regular army, they hedged it about with safeguards to prevent it from becoming a tool of despotism.

Moreover, well before the Revolution the American colonists had already developed two other forms of military organization based on the principle of citizen-soldiers as alternatives to a standing army. The first of these was the local militia, made up of citizens who maintained arms and underwent some degree of training. Headed by local officers who were often elected, these units were usually sufficient to maintain social order and to defend their communities from threats from Native Americans. The second came in the form of ad-hoc volunteer forces usually formed to meet specific military exigencies. These units were usually recruited in communities by prominent civilians who became their officers. A large number of such units fought in colonial wars and in the Revolution. They also played a major role in the Mexican War (1846–48) and, until conscription was introduced, made up almost entirely the Union and Confederate armies in the Civil War. Similar units, notably the Rough Riders, were still active in the Spanish-American War (1898). During the nineteenth century, civilian leaders of some of these units had received at least the rudiments of military education at a few private colleges, most notably Norwich Academy in Vermont. During and after the Civil War, many regular officers were suitably impressed with the fighting quality of volunteers so that they sought to regularize the volunteer tradition. The Morrill Act of 1862 that created the land-grant university system included a provision requiring these schools to provide some form of military training to students so they might later take on leadership roles in volunteer units if needed.[1]

One major problem for the reformers, then, was that any effort to reorganize the army along German lines would be highly unacceptable to an American public that was not only deeply suspicious of regular armies but also felt that the two homegrown civilian-based alternatives were more than adequate for meeting the nation's needs, especially since an ocean separated the United States from any major European power.

The second major factor facing reformers was conservative resistance from within the army itself. There were two aspects of this. First, until well into the 1890s, much of the army's senior leadership was comprised of officers who had served in the Union army during the Civil War. Many of these officers entered the war as part of volunteer units. As historian J. P. Clark points out, having been virtually self-taught, this generation of officers saw little value in reforms that stressed professional military education. The fact that the Union army had been victorious in the war seemed to vindicate their approach to military leadership to the point that they saw no need to change.[2] The second aspect was that the major political power in the nineteenth-century American army lay with the chiefs of the bureaus, such as the Quartermaster Corps, that supported the army. These senior officers, having lifetime tenure in their posts in Washington, had built up close relations with Congress. As James M. Hewes has observed, "Bureau chiefs in office for life . . . had greater Congressional influence than passing secretaries or line officers."[3] As a result, during the 1800s, the bureaus had become virtually independent fiefdoms within the army, and unsurprisingly, the chiefs were hostile to any reform movement that challenged their position.

The reform movement was initiated by the efforts of one officer, Lieutenant Colonel Emory Upton.[4] One of America's most influential military reformers, Upton, born in 1839, had graduated from West Point in 1861 just in time to participate in the Civil War. In the eastern campaigns, he proved to be a brilliant and courageous officer, becoming a brigadier general of volunteers by the end of the war. Upton was greatly impressed by the fighting quality of the volunteer soldiers in the army but was disgusted by what he saw as the ignorance of many senior volunteer officers. He attributed the latter to both the almost dominating role played by political influence in the selection of senior officers, especially in the state militias, and to the lack of any systematic military education.

After 1865, Upton began to develop a program of reform to address the problems he had seen during the war. He started by developing a new and simplified system of infantry tactics more suitable for volunteer soldiers. This was adopted by the army in 1867. After that he turned his attention to the issue of officer education. In 1875 he convinced General William T. Sherman, then the commanding general of the army, to send him to Europe and Asia to study military systems there. In Europe Upton was particularly impressed by the German army and its rigorous system for the professional education of its officers. Returning to the United States, he wrote a report of his trip, later published as *The Armies of Asia and Europe,* in which, among other things, he lauded the Prussians' progressive military-education system, their general-staff system, and their reserve system.[5] In addition, he proposed his own idea for raising an army based on volunteers, which he called National Volunteers since they would be trained by the Regular Army rather than by what he saw as the heavily politicized state militias. Regular regiments would then contain one or two skeletonized battalions of National Volunteers that, given the popular excitement typical at the beginning of hostilities, would be filled with new volunteer recruits.

Upton had also come to see that America's major military failing was a lack of a distinct military policy to guide the development of its assets. The objective of such a policy should be to have the nation prepared for war before hostilities started. Its major elements would be, first, that the Regular Army was to be free of political influences outside of those provided for in the constitution. Second, the nation's existing military force would be supplemented by volunteer soldiers trained by the Regular Army rather than the state militias. And third, the professional officers would receive a progressive military education to prepare them for each level of command.

Upton's ideas initially attracted little attention even in the army. Few officers saw any purpose in a progressive education system aimed at higher command in what was essentially a frontier constabulary force and in which few could expect to be promoted beyond captain. Frustrated, Upton planned a second book in which he would make his appeal for a modern European-style military policy directly to Americans rather than as a gloss on an official report. The new work, to be called "The Military Policy of the United States from 1775," was to excoriate the nation for never having developed such a policy while advocating his own ideas. Upton, however, died in 1881 before he could finish it himself.[6]

Yet, within a few years of his death, Upton's vision of an American Army led by a new breed of officers who identified themselves primarily as educated military professionals began to attract a growing number of adherents. These men could be called the "new professionals." A small trickle of such officers began to follow Upton in making trips to Germany to study its military system. Initially, the new professionals were just a tiny minority in the army, but their numbers grew, and their influence grew even faster. That influence depended on their organization and their control of powerful positions in the army. Their organization was founded in the new military schools and professional associations that they helped establish in this period. The most important of these organizations was the Military Service Institute, founded in 1879. Headed by General Sherman, the institute gave respectability to the idea of officership in the army as a learned profession, while its organ, the *Journal of the Military Service Institute*, became the major intellectual clearing house of ideas concerning reform. Other new professional associations, such as the Cavalry Association founded in 1885 and the Infantry Society founded in 1893, along with the journals sponsored by these groups, provided the new professionals with additional opportunities to form networks, read the ideas of others, widen their circle, and establish their reputations through publications.

The influence gained by the new professionals by means of their leadership in these associations was then reinforced by their slowly taking control of the Adjutant General's Office. Located close to the office of the secretary of war, the Adjutant General's Office was seen as the premier bureau in the post–Civil War army and the only one concerned with the overall direction of the military. As such it attracted reform-minded officers and, by the 1880s, became a center for institutional change.

By the 1890s, this movement had coalesced to the point that its adherents could begin to articulate a program of reform largely based on Upton's ideas. The elements of this program clustered around the general idea that the Regular Army should be transformed from a western constabulary and garrison force into a small but compact European-style mobile striking force. This would call for a number of major changes, including the reorganization and concentration of the army, then organized around regiments, into tactical units such as divisions and corps; a shift of focus in its leadership structure from administration to strategic direction; the development of a professional, educated officer corps; and the creation of a means by which the limited strength of the peacetime army could be temporarily augmented in time of an emergency by militarily trained civilian reserves.

Progress toward achieving these goals was made in several directions during this decade. In particular, the army began to systematize its professional-education system. In 1890, officers below the rank of major were required to pass a written test before being considered eligible for promotion. To help prepare for this examination, authorities encouraged regiments to create "lyceums" as the basis for an informal junior-officer educational system. At the same time pressure grew for creating more branch schools, such as the older School of Artillery at Fort Monroe, Virginia, while the existing School of Application for Infantry and Cavalry at Fort Leavenworth, Kansas, was gradually upgraded into a more academic staff college. Finally, some officers began to call for the establishment of an Army War College as a counterpart to the recently formed Naval War College.

Thus, in the later 1890s, the new professionals began to feel confident that they had the organization, power, and articulated program necessary to carry out a major reform of the army along Uptonian lines. They were still a distinct minority, but the disaggregated structure of the army and its tradition of quiet loyalty deprived any opposition of a focal point to oppose the reform movement now emanating from the Adjutant General's Office. The reformers, therefore, were far more concerned with congressional and public apathy or even hostility to updating the military. While army leadership could carry out many reforms internally without the sanction of Congress, most major programs would require legislative action. Yet in the previous three decades, the army had enjoyed little success in getting reform measures through Congress. A major effort to make use of the rising war sentiment in 1897 to push through such legislation also foundered.

The cause of the failure was opposition from the increasingly energized National Guard, as the former state militias were now called, which underscored the fact that it would now be necessary for army reformers to take this service into consideration in any plans for further development of a military reform program. As professionals, many officers in the Regular Army had little more than contempt for the Guard. Seen as both the institutional descendent of the American militia tradition and the product of state-centered political patronage, they considered the Guard to be the embodiment of military amateurism. Since such amateurism directly denied the value of the systematically acquired military education that the new professionals considered central, the Guard was anathema to most of the reformers. Finally, as Michael Neiberg points out, regular officers were suspicious of and prejudiced against the democratic character of guard units, with the election of officers and the familiarity inherent when officers and men came from the same community.[7]

This contemptuous view of the National Guard was, in many respects, neither fair nor accurate. While many guard officers did owe their position to patronage, many were also sincere military enthusiasts who sought to be as well trained and professional as time and resources would allow. And while it was still a state organization, the National Guard, as its new name implied, was also acquiring a sense of national identity, which was institutionalized by the creation of the National Guard Association in 1879. Finally, guardsmen saw themselves as the embodiment of the citizen-soldier, a military tradition they considered to be uniquely American, just as many felt that the European-inspired military vision of a professional soldier was distinctly un-American. Thus, in early 1898 the Guard was able to take advantage of its powerful state political backing and of its attractiveness to many in Congress as a truly American fighting force to defeat the army's reform plan, instead winning for itself the reserve role in any significant war in the future. This victory was an educational experience for the new professionals, who now understood the need to work in cooperation with the Guard in developing further reforms.

America's experience with the Spanish-American War precipitated a major surge of military reform. While American arms had been gloriously victorious, the chaos that surrounded the mobilization for the war made clear how unready the nation had been and still was for any significant military emergency. Together with the support of President Theodore Roosevelt and a strong Republican dominance in Congress, military reformers were able to secure a series of major changes in the period between 1901 and 1903 that gave them much of what they wanted. While Roosevelt's secretary of war, Elihu Root, has been given the credit for these improvements, most of the legislation behind them was actually written by the reformers. The so-called Root Reforms included the

Army Reorganization Act of 1901, which allowed for the expansion of the army to 89,000 men and called for the creation of the Army War College, providing the capstone to efforts to create a system of professional education, starting with the regimental lyceum and ending at the War College. The key reform, however, was the General Staff Act of 1903. This measure encompassed a nearly revolutionary restructuring of the army. The existing army had long been largely an administrative organization, providing a variety of military activities associated with controlling the frontier and guarding major coastal harbors, all of which was controlled by the administrative bureaus in Washington. The General Staff Act transformed it into a tactically organized military organization controlled by the General Staff, to which the bureaus themselves would be subordinated. These reforms were made politically possible by the support of the National Guard, which, in turn, got the Efficiency in Militia Act of 1903, providing for the federalization of the Guard in a time of emergency and thereby officially making it the nation's reserve force. Finally, in 1904, at the culmination of the reform process, Root published Upton's *The Military Policy of the United States* as a tribute to the man credited with the vision upon which the entire reform movement was founded.[8]

The Root reforms were both an end of one phase of the army reform movement and the beginning of a new phase. They largely fulfilled the vision of the new professionals, but those aspirations were largely limited to the concerns of the late nineteenth century and the strategic situation created by the Spanish-American War. And now with their agenda largely fulfilled, most of these officers retired from promoting further reforms during their careers.

The new professionals were succeeded by a generation of military reformers who might be called the "young professionals." These officers were largely the product of the new military schools, which gave them a core of similar ideas and created a sense of corporate identity, self-assurance, and superiority sometimes bordering on arrogance. Convinced that they had received the revealed word in modern military matters, they impatiently favored revolutionary over evolutionary change.[9] Inspired also by the publication of Upton's book, the young professionals made the establishment of a national military policy the focal point of their desired revolution. As their influence grew, this effort increasingly became the central long-term concern of reformers within the army's leadership. As with Upton, the young professionals considered the purpose of a military policy was to prepare the nation for war by the systematic arrangement of all military organizations in the country around a single plan for mobilization. Despite the Root reforms, the country's military matters were still handled on a piecemeal basis, with the role of the National Guard as one of the most anomalous of the pieces. This concern for the systematic organization of the nation's military resources became far more acute after the Russo-Japanese War (1904–5). In this conflict, as well as in the earlier Sino-Japanese War (1894–95), a small but well-prepared power quickly defeated a larger but unprepared power. Moreover, in fighting the Russians, the Japanese were able to transport an army over water and still defeat them, a fact that seemed to demonstrate the actual vulnerability of the United States to an invasion by an overseas power. This was followed in the United States by a brief war scare with Japan, provoked by the treatment of Japanese nationals in this country. These events created a concern that the mobile striking force provided for by the Root Reforms would be inadequate in the face of a maritime invasion.[10] Many in the army began to visualize the United States as a wealthy but virtually unarmed plum ripe for the picking by any aggressive major power. For the young professionals, what was now needed was a way by which the country could quickly raise an army of 200,000–400,000 men. Thus, after 1907, the question of how to create a reliably trained reserve force became the central issue of any discussion of a national military policy. This again called into question the issue of the reliability of the National Guard while making the various reserve systems used in Europe, in which men were called to the colors for several years and then returned to civilian life to serve as a trained reserve, increasingly attractive.

This movement began to coalesce with the appointment of Major General Leonard Wood as chief of staff of the army in 1910. Wood was a dynamic, energetic, and highly charismatic figure who was ambitious to bring about dramatic change to the army. This would have made him a natural ally of the young professionals. This alignment, however, was slow in developing. While the major goal of the young professionals was the creation of a national military policy, Wood's interest in that idea was tepid at best. He was, by temperament, far more an independent crusader for projects rather than the creator of systems and organizations that could, finally, restrict his own freedom of action. Hence, rather than establish a comprehensive national military policy, he preferred to create a Council of National Defense, made up of both civilian and military leaders, which would garner political support for his individual ideas for military change.[11]

Wood's initial efforts to go it alone, however, failed. A naïve plan to mobilize support for the creation of a Council of National Defense by releasing to Congress and the press a secret report demonstrating the nation's vulnerability to invasion blew up in his face due to his failure to consult with President William Howard Taft ahead of time.[12] This was followed by an effort to increase the military reliability of the National Guard by further federalization backed by drill pay.[13] This, too, failed when it was derailed by the powerful state adjutants general, who feared loss of control.[14]

Wood's dalliance with the National Guard also strained his relations with the young professionals. They fully shared the Regular Army's lack of confidence in the military value of the Guard, and Wood's failure contributed to a growing consensus among them to abandon the Guard as a reserve force and focus instead on creating a European-style reserve system.[15] Left to themselves, the young professionals at the same time made further progress in defining the elements of their own reform agenda. In addition, the experience gained by working with various aspects of military policy in the General Staff during 1911 increased their sense of confidence that an actual national military policy could be formulated. Thus, by the end of that year, Wood was in danger of being left behind by the reform movement that he was supposed to be leading.

Wood and the young professionals in the General Staff were brought together in 1912 in the face of a sudden political threat to the entire reform program. The threat came primarily from growing hostility to their efforts within the army. One source of this opposition came from the administrative and logistical bureaus, whose accustomed dominance in the army was undercut by the General Staff Act of 1903. Despite the provisions of that law, these offices still retained significant power in Washington. Further resistance came from traditionalists who still made up the bulk of the officer corps. Their major concern was the growing interest in the European-style reserve program. For them, the central and most attractive feature of the old army was that it involved working with long-term and highly trained enlisted men who remained satisfactorily deferential to the officers. The idea of these career soldiers being largely replaced by men enlisted for only a short term for training purposes seemed to imply a new culture that was neither comfortable, rewarding, nor even martial.[16] Active opposition from the traditionalists had largely been muted by the fact that they were disaggregated, voiceless, and traditionally at odds with the bureaus. But the growing evidence of Wood's commitment to a program of far-reaching reform, as well as his own personal arrogance, began to draw these two sources of resistance together, making an effective resistance movement possible if a leader and an issue could be found.

Toward the end of 1911, that leader appeared in the person of the army's adjutant general, Major General Frederick C. Ainsworth. Adjutant general since 1907, he had built a reputation as a reformer by making the administrative activities of the agencies he headed more efficient. In addition, Ainsworth was highly skilled at cultivating good personal relations with congressmen, who thought highly of him. He also deeply resented the fact that the General Staff Act had ended the supremacy of his office in the army. By 1911, he had become aware of the growing anger among the traditionalist officers regarding the reserve issue and saw that he could restore the leadership of the Adjutant General's Office by using this discontent and his own relationships in Congress to overthrow the supremacy of the General Staff.

In doing this, Ainsworth was also aware that the new Democratic majority that took over in the House of Representatives after the 1910 elections could easily be made sympathetic to his ideas. Taking advantage of the party's interest in cost reduction, Ainsworth helped the Democratic chair of the House Military Affairs Committee, James Hay of Virginia, develop a package of proposals that would constitute a specific Democratic military-reform program. While the proposals were suggested to Hay principally as a means of reducing costs, their real purpose was to reduce the power of the General Staff. The heart of the program was a consolidation of the bureaus and the General Staff into a single office dominated by the adjutant general. In addition, to gain the support of the traditionalists in the army the reforms also proposed increasing the initial enlistment contract from three to five years, which would not only reduce recruiting costs but also derail the development of any European-style reserve system.[17] For his part, Hay used committee hearings and questionnaires sent directly to field officers to give them a chance to voice their opinions on the enlistment issue and to demonstrate that Wood did not speak for the army.[18]

Both Wood and the young professionals saw the dangers posed by the Hay proposals to be introduced in Congress in December 1911, but they differed as to how to respond. Wood planned a multiple counteroffensive to undercut Ainsworth's influence among the traditionalist officers while presenting Congress with his own cost-cutting program based on closing obsolete bases and creating a Council of National Defense.[19] The response of the young professionals, who had little enthusiasm for either closing posts or creating the council, was to develop and publish a statement of a comprehensive military policy that would demonstrate the ability of the General Staff to take the lead in meeting the nation's military needs.[20] Sensing possible public-relations value in such a document, Wood accepted their idea and appointed a committee of four General Staff officers—Colonel R. P. Davis from the coast artillery, Captain William Lassiter from the field artillery, Captain George Van Horn Moseley from the cavalry, and Captain John McAuley Palmer from the infantry—to undertake the project.

The three captains selected were among the most brilliant of the young professionals then making their way through the General Staff. Both Lassiter and Moseley eventually became major generals and played critical roles in the development in the army in the interwar period. And although he only reached the rank of brigadier general during his military career, Palmer, the archetypical military intellectual, was by far the most influential officer in shaping the army's ideas about military policy going into the 1920s and was responsible for the most important and innovative elements of the committee's eventual statement.[21]

As a first effort to design a national military policy, the document prepared by the four officers, later published with the title *Report on the Organization of the Land Forces of the United States* (hereafter referred to as the *Report*), was surprisingly successful. It provoked controversy but finally received a reluctant and highly ambiguous acceptance by the General Staff. Over the next eight years, it remained a major influence in further efforts by both the General Staff and Congress to formulate a military policy. Finally, its basic conceptual elements became part of the National Defense Act of 1920 and have served as the nation's fundamental military policy ever since.

The *Report* stated that the basis of any national military policy should be to provide a military force sufficient to defend the nation from a threat from any major European power or Japan without placing a major strain on the economy. The proposed solution was to provide for an economically minimal Regular Army to meet limited needs, such as an expeditionary force, but that could be readily expanded to up to 300,000 or more men in the event of a national emergency. This would be achieved by the creation of a three-tiered force structure would be made up of the following:

1. A Regular Army organized in divisions and cavalry brigades and ready for immediate use as an expeditionary force or for other purposes for which the citizen soldiery is not available, or for employment in the first stages of war while the citizen soldiery is mobilizing and concentrating.
2. An army of national citizen soldiers organized in peace in complete divisions and prepared to reenforce *sic* the Regular Army in time of war.
3. An army of volunteers to be organized under prearranged plans when greater forces are required than can be furnished by the Regular Army and the organized citizen soldiery.[22]

The bulk of the *Report* was devoted to how the "mobile army," to be made up of Regular Army troops stationed in the country, would be tactically organized.

It was this part of the *Report* that attracted the most attention of other senior officers and was the source of the most controversy.

The second and third tiers of the proposed force structure would be made up of two different types of reserve forces. The second tier was to be an organized manpower pool available as a means of expanding the Regular Army from a somewhat reduced and skeletonized peacetime force to full wartime size at first and then providing replacements for losses incurred in the initial phases of a conflict. In this regard, the *Report* followed the line favored in published discussions that this reserve force be raised in roughly the same way that the major European powers did. It proposed that the existing three-year enlistment be increased to six years, half spent with the colors and the balance as a ready reserve. Since enlistments in the U.S. Army were voluntary rather than compulsory as in Europe, the authors did not think American public opinion would oppose this plan.

The other reserve force, the third tier, would be a large citizen army raised in response to a major war. The idea of a citizen army was Palmer's distinctive contribution to the report and the heart of what he considered to be a proper military policy for a democracy. In the reforms at the turn of the century, the National Guard had been given the role as the primary reserve force. For the *Report*, however, Palmer analyzed exhaustively the constitutional limitations that restricted the usefulness of the Guard, especially in conflicts outside the borders of the United States and concluded that these limitations were not only problematic but also not easily overcome by further legislation. At the same time, he realized that any effort to create a large reserve force by means of rotating enlisted men through the Regular Army for their training would be toxic with the American public, smacking of European militarism. To be accepted by the public, he argued, any citizen reserve force would have to be seen as part of a distinctly American military tradition. As stated early in the *Report,* "The practical military statesman ... does not propose impracticable or foreign institutions, but seeks to develop the necessary vigor and energy within the familiar institutions that have grown with the national life."[23] The *Report* then went on to point out that volunteers had been the traditional American means of augmenting the country's small Regular Army in all the wars of the nineteenth century. Therefore, the major reserve force should be a citizen army made up of volunteers, the insinuation being that this part of the proposal was nothing more than a codification and institutionalization of traditional American practice.

But the authors then pointed out that current threats to the United States meant that this tradition had to be modified in two ways. First, the volunteers would have to be more than a mere manpower pool upon which a reserve force could be built when needed. Given the complexity and size of modern military units, effectively mobilizing such a force would take far too long. Instead, the volunteer citizen force would have to be already organized on paper into its own tactically structured army, a virtual citizen army. Upon mobilization, each volunteer would report to his specifically designated unit headquarters for further training. This post would already contain prepositioned supplies and munitions and a core of trained reserve officers. To augment the latter, the *Report* suggested that the training ongoing in land-grant universities be organized and put under some degree of federal control to produce the desired military results, a foreshadowing of the Reserve Officer Training Corps (ROTC) program established later. With all this set up ahead of time, the *Report* confidently predicted, a well-trained volunteer citizen army could be ready to take the field in just six months.

The second modification to the American volunteer tradition was trickier. For the citizen army to be ready to take the field in just six months, volunteers would need to have already had six months prior military training during peacetime. So, creating this quick-mobilizing reserve army would involve the Regular Army providing military training for a large number of civilians in peacetime. Yet instituting any such training would again raise the specter of the army militarizing society, so the question of how the volunteers would receive prior training remained unanswered.

Finally, it should also be noted that while the *Report* itself was largely the result of the efforts by the rising military professionals to reform the army along the lines proposed by Upton, there were other national forces working along the same line as well. As J. P. Clark has noted, the efforts to rationalize the army's structure was also influenced by the rising culture of progressivism in the United States. On a parallel track, James Hewes argues that the reforms were also the product of the efforts of political and industrial leaders to reorganize the army along efficient business lines.[24]

Meanwhile, the legislative battle over Ainsworth and Hay's reform bill began in the House of Representatives in December 1911. The fight was tumultuous and bitter. At one point, Wood was able to push Ainsworth into a position that forced him to resign as adjutant general. This served not only to increase the bitterness of the struggle in Congress but also to focus it on Wood himself; it became so personal that a move was made to include a description of the requirements for chief of staff that would have made Wood ineligible. But with the patient intervention of both Secretary of War Henry L. Stimson and President Taft, the situation was ameliorated, and a much modified Hay bill finally passed with little damage done to the General Staff. Yet it did include provisions that the enlistment contract be extended to four years so as to preclude the creation of a European-style reserve.[25] The work of Palmer's committee played little role in all this, but its recommendations remained to serve as the basis for future reform efforts.

With the end of the struggle over the Hay bill, the effort to create a national military policy entered a new phase that culminated in the summer of 1916 with the actual passage of a legislation creating such a policy. As before, Wood and the young professionals in the General Staff tended to go their separate ways. But they remained committed to the overall project of basing America's defense needs on some kind of citizen army and remained focused on the principal issue of creating a large pool of trained manpower available as a reserve. Yet their approaches were different. While the General Staff continued to seek a legislatively approved policy based on the concept of a citizen army, Wood sought to create the foundations of support for such a policy by popularizing both the army and military service.

The general did this, in part, through a major public-relations campaign largely carried out by himself and aimed at convincing American elites of the value to society of the army itself and of providing military training for the country's young males. He pursued a vigorous schedule of speaking at chambers of commerce, boards of trade, and university graduations. Yet his most significant effort at popularizing military training was the idea of offering male college students voluntary military training at their own expense at summer camps at Plattsburgh, New York. While the original idea behind the camps was to develop a group of men with sufficient training to make them officers in volunteer units in the case of war, for Wood, the main goal was "planting in every university and college a true knowledge of what our military policy has been and what it should be."[26]

Wood also worked to popularize the idea of universal military training. He had been interested in this idea from the beginning of his tenure as chief of staff. The concept was, indeed, beginning to gain acceptance among American elites who were concerned about the social ramifications of the rapid urbanization and industrialization of U.S. society. There was particular concern that malnutrition and poor living conditions in cities was leading to a growing physical degeneration, a concern that fueled the movement to place physical-education programs into the public schools. They worried, too, about growing urban unrest and the need to "Americanize" the massive influx of immigrants. Wood spoke to all of this in his effort to promote universal military training.[27]

The general's major concern in all of this, and one he shared with the General Staff, was how to provide for a federally trained and controlled manpower reserve in the event of a major war. Although he did not share the highly negative feelings prevalent in the staff regarding the unreliability of the National Guard, he shared the fear that the organization could provide neither the troop numbers nor the assurance of quality performance that would be needed. Wood's initial approach had been to create a trained reserve by using the European military method of short-term enlistments followed by long-term reserve obligations. But, as noted, the legislation supporting this idea became a casualty in the struggle over the Hay bill in 1912.

Therefore, Wood, like Palmer, turned to the more traditional idea of volunteers. In the spring of 1914, he was successful in getting Congress to approve the Volunteer Act. The chief purpose of this measure was to secure a recognized place for volunteers in U.S. defense efforts in the event of a major war. While the act reaffirmed the position of the National Guard as the second line of defense in the event of such a conflict, it provided a distinct provision for federal volunteers as a third line. While the law did not provide for any peacetime training of potential volunteers, it did legitimize for the first time the basic three-tiered structure upon which ensuing military-policy efforts would be based. [28]

While Wood had spent 1913 and 1914 popularizing both the army and universal military training, the General Staff sought to pursue the development of a national military policy. This task was given specifically to the War College Division of the staff. This unit was the chief planning body in the General Staff and, as such, had a magnetic attraction to younger and more intellectual staff officers convinced that the army needed radical change. So for the next four years, the War College Division became the center for the pursuit of a national military policy.

Officers in the division initially intended to use the *Report* as its guide. But as they sought to translate its generalities into specific provisions, they began to lose confidence in some of its basic premises. Overall, they increasingly felt that the main problem with the military policy outlined in the *Report* was that it sought to create a single mobile striking force out of two quite different bodies, the professional Regular Army and a citizen army or the National Guard, raised and trained on the basis of voluntarism. As military professionals grew more scientific in outlook, they became increasingly suspicious of the contingent and more assertive in the demand that military policy be based solely on assured forces. By the fall of 1914, this concern, the outbreak of war in Europe, and collapsing army confidence in the reliability of the National Guard or any other kind of volunteer force led the General Staff to turn to the development of a new military policy. The staff developed a proposal that now suggested the reserve force, to be called the Continental Army, be recruited by conscription rather than by voluntary enlistment. [29]

Yet both President Woodrow Wilson and his secretary of war, Lindley M. Garrison, were opposed to any policy based on raising armies by means other than voluntarism. So, from 1914 through the first half of 1916, the focal point of the effort to develop a national military policy was a struggle between the War College Division and Garrison over the issue of whether the major reserve force would rely on conscription or voluntarism.[30] Things initially went well for the division in this struggle. It was able to make use of Senator George Chamberlain, a Democrat from Oregon, who was chairman of the Senate Committee on Military Affairs and an ambitious maverick with considerable interest in military matters, as a means to get independent access to Congress.[31]

The confrontation between Secretary Garrison and the General Staff came to a head in late 1914. The staff, now fully committed to abandoning the *Report*, called publicly for a new comprehensive military policy based on doubling the Regular Army to 205,000 men supplemented by a force of 300,000 reserves, trained through two to three years of service in the army, to serve as a manpower pool, with the National Guard relegated to an undefined secondary status.[32] When Garrison failed to support this proposal and, instead, proposed to Congress a minimum reform bill, the staff turned to Senator Chamberlain, who successfully pushed for the defeat of Garrison's proposal.[33]

This was a bitter experience for Garrison and a warning that he was losing control of the army. As a result, the secretary suddenly reversed himself and sought to regain authority by taking over the leadership of the movement for comprehensive reform, with hopes of limiting its scope by defining the project himself.[34] But the War College Division was no longer willing to be limited in any way in carrying out a project that represented an ideal long sought by army professionals. Moreover, by early 1915, the mood in the country was changing dramatically. The unexpectedly titanic nature of the war in Europe and the size of the forces involved, as well as the sinking of the *Lusitania* by a German U-boat, created a sudden panic in the United States about its vulnerability. This precipitated what was called the "preparedness movement" as well as a dramatic upsurge of public interest in universal military training, creating a political force that seemed to verge on becoming irresistible. Taking advantage of this, Brigadier General Montgomery M. Macomb, the head of the War College Division, had a committee prepare a draft army-reorganization bill to be ready for the next session of Congress, with Chamberlain agreeing to sponsor it.[35]

But the critical question for both Secretary Garrison and the War College Division remained how the reserve pool of trained manpower would be created. While Garrison remained committed to the voluntarist approach also held by

President Wilson, the division had already given up on any idea of raising such a trained reserve force by any means other than conscription. In discussion with Garrison, Macomb pointed out that an earlier study had shown that the existing voluntary recruitment system could sustain an army of no more than 140,000 men, thus additional men would have to be found outside any reserve system based on voluntary enlistment in the Regular Army.[36]

Garrison responded to this unwelcome news by reviving and remodeling an idea once entertained in the War College Division. The secretary proposed that the remaining manpower requirements would come from a new voluntary citizen-soldier force, which he also came to call the Continental Army, to be independently recruited and trained by the Regular Army. He pressed Macomb and the division to accept it. But while the division had once favored a variation of this idea, there was now little enthusiasm for it, given its voluntarist basis. Instead, division members remained convinced about the need for conscription to raise a federal reserve force. But they were also aware that the political climate in the country was still dominated by a traditional distrust and hostility to anything that could be seen as militarism. So, they hedged by tacitly agreeing to remain quiet on the issue while reserving the right to testify against a voluntary program if a change in public opinion allowed it.[37]

Then, in July 1915, aware of the growing pressure of the preparedness movement, President Wilson called on both the secretary of war and the secretary of the navy to submit proposals to him to form the basis of any future preparedness legislation.[38] Garrison submitted a proposal prepared by the War College Division, but Wilson rejected it. In September Garrison instead recommended a policy statement he had drafted himself along far-more modest lines and based on his Continental Army idea.[39]

General Staff members were so outraged by Garrison's action that any possibilities for further cooperation were all but ruined. The secretary's unilateral action was not only an insult to their professional pride but had also torn their own plan to shreds. Their anger only deepened as it became clear that the president would actually adopt Garrison's program. As a result, Macomb and his division began to resort to a campaign of orchestrated leaks to the pro-preparedness press designed to discredit Garrison's program, allowing the division to put forward its own military-reform legislation to bring the nation as close to conscription as the public would allow. This campaign soon began to focus on the Continental Army, which everyone acknowledged was the most vulnerable element of Garrison's proposal and encapsulated his hopes that a modern military policy could be framed on the basis of voluntarism.[40] The division then looked to Senator

Chamberlain as the means of getting a General Staff program before Congress. Chamberlain was willing to assist, but he and the division understood no program tied to conscription could yet get a hearing. So, the War College proposal was divided into two bills, an army-reorganization bill that included no provisions regarding citizen-soldiers, and a second bill, to be held back initially, that would commit the nation to some form of universal military training and the selective conscription of reserves.[41]

By early 1916, the situation for the division and its program looked decidedly favorable as the military-affairs committees of both chambers of Congress began hearings on Garrison's bill. Public opinion had turned against the Continental Army idea, leaving the secretary's program in deep trouble. At the same time, the Chamberlain reorganization bill seemed to benefit from its clear identification with the General Staff. The testimony of the division members in both houses was so impressive that there was considerable hope that the program they advocated could be passed.[42]

The momentum that seemed to be gathering behind the division's program was suddenly checked, however, by developments in the House. Congressman Hay, who was handling the Garrison bill, told President Wilson that he could not get it through unless he dropped the controversial Continental Army provisions and provided the necessary citizen-soldiers by further federalizing the National Guard. This outraged Garrison, and, when he failed to get from Wilson a virtual pledge of unconditional support for his bill as written, he resigned.[43]

Then, at the moment of its triumph, the War College Division lost control of the issue in Congress. The failure of Garrison's Continental Army plan led not to acceptance of the division's plan for a reserve based on universal military training as hoped, but to the use of the National Guard as the nation's reserve force. With this, things moved quickly, and on June 2 Congress passed a bill that became known as the National Defense Act of 1916. The measure provided for the gradual expansion of the Regular Army to 175,000 men over a five-year period and gave the role of the citizen-soldier reserve to the National Guard. No other citizen-soldier force was created, although there was a general statement noting the universal obligation of all men to serve that was said to be implied in the Constitution. But the act also created the ROTC, which would provide at least a pool of reserve officers who could serve as the nucleus for a major buildup of forces during an emergency.

Overall, the National Defense Act fell far short of what the officers in the General Staff sought, especially with the National Guard being given the role of the citizen-soldier reserve and the continued reliance on voluntarism as the basis for military service. Nevertheless, the army finally had what it had sought for nearly forty years, a nationally accepted military policy. But it was not a policy that the military professionals were ready to accept as written, and they remained committed to substantially remodeling it should the opportunity arise.

Two major opportunities to carry out such a remodeling seemed to appear almost immediately. The first was the mobilization of the National Guard to deal with the Mexican border emergency during the summer of 1916. Pancho Villa's raid on Columbus, New Mexico, created considerable excitement in the United States and led President Wilson to call up the entire National Guard to form a force capable of guaranteeing the security of the border while a Regular Army force pursued Villa into Mexico. This mobilization initially seemed to be a success.[44] But as the period became more prolonged, guardsmen began to complain. The proponents of universal military training sensed this as an opportunity to demonstrate the Guard's unreliability as a reserve.[45] By December, the chief of staff, Major General Hugh L. Scott, charged in hearings before the Senate that the mobilization had proven not only the deficiency of the National Guard but also the bankruptcy of the entire volunteer approach and called for replacing the Guard with a citizen force based on universal military training.[46] By then, Congress seemed ready to revise the National Defense Act by replacing the Guard sections with provisions likely to produce a more dependable and less politically vocal alternative.[47]

The second and more significant opportunity came with perceived changes in the public mood. While the national press was coming to favor universal military training, there were indications that public opinion was changing, too. By late 1916, Scott sensed that it had shifted to such a degree that it made legislative consideration of universal military training a real possibility and decided to have ready a more compelling case for it if an opportunity arose. He called on the War College Division to prepare a new study of their previous policy recommendations. By early December, as it became clear that Chamberlain and others in Congress were planning to submit actual universal military training legislation, Scott gave the project the highest priority.[48]

One of the officers assigned to the project was Palmer, now a colonel, who had returned to the War College Division in 1916. As principal author of the *Report*, he was unhappy that the General Staff, in developing its program, had abandoned what he considered to be that work's central feature—the citizen army. Being unable to do anything about it now, he, instead, turned his attention to the issue of universal military training. While his proposal for a citizen army in the *Report* had been based on voluntarism, by 1916, Palmer had become one of the most vocal military advocates of compulsory training. In doing so, he largely worked outside the army with civilian groups in the preparedness movement and, in particular, with the Military Training Camps Association (MTCA), which had taken the lead nationally in calling for a policy of universal military training.[49]

In the War College Division, Palmer was assigned to the committee designated to draw up the new report demanded by Scott. He soon found that his fellow members were favorable to the idea of a citizen army, which would now receive its preliminary instruction through universal military training. The division was able to present the chief of staff with a preliminary report in December, proposing a new military policy based on a worst-case scenario of an attack by two major powers and aimed at mobilizing an army of four million men. This force would be structured as a Regular Army and a National Army. The Regular Army would be given responsibility for garrisoning outlying forts, mounting minor expeditions, and training. The National Army would have its own internal structure to allow for a rapid mobilization, as Palmer had advocated in his 1912 work.[50]

General Scott approved the program, demonstrating considerable interest in Palmer's National Army concept, and called on the War College Division to produce a more detailed plan within little more than a month.[51] The committee, however, found it difficult to meet this timetable. Since both the idea of a citizen army and a universal military training program were new concepts, the committee felt compelled to work each out in detail. As a result, even though the members worked on weekends and through the Christmas holidays, the detailed plan was still incomplete.

The committee finally finished its plan on January 27, 1917 and circulated it for comment. It was based on three principles: "universal liability for training in peace and service in war, decentralization of administration in peace and war, and localization of organization." Under the plan, all able-bodied males would be called up in their nineteenth year for eleven months' training, to be followed by two weeks of training in their twentieth and twenty-first years. They would serve in a "First Reserve" for four years and one month, then in a "Second Reserve" for another seven years. After that, they would be part of an "Unorganized Reserve" until reaching the age of forty-five. Both the First and Second Reserves were to be fully organized in local units. Officers were expected to be graduates of the newly created ROTC program. The National Guard would, in the meantime, revert to its older status as a state constabulary.[52]

But by the time the proposal reached the new secretary of war, Newton D. Baker, in mid-February, the international situation had changed dramatically. Germany's announcement that it would resume unrestricted submarine warfare led to a crisis in its relations with the United States, making war imminent. The emergency and subsequent hostilities became a fatal interruption in the growing momentum enjoyed by the universal military training movement just when it seemed to be on the verge of success. The cause of this lay in three factors: the attitudes of Wilson and Baker toward the issue of universal military training, the particular framework of events leading to the decision to base wartime military policy on selective service, and the absorbing character of the war itself.

Neither Wilson nor Baker were philosophically opposed to the idea of wartime conscription, but they were not at all enthusiastic about universal military training as a permanent program. As progressives, they were both attracted to ideas of rationalizing social-structural activities and saw the government as capable of doing good. Baker appreciated the military ethos of self-subordinating service and, even before the war, saw in army life a chance to provide youth with appropriate vocational, civic, and moral education.[53]

But both held major political and policy objections to universal military training as a permanent program. Despite the almost unanimous support given by the press for the policy in 1916 and earlier, Wilson and Baker could sense that garnering actual political support for such a proposal was impossible.[54] Moreover, both were convinced that the nation would balk at universal military training once the fiscal cost was revealed. Nor were either of them convinced that the nation needed such massive protection.[55] Finally, and most importantly, by 1916, Wilson had already developed the hope that the peace that would follow the war would be favorable to the creation of a new world order based on international cooperation. Therefore, he and Baker were opposed to the creation in wartime of any permanent postwar military policy predicated on any sort of contrary global vision.[56]

By the time Baker forwarded the General Staff bill to Congress, the issue was becoming moot. The nation's interest was rapidly shifting from preparedness in general to preparation for fighting a specific war. Shortly after the February 1 rupture with Germany, Baker ordered the General Staff to prepare a plan for raising an army of 1,000,000 men by means of expanding the Regular Army and National Guard to 500,000 combined and supplementing that with a second batch of 500,000 men—all to be raised on the principle of voluntarism. The General Staff, however, was still determined to use the global situation to establish a military policy based on compulsory training. It developed the plan it forwarded to Baker on its own recently submitted universal military training proposal while arguing strongly for the use of conscription rather than a voluntary system.[57] This did not satisfy Baker, who sent the staff back to develop a plan based on voluntarism.

With the president's call on March 21 for a special session of Congress to meet on April 2, it became clear that war was inevitable. On March 23 Baker gathered a group of senior General Staff officers into a special committee to create an army of 1,500,000 men, though still on the principle of voluntarism with a recourse to a draft only if that failed.[58] For a short while thereafter, the secretary continued to press for a mobilization plan based on voluntarism. But those hopes ended later that year with the passage of the Selective Service Act on May 18.

The Selective Service Act and the rush to get ready for war effectively ended the hopes of the universal military training movement. Backers tried to remain hopeful and attempted to seize any opportunity to get the idea back on the national agenda but failed. Chamberlain and others in Congress again attempted to get universal military training bills onto the congressional agenda but also failed. By June 1917, it was clear to the War College Division that the issue was dead. The service journals continued to hold out for a short while longer, seizing on any piece of evidence that suggested there was still public support for compulsory training. Yet the situation was clearly hopeless, as Baker made it clear that the War Department would make no recommendation regarding a permanent military policy until after arrangements for peace were concluded, hinting strongly that such a policy would in no case include universal military training.[59] This remained the policy throughout the war so that the task of finally creating the long-sought national military policy based on a federally trained citizen army was postponed until afterward.

The sudden end of the war in November 1918 took the army and the General Staff very much by surprise. Despite the great Allied battlefield successes in the late summer and fall, as late as October the General Staff was still expecting fighting to last well into 1919. But by the middle of October, both Baker and the members of the General Staff began to see the need to initiate planning for a postwar reorganization of the army. He and President Wilson were concerned about the likelihood of social unrest in central Europe after the war and sought to ensure that the United States had military forces necessary to secure the peace there until the desired League of Nations was established.

Leadership in the General Staff was now in the hands of General Peyton C. March. He had come to the staff in March 1918 to tighten the organization of its efforts to support the American Expeditionary Force in France. Prior to this, March had had little experience with the staff and was not part of the prewar efforts of the War College Division to create a new military policy based on a federally trained citizen-army reserve. Instead, he favored the idea of a large and partially skeletonized Regular Army that could be expanded in wartime by means of a draft. Thus, he and Baker easily agreed on an army-reorganization program that would lead to a military of 500,000 men.[60] But while Baker and Wilson saw this army as only a transitional force, March saw it as part of a permanent military policy for the United States.

March worked out his basic concept for the postwar army quickly in concert with his assistant chief of staff for operations and training, Major General Henry Jervey, Jr., in October 1918. Jervey then transmitted it in a terse and informal memorandum to Brigadier General Lytle Brown, who was then the director of the postwar successor to the War College Division, the War Plans Division, as "further reference to the study of plans for demobilization." The March plan based future U.S. military policy on the cadre principle, calling for

> the permanent establishment in this country of a *single Army complete* in the framework of all divisional, corps, and army units, but at a reduced strength so that the total of the *one Army* would be 400,000 to 500,000 men." "The idea," Jervey went on to explain, "is to have a framework all ready for an immediate expansion in case of need but not to have too many individuals permanently in military forces.[61]

The terseness of Jervey's directive, together with a lack of further guidance from March, soon led to a significant strain in the relations between the chief of staff and the War Plans Division. For March and Baker, time was of the essence. For different reasons, both wanted to get a reorganization bill to Congress as soon as possible. March wanted rather brief and general organic legislation that would leave the details to be worked out at the discretion of the president. The officers in the War Plans Division, on the other hand, believing that the terseness of the directive gave them leeway to plan the long-desired military revolution that would cap with complete triumph the long search for a national military policy, chose to be thorough and meticulous in drafting legislation. Moreover, the experience of the war and of the new weapons introduced in combat, together with the intention of actually carrying out a revolutionary break with the past, meant that the division saw itself plunging into the unknown.[62] As a result, the project quickly blossomed into a massive undertaking, spinning off an ever-increasing array of subordinate studies while the division officers stumbled through nearly metaphysical discussions as to the nature of the knowledge upon which policy could be developed.

Meanwhile, March, who justifiably feared that the mood in Congress would soon turn against the army, had directed that the division have a draft of a bill presented to him by the beginning of January 1919. Given the complexity of the project it had created for itself, the division was unable to give him much more than a hastily drawn up draft of legislation based upon disconnected fragments of an incomplete study.[63] Frustrated that he could not get anything like the legislation he wanted when he needed it, March ignored the division's proposal and, in early January, gathered a few top General Staff officers and proceeded to write a reorganization bill himself. After he gained Secretary Baker's approval, he submitted to Congress the draft of what became known as the March-Baker bill.[64]

Members of the War Plans Division were deeply angered with the summary treatment accorded to their own proposals by General March. They were embarrassed by the fact that, at the end of December 1918, they still had only a highly fragmented and not altogether comprehensible study to show him and expected the very rough draft to be returned with demands for revision, perhaps even disapproved altogether. They did not expect that both the division and its study would be ignored. The division made further efforts to gain March's attention for a number of months until they finally gave up in May 1919 and unenthusiastically worked in support of the March-Baker bill.[65]

March's draft bill met with almost immediate hostility in Congress so that after only a few days of hearings, Congressman Stanley H. Dent, Democrat from Alabama and chairman of the House Military Affairs Committee, told Baker that he doubted that the measure could be passed before the end of the term.[66] Meanwhile, by May, the army no longer had the field of reorganization entirely to itself. Other groups in society with an interest in the issue had now had time to begin mobilizing political strength to make their voices heard.

The most important of these was the National Guard. Most guardsmen who had fought in the war came out with a deep distrust and hostility toward the Regular Army. But they initially had little means of exerting political pressure on the formation of national military policy. The mobilization for the war had all but destroyed the state organizations, and the army did little to help them recover. Congress's summer recess, however, provided the Guard time to recover at both the state and national level and to begin to mobilize its own political forces. It soon began to turn its attention to the efforts of the War Department to craft a new national military policy, becoming deeply suspicious that the emerging legislation would include no provisions for a National Guard. Such suspicions were entirely justified. Many of the Young Turks in the General Staff saw the "state troops" as an anachronism that should be swept away in the hoped-for postwar revolution within the army. And despite their many differences, the War Plans Division and General March were in at least tacit agreement in that the National Guard did not factor in their respective army-reorganization plans. As a result, the Guard began to develop its own ideas about postwar army reorganization and to mobilize political support against plans developed by the War Department.[67]

The congressional summer recess brought all legislative efforts to a close. By the time Congress reconvened in August, control of the formulation of military policy appeared to have passed out of the hands of the General Staff. The draft March-Baker bill was introduced into both the Senate and the House on August 4. For the next four months, it underwent extensive hearings in both chambers that were marked by considerable hostility to both the bill and the General Staff and by confusion and hesitancy on the part of many of the officers called upon to testify.[68] While General Staff members did not attack the bill, their obvious hesitancy and the tepidness of their support led to charges that they were being gagged by General March. By early October, the House and Senate Military Affairs Committees were sufficiently impressed by the opposition to the bill that both decided to abandon it and write their own legislation. But each decided on a different approach to the task. By November, the House Military Affairs Committee began writing what would be essentially a series of amendments to the National Defense Act of 1916.[69] The General Staff readily provided professional assistance to this effort, lending to the committee the services of Colonel Thomas M. Spaulding and Colonel Thomas Hammond.

The Senate effort, headed by the chairman of its military-affairs committee, Senator James W. Wadsworth, Jr, Republican from New York, had given up on the March-Baker bill in early October and decided to draft legislation strikingly different from that bill. Earlier, several General Staff officers quietly suggested to Wadsworth that he call on Palmer to testify regarding the March-Baker bill. The colonel appeared before the committee and electrified it by announcing his near total opposition to the proposal and outlining the ideas he had been advocating within the General Staff for over a year, and had originally outlined nine years earlier in the *Report*. In this case, however, Palmer put heavy emphasis on two essential points. His first was that any national military policy had to be based on universal military training. His second was that U.S. military policy should be based on a truly citizen army. He then spelled out the essential characteristics of his vision of a citizen army as one in which citizen-soldiers and officers who would largely be self-trained would occupy all the positions in the army from bottom to top.[70]

In all this Palmer was immensely successful. Committee members were charmed by his manner, delighted by his opposition to the General Staff line, and impressed by his broad vision of military policy that seemed so congruent with their own outlooks. Over March's angry objections, Palmer was detailed to the Senate committee, finding considerable freedom to write his own ideas into prospective legislation without General Staff opposition.

Once the hearings were over, both military committees decided to write their own bills, leaving that task to subcommittees. This meant, in fact, that the actual drafting of legislation was left largely in the hands of the military advisors to the committees, Spaulding and Hammond in the House and Palmer in the Senate. In this arrangement the three military advisors were able to work cooperatively. The result of all this was two bills that, as they were emerging, were becoming increasingly similar in detail while still divergent in principle and structure.[71]

Of the three officers, Palmer on the Senate subcommittee enjoyed far more freedom in drafting its bill than did Hammond and Spaulding on the House subcommittee. The colonel had won the confidence of Senator Wadsworth and the subcommittee members, who saw his ideas as reflections of their own and left him largely free to write the bill he wanted, forwarding it section by section to Wadsworth for approval. In the House, the drafting subcommittee was chaired by a Republican, Daniel R. Anthony of Kansas. While Anthony's district included Fort Leavenworth, he was not friendly to the army and was far more concerned with creating an atmosphere that would favor the revival of the National Guard. Hence, he was hostile to both universal military training and to any army reserve organization that would rival the Guard.[72] Therefore, as both draft bills were reaching conclusion, the officers in the General Staff began to unite in support of the Senate version.[73]

While army leadership slowly united behind the provisions in Palmer's draft, the legislation itself began to face increasing opposition from outside the army. The result is that the legislative history of the bill from early February of 1920 until it's final consideration in conference committee was dominated by outside forces. The opposition was primarily focused on two interconnected issues— universal military training and the National Guard—and military supporters of the draft bill, especially Palmer, found most of their time consumed in a largely losing struggle over these.

The most controversial of the two was universal military training. Overall, the end of the war and of the preparedness movement meant that public support for the idea was rapidly fading. Hostility to the proposal was already so strong that House Democrats in caucus voted overwhelmingly to make opposition to universal military training a party issue. With that, support for it collapsed.[74] In the Senate, debate on its version of the bill was delayed by consideration of the Paris peace treaties and did not begin until April 1920. By then, the political current against universal military training was so strong Colonel Palmer feared that a move to delete those provisions from the bill would also root out the provision for the Organized Reserve, which was the heart of his citizen-army plan. As a result, he countered an anticipated motion to delete universal military training by drawing up a set of amendments making such training voluntary rather than compulsory. His plan worked. Some senators grumbled that voluntary military training made as much sense as voluntary taxation, but it was difficult to vote against voluntarism. Palmer's amendments passed, saving the Organized Reserve.[75]

The second issue was the National Guard. The Guard was continuing to mobilize its adherents and political support to ensure that it would not be ignored in any future military legislation. This actually took Palmer by surprise. As was the case with the March-Baker bill, the colonel's proposed military policy had no provision for the Guard. While having come out of the war sharing the respect held by many other senior regular officers for guardsmen as soldiers, he still saw the state organizations and their hierarchies as political and patronage organizations rather than genuine military units. He naïvely assumed that what he called "the best element of the old National Guard" shared his views and would prefer to serve in his planned Organized Reserve. Thus, by the time Palmer realized the extent of the Guard's growing influence, its political position had become almost unassailable. It threatened to bring this political power into opposition to universal military training unless the Guard itself was made part of the national defense policy and given the role of second line of defense. With this, Palmer and his Senate allies capitulated and wrote the Guard into their policy proposal.

The final legislative problem was that army reorganization legislation had been treated in the House as an update of the National Defense Act of 1916, so the House bill was written as a series of amendments to that law. The Senate bill, on the other hand, treated army reorganization as an entirely new piece of legislation. For Palmer and the rest of the enthusiasts in the General Staff, the "revolutionary" character given to the legislation, making 1920 year one of an entirely new military policy, was vastly superior to the "evolutionary" character given to the House legislation. But that cause was lost as well in conference committee, and the final legislation was written as a series of amendments. It was then passed by both chambers on June 4, 1920.

The final form of what became known as the National Defense Act of 1920 was, obviously, a major disappointment to Palmer and many other upper-level army officers. Without a provision for universal military training, the citizen army—the heart of the colonel's proposal—survived only as a hollow shell made up solely of reserve officers. Moreover, this force had to face the National Guard

as a politically powerful rival citizen component in the army. Yet while Palmer
and his colleagues failed to get the national military policy they wanted, they
did succeed in getting the rest of the army, as well the U.S. government and the
nation, to accept the idea of a citizen army rather than a Regular Army as the
basis of U.S. military policy.

What was important about the National Defense Act of 1920 was not so
much its separate parts as how it was perceived. While the fact that it was written as a series of amendments to the 1916 act made it difficult to see the conceptual basis, its central features were clearly visible. The revised act provided for a
national army to be made up of three components: the U.S. (Regular) Army of
280,000 men and officers; the National Guard, which was expected to eventually reach 435,000 men; and a reserve force made up of the Officer Reserve Corps
to serve as a skeletal organization that could be rapidly expanded in the event of
war. Finally, the details for the actual reorganization of the army were left to the
president, giving the General Staff the virtual freedom to reorganize the army
within the guidelines set by Congress.

The perception of the 1920 act is more difficult to discern but a far more important matter. If the envisioned citizen army were to succeed, the revolutionary
character of this measure had to be understood and accepted by the army, the
government, and the nation. But the disaggregated form of the act as a series of
disparate amendments made it extremely difficult to perceive. During the rest
of the 1920s, Colonel Palmer worked tirelessly to help both the army and the
American public understand this. He was aided by the fact that General John J.
Pershing, who succeeded General March as chief of staff, understood and warmly
supported the concept. In addition, the officers in the General Staff who had
worked for years to establish this new military policy understood it as well. Finally, with all its drawbacks, many in the army saw sufficient positive features in
the 1920 legislation, leading them to embrace it. For all army officers, the nineteen
months between the end of the Great War (or World War I) and the advent of the
National Defense Act of 1920 had been a difficult period marked by confusion
over demobilization, the end of wartime promotions, and what seemed to be a
growing lack of public interest in the army. In this regard, they were eager to see
the act as the beginning of a new period of stability and development.

I

Creating the Citizen Army, 1919–1925

CHAPTER ONE

Disappointment and Disillusionment

The Army and the Nation, 1920–1925

D ESPITE THE DISAPPOINTMENTS FELT about the National Defense
Act of 1920, it was still greeted with significant enthusiasm in the army,
both for the provisions it contained and for the hopes it offered in terms
of finally providing stability and the legislative, political, and popular foundations on which to begin a process of rebuilding after the demoralizing experience
of the immediate postwar years. Far more important, the act provided the army
with a major new mission—training the civilian components of the new citizen
army. This seemed to promise not only to be highly satisfying professionally but
also to provide the military widespread support from the American public.

The army's experience in the first five years of the 1920s tested these hopeful
expectations. These years were dominated by two developments: the experience
of organizing the civilian components and the efforts to establish a positive relationship with the government and with the American public. Regarding the
latter, the hopes of widespread governmental and popular support were cruelly
shattered. This disillusionment came quickly and dominated the army's first two
years after the act's passage. Indeed, these initial years of the new order turned
out to be one of the most dismal periods in the history of the interwar army.

The major problem at this time was that the political and popular landscape
had undergone an immense change after the war, especially as the new decade
opened. The Republicans' landslide victory in the 1920 election made them the
dominant party in Washington throughout the decade. While the party had
almost always been friendlier to the army than the Democrats, the postwar Republicans were highly focused on instituting government efficiency and economy that could result in tax reduction. At the same time, the public was becoming increasingly isolationist and had little interest in building an army suitable
for fighting another major international war. As such, Americans began to look

on the army as, at best, a necessary evil, the expense of which ought to be reduced at every opportunity. Many in Congress were all too happy to cater to this mood.

GIVEN THAT THE primary reason for the deterioration of the army's relationship with Congress rested on the issue of financial support, the confrontations were chiefly focused on the annual appropriations bills. In that regard, Congress made it clear as early as the fall of 1920 that it did not feel bound to support the personnel levels of 18,000 officers and 280,000 men authorized in the National Defense Act. Even before President Wilson signed the act, Congress passed an appropriation bill providing funding for only 175,000 men and 17,000 officers.[1] Secretary of War Baker thought that the defense act allowed him to continue to recruit the army to the levels authorized.[2] This led to an immediate confrontation with Congress in which Baker was called before House Military Affairs Committee to explain why he was recruiting an army in excess of that allowed in the appropriations act.[3] The secretary gave in, while an angry Senate debated as to whether he had violated a law.[4] Then, in July 1921, a new appropriations act reduced the army further to 150,000 men and 14,000 officers.[5] The following year, operating in the warmth generated by the success of the Washington Naval Disarmament Conference, members of the military subcommittee in the House were ready to cut the army again. This led to a bitter fight, but in the end Congress passed an appropriations bill reducing the army to 125,000 men and fewer than 12,000 officers.[6]

On top of this, in 1921, lawmakers passed the Budget and Accounting Act that called on the government to submit to them a single unified budget and created a new bureaucrat, the director of the budget, to carry this out. In addition, Congress reorganized its committee structure to ensure that it would produce a coherent budget. In the past, matters concerning the army in the annual appropriations bill were handled in the military-affairs committees. These panels traditionally attracted congressmen and senators with a distinct interest in military matters, so that members were usually knowledgeable about and, on balance, friendly to the army. Under the new arrangement adopted in early 1921, all matters dealing with appropriations went to the appropriations committees in both chambers, which then had military subcommittees deal with army matters. Appropriations committees tended to attract congressmen interested in economy in government; thus, those assigned to military subcommittees were less interested in and knowledgeable about matters other than financial.[7] As a result, the army suddenly found its budget estimates facing scrutiny first by an economizing director of the budget and then by congressional subcommittees prepared to be hostile.

The 1922 reduction came as a shock to the army. Beyond the actual reduction of officers, it also specified the number to remain in each grade, thus requiring the separation or demotion of nearly 2,300 officers. Overall, this crisis was devastating for army morale. Nearly one out of eight officers was affected, and many more felt threatened. Moreover, this was the third personnel reduction suffered by the army in eighteen months. All of this seemed to dash any hope that the 1920 National Defense Act was going to provide any stabilization or a chance to build a new force. Both Secretary of War John W. Weeks and Chief of Staff General Pershing stressed the negative effect on morale in their annual reports, and professional journals viewed the act as monumental in consequence.[8] The army exploded in anger over the measure. While most of this was contained in the service publications, some expressed interest in taking political action while Pershing learned that servicemen in Congress were beginning to organize as a bloc.[9]

The impact of the three reductions between 1920 and 1922 went beyond the need to force officers and enlisted men out of the army. Each led to a consequent reorganization. These restructurings often wiped out a year's building efforts within organizations, leaving them in worse shape than before and with considerable internal frustration. This sense of growing destabilization was aggravated by the efforts already underway to reorganize the army in accordance with the National Defense Act, which involved an unusual number of reassignments and transfers. Moreover, concurrent efforts to reduce transportation outlays shifted some of the associated cost burdens of such moves to the officers themselves. Finally, reductions in military personnel were more than matched by those in the army's civilian workforce, increasing the duties for officers and men already overworked. On several occasions, senior officers making surprise post inspections found lieutenants having to take turns at evening guard duty. The budget reductions of 1921 and 1922 set the pattern for the relationship of the army with the president and Congress for the remainder of the interwar period. As William Odom points out, "the tiny appropriations for military activities largely shaped the history of the interwar army." Then, in his conclusion, he charges, "First and foremost, budget limitations explain the army's failure to develop adequate doctrine in the interwar years."[10] Finally, on a day-to-day basis, as Secretary of War Weeks noted in his annual report for 1922, "economy has literally become the primary consideration of every departmental undertaking."[11]

The highly negative consequences of these reductions on morale was aggravated by issues outside of appropriations. Living quarters were a major problem. The postwar policy of concentrating units in the regional division cantonments built during the war meant that officers and men had to live in structures generally meant for temporary use. As these buildings rapidly deteriorated during the ensuing years, housing issues became increasingly demoralizing. Officers seeking to live off post with their families often found options limited and rents unexpectedly high. The massive personnel turnover in the army since 1918 also put a severe strain on its internal cohesiveness. By the summer of 1922, the old army that existed prior to America's entry into the First World War had all but disappeared. Seventy-five percent of current officers had joined the military during or after the conflict, while the bulk of enlisted men had joined postwar. Normal socialization processes were seriously disrupted. The homogeneity of thought and outlook developed over a long period of time by means of shared education and experiences was all but lost in the officer corps, only a small percentage of whom shared a West Point training in common.

This internal dysfunction was aggravated by personnel issues, the most significant of which was implementation of the single-list promotion system called for by the National Defense Act. Prior to 1920, promotions occurred within individual branches and bureaus, a system that worked to the advantage of officers in the bureaus and to the disadvantage of those in the combat branches. The new system placed all officers on a single list by date of rank, thereby ending the latter's disadvantaged position. While the single list was favored by many, its implementation was a source of bitter controversy. Position on the final list was, of course, vitally important, hence all officers were personally interested in the process by which sequence was determined. Unfortunately, given the anomalies regarding the composition of the officer corps in 1920, producing a list that would satisfy everyone as fair proved to be extremely difficult. The necessity of collating the officers of a number of different branches, each with its own particularity; the war, which had resulted in a vast influx of new officers under variety of circumstances; numerous cases of officers departing after the war and then returning; and a perception of sloppy recordkeeping made the development of a seemingly fair system for recognizing longevity of service all but impossible.[12] The result was myriad cases of officers who were increasingly outspoken over presumed injustices. By April 1921, dissatisfaction over promotion had reached the point that some lieutenants and captains began organizing to protest to Congress.[13] Other officers took to the courts to bring suits regarding the single list.[14]

The most important outside cause of low morale, however, was the growing perception that Americans were uninterested in the army or even hostile toward it. When Colonel Palmer submitted *America in Arms,* a revised edition of an earlier book, to his agent in 1924, the man could find no publisher for it, reporting to his client, "interest in the Army . . . is at its lowest ebb."[15] The perceived promise that the army would be accepted as an integral part of society seemed inherent in the military policy of the National Defense Act 1920, causing many officers to receive it enthusiastically. Signs that traditional antimilitary attitudes were reasserting themselves, therefore, threatened the entire myth structure surrounding that legislation, creating a further source of depression.[16] More important, any military policy under the defense act would work only with sufficient public interest to ensure a solid stream of volunteers into the civilian components. As Pershing said in a public speech, "The success of our National Defense plan depends on the quality of our citizenship."[17] Hence, evidence of public indifference to the army was more than a major disappointment in regard to the act's promises, it could also spell doom for the policy on which the act itself was based. Yet many in the army could sense that public interest in the military was continuing to fade. By 1923 and 1924, articles warning citizens to wake up to the need for preparedness once again appeared in professional journals, while those discussing how pursuit of the military policy established in the National Defense Act would end the army's isolation diminished.[18]

The General Staff tried several ways to counter this perceived indifference or to explain it in a manner that would preserve confidence in the defense act. One such approach was to argue that this apparent indifference was actually a failure in the army's public relations. Thus the solution was for the army to become more savvy and develop additional publicity. Articles appeared in professional journals discussing how commanders could get items into the local press and encouraging officers to go out and spread the army message to service clubs and other organizations.[19]

Some blamed this indifference on rising materialism in the United States, arguing that opulence eroded citizen interest in the common good.[20] But by far the favored response was to blame public apathy on alleged conspiratorial activities of dissidents, particularly communists and pacifists, to deliberately mislead Americans. While military journals generally stayed well clear of political issues, beginning in 1920 their interest in dissident activities, increasingly interpreted as being aimed at undercutting citizens' respect for and interest in the army, began to blossom in a way seen neither before nor after this period.

The army had always identified with conservative and institutional forces in society and was never particularly tolerant of political dissidents. Even before the war, professional journals had occasionally voiced criticism of dissident movements while praising patriotic movements. There were, however, two major changes in the thinking of army personnel, both of which followed the reductions forced by Congress, though not linked to them directly. One was a new tendency to connect the emergence of the Soviet Union and Bolshevism to American dissidents as part of an international conspiracy of native dissidents funded and directed by Moscow. As the editor of *Infantry Journal* put it, "This is the boring from within process that we have heard so much about."[21] The second was a rising concern with the threat posed by organized pacifism. This was precipitated by the 1921 Washington Naval Disarmament Conference, so, the concern in the army initially was limited to countering the idea of disarmament rather than pacifism itself.[22] This effort to explain public apathy or even hostility to the army on alleged communist conspiracies or pacifist agitation continued well into 1923, then slowly died as relations between the army and the Congress improved.

Overall, outside of the conflict with lawmakers over appropriations, the major sources of army discontent in 1921 and 1922 were clearly temporary in nature and largely the product of reorganizations. By late 1922, the army worked out most, though not all, problems as it had found ways to cope with them. Yet while temporary, the disruptive issues were intense and often mutually reinforcing, producing deeply felt frustration and widespread pessimism. As a result, the initial enthusiasm generated by the presumed opportunities of the National Defense Act was severely dampened.

In 1923 the situation of the army began to improve. In his annual training message to the army in January, Chief of Staff Pershing admitted that the past year had "been one of uncertainty, hardships, and disappointments." He then declared, "we have entered a new year of great promise" and listed numerous reasons for his hopeful prognosis.[23] Pershing was not alone in this optimism. It was also voiced in service journals, and indeed, they were right.[24] The situation for the army did begin to improve markedly toward the end of 1922, so that the next two years, 1923 and 1924, could be seen as a kind of golden age for the National Defense Act army. It appeared that the great promise of the 1920 legislation finally seemed to be coming true. This sense of well-being was the product of three quite noticeable trends. First, relations between the army and Congress visibly improved. While these relations continued to center on appropriations, the wording of the budget act as accepted and interpreted in both Congress and the army meant that the legislative process itself no longer stirred discontent, even though they differed on the level of funding required. Second, the long-awaited stability had arrived. In 1922 the army underwent its last mandated reductions and subsequent reorganization. Hence, the military could now focus its attention on carrying out its assigned missions in the defense act, especially training the civilian components. By 1924, the army had developed a training cycle, with a focus on summer camps. While exhausting, the annual cycle and camps provided officers with considerable satisfaction with their accomplishment and an overall sense that the army had definitely entered a stabilizing building period. Third, efforts were being made to reduce the remaining sources of discontent, including poor housing. So, the 1923–24 period was seen as one of growth, stability, purpose, and hope.

The most visible, if not most significant, of these characteristics was the improvement in relations with Congress. This was due largely to both the army and, especially, Congress reaching a modus vivendi regarding the new budget system. Under the system, all branches of government submitted estimates of appropriations to the director of the budget, who then fit them into the president's overall budget programs. The services were then requested to support the final budget proposal before Congress. While the army followed the system in the fall of 1921, many lawmakers refused to be bound by it, feeling that Congress still had principal control over the purse strings. Thus, in the appropriations for fiscal year 1922–23, the army had to go through the humiliation of seeing its estimates cut twice, first by the director of budget and then by Congress, with the latter resulting in the painful reductions of 1922. By the fall of 1922, House members had been brought into line on the issue of the budget process, and the army was reassured that they understood that the estimates submitted were the president's, not the War Department's, resulting in little likelihood of further drastic cuts.[25]

In the meantime, patterns of activity within the army were also regularized in a way that provided a significant number of officers and troops with a focus for activity in areas that seemed rewarding and constructive. The main focal point was the training of citizen components in summer camps. These began for some of the component units in 1921 and spread and expanded thereafter, with the rhythm of the army year beginning to develop around them. In the fall, the General Staff would draw up overall training regimens for the civilian components based on its own plans as well as on anticipated appropriations. These would be disseminated along with tentative appropriations to corps-area commanders during the winter. The corps-area commanders would select camp commanders and staff, assigning them specific training duties, as well as officers and troops to assist. Camp commanders and their staff would develop training plans for each group assigned to them. Shortly before the citizen units showed up, officers and troops assigned to assist in training would arrive. By mid-summer, when this training was in full swing, 50 percent or more of the combat troops on duty with the Regular Army in the United States would be involved in instruction.

At the completion of the camps, camp commanders compiled reports and recommendations for improvement in subsequent years. These were combined with feedback from the chiefs of branches on training and served as a major input in the General Staff development of training plans in the fall as the cycle began again. Within this cycle, all other events, including school programs within the Regular Army and personal leaves and transfer dates for officers, were fixed by the schedule of summer camps.

The good years ended with a major effort to invigorate public interest in the vision of the citizen army. This effort was a so-called Defense Test held in September 1924. Ostensibly, the purpose of this exercise was to test mobilization plans and the ability of civilian components to meet objectives by having an actual one-day test mobilization. It was intended to be highly visible, having been scheduled for September 12, 1924, the sixth anniversary of the Battle of Saint-Mihiel and, more than coincidentally, the day prior to Pershing's retirement as chief of staff. As such, it was basically planned to be a nationwide patriotic fete to honor the army and Pershing as well as a symbolic proclamation that the structure called for in the defense act was now in place.[26] Much of the army's activity in 1924 was based on making the defense test a success. All field-training activities outside of summer camps were canceled in preparation. Much of the planning for the test focused on community involvement so that the day on which local units mobilized would be marked by parades, patriotic speeches, and other forms of public manifestations of support.[27] The announcement of the test aroused significant opposition from pacifist groups. This delighted the army, anticipating that it would give the defense test additional significance as a public victory over pacifists.[28]

The day itself was a great success. Community committees, headed by local notables and supported by local social organizations and industries, planned parades and ceremonies. Local National Guard and Officer Reserve units mobilized conspicuously, with public displays of weapons in a holiday atmosphere. Nationwide, the army estimated that nearly seventeen million people in over 6,500 communities participated in the festivities in some way or another.[29] Looking over the results, Pershing remarked with satisfaction, "I believe it has come to stay," and plans were made to hold a similar defense test annually.[30] But, like many of the other efforts to portray the integration of the army with the people inherent in the National Defense Act, the defense test was only an illusion. Americans were willing to take a paid day's vacation from work to celebrate victory in the world war and to cheer on their friends and neighbors in the National Guard and organized reserves. But they were not willing to do it annually. The defense test held in 1925 was a dismal failure in this regard; plans for a defense test in 1926 were quietly dropped.

Thus, while the golden age of the new citizen army ended in an apparent public triumph, that success was—like much of the rest of the golden age—an illusion, leaving the army's confidence in its relationship with the American public fragile and highly vulnerable to its first encounter with reality. The major source of fragility was the officers' considerable doubt that Americans really wanted the citizen army they were attempting to build. While efforts in Congress to reduce the Regular Army's size ended in 1922, officers could find precious little evidence anywhere else that the public was interested in cooperating with the military in building an adequate defense structure based on citizen-soldier components. As a result, the stabilization of 1923–24 did little to reassure them that there was any real purpose in their enterprise. Further strain from additional evidence of public indifference could easily lead to a state of crisis, as the army would lose confidence in the military policy to which it had committed.

The experience of the army in 1925 produced that strain, creating a near crisis of disorientation and confidence as the military policy seemed to be failing. Morale again sagged. The number of officer resignations, which had been declining in the past several years, rose by 10 percent in fiscal year 1925 and by nearly 30 percent in fiscal year 1926, while desertions among enlisted men followed a similar trend.[31] Some of the causes of the problem were familiar, with money at the top of the list.[32] But others were new. The court-martial of air advocate Brigadier General Billy Mitchell was a source of discomfort to those involved and a source of division in the upper circles of the army.[33] There were also growing complaints about the extraordinary and exhaustive effort required annually to run the summer training camps. For enlisted men, these meant long marches to and from the camps, four-to-six-month separations from family, hard physical labor, and long periods of living in tents.[34] Moreover, other units, already skeletonized by personnel reductions, were drained further by the needs of the camps. For officers, they meant major annual disruptions of both their professional and personal lives, as their own training and that of their units had to take place in less-desirable periods. In 1924 all summer leaves were canceled to provide officers for the camps.[35] As a result of all this, one military journal editorialized at the end of 1925 that efforts to carry out the mission of training civilian components were "wrecking" the army.[36]

But the major problem that dominated the army's experience in 1925 was, again, its relations with the government. In this regard, there was significant disorientation caused by the fact that friends and enemies seemed to change places. Traditionally, the army tended to see itself as part of the executive branch of government, so that the president, as commander in chief, was an ally. Congress, on the other hand, as the parsimonious controller of the purse strings, was the enemy. In 1925 the two seemed to switch roles. One main reason for this was the 1921 budget act, which, as interpreted by the president, the director of the budget, and Congress, made the director, as an agent of the president, the true controller of the purse strings. While this had been apparent in 1923 and 1924, it was not a source of antagonism since the army had not demanded of the president more than he was sure to grant. So, once Congress had accepted the new budget system, little was left for Congress and the army to contest.

As was the case earlier in the 1920s, the primary factor in the 1925 crisis was again the budget, but this time the dispute was between the army and the president. Tensions were precipitated by demands from the new president, Calvin Coolidge, for more significant cuts in the army budget. The dispute was distressing not only because Coolidge's demands threatened the army with new reductions and destabilization reminiscent of the reductions of 1921 and 1922 but also because they came from the president. While the army had learned, to some extent, how to deal with a querulous Congress by referral to the president's policy and appeal to public opinion, it was at a loss as to how to deal with a seemingly unreasonable president.

The situation was complicated by two other factors. First, ever since the passage of the National Defense Act of 1920, the army had, to some extent, been living beyond its means. While it carefully kept expenditures within limits set by annual appropriations, it was still able to draw freely on a large store of surplus uniforms, supplies, and munitions left over from the war. These leftover materials were particularly useful in subsidizing the training of civilian components. But this practice carried with it the danger that, when these stocks were exhausted, the army would need a sudden increase in appropriations to maintain the same level of training. Beginning in 1924, Secretary of War Weeks included in his annual reports a warning that the exhaustion of stocks would necessitate an increase in expenditures in hopes that this would make such a future increase more acceptable.[37]

The second factor was increasing anger in the army over the nature of budget practices, which seemed designed to shield those who were making the cuts, including the president and Congress, from having to take responsibility for them. Under the new guidelines issued by President Coolidge, the army was to keep secret the estimates it sent to the director of the budget. The director would then cut the army's estimates and send his recommendation to the

House Appropriations Committee, still under the wrap of secrecy. In the military subcommittee, the army was restricted to testifying in support of the budget director's proposal, with all such testimony given in secret. The substance of the hearings and subcommittee budget recommendations were then sent to all House members in massive volumes only a few days before the scheduled vote. But if the subcommittee made no substantial cuts, the figures were said to represent all that the army asked for. Hence, if the budget passed as presented, the army bore the responsibility for living within the appropriations approved.[38] During the winter of 1924–25, the navy attempted to revolt against the system by having a friendly congressman on the House Naval Affairs Committee demand an end to the secrecy of these procedures, but the administration successfully squelched the initiative.[39]

The major crisis in the relations between the army, the president, and the director of the budget came in the summer of 1925. In May the budget director, Herbert M. Lord, notified the army that the president wanted to cut taxes and so was calling for another reduction in spending.[40] The War Department responded that, due to the near exhaustion of surplus items, it would actually require a $16 million increase over the amount appropriated for fiscal 1926. Lord, in turn, demanded a list of all training activities, both for the Regular Army and for the civilian components, with the intention of slashing them in half. He threatened to reduce the army school system, the value of which he did not see.[41] The General Staff was outraged that the budget director had now taken upon himself the power to determine army policy. In the face of this uproar, the president backed down. Instead, Coolidge sent a letter to the secretary of war calling on the War Department to propose reductions in its own budget amounting to $35 million over three years.[42]

The president's request created a crisis in the General Staff, seen in two weekly meetings of its Legislative Committee.[43] The need for $16 million just to stay even and Coolidge's demand for an eventual $35 million reduction, together with Lord's cavalier attitude toward the training of civilian components, brought the General Staff to reconsider seriously for the first time its support of the National Defense Act and even its traditional loyalty to the president. In wide-ranging discussions, some members of the committee proposed severe reductions in the civilian components to save the Regular Army. Others proposed a rebellion along the line of that taken by the General Staff in 1915 against Secretary of War Garrison. They would propose a budget based on the 13,000-officer, 150,000-man army that reflected the staff's professional opinion as to the minimum necessary to carry out the missions assigned by the National Defense Act. If this was cut by the director of the budget, a member of Congress would call upon the General Staff for a report as to the army's ability to carry out the military policy in the National Defense Act. Such an inquiry would then allow the army to avoid the rule of secrecy imposed by the administration.[44] After a period of indecision, the committee decided to take a far more moderate path, developing a budget recommendation that included an increase, although not the full $16 million it felt was needed.[45] Rumors then surfaced that Lord proposed cutting even that budget by $7–8 million, sending the leadership of the General Staff into a new round of meetings. They were, again, divided between one group who looked for new ways to economize and save as many Regular Army personnel and civilian components as possible and a second, more radical group that called for deeper cuts in personnel coupled with a proposal that Congress repeal the National Defense Act, since the army could no longer carry out the mission that law assigned it.[46] In the end moderates again carried the day, leading the War Department to further reduce costs by suspending recruiting in the National Guard, reducing the size of the Regular Army to 115,000 men, and trimming allotments to other components.[47] While this measure ended the immediate budget crisis, the experience left army leadership angry with the Coolidge administration and with a significantly reduced sense of commitment to the defense act.[48]

While it may have seemed disorienting to be in conflict with the executive branch in regard to the budget, this was, in fact, only one area of such conflict. Individual officers and servicemen also found themselves for the first time at odds with several executive agencies, including the Internal Revenue Service and the newly created Comptroller General, whose fiscal policies appeared in the army to be capricious and arbitrary.

What was probably most disturbing to army officers was the sense that they had been abandoned in the face of a new foe. As professional agents of the government, and especially its executive branch, officers felt they had a right to protection by that branch from outside attacks. In the past, the president had often come to the army's aid when it was beleaguered, especially by Congress. The fact that the president now was unwilling to protect the military from his own administrators, leaving officers to fight in their own defense by means of test cases in the courts supported by round after round of contributions to legal funds, left many feeling abandoned.

Army officers responded to this demoralizing situation in several ways. One was a reappearance of some forms of conspiracy theory and renewed attacks on pacifists. Antipacifist agitation had all but disappeared from the professional journals by early 1925.[49] It began to appear with increasing frequency in the second half of that year after Coolidge's budget battle with the army. Moreover, the nature of the attacks had changed. The old vision of pacifism as a dupe of an international communist conspiracy had all but died. Instead, pacifism now was linked with materialism and efforts at economy.[50]

But the most important response, although in line with others, was a notable decline of interest in and enthusiasm for the National Defense Act and its military policy. Colonel Thomas Hammond, one of the officer architects of the defense act and other legislation surrounding it, was still speaking in its behalf at the end of 1925. *Infantry Journal* reprinted part of one of his speeches in November 1925.[51] But that was the last article favorable to the act to appear in the publication for a long time. Elsewhere, army officers in public addresses and articles were beginning to show a real skepticism of the military policy of the National Defense Act. Major General John L. Hines, as deputy chief of staff, stated to a supportive audience at the national convention of the National Guard Association in December 1924: "I consider the National Defense Act of 1920, . . . a splendid piece of legislation. It is good, however, only to the extent to which it is backed up by the people of the United States. Otherwise, it is a dead letter and worth no more than the paper on which it is printed."[52] Editorials in many of the service journals made the same argument, that the military policy of the defense act, however desirable it may have been, was dependent on popular support for its success. Yet that backing was nowhere visible.[53]

There was also, in speeches and articles, a noticeable return to the vision of the military profession as one isolated from the public. This was seen a bit in the fall of 1922, after the officer elimination and demotion crisis. In 1925, articles began to appear with significant references to the nation's traditional unwillingness to adopt a realistic military policy.[54] By late 1924 and throughout 1925, this outlook started to become common in speeches by military leaders and in articles in military journals.[55]

Thus, while the Regular Army began the project of organizing the new citizen army called for by the National Defense Act of 1920 with the happy expectation that it would enjoy the full support of the both the American government and people, by 1925, it was clear that there would be no such support. This was a severe disappointment, leaving the army and its leadership with the question of whether to continue with these efforts or to give up and return to basing U.S. military policy on the traditional model of a Regular Army that could be expanded in time of emergency by means of volunteers or conscripts.

CHAPTER 2

The Heart of the Policy

Creating the New Citizen Army

T HE NATIONAL DEFENSE ACT of 1920 was all but revolutionary in that it changed the mission and character of the Regular Army. Instead of serving as the professionally trained ground force in the nation's defense structure, the military took on as its most basic mission the education and training of the civilian components of the new citizen army, making it, in Pershing's words, "a great institution of military instruction."[1] During the entire interwar period, the Regular Army continued to regard this mission as its chief and defining responsibility, even at the expense of its own training and development.

The defense act called for the creation of a citizen army, to be called "The Army of the United States," that would be made up of the existing Regular Army and four civilian components: the National Guard, the Officers' Reserve Corps (ORC), the Reserve Officers' Training Corps (ROTC), and the Citizens' Military Training Camps (CMTC), the last of which had an anomalous relationship to the entire program. Creating this new citizen army involved reorganizing the Regular Army, developing the citizen components, and properly assembling them into the Army of the United States.

Once the National Defense Act had been passed, it fell to General March and the General Staff to reorganize the existing army along the new lines required by the act. While the defense act was passed in opposition to his own plans for reorganization, once it became law, March moved immediately and loyally to implement it. Most of the conceptual planning and actual reorganizational work was carried out during the remaining portion of his tenure as chief of staff, leaving it to his successor, General Pershing, and the new secretary of war, John Weeks, to complete these preliminaries and begin implementation.

In his annual report, submitted just weeks after the defense act was signed, March indicated the General Staff's full support of building a citizen army, stating with enthusiasm, "In the furtherance of this end the field open to the Army is one of great possibilities." He noted his approval that the new law meant that the army's traditional separation from society would come to an end.[2] Moreover, the officer who would be most responsible for implementing the program, the director of the War Plans Division, Major General William Haan, had long been a genuine and enthusiastic supporter of the legislation. Haan, who in the war had commanded the 32nd Division, composed of National Guard units, was a firm disciplinarian with a rigorous professional outlook. Yet his duty with the 32nd had led him to appreciate the citizen-soldier, and his temperament led Haan in the direction of cooperation and conciliation rather than domination. The result was that, in the same way the character of General March had shaped the centralization of authority in the General Staff in the war's final months, the character of General Haan largely shaped the work of establishing the foundation of the military policy under the National Defense Act.

Once the defense act was signed, Haan created a committee involving major interest groups, including the General Staff, Pershing's staff, the general-service schools, and the Infantry School. The panel soon addressed concerns on the basic concepts. From there, two major committees of the War Plans Branch of the War Plans Division carried the work forward. An Organization Committee worked on the tactical structure of the Regular Army and the tactical units that would make up the Army of the United States. Its members found their efforts frustratingly interrupted by the force reductions ordered in the 1920 and 1921 Army Appropriation Acts so that much of their work had to be redone. A Committee on War Department and Defense Projects carried out most of the plans regarding the integration of the National Guard, the Organized Reserve, and the Regular Army into the unified citizen army and allocating units of each to the new corps areas. These corps-area commands replaced the older territorial departments on September 1, and within three weeks they received instructions on the overall development of the U.S. Army. The plan for restructuring the National Guard was published in October 1920. and in February 1921 the basic organization of the Organized Reserve was completed, with unit allocations sent out to corps-area commanders shortly thereafter. The entire plan was then explained to state governors in a letter sent out at the beginning of June.[3]

The plan was quickly accepted. The goal of the General Staff was to develop the framework for a citizen army of 2,000,000 men that could be mobilized quickly in the face of a great emergency such as the past war. This force was to be made up of six field armies of three corps each, with six divisions in each corps. Of the requisite fifty-four divisions, nine would come from the Regular Army, eighteen from the National Guard, and twenty-seven from the Organized Reserve. The 280,000 men allocated to the Regular Army would allow the creation of nine divisions at full strength. The National Guard was to be expanded to 424,800 men by 1924 and would be organized into the eighteen divisions, all to exist at full strength. The Organized Reserve units, on the other hand, would be skeletal organizations only, consisting of reserve officers and a few enlisted specialists. Reserve units were formed on the assumption that, in an emergency, the manpower to fill them would come from a draft and that they would initially be mobilization and training commands. All units in this "Six-Army Plan" would be localized. The Regular Army divisions would be stationed in World War I cantonments in each corps area. The National Guard and Organized Reserve divisions were broken down into myriad local units that could be mobilized within the corps areas at the outbreak of a war. For less than a major emergency, only Regular Army and National Guard units would be mobilized, while minor emergencies would be handled by an expeditionary force made up of regular units only.[4]

In the meantime, the General Staff itself was reorganized along lines similar to those used by Pershing in France during the war.[5] On September 18 the chiefs of branches offices for the combat arms were created. At the same time, the basic organization of subordinate units, such as branches, arms, and services, was standardized.[6] As a result, at the end of fiscal year 1921, as both March and Haan were ready to step aside for their successors, the military was tactically organized into a single Army of the United States comprising three basic components. In some respects, all that was left to do was to organize and fill the citizen components.

Pershing's first major concern when he became chief of staff was to finish the work of reorganizing the General Staff along the lines of the Allied Expeditionary Force (AEF), which he had commanded in France, with a nucleus general headquarters to support him as commanding general. Within a week he had a board of senior officers, organized under Major General James G. Harbord, to carry out this reorganization.[7] The basic structure of the General Staff was altered to conform to that of Pershing's AEF staff, with the same titles and the same G1 to G5 designations.[8] Moreover, this new organization was to be used as a model for the corps-area commanders' staffs. Otherwise, the basic structure of the General Staff created by March remained largely unaltered. The War Plans Division (G5) was organized so that it could serve as a nucleus of a general headquarters but was otherwise an integral part of the General Staff, sharing in its work. Thus, the resulting arrangement retained much that existed under March. Moreover, it was clear that the General Staff would continue to supervise the bureaus; the goal of the reform was to make it better able to do so.

Pershing's real influence on the General Staff in the first years as chief of staff, therefore, was not in reorganization, as much as that might have interested him, but in the process of implementation of the National Defense Act by setting up the civilian components of the Army of the United States. As noted earlier, much of the preliminary conceptual and organizational work for this had already been accomplished during March's tenure. The major contribution of Pershing and his staff was the decentralization of the program by placing the major responsibility for its execution on the shoulders of the new corps-area commanders. Based on the Six-Army Plan, the country was divided into nine corps areas, each with its own commander responsible for much of the military activity therein, including the training of the civilian components. By the time Pershing had become chief of staff, much of the initial work establishing the corps areas was already completed. The corps areas themselves were designated and the Regular Army units assigned to them for training the civilian components as well as the assignment of the Organized Reserve units.[9] What remained was to organize the corps-area training structure, especially the training centers. The governing instructions to corps-area commanders regarding their training responsibilities were issued in September 1921. These instructions were brief, leaving much room for the commanders' initiative, pointing out only the work to be done and calling for "*brief*" monthly reports on progress.[10]

With the organization of the corps areas already completed, the General Staff under Pershing turned its attention to the creation of the training centers. Each was to be the corps-area commander's headquarters and planning center. Regular Army recruits assigned to corps area would be trained there, as would Organized Reserve and National Guard units when appropriate. Regular units responsible for training civilian components would be stationed at each as well. Finally, in a war, the training centers would function as mobilization centers for the corps area. Basic instruction and regulations for the organization of the training centers were issued to corps-area commanders in October. While assignment of regular units was significantly disrupted by the three reductions in the army, most training centers had sufficient units assigned to allow them to begin full-scale summer training in 1922.[11] Once the corps-area training structure was in place, Pershing and the General Staff left it alone and involved themselves with policy issues in regard to the civilian components, including educating the Regular Army that their training was now its central mission.

Pershing also took an interest in aspects of the further development of the civilian components themselves. In November 1922 a general policy was developed regarding the length of tours and the responsibilities of reserve officers serving on duty with the General Staff as required by the National Defense Act.[12] Initially, reserve officers were concentrated in the Personnel Division and, especially, the Operations and Training Division, since those sections dealt with most of the policies regarding the National Guard and Organized Reserve. After a year, Pershing changed this policy so that reserve officers were assigned for orientation purposes to all branches of the General Staff.[13] He also intervened personally in National Guard and Organized Reserve matters regarding officer assignments to ensure that the Regular Army's best officers served in training components. The chief of staff also pushed the general-service schools to develop career courses for guard and reserve officers so that they could gain access to the General Staff Eligible List and serve on the staff in wartime.

But Pershing's main concern with the civilian components at this time was to convince officers in the Regular Army to accept what was then called the "one-army" spirit. As he explained to one correspondent even before he had become chief of staff, this meant "that all officers whether of the Regular Army or of the Organized Reserve should be for the Army of the United States as a whole, and not mere partisans of the branch of the service to which they may belong."[14] At the same time, he told the chiefs of branches that he expected them to promote the "one army" spirit when visiting their units and supported the creation of the Army Association of the United States as an organization representing the "one-army" idea.[15] Pershing also relied heavily on Colonel Palmer to propagandize the "one-army" spirit. At Palmer's request, the general appointed him aide-de-camp with few duties other than to speak and write on behalf of the "one-army" vision of the National Defense Act.[16] For the next year, Palmer wrote articles for popular and service journals and spoke to citizen and military groups as well as contacting those in Pershing's broad network of friends and acquaintances.[17]

Finally, all officers were encouraged to advocate for the "one-army" idea as well. The requirement that they clear any articles with the War Department before publication was dropped. Instead, it was made clear that officers were not only allowed to publish but also encouraged to do so, especially if the work would acquaint a wide audience with the War Department's "one-army" policy.[18] By early 1922, articles on the topic began to appear in service journals. By October, the War Department was emphasizing that officers were expected to take an aggressive role in promoting the "one-army" idea to any audience available.[19]

Although Pershing's commitment to the citizen army was vigorous, it was, nevertheless, less than complete. It was one thing to urge the General Staff and Regular Army officers to adopt the "one-army" spirit and to demand that army attention be focused on training of civilian components. It was another matter,

however, to sacrifice units, promotion, and morale to this policy. This problem
was evident even before Pershing became chief of staff, as it became clear that
the Regular Army was to be reduced from 280,000 to 175,000 men. After several
exchanges between the Operations and Training Division and the War Plans
Division on how to effect such a reduction, they reached a tentative decision in
favor of demobilizing five divisions in order to save the training centers.[20] Nevertheless, opposition to this approach developed within the General Staff, while
the chief of infantry also opposed it, favoring, instead a skeletonizing of all divisions.[21] Although the Operations and Training Division proposal was accepted,
concessions were made to the opposition.[22] Palmer saw that another reduction
would lead to pressure to save as many units as possible through the sacrifice
of the training centers and their mission. He sought to avoid this by building
sanctions against it. The colonel drafted a general order by which the secretary
of war indicated that his interpretation of the National Defense Act was that the
focus of Regular Army activities was to be on building the citizen components,
the number of officers authorized in the act having been made purposely high
for the express purpose of carrying out this training.[23]

Palmer then continued to plump for the idea in speeches and publications.
Nonetheless, all of this was to no avail in the face of the 1922 reductions. Palmer
urged Pershing to reduce and eliminate the number of divisions in the Regular Army in order to save the training forces. But since that likely meant the
further elimination of some officers and the demotion of others, most in the
General Staff opposed this idea. Hence, Pershing agreed instead to carry out
the 1922 reductions by abolishing the newly created training centers, making
the remaining partially skeletonized forces responsible for training. Given the
disastrous state of officer morale in the summer of 1922, this was probably a
wise policy and probably had less disruption on the training of components
than Palmer feared. But it showed the degree to which outside pressures could
place significant strain on the commitment of the Regular Army to its new
training mission. Even so, as William O. Odom has pointed out, the Regular
Army continued to support the citizen components even at the sacrifice of its
own training and development.[24]

While the work of organizing the Army of the United States and reorganizing the Regular Army was carried out chiefly by the General Staff, the creation
of the individual citizen components required the development of a cooperative
relationship between the staff and those units themselves. This was achieved,
though in some cases not without some initial difficulty. The process of development was also hindered by the turmoil and stress that beset the army in the

first half of the 1920s. As a result, although the process of developing the citizen components was virtually completed by 1925, its success varied between the components themselves.

The National Guard

Despite the acrimony existing between the National Guard and the Regular Army up to 1920, the two organizations were soon able to build a working relationship that became all but cordial by 1925. They also succeeded in building a new guard organization and fitting it into the National Army structure envisioned in the National Defense Act. But, by 1925, critical deficiencies began to appear in the Guard with regards to recruiting and, especially, in training that led to a growing concern as to whether it could actually carry out its assigned wartime mission.

The immediate foundations upon which the collaborative reestablishment of the National Guard as a civilian component of the Army of the United States was to be built were scarcely auspicious. Relations between the Regular Army and the Guard were already strained to the utmost on the eve of World War I. Then the experience of the Guard during the war severely aggravated this strain. Guardsmen were drafted during the war to serve as individuals rather than being allowed to volunteer as entire units, as Pershing and other army leaders decided that divisions formed pursuant to existing American military policy were too light to be effective and needed to be increased in size. As a result, many guard divisions and smaller units were broken up to form new and larger multistate divisions.[25] These were then given numerical designations that in almost no way indicated state or guard origins. While the War Department expressed regret at the damage done to unit and state pride, guardsmen were outraged.

During the war, many senior regular officers who fought in close association with guard units emerged with a profound respect for them. Guardsmen, on the other hand, found far less reason to change their minds about the arrogant and narrow-minded professional intolerance they found in many regulars, especially rapidly promoted field-grade officers on staffs, some of whom became legendary in their repeated expressions of contempt for the Guard.[26] Finally, the war all but destroyed the guard units and organizational structure remaining in the country. The draft in 1917 took the younger men out of most units, and the extension of the draft age to forty-five years old in August 1918 stripped most units of all but a few older men.[27] Moreover, the National Defense Act of 1916 and the Selective Service Act of May 18, 1917, provided that guardsmen who had

been drafted into federal service lost all guard identity and, at the end of the
emergency, would be discharged as civilians rather than returned to the Guard.

The immediate postwar experience of the National Guard aggravated the
strained relations with the Regular Army even further. The Guard, or what was
left of it after war and demobilization, was fearful that it might not even have
a future. While it was certain that any final military policy adopted by Congress would continue provisions for a regular army, there was no such certainty
that the Guard would not be reduced to the role of a state constabulary. The
March-Baker bill included no provision for the organization. Colonel Palmer,
in drawing up legislation for the Senate Military Affairs Committee, explicitly
omitted the Guard. In this atmosphere, the Guard became increasingly restive,
using its political influence to exert pressure for the preservation of its clauses
from the 1916 defense act. Their efforts found much support in the House of
Representative and were responsible for many of the provisions in National Defense Act of 1920 under which the Guard would be reorganized.

Outside of the legislative issue, relations between the Guard and the Militia Bureau, the agency within the General Staff with responsibility for Guard
matters, were also strained by the perception that the bureau was doing little
in terms of reconstructing the Guard. During the interwar period, it consisted
of four guard officers and twenty-six regular officers.[28] Although the regulars
often shared the prejudices of many of their colleagues toward the Guard, they
were still closer to guard personnel and more in sympathy with them. Hence,
even without policy guidance, the Militia Bureau sought to encourage states to
reconstruct their guard units while offering whatever support it could. At the
same time, it also pushed the War Department toward a military policy that
would include provisions for the Guard. Lacking influence within either the
General Staff or the War Department, however, the Militia Bureau was initially
able to do relatively little to support guard reorganization.

Outside the bureau, however, state pressures began building in the spring of
1919 to push the General Staff toward a commitment to reestablish the position
of the National Guard as the main reserve force. By the middle of May, Secretary
of War Baker grudgingly accepted the idea that the Guard was to be reconsti-
tuted at the federal as well as at the state level with the National Defense Act of
1916 as its basis.[29] By June, the Militia Bureau had worked out a provisional policy for the Guard that took into account the legal provisions of the 1916 defense
act, the tactical experience of the war, and the special conditions under which
the Guard operated. In so doing, it raised most of the issues that dominated the
guard experience in the interwar years. While the 1916 act allowed the Guard a

strength of 424,800 troops, or 800 men for each congressman and senator for each state, the Militia Bureau anticipated that Congress presently would not fund such a large force, nor could such a force be organized immediately. Thus, it suggested that the army initially plan the organization of the Guard on the basis of 200 men per congressman and senator. It also suggested that it be organized on the same tactical basis as the Regular Army to avoid any repetition of the wartime reorganization that had proved so painful in 1917. On the other hand, it was clear that guard units could never be recruited to the strength of regular units. Many communities were too small to support such numbers, and most armories were built to accommodate smaller organizations. Hence, the Militia Bureau recommended that guard companies be given federal recognition and support at a level of 65 men and that a National Guard reserve be maintained sufficient to raise companies to 100 soldiers in the event of war.[30]

Meanwhile, elements in the Guard hostile to the Regular Army and, especially, to the General Staff gained control of the nearly moribund National Guard Association. They worked to mobilize guardsmen to fight for their interests in the fall of 1919 as Congress began to consider military-policy legislation. This political mobilization was difficult since it lacked a target. As a result, anger was actually channeled against the Militia Bureau, which was unfairly subjected to a variety of criticisms aimed to show that an agency headed by a Regular Army officer could never understand or meet the needs of the National Guard.[31] So, during the fall of 1919, as Congress considered military policy, the Guard's two main political objectives were preserving the Guard provisions of the National Defense Act of 1916 and placing one of its officers at the head of the Militia Bureau.

By then, however, the anti–General Staff radicals began to lose control of the National Guard Association to moderates who advocated a more cooperative relationship with the staff. Recruiting for the Guard had not been successful, especially in the summer and fall of 1919.[32] Cooperation in this area then began to pay dividends. In the spring of 1920, the Regular Army began to assist the Guard in recruiting while publicizing plans to give guardsmen some summer training. As a result, enlistment numbers began to rise rapidly.[33] A more cooperative spirit also helped in Congress, where there was still much support for a version of a military-policy bill that would leave the guard provisions of 1916 intact and for placing a guardsman at the head of the Militia Bureau.[34] As a result, even though the Guard and the army remained in opposition on many issues related to the pending national defense legislation in the spring of 1920, their relationship became increasingly cordial and cooperative.

As completed, the National Defense Act of 1920 contributed to this growing cooperation by providing compromises on major issues that were satisfactory to both sides. It required the Militia Bureau to be headed by a guardsman, but it gave the General Staff considerable control over the selection of that officer. It called for the appointment to the General Staff of guard officers to deal with issues specifically related to their organization. The Guard was also allowed a temporary variance of 10 percent in the requirement for a minimum of 65 men a unit to qualify for federal support. Moreover, units were given a year to reach this standard; in fiscal year 1920–21, units needed to contain only 50 men to qualify. Finally, since the Guard was to play a role as a reserve available for immediate use, it was generously allowed the authorized strength of 800 per congressman and senator as provided in the 1916 act.

With the passage of the National Defense Act of 1920, the focus of attention in both the General Staff and the National Guard was on building the new Guard within the framework provided by the new law. Over the next five years, this centered on three major issues: recruiting, organization, and training. But as would be expected, in the first years the focus was on recruiting and organizing. The provisions of the defense act had given the Guard nearly all it had asked for, including a critical mission and an ambitious recruiting goal. This fostered a new spirit of cordiality and cooperation that increasingly seemed to infuse relations between the Guard and the Regular Army, creating an initial euphoric enthusiasm in the Guard as it set out to recruit under the act. This effort then met with at least the appearance of impressive success. During fiscal year 1921, the size of the Guard increased by over 100 percent, from 55,883 to 113,640 men, and the Guard enjoyed another 42-percent growth in fiscal year 1922 to 159,658 troops.[35] This increase was matched by expanded breadth for the organization. In June 1920, only thirty-four states had units. At the end of fiscal year 1922, only Nevada lacked units, and twenty states had organized all the units allocated to them.[36]

Yet the statistical results masked several basic problems. Despite this initial rapid growth, army leaders began to question whether the National Guard would be able to recruit much above its prewar levels. For the pessimists, the initial surge in guard enlistments in 1921 was seen as a response to the end of uncertainty and other matters that had depressed recruiting earlier. Moreover, most of the growth came from the development of new units rather than the expansion of established ones. By July 1921, it was necessary for the chief of the Militia Bureau to request a one-year extension of the special provision that gave tentative recognition to units with as few as fifty men per company.[37] A similar request was made in 1922.[38] Finally, as Congress began cutting budgets, it became increasingly less willing to fund the rapid expansion of the Guard.[39]

The recruiting problem reached a crisis stage in 1922 with the army reduction called for by the Congress. Officers in the General Staff and elsewhere had always been skeptical as to whether the National Guard could ever recruit the authorized 424,800 men and felt that a force half that size was adequate.[40] By the end of 1921, General Staff leadership was convinced that a severe reduction was needed and hoped the Guard would take the lead, not wanting the reductions to appear to be an anti-Guard action on their part.[41] Early in 1922, the situation became more critical as it became increasingly clear that Congress would again reduce existing officer strength, which led to efforts to find ways to economize on the use of officers. The General Staff began to consider vastly reducing recruiting by the Guard. Secretary of War Weeks took the lead in this. After Congress passed the 1922 army reduction, Weeks assembled a committee of guardsmen and members of the General Staff to suggest appropriate action. The panel began meeting on November 13 and had a recommendation ready by January 15, 1923. It called for a reduction of the final overall size of the National Guard to 250,000 troops, which would still provide for enough men to staff the eighteen infantry and four cavalry divisions called for in the Six-Army Plan at maintenance rather than full strength.[42]

Most guardsmen considered the new goal reasonable in the light of national and state economic-retrenchment policies, the growing recruiting problems, and the reduced size of the Regular Army. Yet the reduction all but enshrined the 65-man rather than the 100-man company as the standard National Guard unit. In an emergency, these companies would have to be expanded to a war strength of 200. It had been anticipated originally that much of this expansion would be carried out by units of National Guard reserve, men who had been trained and still attended summer camps but belonged to no distinct unit. Yet that program was a total failure, with less than a thousand enlisted. Thus, while it was never admitted, the reduction of the final objective meant that in an emergency, Guard units would be so diluted by a massive input of untrained volunteers or draftees that their immediate fighting power would be negligible. This, in turn, meant that the Guard would never really be capable of meeting its mission as an immediately available combat-ready force.[43]

This decision, however, was vindicated by the results of recruiting efforts in 1923. Major General George C. Rickards, chief of the Militia Bureau, had called for appropriations to provide for a nearly 20-percent expansion of the National Guard, from 159,658 to 191,000 men, but by the end of the year, guard membership was up by less than 1,000 men to 160,598.[44] Several factors explain this unexpected collapse in recruiting. For one, by 1923, the three-year enlistment of nearly 15,000 guardsmen who had signed up in 1920 expired, and most left. Moreover, curtailing the manpower objective meant that many states received no new allotment of units. Finally, budget retrenchments in many states made legislators less willing to invest in armories. These factors tended to diminish the number of new units created, and new units had always been the major source of increased numbers for the Guard.[45]

Underlying these external factors, however, was an internal problem. The National Guard was losing its overall attractiveness. The fact that the total number of guardsmen remained level between July 1, 1922, and July 1, 1923, at the same time as the number of units increased meant that average unit membership actually fell. There were several reasons for this. Twenty years earlier, the Guard, with drills, uniforms, and parades, was one of the more exciting preoccupations offered in many communities.[46] By the early 1920s, movies, organized sports, and other activities had appeared as rival forms of public entertainment. Labor remained hostile to the Guard, so union members rarely joined. On top of this, life in the Guard was rather demanding and boring. In the early 1920s, training concepts in the Guard were still fairly primitive and focused on parade drill, so training seemed more like useless work than military instruction. On top of the one and a half hours of drill each week, most officers were expected to put in another hour and a half without pay to complete paperwork and plan for future drills, not to mention several additional hours a week on a correspondence course for professional advancement. Thus, many found the time commitment eating up two to three nights a week. As a result, guardsmen began to lose interest and dropped out when the opportunity presented itself. Turnover rates in many units in 1923 approached 50 percent, creating problems in stability and training.

The recruiting crisis of 1923 was overcome to some extent in 1924 as measures were taken to increase public interest. As a result, the National Guard enjoyed a 15-percent expansion in fiscal year 1924. The enthusiasm created by this expansion was, however, dissipated early in the next fiscal year when economic retrenchment in Congress limited available funds, and the Militia Bureau was forced to suspend recognition of new guard units, leaving enlistments nearly static.[47] Even before this freeze, however, many in the General Staff, and in the Militia Bureau, began to regard the prospect of even reaching the reduced goal of 250,000 guardsmen by July 1926 as unlikely.[48]

On the other hand, even though the organization of the National Guard into tactical units that would fit into the overall Six-Army Plan was a massive job, it was handled smoothly in a manner that continued to maintain the confidence of both regulars and guardsmen. The problem was fraught with political difficulties. While dividing the corps allotted to the Guard in the National Defense Act into specific divisions and allocating units of each to states was relatively easy, getting the states to go along with this was difficult because the process would necessarily involve an amalgamation of some traditional units while extensively changing the functions of others. In addition, while the General Staff had to plan the organization of a 424,800-man Guard, the schedule for reaching that strength stretched over four years, so unit allocations had to be introduced incrementally to preserve the Guard's overall balance during this expansion.

Despite the massiveness of the undertaking, the initial organization was done rather rapidly. By the middle of July 1920, a committee in the General Staff had worked out the basic policies along which the National Guard would be reconstructed. Following the War Department's commitment to decentralization, the plan gave corps-area commanders broad authority in local reorganization, leaving the staff and the Militia Bureau responsible only for policy development and administrative oversight.[49] The task of distributing the units among the states was far more complex, but that was worked out chiefly by the Guard itself. Palmer had insisted that this be worked out by a board on which guard and reserve officers would predominate. By December, after initial discussions with state governors, this board, acting through the chief of the Militia Bureau, distributed major allotments to individual states. Then state boards, made up almost entirely of guard officers, distributed allocations of company-size units to localities.[50] The task of supervising the formation of local units and recognizing them belonged to corps-area commanders. Even though this process involved the distribution of over 2,500 units in a ticklish political setting, it went surprisingly smoothly.

After the initial organization of the National Guard, the only major organizational problem remaining to be worked out centered on the relationship of the Militia Bureau with the corps-area commanders. Much of this problem stemmed from fears in the General Staff that, with a guardsman at its head, the bureau would soon become the headquarters for an increasingly autonomous Guard. Such concerns were aggravated by overall anxieties regarding decentralization and by personality clashes. Rickards, who became the first guardsman to serve as chief of the Militia Bureau, came to his post with a long and distinguished career and significant backing within the Guard. He also viewed himself as an advocate for the Guard, which introduced further strain between his office and the General Staff. The result was an ongoing struggle between the bureau, which wanted to keep as much control over the Guard in its hands as possible, and the staff, which sought to delegate as much authority as possible to corps-area commanders.[51] The issue was finally resolved by a committee of regular and guard officers who worked out a compromise that shifted more authority to the corps-area commanders, making the local guard units so dependent on them that the development of an autonomous Guard became virtually impossible. Rickards protested the decision but lost.[52]

Despite this source of rancor, the General Staff and Chief of Staff Pershing made major efforts to further the development of cordiality and trust in the relations between the National Guard and the Regular Army. Recruiters were encouraged to cooperate with the Guard and were recognized when they did so. Finally, and most important, Pershing insisted that officers serving with the Guard be among the best in the army and be informed that the army considered such duty to be of the highest importance. He also ordered the compilation of a roster of these officers so that everyone on it with an effectiveness rating of less than average could be relieved. He then went through the list himself, checking off names of officers he wanted released from service with the Guard.[53]

Organizational developments between 1923 and 1925 were far less discouraging than the recruiting efforts. Indeed, the slow growth in recruiting was one of several factors that led to a sense of stability in the National Guard by the end of 1925. At the same time, histories of the Militia Bureau began to appear in professional journals, signaling that the office was becoming accepted as part of the army leadership structure.[54] Guard regulations were revised as were those for mobilizing its units. At local levels, the bureau encouraged guard units to write their own histories and apply for coats of arms as a means of creating a sense of permanence and unit identification. At the same time Congress authorized commissions in the Army of the United States for the Guard, which gave guardsmen a better sense of belonging to a single whole, as did its participation in the defense test in 1924.[55]

While the growing sense of stability in the organization to some extent balanced the more volatile and depressing situation in terms of recruiting, both issues were old problems that officers in the National Guard and the Regular Army could understand if not entirely control. Yet by 1925, a new problem began to appear in the Guard that became a growing source of concern among regulars, since it called into question the basic ability of the Guard to fulfill its primary mission. The trouble was with training. To fulfill its mission to serve as a force immediately ready for emergency combat situations, the better part of the Guard would have had to have undergone a significant degree of both individual and unit training. This was a challenge.

In the initial years of reconstructing the National Guard, little attention was given to training since the problems of recruiting and organization were so immediate and compelling. Moreover, many assumed that the ranks of the Guard would be filled by war veterans who had already undergone considerable training. This, however, failed to happen, with new recruits increasingly being younger men without military experience. By the summer of 1921, 80 percent of guardsmen had no previous military training, which meant that the Guard had to provide them training to make its units immediately available in case of war.[56] Observers saw the issue largely as one of time. A guardsman trained only an hour and a half a week and fifteen days in the summer. Even if he attended every drill, this would provide less than two hundred hours of training a year, scarcely enough to prepare a man or a unit for combat, many believed.[57] For several years, hope was that the problem would be solved by a rapid expansion of CMTC, which at least would provide the Guard with a source of partially trained manpower.[58] This, however, failed to happen.

As these initial expectations dissipated, problems associated with training became clearer in both character and complexity. Time remained a critical issue, but there was also the question of who would carry out the training. Palmer envisioned a citizen army as self-trained, with the more able and ambitious moving ahead in rank by training themselves to a point that they would take charge of instructing others. The assumption that the National Guard would train itself, however, proved flawed in several ways. First, it put too heavy a burden on the leadership. Officers needed to spend time not only in supervising the one and a half hours of drill one evening a week but also in preparing training programs on both an annual and weekly basis. In addition, they had to work on the correspondence courses necessary for their own professional advancement. While some guard officers had a sense of professionalism and commitment sufficient to inspire them to devote this time and energy, many others did not. Moreover, even those willing to put in the time to do the job right often lacked the experience needed to develop a compelling training program. This was aggravated by the fact that, due to the high level of turnover, a typical National Guard unit consisted of both veteran noncommissioned officers (NCOs) and raw recruits. Such variations in experience meant that the unit could not train together but had to follow several different training plans simultaneously. Finally, although the Guard was furnished with regular officers and NCOs to assist with training, the regulars often lacked the understanding, patience, and tact needed in working with part-time volunteers. The result was often not just friction but also frequent efforts by the regular officers to take over the job of training themselves.[59]

Through the summer of 1922, the General Staff limited itself to supervising the conduct of summer camps, where almost all efforts were focused on recruit training. The army also made spaces in its own special-service schools available to the National Guard in an effort to provide training for its officers, while Pershing attempted to get curricula for regular officers in special summer schools revised to include more instruction related specifically to guard training.[60] By 1923, it was clear that, to provide an adequate system of training for the Guard, the General Staff would have to coordinate the supervision of the entire training year so that summer camps supplemented rather than duplicated the work done in armories during the year.[61] The Operations and Training Division, therefore, began to coordinate efforts by publishing an annual training directive focused on the objectives to be met in both the Regular Army and the summer training camps.[62] While dissemination of the plan in 1923 was too slow and the plan itself too rigid to influence instruction in armories that year, the distribution of the following year's plan was speeded up, and the plan itself made more flexible, providing unit commanders basic training objectives to serve as the focus for their own preparations.[63]

But while the General Staff and the National Guard had developed a comprehensive training system by 1925, there was still growing skepticism within the Regular Army that the Guard was getting the necessary training to fulfill its mission. This pessimism was seen in a sudden rash of articles on training that appeared in the professional journals in 1925. While their tone was always positive and dealt with problems solved, the articles also discussed in detail the problems yet unresolved and with an undercurrent of doubt. Few saw any answers to the time problem, compounded as it was by the high turnover rate. This meant that most guard units were deeply involved with recruit training and could rarely be counted on at any given moment to be ready for immediate combat. In addition, while most guard officers needed to carry on their own professional training through the correspondence-school system, many took little interest in the courses.[64]

Finally, in the minds of many regular officers, the training deficiency and high turnover in individual units greatly aggravated the dilution problem inherent in mobilizing National Guard units by filling them to war strength with untrained conscripts. Considering that, at any given time, a significant number of the men in typical guard units were themselves recent recruits, filling a sixty-five-man unit to its war strength of two hundred by adding raw draftees meant that far more than just two-thirds of the men in a unit would be untrained.[65] And, since even the members of the more experienced cadre had only about 150 hours a year of training themselves, it seemed highly questionable whether, in an emergency, they would be able to train the newcomers while still functioning as a readily available combat unit. Hence, while the ethos of the "one army" spirit made it virtually unprofessional for regular officers to openly criticize the Guard, the sudden interest they expressed in the issue of guard training in 1925 would indicate that the Regular Army's traditional skepticism that the National Guard had the ability to carry out its mission was rapidly returning.

The Citizens' Military Training Camps (CMTC)

Of the four citizen components for which the army took responsibility under the National Defense Act 1920, the most anomalous was the Citizens' Military Training Camps. These were authorized under section 47(d) of the defense act, which, while it was quite precise in fiscal matters, was rather vague as to the purposes of the camps. This vagueness was largely due to the fact that the impetus for the CMTC came from two sources. Narrowly interpreted, the obvious intention was to provide for a continuous source of reserve officers and noncommissioned officers, especially after the veterans of the war surpassed the age of useful service. But the concept of summer training camps had its own history that suggested to many a far broader purpose for the CMTC. The idea was tied to General Wood's Plattsburgh experiment and through it to the preparedness movement and the effort to establish universal military training. For many of its supporters, section 47(d) was to be the wedge that would reopen the way to the establishment of universal military training. Pursuit of both the narrow and the broader objectives made the camps a distinctly ambiguous undertaking. The thirty-day events were expected to turn out officers and noncommissioned officers for the Organized Reserve in the way that wartime officer-training camps had, yet, at the same time they were to provide civilian attendees with an exciting experience that would popularize military service to the point that the country would accept it. In short, camp commanders were not altogether certain whether they were to emphasize the "military training" or the "camp" aspect of the CMTC.

This anomaly became apparent as the army prepared to hold its first set of camps in the summer of 1921. The key structural device masking the ambiguity of the camps' purpose was in the organizational focus around three different courses—the "red," the "white," and the "blue." While the color scheme suggested that all three were meant to be part of a greater whole, such was not actually the case. The red course was for the civilian initiate, focusing on boys in their late teens and basically organized to be an enjoyable introductory orientation and indoctrination program. The white course was developed to produce non-commissioned officers, while the blue course aimed to produce reserve officers. Hence, while the CMTC color scheme suggested that it was a three-year program of instruction in which candidates would pass from the red to the white to the blue over time, actual cases of such progression were, in fact, rare.

Moreover, while a few officers such as Palmer had hoped to see the program emphasize the white and blue courses as the means to build up the Organized Reserve, the General Staff opted to emphasize the red course almost to the exclusion of the other two.[66] The overall objective behind this was to popularize the idea of military training by spreading the exposure to a special CMTC version of such training as widely as possible. This was explained clearly to corps-area commanders before the camps opened in 1921 in a General Staff directive that stated, in part, "it should consistently be kept in mind that the purpose of the camps is not so much to give 10,000 men 30 days of practical military instruction as it is to demonstrate to the country the merit of these camps."[67] When it became clear that Congress would likely appropriate no more than $1 million for the program, these plans were modified to ensure the widest possible distribution of camp experience, with each corps area given a quota and orders to promote a broad geographic representation in the camps.[68]

At the same time, while those in charge of the camps received explicit instructions on subjects to be taught, they also understood clearly that the main measure of success would be "the enthusiastic approval" of those attending.[69] While the schedule developed by the General Staff included five hours of instruction in military matters each day, a lot of time was still left for physical training and athletics. Prospective attendees were promised a wide range of sports activities.[70] Movies, vaudeville performances, or talks about the war were scheduled for most evenings.[71] The military training itself was to be rigorous but not exhausting, and camp commanders were warned to ensure that no campers were injured.[72] Training included a heavy emphasis on the rifle and on marksmanship, perceived by the General Staff as being popular among teenage males. Finally, camp commanders were instructed to pay attention to the quantity and quality of the food and to ensure the presence of adequate medical personnel.[73] Overall, the four-week experience was intended to be quite a bit more like a camp getaway than actual military training.

The General Staff initiated the program with a massive recruiting effort for the 1921 camps at the national, state, and local levels. It aimed to ensure not only that they would be able to recruit a social and geographic cross-section of American male teenagers, but also to put pressure on Congress to increase appropriations for future summer camps by demonstrating their popularity. Corps-area commanders were encouraged to recruit attendees vigorously: "No mark is too high and it will not be inappropriate if there are at least ten eligible applicants for each accepted position."[74]

The 1921 camps appeared to have been a tremendous success. The publicity campaigns, together with the efforts of recruiters and civilian groups, produced the much-hoped-for oversubscription of applicants. Over 130,000 males expressed interest, of whom over 40,000 actually applied and 11,202 were finally selected, with 10,681 actually attending the camps.[75] Soothing letters went out to the unsuccessful applicants, promising preferred treatment in the competition for the 1922 camps.[76] Moreover, the actual participants were extremely pleased with the experience. Numerous letters arrived from parents happy with the noticeable growth in physical and personal maturity of their sons, while the army itself proudly noted that the campers had, on average, gained an inch in height, 2.75 pounds in weight, and an inch in chest expansion during their camp experience. State governors were canvassed on their response to the program, and thirty-seven of thirty-eight gave it an enthusiastic endorsement.[77]

Counting on the 30,000 unsuccessful candidates as a backlog and expecting the popularity of the camps to create a word-of-mouth campaign that would bring in a host of new applicants, the army was confident that the CMTC program was headed in a direction of rapid expansion.[78] But while there was enthusiastic discussion in the General Staff of expanding the program participation to 50,000 campers in 1922 and up to 100,000 in 1924, this was dampened by a realization that Congress would not appropriate the necessary funds. As a result, the army finally requested appropriations for only 30,000 campers in 1922.[79] The apparent success of the 1921 camps also had other ramifications. It fixed for the next two decades the dominance of the red course as the quintessential feature of the CMTC program. While the white and blue courses debuted in 1922, they received little attention outside of the cavalry and field artillery participants. In the infantry camps white and blue participants were used as NCOs for the red course.

With confidence in the assumed popularity of the CMTC program, the army entered 1922 focused chiefly on the issue of how to carry out the anticipated rapid expansion of the camps that summer. Congress had generously doubled the appropriations for the camps for 1922, but the army hoped to triple enrollments. This led to a search for economies. The most important issue, however, was to ensure the camps' popularity. Directives from the General Staff emphasized "the necessity for making instruction popular and maintaining enthusiasm in the daily work."[80] At the same time, the War Department notified congressmen of the intention to expand enrollment in the camps to 30,000 and reminded them that the popular program had attracted many more applications than that in 1921.[81]

This confidence was abruptly shattered in late spring, as recruiting reports began to indicate surprising indifference to the program. By May 1, 1922, with the army halfway through a sixty-day recruiting campaign, only 4,000 boys had applied.[82] A variety of factors contributed to this sudden and totally unexpected decline, but the most important was that the army fell victim to its own oversubscription campaign. Those rejected from the camps in 1921 were quite alienated by that, and few reapplied. Moreover, the high rejection rate that year discouraged others from applying the following year. It also angered and discouraged many of the civic groups and individuals who had worked hard in 1921 to encourage recruits.[83]

This emerging enrollment crisis was seen as an extremely serious matter by the army, stretching well beyond mere embarrassment. The underlying purpose of the CMTC program was to prove that military training would be both popular with young American males as well as beneficial, thereby building public support for the eventual introduction of universal military training. An enrollment failure in the second year would destroy that perception. Understanding the importance of the crisis, Pershing and the General Staff gave it their full attention. All corps-area commanders were called upon to invigorate recruiting and to cooperate with supporting civilian groups. At the same time, President Warren Harding was urged to call on the governors of all the states to aid in the recruiting push.[84] All these efforts, together with a fifteen-day extension of the application period, led to a final enrollment of 28,000 boys, 6,000 of whom failed to show up at the camps.

The army put the best face possible on the results, emphasizing in its reports that the 22,000 boys who actually attended marked a doubling of the program in just one year. But officials were shaken by the experience. This failure, together with the far more important reduction in the size of the officer corps ordered by Congress, made the summer of 1922 a real nadir in the army's experience and in its self-confidence. The sense of despair was heightened by a General Staff study, conducted in the spring of 1922, that concluded that the need to replace the aging world-war veterans with new reservists would require that the camps be expanded immediately to 100,000 participants a year.

The General Staff responded to this by increasing the control of civilian organizations over the camp enterprise.[85] While efforts were made to include a number of such organizations in this effort, reliance was placed chiefly on the MTCA, which was given even greater control over the program, especially in recruiting. Leading members of the MTCA were now to be designated as "War

Department Civilian Aids for Military Training" and given special access to corps-area commanders regarding recruitment.[86]

The introduction of the white and blue courses in 1922 posed other problems for the program. Since graduates of these courses would hold NCO rates and reserve-officer ranks within their respective branch, the branch organizations had considerable influence in the activities of those camps. They also became increasingly critical of the red course for not offering enough training to allow graduates to enter the white course. One result was that the red course was divided into two separate portions, a thirty-day basic course, which remained focused on the objective of popularizing military training, and a thirty-day advanced course, which aimed at preparing campers for the white course the following year.[87] The result of this, and the sharp discouragement over enrollment in 1922, was that the CMTC program slowly began to shift its emphasis a bit from popularizing military training to serving also as a four-year program to produce reserve officers.

Despite the setback in 1922, the army adhered to its goal of reaching a training level of 100,000 in the CMTC camps, as this was now seen as necessary to produce the number of reserve officers needed to support current mobilization plans. At the same time, it stepped up recruiting efforts for the camps. New publicity ideas, including a nationwide contest in which teenage females wrote essays on "Why the young man I know should attend a CMT Camp" and an offer from Babe Ruth to give an autographed baseball to the outstanding boy in each camp, were introduced.[88] This new campaign was a smashing success. While the General Staff had planned for 30,000 campers, it stretched funds in every possible way to accommodate the 33,000 who actually attended. Within the staff, hopes for reaching the goal of 100,000 reignited.

Despite this success, however, by 1925, the CMTC program began to feel the pain of the army's deepening budget crisis. The general depletion of war surpluses that plagued the ROTC also affected the CMTC. Therefore, while the General Staff planned only a modest increase in camp attendance to 35,000 in 1926, it was clear that even this figure could be achieved only with drastic economies. Thus, the initial hopes that the CMTC program would reinvigorate the prewar public enthusiasm for universal military training began to dim rapidly.

The Officers' Reserve Corps (ORC)

Even before the World War, General Staff officers concerned with formulating a military policy based on a citizen army were aware that this new force would require a reserve officer pool made up of men who had at least a significant modicum of military training. Therefore, in planning the creation of a military policy after the war, both General March and the General Staff agreed on the need to create a large Officers' Reserve Corps. The existence of such a corps was already sanctioned in National Defense Act of 1916. Yet the structure and future of any such military force remained disturbingly unclear in the year and a half during which the National Defense Act of 1920 was being developed. Thus, recruiting and organizing an ORC in this period was difficult.

Almost immediately after the war, the army began recruiting officers leaving active service to join the ORC, taking advantage of the demobilization process. By early February 1919, March could report that over 10,000 officers had applied for reserve commissions.[89] On the other hand, the army's goals for the ORC were even more ambitious. March and the General Staff tentatively decided that the country's future military policy should be based on raising a citizen army in times of emergency of 2,000,000 men. That would require an ORC of 150,000 officers, half of whom, it was hoped, would be signed up by the end of December.[90] Happily, recruiting reserve officers at this time was not difficult. Many had a positive feeling about their wartime experience and were eager to continue a military connection. Moreover, an officer's commission still conferred status in many areas of American society. Hence, the recruiting goal of 75,000 reserve officers was met by December 1919, with the expectation that, by the completion of demobilization, 82,000 more would join.[91]

The more difficult problems were associated with organizing the ORC in a period of uncertainty and, more importantly, building a tight institutional bond between it and the Regular Army. Organization problems initially included coping with the paperwork involved with an organization that was attracting four hundred applicants a day at a time with the army itself rapidly diminishing in size. The Personnel Section of the General Staff, which had the responsibility for approving applications, was swamped.[92] But the greatest problem by far was binding the ORC to the Regular Army and to the War Department. Since these were without a military policy, while they might be able to form an ORC, they could give it little in terms of a mission or other ways to provide activities that would establish bonds.

As feared, reserve officers did come to feel abandoned and responded by forming chapters of a Reserve Officer Association (ROA) on a local, then a state, and, finally a nationwide basis.[93] The General Staff was unhappy about this, arguing that "Reserve Officers should feel they are a part of the Regular Army, not a separate and distinct class."[94] But by then the damage had been done, and the development of a separate corporate identity among reserve officers would remain a persistent aspect of the character of the ORC for the interwar period.

This period of confusion and perceived neglect came to an end in June 1920 with the passage of National Defense Act. It provided not only a role and mission for the reserve officers but also, in fact, made them the heart of the new military system. While the Regular Army and National Guard were designed, in part, to provide forces to be used in minimal exigencies, the central purpose of the new system, as the act's authors and supporters tirelessly reiterated, was to provide the structure, planning, and machinery to allow the huge citizen army that fought the Great War to be mobilized again in the future if needed, only more quickly and more effectively. The key to this accelerated mobilization was having the tactical structure of a fully organized army already in place in the form of paper units staffed by reserve officers and a few key enlisted men. The role of these officers in an emergency would be to receive, arm, and train recruits raised by selective service. Therefore, they were no longer thought of as auxiliaries to be called up to fill out the Regular Army as it went off to fight the nation's wars; instead they were to be the leaders of the citizen army that would fight the wars. As a result, the success of the national defense program created by the act rested, in large part, on the ability of the army to recruit and train a force of reserve officers sufficient to create such a citizen army.

Although the formation of the reserve officer units was critical for the success of this new program, little apparent effort was made in terms of actually organizing such units for over a year. As with the case of the reorganization of the army itself, creating a vast new military organization such as the ORC required a great deal of preliminary planning to be carried out before efforts could begin in creating any actual units. For instance, all major decisions about the size and character of the overall Army of the United States, of which the Organized Reserve would be a part, had to be worked out in advance, as did principles upon which reserve units would be based. Thus, much of fiscal year 1920–21 was consumed with drawing up blueprints for the ORC. While this delay is understandable, it led to further discontent among reserve officers, as recruiting levels fell and several thousand finally resigned.[95]

Even the development of the planning process was difficult. According to the National Defense Act, all plans regarding the formation of the ORC were to be worked out by committees composed of both regular and reserve officers. As a first step in the development of the Organized Reserve, the War Department solicited recommendations from governors of reserve officers in their states who might be suitable for service on such committees.[96] These panels, once formed, began working in September 1920 to write tentative regulations to govern the foundations of the ORC as well as distribution tables that would list its various branch units and assign them to paper divisions spread throughout the United States.[97] A preliminary draft of Special Regulations 46, dealing with the organization and administration of the Organized Reserve, was completed and distributed for comments on December 1, 1920.[98] Afterward, the final regulations were released on February 16, 1921.[99]

These regulations were designed to allow the Organized Reserve to fulfill both explicit military objectives and implicit political objectives. The military objectives involved the creation of sufficient paper units to create twenty-seven divisions, three in each corps area, as well as cavalry, headquarters, and other organizations. While much of this work was mechanical, the War Department was concerned about reserve units being able to build a sense of unit cohesion and esprit de corps. Therefore, they were given divisional and regimental numbers designating them as units that had actually fought in the war to provide a sense of organizational history.[100] Finally, the implicit political objective of the Organized Reserve was to create a tangible link between Americans and the army by providing local reserve organizations with which the local population could identify and in which they could take pride. Therefore, developers took great care, insofar as possible, to form divisions and especially tactical units within state lines while assigning subordinate units to distinct regions within a state, seeking to establish an organized reserve presence in every part of the country.[101]

The work of assigning units to locations began in April 1921. Corps-area commanders received copies of Special Regulations 46 as well as tables indicating divisions and other units assigned to them.[102] They, in turn, created boards made up of reserve officers for each state in their area to work out the distribution of units within states. These panels also included a regular officer, who came to meetings equipped with a distribution proposal, leaving the boards with the duty of largely approving the plan worked out by regulars in corps-area headquarters.[103] The corps-area plans were then sent in June to the War Department, where they were carefully scrutinized and the necessary modifications worked out with each commander by the end of the month.[104]

With organization plans completed, the War Department was ready in July 1921 to begin the actual organization of the ORC units. While corps-area commanders were responsible for organizing the units in their areas, they were assisted by special teams of regular officers sent in for this purpose. Forty-two such support groups were created, consisting generally of a colonel, three other field-grade officers, and several sergeants to carry out the clerical work.[105] Despite the care taken in the initial planning, these teams usually found the situation facing them chaotic. With no funds authorized for renting office space, they had difficulty establishing an actual headquarters. Nor was adequate information provided. Most teams were given only a list of names and addresses of reserve officers, often inaccurate, from which to select officers for the reserve units. As a result, personal-qualification files had to be built slowly using questionnaires. Attitude problems hampered all efforts, as it was often difficult to get local reservists to take the idea of creating an Organized Reserve seriously. Correspondence with local reserve officers was answered slowly, if at all.[106] Nevertheless, by December 1921, the initial organization of all twenty-seven infantry divisions had been completed, and recruiting programs were underway in most areas.

The organization of units also demonstrated quickly that the military and political objectives of the Organized Reserve program were, to some extent, at odds with each other. As state and local boards continued to create subordinate tactical units throughout the summer and early fall of 1921, the War Department discovered that corps-area commanders and state boards were concentrating units in and around large urban centers for efficiency in terms of administration and training. As a result, many rural areas were left with no Organized Reserve representation at all. While the War Department had sympathy with the considerations that led to such concentration, officials felt that the "opportunities for the creation of and development of local community interest" took precedent, and they called upon corps-area commanders to give the "maximum distribution of subordinate units" high priority.[107] To reinforce this call, the War Department sent back those organization plans that called for such concentration of units.[108]

By the beginning of 1922, the initial development of the ORC had proceeded to a point that most of the major problems had been overcome. The General Staff felt it could now turn its attention to recruitment and to addressing new issues within the reserve component as they emerged.[109] Recruiting for the ORC had slowed precipitously at the beginning of 1921 as demobilization came to an end and persistent inactivity within the component reduced morale. By February 1921, the ORC had a reported strength of only 70,000 officers. While the War Department reduced its initial recruiting goal to 100,000, there was growing concern as to whether even that goal would be reached and, even if achieved, maintained.[110] The recruiting effort during demobilization had already brought into service the most willing officers, those who had highly positive feelings about their service in the war and were eager to continue that service in some way. The army now had to approach those veteran officers who, for one reason or another, had not chosen to join when demobilized. This phase was slow in results.[111] At the same time, the army reductions that began in 1921 reduced the number of officers available for recruiting duty.[112]

Toward the end of 1922, another major problem began to emerge, as units requested funding for headquarters and for supplies such as rifles, uniforms, and other equipment. As far as the War Department was concerned, the ORC was a purely paper organization. A local company might consist of a handful of officers with headquarters in the living room of the company commander, who would likely maintain files in his personal desk or file drawers. Their duties were to train personally for responsibility during mobilization and to lead units afterward. The bulk of this training would be carried out through correspondence courses. As such, units were not expected to have much need for proper headquarters space, let alone weapons and uniforms. Initial requests, therefore, were viewed skeptically by the General Staff.[113] But officers in the Operations and Training Division defended the requests, arguing that office space and equipment were vital to helping tiny independent units overcome a sense of isolation and to give them a feeling that the ORC really existed, that they were a real unit in a real organization. In short, a headquarters with racks of rifles and flags would provide the morale and sense of esprit necessary for widely dispersed, largely paper organizational units to survive and maintain individual training. As a result of this argument, weapons were allocated and funds found for renting space for headquarters.[114]

The most important single problem in the reserves, however, was the issue of summer training. From the beginning, the heart of the reserve program was to be a fifteen-day summer training camp. The ostensible purpose of this training was to keep officers current on new weapons and doctrinal developments as well as to give them instruction and experience in the mobilization and training duties they would face in an emergency and in the combat leadership they would face afterward.[115] Summer training sessions were organized to do this. Early camps included terrain exercises, focusing on problems in minor tactics, along with drills and demonstrations of new weapons. Later, as training became more sophisticated, three types of camps emerged for reserve officers. These were branch training camps for instruction in combat leadership; unit camps, in which an entire unit would train for the mobilization duties for which it was responsible; and reserve leadership camps to train reservists for wartime duties as regular officers. Theoretically, by attending each of these camps, a reserve officer could have significant training and experience in the three major dimensions of his assignment.[116]

But training was only part of the reason for camps. In some respects, the main purpose was to boost the morale of reserve officers by letting them put on a uniform and be officers in the field for two weeks, demonstrating that the ORC really existed and that their volunteer service in the reserves was appreciated and mattered. Hence, those who ran the camps understood that it was more important that the reserve officers enjoy their experience than that they gain the maximum training possible.[117] Thus, while authenticity was achieved by the lure of tent encampments, the routine was not demanding, especially physically, with emphasis placed on the social side.[118] Major General John L. Hines, while he was commanding general of the Eighth Corps Area, understood this when he wrote to Chief of Staff Pershing informally about the reserve officers camps in his area in 1922: "We made them comfortable and had a very good mess for them. We gave them a reception and dance, and I believe the schedule of instruction was very good considering that it was the first one and, therefore, perfection could not be expected. . . . I made it plain to all officers engaged in the work that I thought it absolutely essential that these officers go home feeling that they have been treated with every consideration."[119]

Given the personal value of the summer camps both in terms of training and morale, the War Department considered it essential that each reserve officer be able to get to them at least once every three years. Yet Congress never allocated anywhere near enough money to allow a third of the ORC to go to camp during a summer. In 1922, the first year for the camps, the House of Representatives struck their appropriations out of the budget entirely, and the Senate could restore only enough to allow 4,500 reserve officers to go for summer training.[120] While Congress was more generous in later years, the goal of reservists attending a camp once every three years never came close to realization.

The General Staff was aware of the danger that, without sufficient experience of serving with the Regular Army to create bonds of affinity, reserve officers would fail to identify as part of the single Army of the United States and would, instead, develop a separate corporate identity similar to that of the National Guard. Since Congress did not provide even a minimum opportunity for camp attendance, the army tried other approaches. When possible, representatives of the General Staff would meet with reserve officers in an area for one-or two-day conferences whose subliminal theme was the necessity for those in the ORC to identify with the army as a whole.[121] On a more symbolic level, the staff amended uniform regulations so as to remove the "R" from the "U.S.R." that the reserve officers had worn on the collars of their uniforms, thereby making the reserve uniform insignia indistinguishable from that of the regular officers.[122] Finally, the Army Association of the United States and Reserve Arms was formed, which, it was hoped, would provide a means to include guard and reserve officers with regular officers in a single professional organization.

None of these efforts, however, proved sufficient to stem the development of a sense of individual corporate identity within the ORC. During 1921, chapters of the ROA sprang up at local and state levels. The following year, the state ROA of Nebraska called for the formation of a national organization. Despite its misgivings, the War Department did not attempt to stand in the way.[123] The founding congress of the national ROA was held in Washington on October 2-4, 1922. Once formed, it began calling for the creation of special federal office for reserve affairs, a step opposed by the General Staff as leading to the further development of a separate corporate identity within the ORC.

Starting in 1923, the General Staff began to shift its attention from recruiting and organizing units towards individual officer training and giving the ORC a more professional tone. The central focus of this effort was to encourage voluntary training largely through correspondence courses, expecting that those with the interest and ability to carry out such self-training would emerge as the leadership of the Organized Reserve. In addition, it was felt that the Organized Reserve would never be accepted by regular officers unless reserve officers achieved a respectable level of professional development. Finally, while the ORC at that time consisted almost entirely of veteran officers from the war, the General Staff always saw this as a temporary situation that would come to an end as the veterans aged out. To function as an ongoing citizen army, the ORC had to create a leadership structure out of ROTC and CMTC graduates who could not draw on previous wartime experience but had to rely entirely on the voluntary training program.[124] The first step to produce this new emphasis on professionalism was a revision of the regulations for the ORC. The principal focus was to create a more specific and stricter set of qualifications needed for promotion. Overall, the two basic qualifications required were completion of the requisite correspondence courses and, especially, "demonstrated ability to command." The latter quality, of course, could basically be manifested only in summer training camps.[125]

Along the same line, there was growing concern in the General Staff that ORC units not become top heavy in rank. In fact, staff officers hoped that, in the event of an emergency expansion, there would be enough positions open in the upper levels of Organized Reserve units to allow for the insertion of a few regulars and the rapid promotion of proven junior officers.[126] This attitude grew stronger as the first mobilization plans began to reach final shape in late 1923 and early 1924. This new emphasis on maintaining room for expansion in the upper ranks was soon felt within ORC units. In 1921 and 1922, when emphasis had been on recruiting officers for the reserves and creating actual Organized Reserve units, the War Department was somewhat liberal on questions of assignment of officers. The policy then was, if a unit had a vacant position in which an authorized table of organization called for an officer of a certain grade with certain qualifications and it could find no officer of that grade with those qualifications in its area, then it could assign an officer of a different grade with nearly those qualifications.[127] In short, colonels could fill positions reserved for captains. Late in 1923, the General Staff reversed itself and began to follow a new policy whereby the only officers who could be assigned to a position in a unit were those holding both the requisite qualifications and the requisite grade. Others might be allowed to fill vacant positions for which they were otherwise disqualified on the basis of grade, but they would be listed only as being "attached" to the unit, not "assigned" to it. Furthermore, each unit was to be allowed a distinct quota of officers in each grade, and any unassigned officers in excess of that quota were to be listed as "surplus." To give emphasis to the distinction between "assigned," "attached," and "surplus" officers, unit commanders were required to submit reports listing those in their units in each category.[128]

This policy change, which was seen as forcing older and more senior officers out of the reserves, produced enormous anger in the units. "Attached" status was seen as derogatory, and many senior officers who had played major roles in their units now either lost interest or displayed their anger openly.[129] By the fall of 1924, the growth of discontent and demoralization was seen as significant enough that the General Staff began to reconsider its policy but found they it difficult to discover a formula that would satisfy the reserve officers while keeping unit organization within the dictates of the mobilization plans.[130]

As with the other components of the army, 1925 was a year of crisis for the Organized Reserve. In this case, however, budget issues were less important. While fiscal constraints further reduced the number of reservists who could participate in summer training, the emerging crisis was growing doubt as to the viability of the entire Organized Reserve program. This was created by two major issues. The first was growing tension developed between the reservists and the General Staff regarding the demand for specific reserve officer representation in the War Department. The second was increasing evidence that reserve officers were not undertaking the self-training needed to perform their roles in the event of an emergency. By 1925, these had ripened to the point that many in the army saw in the reserve project yet another reason for doubting the validity of the entire citizen-soldier concept upon which the military policy of the National Defense Act was based.

The movement among reserve officers for specific representation in the War Department or on the General Staff had two principal aspects. One was the growing consciousness among reservists that they formed part of a specific component in the Army of the United States with a specific mission that was distinct from that of the Regular Army. Second, this sense of corporate identity was strong enough to cut across branch lines to the degree that most reserve officers thought of themselves as "reservists" far more than as "infantry" or "cavalry." Hence, they wanted matters related to their training and administration to be handled by officers specifically devoted to the reserves rather than by branch chiefs.

After 1922 this movement began to build momentum. In 1923 the national ROA, acting chiefly as a political lobby for reserve officers, still focused its efforts on getting Congress to authorize more money for summer camps.[131] But by 1924, it renewed the call heard two years earlier for a distinct representation of the Organized Reserve in the War Department on a similar basis as the National Guard. But now the organization specified that it wanted the creation of a new post in the General Staff, the assistant chief of staff for reserve officers, to be headed by a general from the Organized Reserve.[132] By March 1925, the ROA submitted a formal request to the secretary of war for the creation of a specific bureau for the reserves, similar to the Militia Bureau, that would give the Organized Reserve its own distinct national leadership.[133]

While leaders in the General Staff were somewhat aware of the pressure building within the Organized Reserve for a more autonomous existence, they were still surprised and shaken by this demand. From their point of view, this struck at the heart of the military policy established by the National Defense Act. The defense act provided for a single Army of the United States made up of several components, in which the mission and role of the Regular Army was to provide the professional guidance in training and development of all components. The task of the General Staff was to deal with the concerns of all components, not just those of the regulars. It was this conception of the staff that had prompted such bitter opposition among regular officers in the War Department to putting a National Guard officer at the head of the Militia Bureau, which they looked at generally with some hostility. The purpose of the bureau, from the point of view of the regular officers, was to provide professional guidance to the development of the National Guard as a component of a single U.S. Army, not to serve as the political representative of a military organization in competition with other components. Regular officers now saw in the demand to create a reserve bureau a similar threat to give the General Staff an increasingly political character while limiting its ability to guide and control the development of the Organized

Reserve. Were such developments to continue, the whole idea of the Army of the United States as a cooperative union of three components could be threatened, as each would then be driven into a competitive stance in relation to the other two. And in such a contest, the Regular Army would be not only the smallest component but also the only one without outside political leverage. All these considerations led Brigadier General Hugh A. Drum, then the assistant chief of staff for operations and training to conclude somberly, "while considerable experience has been had with the Reserve project, positive conclusions as to its future development cannot be made at the present time."[134]

Drum sought a solution for the problem that would still reflect what he and other officers in the General Staff saw as the "one army" spirit of the policy upon which they felt the National Defense Act was based while also satisfying the growing demand within the ROA for some form of visible corporate representation. The key to his plan lay in the few National Guard and Reserve Officers already assigned to the General Staff in compliance with the defense act. In the past, no policy had been developed for the use of such officers on the staff so that, while occasionally called together for consultation on reserve matters, particularly in drawing up regulations, they were otherwise merely assigned to work as needed. Drum suggested that these officers instead be assigned primarily to duties clearly associated with the Organized Reserve in a way to give them greater visibility. This, he hoped, would satisfy the demand for representation while demonstrating the idea that the General Staff was made up of and represented the Army of the United States as a whole.[135]

Drum's idea did not win immediate acceptance in the General Staff, where most officers doubted that merely giving the reserve contingent greater visibility in roles directly related to their component would satisfy the dissidence reflected in the ROA.[136] The reservists actually on the staff also felt it was inadequate, so the issue lay unresolved throughout the summer of 1925.[137] But by September, the staff had come to support Drum's plan, with the additional provision that the War Department would seek appropriations to increase the number of reserve officers on the staff, some of whom would be sent to the offices of branch chiefs so that, over time, they would develop greater branch identity as a counter to their corporate identity with the reserves.[138] While this solution seemed to put the issue to rest at least temporarily, it contributed to a further erosion of confidence among regular officers on the General Staff regarding the viability of the Organized Reserve project.

The issue of reserve officer training also seemed to come to a head in 1925 and significantly furthered that erosion, carrying it well beyond the ranks of

the General Staff. At issue was not so much the training that took place at summer camps as the inactive training regarding the correspondence courses reserve
officers were expected to carry as the heart of their professional development.
The staff, working together with army schools, had created an elaborate system of correspondence courses and sub-courses to allow for this self-paced and
self-directed professional development. The courses were geared to allow any
officer willing to devote about two hours a week to their study to complete the
educational work needed for promotion by the time it was due.[139]

By 1925, this issue of inactive duty training was becoming critical. For one
thing, it was understood that in the next decade, the character of the Organized
Reserve would undergo a major change as the World War veterans gradually
retired, to be replaced by graduates of ROTC and CMTC who lacked wartime
experience. Hence, with the rise of a new generation of reservists who could
no longer rely on such experience, a successful inactive-duty training program
was vital if the reserve program were to produce officers with even a minimal
competency to lead a citizen army in war. Yet it was becoming clear by 1925
that the correspondence-course system was not working. As early as 1923, the
commanders of summer training camps complained that many reserve officers
who attended were unready for training since they had not completed relevant courses.[140] By 1924, Drum was directing commanders of corps areas to put
special emphasis on inactive training of reserve officers.[141] By the fall of 1925,
concern about the low level of participation in the correspondence courses had
extended well into the army itself. In its September issue, *Infantry Journal,*
which almost always avoided printing anything critical of any army component,
published a scathing critique of the entire reserve program, pointing to the fact
that only 12 percent of reserve officers were even enrolled in correspondence
courses, with only 6 percent finishing them.[142] At the same time, Pershing, in a
gentler tone, reiterated that the Organized Reserve was "something more than
a social organization, something more than an organization in which a man can
occasionally wear his uniform. It is an organization that demands an interest,
that demands study."[143]

While Drum and others sought ways to improve reserve officers' participation
in the correspondence courses and to reduce their sense of isolation, confidence
in the Organized Reserve reached a low by the end of 1925. In an otherwise positive address to the ROA at its annual convention in October 1925, Major General
Hines, having succeeded Pershing as chief of staff, admitted to being discouraged by the overall progress of the reserve project.[144] Moreover, by the end of the
year, it was becoming increasingly clear that the allocation of Organized Reserve

units developed in 1921 under the principle of localization was unrealistic for carrying out an actual mobilization based on a draft of available manpower.[145] While it was likely that a major reallocation of units could solve the problem, this would involve shifting some units from one state to another, a process that would considerably disrupt the development of Organized Reserve. While the problem was not insurmountable, it was still just one more indication that the program and the citizen-soldier concept on which it was based seemed to be at an apparent crisis point at the end of 1925.

The Reserve Officers' Training Corps (ROTC)

Of all the civilian-component training activities undertaken by the army in the period between 1920 and 1925, none was as popular or seemingly as successful as the Reserve Officer Training Corps. There were several reasons for this. Officers could readily see that the viability of a military policy based on a skeletonized reserve force would depend on securing a large, well-trained ORC. Moreover, the students in the ROTC program would train within branches, so that a branch identity and bonding would develop in ways that it did not form within the other civilian components. Finally, the program was popular with the administrations of many universities and colleges. Administrators were both eager to have it on their campuses and highly supportive of it. Thus, for regular officers, the experience of developing the ROTC program provided far greater satisfaction and was far closer to what was expected from the National Defense Act than the experience with the other civilian components.

The tradition from which the ROTC sprang, that of the self-trained volunteer officer who served in emergencies, was far older in America than the more visible tradition of the professionally trained regular officer. And while regular officers in the nineteenth century began being trained at West Point, some citizens interested in leading volunteer military units began to look for their military training from colleges with established military credentials and cultures such as Norwich College, Virginia Military Institute, and The Citadel. By 1862, the first year of the Civil War had demonstrated the value of these college-trained volunteer officers so that Senator Justin Morrill included a requirement for military training in his bill establishing the land-grant colleges.[146]

The impetus for major change in this form of amateur military training in colleges in the early twentieth century came from two sources. One was the educational institutions themselves, many of which were seeking to rationalize and modernize their curricula and wanted to give more coherence and purpose to the mandated elements of military instruction. The second was the army's rising interest in establishing a reserve system based on federally trained volunteers. Articles in military journals concerning reserves up to 1907, however, were limited to the issue of expanding the army for the purpose of fitting out expeditions. But after a brief war scare in 1908, authors began viewing the reserve problem from the perspective of meeting a national emergency arising from an invasion by a major power. As a result, the estimates of the size of the reserve force needed began to expand rapidly. Many of these assumed that reserve officers would be drawn from the graduates of land-grant and other colleges offering federally sponsored military-training programs.

Early in 1915, as the War College Division of the General Staff was formulating its plans for a national military policy, it turned its attention to the military-training programs in the land-grant schools. By midsummer, it had worked out a fundamental scheme based on centralizing control of all military education at civilian institutions into a program to be called the Reserve Officer Training Corps. By November, its plans were sufficiently clarified and detailed that the staff could draft a bill to establish the ROTC.[147] This legislation was then included in the final military-policy bill passed as the National Defense Act of 1916. By March 1917, the enthusiastic reception of the program by colleges and universities led the adjutant general to suggest that its expansion be halted until September, since the number of schools that had accepted the program already would place considerable strains on available manpower. But before this issue could be discussed, the United States was at war.[148]

The world war severely disorganized the nascent ROTC program but did not end it. In June 1917, Secretary of War Baker rejected a suggestion that students enrolled in ROTC be given draft deferments until their officer training was completed. By early 1918, however, it was becoming clear that, along with a system of controlled and rationalized industrial mobilization, the nation needed a system of rationalizing personnel mobilization that would assure a steady supply of officers for the anticipated campaign of 1919 while ensuring that the draft would not prove economically devastating to the nation's colleges.[149]

Out of this concern was born the Student Army Training Corps (SATC). The plan was to allow students in colleges or special technical-training programs to enlist in the army and receive significant drill and training but to remain in school until their education was complete. Chief of Staff March agreed to the idea in late April 1918 and created the Committee on Education and Special Training (COEST) to draw up plans. By September, four hundred of the just under six hundred colleges in the nation had accepted SATC units.[150] The program, however, lasted only six weeks. On November 12, Baker ordered it discontinued, and students enrolled under it returned to civilian life.

With the end of the war and the SATC program, the War Department rapidly bent its efforts toward reestablishing ROTC, and within ten months the program was again fully functioning. Attention then shifted from the problem of reestablishment to problems of administration. During this ten-month period the most visible characteristic of the reestablishment effort was the vigorous leadership of COEST and, especially of Frank Morrow, its chairman. Morrow sought to take advantage of what was seen as a momentary window of opportunity created by specific postwar conditions to create a program that would be far more expansive than that provided for in the National Defense Act of 1916. The result was that ROTC was reborn in an environment of great enthusiasm that favored its successful reestablishment despite the incubus of growing popular indifference to all things military. At the same time, the enthusiasm generated by its rapid expansion precluded any significant reconsideration of the program and its initial inconsistencies. Consequently, problems that were just barely visible in the program's brief life in 1916–17 returned in more magnified proportions in the 1920s as funding diminished.

As the war came to an end, schools that had participated in the SATC program saw the value of ROTC, especially in terms of financial support of students, and expressed the hope that the program would be continued.[151] War surplus equipment and uniforms meant that the resources for a rapid expansion in 1919 were at hand. Morrow, therefore, felt that, with energetic action, an expanded and popular ROTC program could be established in the nation as a fait accompli before Congress even began a consideration of military policy. He easily sold his idea to both the General Staff and to Baker, who authorized the program's reestablishment in November 1919.[152]

Morrow's plans for a rapid and massive reestablishment of ROTC were extremely successful. By the end of December 1919, all colleges that had had units in the prewar period had applied for the reestablishment of those units, while applications were also received for the establishment of nearly two hundred new units.[153] One of the major reasons for this rapid expansion, as Michael Neiberg points out, was the popularity of the program with college and university presidents who saw it as providing much needed discipline, patriotism, and moral guidance for the students involved.[154]

By this time, however, there was growing opposition within the General Staff to Morrow's policy of rapid expansion of the ROTC. Some questioned the wisdom of creating units when there was no assurance that Congress would provide the means to support them.[155] Concerned officers appealed to the chief of staff to halt the expansion until the War Department had a better sense of the future military policy of the country. This appeal was successful, and Morrow's expansion project was slowed considerably. With this, it was clear that COEST's days were numbered, and it was disbanded at the end of August 1920. Nevertheless, before COEST disappeared it had expanded ROTC into a program with over 50,000 students enrolled and within easy reach of Morrow's goal of 100,000 participants. By the beginning of the fall semester, the program had been adopted in 191 colleges and 128 secondary schools, with applications pending for 151 more units. ROTC had also conducted its first summer camp.[156] While all this put a strain on the army in terms of finding officers to support these units, it gave the program a flourishing start when such a popular success was vital to the army. At the same time, this activity left the structure of ROTC unexamined and the army with a program for producing reserve officers that was unnecessarily cumbersome and expensive.

By September 1920, ROTC seemed to be well established, involving at least enough students that initial enrollment goals were met.[157] It also followed the lines provided for in the 1916 National Defense Act. There were two levels of the program, a junior version for high schools and a senior version for colleges and universities. The main, though unspoken, objective of the junior program was to serve as another opening wedge for universal military training. At each institution at the senior level, there were two sequential courses. The first was the basic course, a two-year mandatory program for all male students. Its objectives were to prepare them for the subsequent advanced course and to popularize military training and the army. The second was the advanced course, which was open to selected volunteers from the basic course and, upon completion, led to a commission as a reserve officer.

With ROTC established, attention was turned to the immediate, numerous, and varied problems associated with the initial organization of such an enterprise. The next three years of the program revolved chiefly around the efforts to resolve those issues as they appeared. As a result, ROTC in this period seemed to be dominated by troubles. As one observer wrote in the fall of 1920, "The outstanding feature of the R.O.T.C. situation is that its problems are far from settled."[158] In perspective, these difficulties, while numerous, were basically of a minor and transient nature that ought to have been expected in the initiation of so vast and novel an enterprise. Indeed, given the fact that, by the fall of 1920, ROTC involved well over 100,000 students in over 300 institutions nationwide, and that it offered the officers of the army their first cooperative venture with civilian institutions and vice versa, it is surprising that the problems were so few and, with several exceptions, so minor in character. The most significant fact related to ROTC in this period was that, despite its initial hasty and possibly overextended origin and subsequent growing pains, it continued to thrive during years of federal budgetary retrenchment.

The problems in the program at this time were generally experienced at two levels. The first was with the individual college or university, regarding difficulties related to organizing the program and integrating it into the academic, social, and cultural life of the institution. The second was at the national level, where the problems centered on the management of the entire program and integrating it into the other programs and priorities of the War Department. Of the two, the issues at the lower level were easier and more transient, although it is likely that they did not appear to be so to the harried and frustrated professors of military science and training (PMS&T) who faced them constantly. On the campuses the problems generally fell into two categories. One included those associated with maintaining the program itself, which initially involved matters of supply, the maintenance of uniforms and equipment, and personnel matters. The other included the greater problems associated with creating a new educational program and integrating it into those already established at the institutions in a way that was acceptable to both sides.

In regard to program maintenance and personnel, the most significant issue by far was uniforms.[159] Cadets were expected to wear them to class and drill, which often meant that they were worn two or three days a week. Hence, the individual units, the host institutions, and the cadets all wanted uniforms that were impressive in appearance and fit well. These, of course, were expensive. In planning for the rapid expansion of the ROTC, Morrow and others counted on being able to use existing stocks of war surplus uniforms.[160] Yet this assumption was ill-founded. Wartime uniforms were cut to fit a male population between twenty-one and twenty-five years old. But including the junior units in the high schools, the ROTC population ranged in age from thirteen to twenty-one, and many of the uniforms were just too large to be used and few were suitable for younger cadets. Moreover, wartime uniforms were meant for field service and made cheaply, often fitting poorly and seldom making the impressive public appearance sought by the units and the cadets. Finally, many military schools had their own distinct uniforms and did not want to switch to the use of army surplus regardless of quality.[161]

The army initially responded in 1919 by allowing institutions that so desired to purchase tailored uniforms for ROTC cadets on campus, with the provision that they would be reimbursed by the government for all or part of the cost.[162] But by 1922, repeated budget cuts made these commutations a luxury so that further extensions of the provision were made very sparingly.[163] At the same time, the War Department slowly shifted to issuing new uniforms of its own order rather than using war surplus, which overcame some, though not all, of the difficulties, though requests for commutations continued to be received well into 1924.[164]

Along with the problem of uniforms, there were other initial supply troubles. These were caused by a variety of factors, including the shift in the responsibility for supplying ROTC from COEST to the Adjutant General's Office, the declining availability of clerical staff due to rapid demobilization, and confusion in the use of the nation's railroad system as it was returned from temporary public administration back to private operations.[165] This produced repeated frustrations that were compounded by other changes in administrative responsibility. All of these problems left institutions confused as to whom to contact regarding repeated and lengthy delays in getting equipment.[166]

The most difficult of the supply related issues, however, was the matter of accountability for equipment. Taking the view that ROTC was essentially a college program that the army supported, the War Department required that a school official sign for and accept responsibility for all equipment used in training and be bonded against loss and breakage.[167] School officials, however, tended to see ROTC as a War Department enterprise that was merely hosted by educational institutions. They resented the requirement that they take responsibility for army equipment. The issue provoked continued interchange between the institutions and military officials.[168] Given the basis for the requirement in existing legislation, however, neither side was able to do much about it, leaving it as a source of lingering irritation.[169]

On the academic side, a number of problem areas emerged in this period. One was the overall relations between the War Department and the colleges and universities, especially during a time of great flux for the army. College leaders expected to be personally consulted on matters related to government programs on their campuses. The army tried to meet these expectations as well as it could, at least at the national level, introducing no major legislation and initiating no major policy changes without at least consulting representative groups, such as the Association of Land-Grant Colleges and Universities. At lower levels, however, officers were often more abrupt and peremptory in their dealings with institutions. Moreover, the period 1920–22 saw rapid changes in policies in the army, with officers frequently shifting from one position to another, and a permeating sense of demoralization resulting from the demotions and reductions in officer strength mandated by Congress. All this led to problems of confidence, as academic officials began to wonder if the army could be trusted to keep its promises.[170] Again, these problems tended to work themselves out over time, especially after 1922, as the army's situation became more stable.

The ROTC curriculum also provided opportunities for collisions between host institutions and the army. Desiring that ROTC education be standardized as much as possible, the War Department had highly specific and detailed ideas regarding the curriculum of military-science programs.[171] As a result, this curriculum at any given institution was developed through negotiations between the army's professors of military science and tactics and school faculty members in an effort to revise existing courses in a manner that would fit army specifications, with the promise that they would then be included in the ROTC curriculum.[172]

Another major area of academic difficulty was instruction. Although the officers assigned to duties as professors and their associates rarely had either advanced degrees or any experience with college teaching, they had to teach in situations where they would be compared to academic professionals. Indeed, much of the issue of course credits revolved around the question of the quality of the instruction given in military-science classes. This problem was aggravated in the early years by the frequent transfer of officers.[173] In addition, much of ROTC was structured to be self-taught. Military drill, for instance, was largely conducted by the cadets themselves, with upperclassmen in the advanced course conducting the drilling of lowerclassmen in the basic course. This practice became the source of considerable criticism regarding the level of professionalism in the instruction of military-science students.[174]

Despite all these problems, many on the campuses recognized almost immediately that ROTC was making positive contributions to college life. Students in the advanced course received financial assistance in terms of commuted rations. The physical condition of these students improved, a matter of great concern to educators at that time.[175] Finally, ROTC added new features to the social and recreational life on campuses by sponsoring dances, especially an annual military ball, and athletic teams.[176] As a result, while the harried military professors may have seen the program in terms of a continuous diet of problems and troubles, on the whole, their efforts led to widespread acceptance of ROTC as a permanent and positive part of the educational program on collegiate campuses as well as a further development of that program elsewhere.

On the national level, the main ROTC challenge for the General Staff was creating an administrative structure that would allow centralized control of the program so it could be directed toward agreed-upon goals. Structurally, the ROTC program was organized around three levels of control. At the top, direction and guidance came from the General Staff, in particular from the ROTC Branch of the Operations and Training Division. At the next level, supervision, support, and oversight of individual units was in the hands of the corps-area commanders, all of whom had staff officers responsible for ROTC. At the bottom were the professors of military science and tactics at individual institutions, who were responsible for the direction and administration of their campus units.

While this structure seemed simple in the abstract, making it work in practice was harder. At the top, branch chiefs also wanted some control over the units in their bailiwicks. In addition, the adjutant general and the assistant chiefs of staff for supplies also had some jurisdiction over ROTC. All of this led to some initial confusion as to who reported what to whom and to an increased tendency for those at the top and bottom of the structure to ignore normal army lines of communication and to correspond with each other directly. This problem was finally ended by 1922, as the linkages in the system were finally worked out and clarified.[177] As for guiding the actions of individual units, the General Staff relied on the traditional means of official regulations and inspectors.

While the ostensible purpose of the inspection system was to ensure that the operations of individual units were in conformity with the applicable regulations, the system soon took on a life of its own in terms of directing ROTC activities. The idea of controlling ROTC units principally by means of periodic inspections arose in COEST, with its division of the country into twelve ROTC inspection districts, each headed by a district inspector who reported directly to Morrow.[178] Initially, the purpose of inspections remained largely organizational and intended to be supportive in character. Inspectors were, therefore, charged to be constructive in their approach, acting more as advisors than critics.[179] Later, however, inspections became increasingly oriented around competition between units to be recognized as either a "Distinguished College" among senior units or as an "Honor School" among junior units.

Along with giving programs direction and control, the General Staff also administered summer camps. The army tended to see the summer-camp experience as the keystone of the ROTC program, providing cadets with both practical training and an adventurous experience that would bind them more closely to the army. As a result, the General Staff was eager to offer this to as many ROTC students of both its junior and senior levels as possible, making it mandatory for those in the advanced course. The first camps were held in the summer of 1918;

even amid a war, the army made sure to find the time and resources to conduct camps for nearly 7,000 ROTC cadets.[180] Camps were then held in 1919 and 1920.

The army's experience with ROTC camps in the early 1920s followed the lines of its experience in other ROTC-related areas. Yet the fact that, by 1919, the army already had considerable experience with summer officer-training camps meant that, by 1920, it had already developed a good sense of what these should be like. Hence, there were far fewer problems with the camps than with other areas of ROTC, and those that existed were minor and specific.

The most significant ongoing issue was the division of control and responsibility for the camps. Direct responsibility for developing and administering the programs for each one fell on the commanding officer of the camp and on the corps-area commander. They were guided and supported in this by the Operations and Training Division of the General Staff, which was responsible for policies regarding the conduct of the camps, for distributing funding to support their activities, and for setting general guidelines for the training offered there. At the same time, the camps themselves were organized by the branches, which meant that there were distinct infantry camps, cavalry camps, and so forth. Branch chiefs took responsibility for developing the specific training programs for each. Despite the army's commitment to decentralization, guidance from above in terms of both policies and programs of instruction was often quite detailed and rigid.[181] Otherwise, this division of responsibilities produced remarkably little friction. The only significant ongoing conflict was between the tendency of the branches to make the experience at their camps unique and the desire of the General Staff to standardize them.[182]

By 1922, the camps were governed by a well-developed administrative rhythm. In December, the General Staff would submit an overall summer training plan to all of the components, including ROTC, that outlined general goals and allocated funds.[183] Chiefs of branches would use this to develop specific programs for the ROTC camps under their jurisdiction.[184] All of this would then be sent to corps-area commanders and, through them, to the commanding officers of the camps. At the end of his camp, the commanding officer reported on the experiences and made recommendations for changes. This information made its way back to the General Staff and was fed into the development of the plan for the subsequent year. By the end of 1922, the training-camp program was basically set and had largely become a matter of routine. This pattern was upset only by the intrusion of outside issues, most of which originated with efforts to economize induced by budget restrictions. Otherwise, the camps worked smoothly and successfully. Enrollments grew, as did student satisfaction, so that even in this early period the camps were already a source of pride for the army.[185]

The most significant outside issue affecting ROTC was the budget. As the army was hit with demands for economy, ROTC funding was reduced from $4,000,000 for 1920 to $2,900,000 for 1922. Finally, in early planning for the program, it was assumed that much of the materiel supplies would come at no cost from war surplus. But it was soon discovered that these could not be used as much as expected. So, by the spring of 1921, the General Staff faced the possibility of a shortfall in the 1922 budget for ROTC by as much as $700,000.[186] Although it took a number of measures to reduce the shortfall, the army still had to institute a variety of economies in the program. The major victim of these was the junior ROTC level. Its financial support diminished to the point that the program was soon limited to units in private military academies.[187] With this change, the old prewar idea of using federally sponsored military training in the high schools to popularize universal military training died, a victim not only of the drive for economy but also of the increasing antimilitary climate in society in the 1920s.

But while the three-year period between 1920 and 1922 was filled with problems and challenges for the ROTC program, it was, overall, a period of growth and success. The program, both at the national and unit level, acquired its basic form and largely worked out the problems of jurisdiction and administration. It was popular and grew rapidly. Units were gradually accepted as integral parts of their host academic institutions. Thus, while 1922 was calamitous for the army in many other ways, it could still look to the ROTC program as a success.

Moreover, the next two years were seen as happier and more stable time than the earlier period. Articles in professional journals concerned themselves less with problems and more with celebrating achievements or with describing ROTC as if the institution and its activities had become permanent fixtures. Enrollments in the program continued to grow at better than 10 percent annually; the rate of growth in the number of advanced-course students was even greater. Other statistics, such as camp attendance and number of graduates commissioned into the Organized Reserve, grew as well, though more slowly.[188] Problems continued to exist, and indeed, some significant issues of a more permanent nature began to appear. Yet this did not seem to cloud the happier overall perception that the difficulties that had plagued ROTC in its early postwar years were now coming to an end, that the program had been stabilized, and that it was entering an era of constructive growth.

Problems, of course, continued to exist but were diminishing. On campuses, the major single remaining problem for units was uniforms. The General Staff agreed that measures of economy required that ROTC continue to rely on war surplus uniforms until the supply was exhausted in 1925 or 1926. And although there was a brief flurry of interest in developing a distinct ROTC uniform, the costs were considered too high, the use of regular stock uniforms continued.[189] On the other hand, the old question of accountability for equipment was resolved at the end of 1923, when the responsibility was transferred from the institutions to the military professor.[190] ROTC instructors had been frustrated by the fact that no textbooks had yet been published to cover the courses they taught. By the end of 1924, however, this problem was partially resolved by reorganizing ROTC courses around existing training regulations.[191] At the same time, temporary regulations for the program were revised and issued as AR 145-20, indicating that ROTC was now governed by normal army regulations.[192]

By 1924, two more-ominous and long-term problems began to appear, threatening the vision that the program was, or could continue to be, successful. One was whether ROTC could produce the number of reserve officers called for by the mobilization plans linked to the National Defense Act. As such, the problem had two dimensions: first, whether the total number of reserve officers provided annually would be sufficient to maintain the Organized Reserve at an adequate level, and, second, whether the balance of reserve officers among the branches would be adequate for existing war plans. The Six Army Plan required enough officers in the Organized Reserve to provide for twenty-seven divisions upon mobilization as well as enough to help the Regular Army and National Guard provide their assigned divisions. Original planning presumed that the maintenance of such a manpower pool would require commissioning 10,000 new reserve officers annually, with the bulk coming from ROTC and a far smaller number coming from CMTC. By 1923, this estimate was reduced to 7,000 annually, with 80 percent coming from ROTC. Even though the program's enrollments were rising at an encouraging rate, it was clear that, with the limited number of regular officers available for support duty, this expansion would soon reach a virtual limit that would still be far short of the capacity needed to produce the 7,000 reserve officers annually.[193] The second issue was that the production of reserve officers in certain branches, particularly field artillery, was well below the numbers needed to maintain the balance among the branches in the mobilization plans. Since infantry units were far cheaper than others in terms of equipment, ROTC was soon unbalanced in favor of that branch. Now, due to fiscal and personnel limitations as well as direct legislative prohibitions, this imbalance was all but baked in.[194]

The other longer-term problem was the older issue of budget limitations. Initially, this did not seem overly serious. ROTC remained popular in Congress so that, after the initial decrease in funding experienced in the period 1920–22, appropriations began to increase substantially in 1923–24. The program's major fiscal problem in this period was the longer-term concern of the diminishment of war surplus materials it had used for free in the past. When these were finally exhausted, ROTC budgets would have to absorb new costs. As a result, during 1924, increased emphasis was placed on economy wherever possible. Even the possible elimination of summer camp for students in the basic course came under consideration.[195]

By mid-June 1924, it was becoming clear that ROTC was headed for a major fiscal crisis. The rapid exhaustion of surplus stocks meant that future appropriations would have to be raised dramatically just to allow ROTC to continue its current level of activity. Yet this was still less than adequate to produce the reserve officers needed for the Six-Army Plan. Unless ROTC was expanded by 50 percent, the army would have to accept the conclusion that the Six-Army Plan as unviable, an admission that could, in fact, call into question the ability of the National Defense Act citizen army to provide an adequate defense for the United States.

During 1923–24, Congress and President Harding had been remarkably generous with ROTC, increasing appropriations by 35 percent (from $2,8000,000 to $3,800,000) at a time when fiscal retrenchment was otherwise the order of the day. But Harding's successor, Calvin Coolidge, was far more committed to budget austerity, making it highly doubtful that such a generous rate of expansion of appropriations could be expected in the future. Yet by June 1924, estimates indicated that the need to make up for the exhaustion of surplus supplies and to expand the program to meet the needs of the Six-Army Plan would require an increase in the ROTC appropriation for fiscal year 1926 of $3,250,000, an 85-percent jump, while final exhaustion of stocks a year or two later would call for eventual appropriations of $9,250,000, a 240-percent increase over current levels.[196] Since it was extremely doubtful that budget increases of this magnitude could be wrung out of Coolidge, ROTC went into 1925 headed for a new fiscal crisis that could undermine the army's faith in the entire citizen-soldier concept.

Superficially, 1925 still seemed to be shaping up as a banner year for the ROTC. Enrollments continued to rise, while the closing down of several weak infantry units provided means for a badly needed expansion of field-artillery units.[197] In fact, however, 1925, a crisis year for the entire army, also saw the precipitation of a major crisis in the ROTC program. As with the military itself, this crisis was largely budgetary. Despite the problems arising from the depletion of surplus stocks and the need to expand officer graduations to meet the needs of the Six-Army Program, the Coolidge administration made it clear to the War Department that there would be no appropriations increase at all for ROTC for fiscal year 1926. This put the General Staff into a major quandary. On the one hand, the staff recognized that ROTC required an annual increase to produce the number of reserve officers needed for the Six-Army Plan. On the other hand, due to increased costs arising from the depletion of surplus stores, it would be difficult to maintain ROTC even at its existing level with the appropriations allowed. Hence, after much controversy, the Operations and Training Division decided that the least disruptive course would be to limit the level of ROTC enrollments for fiscal year 1926 to that of fiscal year 1925.[198]

While the division finally accepted this solution in mid-April, it still had considerable difficulty getting other parts of the General Staff and the chief of staff to go along, so this dragged on without resolution until June. There was then further delay as the directive went out to the corps-area commanders that they had to maintain overall enrollments at the same level as in 1925, although they were allowed wide discretion in how they were to do this. These officers appreciated the discretion but not the assignment. Nor were they clear as to what was wanted, leading to a further flurry of correspondence. As a result, the commanders did not begin informing their local ROTC professors of the order to limit enrollment until late July and early August. The professors, in turn, spent a few weeks mulling over how they might implement the limitation on their campuses before going to the president of their respective host institution with the news.[199]

The chiefs of branches in Washington heard about the limitations at the same time the corps-area commanders did. Major General Frank W. Coe, chief of the Coast Artillery Corps, and Major General William J. Snow, chief of Field Artillery, wrote separate letters denouncing the decision. Snow characterized it as "a catastrophe." He agreed with Coe's conclusion that, after the two had urged colleges for so many years to bend every effort to expand the program, to order a halt to that expansion on the eve of a new academic year, with students already enrolled in the program, would "destroy the confidence of college authorities in the War Department's policies."[200] College presidents reacted to the news with equal outrage. The president of Cornell University wrote angrily of his embarrassment with having to drop 129 students who had been accepted in good faith into the advanced program the previous spring.[201] The General Staff was further vexed in dealing with this correspondence by the fact that it was both impolitic and professionally disloyal to place the blame for this predicament on the president's stringent fiscal policies. Yet by the end of 1925, their sense of professional loyalty toward Coolidge was diminishing rapidly and many officers found private channels to communicate to college and university presidents the staff's view of the real cause of this dilemma. As a result, the concluding resolution of the annual meeting of the Association of Land-Grant Colleges and Universities, held in Chicago in mid-November, soundly blamed the president and Congress for the situation of ROTC.[202]

In truth, however, the army itself deserved much of the blame for the 1925 ROTC crisis. From the time of its creation, ROTC had always been a rapidly expanding program that had existed well beyond its means. The rapid expansion of the program and its dependence on surplus stores made it vulnerable to crisis at the first major fiscal-retrenchment program. It is, indeed, doubtful that any U.S. president would have found it politically possible in the 1920s to provide ROTC with the resources needed to sustain the size and rate of growth it had achieved by the beginning of 1925. At that point at least, a more modest program might have experienced a more stable and happy development.

The Army in the Era of Stability, 1926–1929

Creating the Branches

CHAPTER 3

Stabilizing the Relationship

The Army and the Nation in the Era of Stability

T HE SITUATION FOR THE Army of the United States improved considerably in the second half of the 1920s. Although its work and concerns were similar throughout the decade, the spirit that characterized its work changed a great deal after 1925. The first half of the decade was characterized by experiment and building in an often emotionally heated atmosphere, while the second half was marked by stability and calming routine. The nation itself also seemed to be entering a more stable era beginning in 1926. The international turmoil that had followed in the wake of the Great War had largely disappeared, and the international community seemed committed instead to building security by means of cooperation and disarmament. The apparent threats posed by domestic social and labor unrest, so prevalent early in the decade, also seemed now to be receding quickly. At the same time, the spreading economic prosperity, the new cultural world opened by film and the radio, the new personal freedom offered by the automobile, and the growing sense of personal liberation emerging from moral changes during these years created a climate of self-indulgence and lack of concern for matters related to the national community. In this environment, President Coolidge's unspoken promise of an administration that would do as little as possible fit perfectly.

The army appeared to share in this stability, leading to a sense of a return to better times. Relations with both the president and Congress improved rapidly. Coolidge made it clear that while he would permit no increase in the size of the army, neither would he countenance any further decrease. He was seconded in this by Congress, and the size of the Regular Army was finally stabilized at about 12,000 officers and 112,000 men. Both the president and congressmen became friendlier toward the army, with the tone of dialogue between the two parties becoming far more cordial and mutually supportive. At the same time, the army became increasingly reconciled to apparent public apathy, and the concern regarding the failure of public opinion to support the army began to disappear from service publications.

Internally, the Regular Army remained committed to the basic principles of the National Defense Act of 1920, although the enthusiasm associated with building that force and the rosier hopes of the first half of the 1920s were now largely replaced by an approach more routine in nature and tone. The principal focus of the army remained the training of the civilian components, with more than half of its strength devoted to that mission and the rhythm of the fiscal year dominated by its administration. The service journals also paid considerable attention to the civilian components, and relations between regulars and reservists and guardsmen remained good despite occasional strains. At the same time, the new professional-education system worked well, producing a growing professional homogeneity and sense of military competence within the officer corps.

The chief basis for feeling that the army had entered a period of stability was the improved relations with the administration and Congress. The most appreciated aspects of this were the stabilization of the overall size of the army, the support given by both Coolidge and Congress to national defense and the services in general as well as to a number of programs that the army considered important, and the moral integrity of the administration, which restored public confidence in the government and the services. Coolidge's announcement in August 1927 that he would not run for election to a second full term was, therefore, met with genuine regret within the military's upper circles. Although the president's insistence on economy in government had created early strain in his relationship with the army, relations quickly improved once the military adopted a budgeting plan that brought estimates into line with the president's program. Coolidge, on the other hand, provided the War Department with a "continued definiteness of policy" that was credited with creating a greater sense of stability and the capacity to engage in long-range planning.[1] He supported the army's program to improve housing and the recommendations of the Morrow Board that kept the emerging air corps under firm army control while he opposed any further reductions in the officer corps. The support provided by Coolidge's secretary of war, Dwight F. Davis, in these areas was also appreciated, leading the *Army and Navy Journal* to state "there never has been a more attractive man personally in the office of Secretary of War than Dwight F. Davis."[2]

The improvements in relations with Congress were more immediately noticeable. By January 1926, several service publications were already commenting on this new atmosphere. In particular, many members of Congress signaled a willingness to go beyond the recommendations of the Bureau of the Budget if the army could make its real needs known to them. While army witnesses in budget hearings had to be careful that they did not transgress the law requiring them to support the president's budget, the readiness of members and senators to go beyond those limits as well as congressional interest in housing and other matters of military concern was very much appreciated. By May of that year, the *Army and Navy Journal* claimed that Congress had set new records in its support of the army's legislative program and that nearly all legislative proposals submitted by the War Department had received some degree of positive support.[3] This new attitude was the product of several things. The army made a dramatic exposé of the terrible housing conditions prevailing for officers and enlisted. The issue drew popular attention, and congressmen hastened to demonstrate their concern for proper army housing and for the army in general. Several visited army bases to see conditions for themselves.[4] At the same time, army leadership also made it clear that it accepted the president's demand for economy in operations. Under Hines's leadership, it began studying and incorporating business practices in its operations and cutting costs even further, allowing a well-publicized return of over $5 million in savings to the Treasury at the end of the fiscal year.[5]

This improvement in relations was not immediately noticeable. As the political season opened in the fall of 1925, Coolidge demanded that the services absorb another 10-percent budget reduction, leading to increased militancy and opposition within both the army and navy. Determined to oppose the new cuts politically, the General Staff prevailed upon ailing Secretary of War Weeks to allow it to complete a study begun a year earlier, which argued that the military was unable to carry out its assigned missions under the National Defense Act of 1920 on even a minimum basis with a strength of less than 165,000 men and 14,000 officers. Davis, Weeks's successor, refused to recommend these conclusions to the president. But he did pass the plan on to the chairman of the House Committee on Military Affairs and indicated that he personally felt that an increase to 150,000 men and 13,000 officers would be desirable.[6]

The army also began to resort to the political mobilization of the civilian components. State ROA conventions voiced anger about the proposed cuts and issued resolutions in support of an expanded budget, especially for reserve training. As the national ROA convention in Kansas City approached, it was clear that it would issue similar resolutions, with delegates beginning to plan a coordinated political campaign with the National Guard. The attempt to mobilize the Organized Reserve and the Guard in opposition to the proposed budget cuts angered the Coolidge administration. The director of the budget notified the General Staff that officers planning to attend the ROA National

Convention in October were to avoid speaking in any way about the budget.[7] Coolidge himself finally entered the fray in a public speech to the American Legion National Convention, warning that, "any organization of men in the military service bent on inflaming the public mind for the purpose of forcing Government action through the pressure of public opinion is an exceedingly dangerous undertaking and precedent." [8] At the same time, however, he began to retreat on the issue, especially as it was seen that the reservists had gathered considerable public support already. His warning was somewhat offset by news that he intended no further cuts in officer personnel in the forthcoming budget. And, while the final Bureau of the Budget estimates actually did involve an overall cut, it was less than 4 percent rather than 10 percent.[9] Congressmen, on the other hand, were quite friendly to the army, and many encouraged officers to make the services' true minimum needs known.[10] The House then added over $1 million to the army budget, while the Senate, where Wadsworth gave the army an especially friendly reception, added another $3.5 million, erasing the cuts made by the budget director. Overall, in the eyes of the *Army and Navy Journal*, Congress had "dealt as generously with the Army as it could under the Administration's general economy program."[11]

After this near collision with the president, Chief of Staff Hines and others in the General Staff consciously dropped any further efforts at political mobilization on behalf of the army and adopted instead a strategy of cooperation with Coolidge. This policy paid off, as the following fiscal year saw an even greater improvement in relations between the army, on the one hand, and Congress and especially the president, on the other. The main difference between the two years was the absence of mobilized agitation from the civilian components. Hines, in his last year as chief of staff, made the loyalty of the army to the president's program clear, and Coolidge, in turn, became even more solicitous of the needs of the army. As a result, even though the final legislative session of the 69th Congress was a brief one, its results were impressive, leading the *Army and Navy Journal* to label the year as the military's best since the passage of the National Defense Act.

Meanwhile, the recurring budget confrontations and responses to cuts had a significant influence on the way the General Staff carried out planning. Efforts to tighten control over and reduce spending led to greater prioritization, which, in turn, gave the staff greater control over the budgetary process in the army. It also had a clear potential to increase interbranch disharmony and political infighting. Branch chiefs sought to ensure that any new economizing measures would not reduce their own degree of budgetary autonomy. The staff response to this was to rely more heavily on long-term planning. Five-and ten-year projects were created in each major command of the Army of the United States, including the Regular

Army, the National Guard, the Air Service, and others. Annual increments of all the projects were then organized each year as the army's budgetary "program." This system created more predictability in the process while eliminating much of the grounds for intra-army budgetary scuffles. But it also made the process more rigid, allowing little room to add new "projects" such as mechanization. Above all, however, all documents associated with the budget emphasized: "The War Department Budget is that of the President. The needs he approves will be fully supported, but no reference to others will be volunteered."[12]

Yet even with the commitment to support the president's economy program and the new budgetary planning process, annual appropriations remained a source of strain in the relations between the army and the Coolidge administration. This became obvious in 1926. The appropriations for that year included funds to support an enlisted force of no more than 118,750 men. But predicting the cost of maintaining such a large number of enlisted men was difficult, especially when it had to be done almost two years in advance and since a number of variables, such as prices, reenlistment rates, and cost of retirement payments, were hard to control. On the other hand, the army was under pressure to keep expenses down, so the calculations as to the cost of the enlisted portion of the army were pared to the bone.

In the spring of 1926, it became clear that the appropriation for that year would be inadequate to maintain the army at an average of nearly 118,750 men, leaving the General Staff with a choice between reducing the number of troops temporarily or asking Coolidge for supplementary legislation to cover a deficit of close to $800,000. The president disliked asking Congress for such additional funding since it was contrary to both his economy program and to what he considered good business practice in government. Nevertheless, Davis asked him for the legislation, and Coolidge reluctantly agreed, adding, "with regard to the next fiscal year, I expect that the enlisted strength of the Army will be so regulated so as to avoid any possibility of a reoccurrence of a deficiency of this nature."[13] Unfortunately, all the economic factors that produced the shortfall in fiscal year 1926 remained in place for the next year, so that by September, it was clear that the army would face a deficiency of nearly $2 million. Recalling Coolidge's injunction, Hines opted this time to meet the deficiency by reducing the size of the enlisted force to an average of 110,900 troops. Recruiting was halted in late September and resumed on a limited basis only in November. By this time, the financial news worsened still, and a cut to 110,000 men was contemplated as a necessity.[14]

The news that the army was preparing to draw down to 110,000 men caused considerable unhappiness in the ranks. Commanders complained that their units were already so skeletonized that this latest cut could severely undermine their capacity to carry out meaningful training or even maintain their posts. In addition, such a reduction brought back depressing memories of the cuts made in the early 1920s. Finally, there was fear that even a temporary reduction could become permanent as economy-minded politicians might justify further spending cuts on the basis of the army having gotten along with only 110,000 troops.[15]

Despite this demoralization, Chief of Staff Hines refused to go to the president to request deficiency legislation. Instead, he set the General Staff to restudy the entire budget to see if money could be found anywhere to make up the deficit while making it clear in the press that the funding problem arose from the difficulty of making estimates rather than the action of the president or Congress. At the same time, however, Coolidge stated in a speech that he had no intention of cutting the army below 118,750 men. Later he indicated that, while he had not been officially notified about the its problem, he had sympathy for the difficulty the military faced and quietly let it be known that he would support the necessary deficiency legislation. With that, the problem was resolved.[16]

The relationship between the army and Congress also improved in this period. In large part this was due to the activism of several members of the House, particularly W. Frank James, Republican from Michigan, who took a real interest in the army and pushed through a number of bills favorable to it.[17] This new mood of active sympathy for the army led to a shift in the focus of military legislation from appropriations to other issues such as housing, the air service, and promotion. While these were sometimes difficult matters in which many officers had deep personal and emotional investments, they were not ones that pit Congress, Coolidge, or the army against each other the way appropriations did. The air service and promotions, in fact, tended to promote divisions within the army, allowing Congress to play the role of an interested and sympathetic unifier. The extent of this shift of focus and its import was clearly visible during the first session of the 70th Congress, which began in December 1928. Congressional action on appropriations was extremely disappointing, yet this was hardly noticed in the service press, which instead focused on issues such as housing and promotion. And while presidential leadership and congressional performance in these areas were less than hoped, the disappointment was attributed to the complexity of the issues involved, so service attitudes toward Coolidge and Congress remained positive.

This growing harmony between the army and the government began to undergo strain, however, during the first fiscal year of President Herbert Hoover's administration. On the surface, 1929 seemed to be for the army very much like those under the Coolidge administration except far more disappointing. The same issues were still discussed in much the same way, employing much the same rhetoric. Yet many could sense that, below the surface, major changes were beginning to happen. The atmosphere in which the army operated became heavily charged with anxiety as the stability enjoyed under Coolidge seemed to be crumbling.

Although the new chief of staff, Major General Charles Summerall, had occasionally been mentioned as a dark-horse candidate for the Democratic nomination for president in the 1928 election, the army still generally favored Republicans and was particularly partial to Hoover as Coolidge's apparent heir. Democrats tended to be associated in the minds of many officers with pacifism and internationalism, while Hoover was seen as having a sober awareness of the realities of international conditions. The *Army and Navy Journal* even went so far as to say of him, "no sounder advocate of preparedness has ever come into the White House."[18] After Hoover's inauguration, things seemed to continue in the fashion that had become familiar in the past several years. The army put the personnel issues of pay, promotion, and housing alongside appropriations at the top of its legislative agenda and began preparations for the first regular session of the 71st Congress with the usual optimism.[19] Hoover, however, immediately poisoned the waters by first agreeing to participate in new naval disarmament talks in London and, almost simultaneously, announcing that he would create a special commission to carry out a thorough analysis of the army to look for programs that had become obsolete "through the advancement of science and war methods" and others whose development could be further spread out over time. His goal was not so much greater military effectiveness as it was economic efficiency. As with Coolidge before him, Hoover sought to improve the business climate in the country by further tax reduction.[20]

The president's announcement was naive and maladroit. The idea that the army could shift to a mechanized system of warfare and save large amounts of money at the same time demonstrated that the new president understood military realities far less well than his army boosters had believed. The suggestion that "obsolete" activities would be targeted created a mood of defensiveness within the entire army, especially within the cavalry and the coast artillery. The progress made in the past decade by aviation and, more recently, by mechanization and armor, had already raised the specter of branch obsolescence that would dominate the army in the 1930s. Hoover's announcement seemed to legitimize the long-dreaded idea of army modernization through civilian pressure. As such, it aroused latent anxieties and professional defensiveness.

Hoover tried to soften the threatening aspect of his announcement by allowing the army itself to carry out the study. But he also insisted on absolute secrecy, which allowed rumors of all sorts to flourish throughout the fiscal year.

Summerall took the mission of the study seriously and, in December, presented two plans, one that involved a significant expansion of the army, and another that provided for maintaining the status quo with only a modest increase in appropriations.[21] Hoover quietly ignored the plans but refused requests to have them published, allowing them to remain hanging as a source of continuing anxiety within the army.

Within this atmosphere, army leadership still tried to carry out its activities in Washington along the patterns learned under Coolidge. Anticipating a presidential call for continued economy, Secretary of War Davis indicated in January 1929 that the budget estimates to be submitted in late summer would be based on the appropriations made the preceding year. But he allowed the General Staff to request an increase in the size of the enlisted component to accommodate the nearly 5,000 men transferred to the air service. He also set a limit of $350 million on the entire budget.[22] The heart of the army's legislative program that year, as in the several previous years, lay in the personnel issues. Pay now emerged as the issue of major concern. Army personnel had not had a pay raise since 1922, so that the bite of inflation was increasingly felt. For officers, pay was also seen as reflecting social respect; for them, the comparability of an army salary with those of other professions was important. Finally, unlike promotions, where there was yet no consensus within the army as to a solution, both the army and navy, along with four other groups of government employees, had agreed on an equitable solution. All that was needed was for Congress to agree to this. By 1929, congressional failure to grant a pay increase had made the issue an emotional one in the army, which many now equated with the question of congressional evaluation of individual officer's or soldier's worth.

Although the first session of the 71st Congress lasted well into July 1930, it produced few gains for the army. Most importantly, it passed no legislation in the area of pay. There were several reasons for the disappointing progress. But the main reason was the fact that the pay bill came with a heavy price tag, which no one in the administration or in Congress was willing to pay. As a result, the first session of the 71st Congress ended with only another housing bill passed. The anger within the army was seen in numerous letters to the editor in the service press, in a call in the *Army and Navy Journal* for a new political mobilization on the issue of pay, and in Summerall's annual report for 1930, in which he protested against misperceptions of the army budget.[23] Thus, as the 1920s ended, the onset of the Depression brought new strains to the army's relationship with Congress and the administration, signaling that the era of stability was coming to an end.

CHAPTER 4

The Civilian Components in the Era of Stability

F OR ALL FOUR OF the civilian components of the army, the second half of the 1920s was characterized chiefly as a welcome period of stability in comparison to the contentious volatility of the previous years. Budgets stabilized, and the components had learned to live within them. The various problems involved with getting them established and through their growing pains had, for the most part, been worked out as well. Some problems remained and new ones appeared, but these were far less important to those involved in the components than was the sense of stability and progress. This, in turn, produced a greater sense of satisfaction both in the civilian components and with Regular Army officers associated with them.

The Reserve Officers' Training Corps

The sense of stabilization within the ROTC program came about more quickly than might have been expected, given the outrage within the colleges and universities over the 1925 decision to cap enrollments at the previous year's level. Moreover, while growth was now limited, it did continue at a pace satisfactory to the parties involved. By the middle of the decade, the established goal of the program was the commissioning of 5,000 officers a year to sustain the Organized Reserve. The actual production during this half of the decade more than met that goal.

The program's administration had stabilized as well now that it was established. Corps-area commanders and the General Staff monitored ROTC via inspections and other means, doing a bit of fine-tuning in terms of both the development and administration of its curriculum. The most significant internal problems in this period were related to budget expenditures and a growing branch imbalance, with an overproduction of officers in infantry and cavalry at the expense of field artillery and coast artillery.

The main problems facing the program in the latter 1920s came from outside ROTC and the army. These came from two sources, although they were somewhat interrelated. One was growing criticism of the program from college and university administrators. The other, and most visible if not most significant, came from attacks by pacifist groups in society. Although the threat from these groups was probably never very serious, it still became a bit of a force shaping ROTC's development.

The character of outside attacks and the army's response were formed as a result of a decision by the University of Wisconsin in 1923 to end mandatory participation in the ROTC basic course, which had been required for all male students. The Department of the Interior, which administered the federal support program enjoyed by the land-grant colleges under the Morrill Act, had accepted the university's decision. The fact that the government had accepted this ruling emboldened organized opponents of military training on campus. In 1925 a number of these organizations came together to form the Committee on Militarization in Education (CME). Its leaders saw in the compulsory basic-course requirement for all male students the most vulnerable aspect of the entire program, offering the CME its best opportunity to mobilize support against ROTC as a whole.[1] By early 1926, the CME had published and distributed a pamphlet by Winthrop D. Lane. In it Lane pressed the main argument of the CME, that ROTC training led to militarization of students by emphasizing and excoriating the brutality of the program's instruction, noting, in particular, bayonet training on campus.[2] Shortly afterward, Republican congressman George A. Welsh of Pennsylvania introduced a bill to eliminate the compulsory status of the ROTC basic course.[3]

The General Staff was stung by the Wisconsin action, which it viewed as part of a growing movement against ROTC in the country. Noting the existence and activities of the CME and other pacifist organizations, officers in the General Staff and elsewhere quickly came to the opinion that this apparent rising tide of opposition toward ROTC was the product of pacifist propaganda and agitation.[4] Moreover, the staff considered preservation of compulsory basic-course participation essential to the program. Experience with ROTC in schools unaffected by the Morrill Act, and where participation in the basic course was an elective, showed that only about 40 percent of the males would sign up while the number of students attending the advanced course was also lower.[5]

The General Staff initially considered dealing with this problem by a counterattack on the pacifists themselves.[6] By December 1927, however, it had concluded that the best course for the army was to stay out of the issue altogether. During the hearings on the Welsh bill, the administrations of land-grant colleges and universities continued to voice support for the compulsory status of the basic course. Most university presidents were proud of their ROTC units and wished to see them prosper. Many also saw ROTC training as educationally and physically beneficial. That being the case, General Staff officers now felt that the issue ought to be left to the schools and local legislatures to decide rather than have federal authorities play into the hands of the pacifists by making it appear that the War Department was dictating to the schools on the matter of compulsory ROTC.[7] Consequently, after 1927 the issue began to die down. The Welsh bill failed to get out of committee, so that the CME began to fight the ROTC battle at the state level but, again, with little success.[8]

Overall, the CME and other pacifist organizations were never a serious threat to the ROTC in the 1920s. While their publications annoyed army officers and friends of the army, they were published in only a few thousand copies and were seldom influential. In addition, the CME itself was small, with a peak strength of no more than 2,500. As its ventures in Congress proved, the group was no match against the friends of ROTC, especially since the prestigious Association of Land-Grant Colleges and Universities favored the program so strongly. Two things were important about this issue and the army's response to it. One was the tendency of those in the military to blame campus unrest over ROTC on the agitation of pacifist organizations and thereby blind themselves to other more important causes. What was more significant was that the basic course itself was growing unpopular. Male students disliked being dragooned into two years of drill and courses of no interest to them.[9] The army recognized this to some extent, as seen when it quietly ended bayonet practice on campus in 1928.[10] But otherwise, the pacifists became a convenient scapegoat that allowed both the army and the university administrators to ignore many of the real problems facing the program.

The other important aspect of this is the degree to which the army was still beset by political paranoia. Officers were still bewildered and hurt that the military was not accepted or respected by the public it served. The basic, though unspoken, ideological basis for making the basic ROTC course compulsory was universal military training. To a significant degree, both ROTC and CMTC were organized to convince the American public that such training would be both valuable and appreciated by those who went through the experience. Hence, the army went to great lengths to convince itself that ROTC was not only good for students but also an experience that most students appreciated.[11]

Finally, for officers, enlisted men, and cadets involved in the program, the real life of ROTC was lived on the campus and in the training camps. The experience was largely a local one, dependent for its particular color on the nature of the college or university involved and its administration as well as on the intelligence, character, and energy of the officers assigned, particularly the military-science professor. To the extent that a local unit had contact outside of the campus it was usually with the area-commander's staff rather than with Washington. For the campuses themselves, the ROTC programs during the second half of the 1920s enjoyed a period of building and stabilization. The major goal of the General Staff was to provide an institutional climate that would optimize the opportunities for local officers to build their units. It was their success on the various campuses that made the program increasingly popular and virtually invulnerable to outside criticism, despite the unpopularity of compulsory participation in the basic course. And it was their success that allowed the bonds between the host institutions and the army to be stronger by the end of the decade, despite the strains that arose in 1926 and 1927.

The National Guard

By early 1926, it had become clear to the leaders of the National Guard that the second half of the 1920s would be quite different for the Guard than the first half. While they acknowledged that the new budget restrictions would be a major constraint on its development, most guard members also saw the latter 1920s in a generally positive light. Even with the constrictions, for most guardsmen, the period was seen as one of a welcome stabilization that allowed them to improve the Guard's professionalism by working on organization and training. From his post as chief of the Militia Bureau, Major General Creed C. Hammond, took the leadership in this effort during most of this period. He was happy to report annually on the improved condition of the Guard. Thus, for most guardsmen, the second half of the 1920s was still, in tone and feel, a continuation of the "golden age" they had begun to experience in 1923.

A longer-term cause of the stabilization was that most guardsmen were basically happy with the provisions made for the National Guard by the defense act and found professional satisfaction in this. As a result, annual conventions of the National Guard Association (NGA) were generally positive celebrations of progress. Efforts such as those in the ROA to mobilize militant support behind major issues were almost nonexistent in the NGA. Instead, nearly all resolutions of the association focused on technical matters of fine-tuning.

In addition, unlike the ROA, the NGA tended to act as a stabilizing rather than a disruptive force. In part, this moderation was due to its structural aspects. The NGA was nowhere near as strong or as well organized as the ROA. It had no national headquarters, no permanent staff, no journal, and no grassroots organizations. Although it did have a president and an executive committee, these rarely acted on their own authority. Instead, the central organ of the NGA was its annual three-day convention, the resolutions of which provided the annual agenda for the association leadership.[12] Moreover, unlike the Organized Reserve, the National Guard was essentially a state organization, so its national representation could be no more than confederative in character. In addition, the Militia Bureau also acted as a national leadership body for the Guard. The access to the General Staff enjoyed by the bureau gave it an ability to act effectively on behalf of the Guard that severely diluted any perceived need for another national body. Overall, then, this was a period of improving morale and greater attention to building the organization that guard leaders found professionally satisfying both in terms of the work involved and the results achieved. The outcome was not only a significant improvement in the training readiness of guard units but also a further federalization of guardsmen's attitudes and professional identification.

The stabilization was also aided by finding a resolution to the expansion of the National Guard. Earlier, in 1923, feeling that the Guard would never be able to expand to number 424,800 men as set out in the National Defense Act, the War Department temporarily set aside those provisions and, instead, called on the Militia Bureau to plan for an expansion to 250,000 guardsmen. Then, in 1924, responding to Coolidge's calls for economy, the department suddenly announced the end of recognition of any new units, thereby all but freezing guard development at 183,519 men.[13]

Initially, this suspension of new units seriously eroded guard morale. Not only could it be seen as something less than a vote of confidence in the organization, but it also disoriented the working goals of the Guard and its leadership. Up to that time, the Guard had been developing toward the organization prescribed in the defense act and the 1923 modified plan. The 1924 suspension, however, provided no new set of goals.[14] Hence, for several years, guard leadership saw the suspension as a temporary matter to be overcome by pressure on Congress.

The Militia Bureau, being closer to the General Staff and to political realities, was not so sanguine. Instead, under General Hammond's leadership, the bureau moved to find a way to live under the new budgetary regime. Hammond's solution was twofold. First, he continued to adhere to the 1923 modified plan and still build the divisions it indicated, albeit on a skeletonized basis. The 250,000-man modified plan had been based on maintaining guard units involved at authorized peacetime strength levels. But the Militia Bureau thought that those operating at barely above what was called "maintenance levels" could still carry on the training needed to enter an emergency on a combat-ready basis. Units at 110 percent of maintenance levels were only two-thirds as large as units at authorized peacetime levels, making the achievement of the modified plan almost possible within the 183,000-man limit established in 1924.[15]

After a year of study on this issue, Hammond slowly began to put his plan into action. On July 31, 1925, a War Department directive established 110 percent of maintenance level as an upper limit for unit expansion, although units above that threshold were not required to discharge personnel. On January 9, 1926, Hammond asked the secretary of war for a small extension of the initial limit to 185,730 to allow the Guard to create the new units necessary to round out battalions still being formed. By April, the Militia Bureau had created a priority list for units still needed to create the balanced and combat-ready force of the eighteen divisions called for in the modified plan.[16]

In 1927, in a continuation of his rounding-out program, Hammond successfully pressed for an expansion of the National Guard to around 190,000 for fiscal year 1930.[17] This success whetted the appetite of guard leadership for further expansion. Many guardsmen came to the 1928 NGA Convention convinced that the Guard should be given yet another 10,000-man increase. Hammond and other leaders were dubious that such an increase would be approved and convinced the NGA to trim the figure to 5,000.[18] Following a resolution from the convention to that end, Hammond submitted a new request on November 21, 1928, for a further expansion of Guard numbers to 195,000 men.[19] This request, however, was not successful, and leadership decided to wait for the inauguration of the Hoover administration before any effort was made in behalf of further expansion. The NGA appeal to Hoover's secretary of war, however, was also rejected. Shortly afterward, Hoover initiated his request that the General Staff consider ways in which its budget could be further reduced. With this, hopes for further guard increases in the immediate future died.

Although enlistments stagnated in the second half of the 1920s, what was most important to guardsmen and leaders was that they could see appreciable improvement in their units as well as in the Guard overall. Nationwide, the building of the basic structure for the National Guard force of eighteen divisions was nearly completed.[20] There was also a major improvement in the available level of supplies, equipment, arms, and ammunition. Building on work already done, the Militia Bureau promulgated a new table of equipment for guard divisions in 1926 that put them on the same footing as divisions in the Regular Army. This was supplemented later by a new table of supplies. Together, the two new tables provided local guard leadership with clear outlines as to the equipment and supplies they should order. At the same time, this allowed a major decentralization of the process since corps-area commanders were authorized to

issue supplies and equipment authorized under the tables without getting further authorization from the Militia Bureau. All this also reinforced the new idea
that the primary objective of guard activity now was building up readiness.[21]

At the same time, inspectors found the quality of National Guard units
was improved, while the number of units rated "unsatisfactory" declined to a
"very small" number. Several reasons explain this improvement. The fact that
few new units were being recognized made communities more supportive of
existing ones, which felt themselves existing in a more competitive environment.
With numbers stabilized, it became much harder to get into a unit, and the
Guard could be more selective of its officers. In addition, by 1929, the Guard had
begun to purge its own deadwood.[22] But the greatest reason for better units was
improved officer quality, resulting largely from the reduction of turnover. The
annual officer turnover rate fell from 45 percent in 1924 to 15 percent in 1928. At
the same time, officer attendance at drills and summer camps increased to the
point that there was fear of a need to cut the number of drills in order to avoid
a budget overrun.[23] Thus, officers were more experienced, more interested, and
more involved with their units.

But despite the gains and progress made in organization in the second half
of the 1920s, the most-visible area of progress, and from which officers and
guardsmen gained the most professional satisfaction, was training. Annual reports from Chief Hammond, from the Operations and Training Division of the
General Staff, and from the chief of staff in these years unanimously agreed that
the training readiness of the Guard had never been higher. Even giving some
allowance for the kind hyperbole that makes its way into such official reports,
the unanimity and the focus on training, along with similar recognition from
regular officers writing in professional journals, indicated that the Guard had
not only made notable training improvements but also made training more central to the experience of guardsmen.

The chief causes of this improvement lay in changes initiated in the National
Guard training program, beginning in 1924 and 1925 but especially those implemented in 1926 and subsequent years; the opportunity to focus on training
afforded by the end of unit expansion after 1924; and to Hammond's leadership
of the Militia Bureau during this period. The general was not so important in
the initiation of the early stages of the new program, but he was responsible for
its successful implementation and further development.

The training program developed by Hammond and the General Staff evolved
in three rather distinct phases. The first centered on a shift in training objectives.
Earlier in the decade, the principal training objective of the National Guard

was "to prepare [the] command for efficient active field service." Yet given the extremely limited time available for training and the extremely high rates of personal turnover then, the results of progressive training programs built around these goals continually fell woefully and frustratingly short.[24] In late 1924 the General Staff decided that, under given conditions, guard units should initially focus on a more intermediate goal of providing "basic training," the instruction a soldier would likely receive during his first three months of service. The change was made under the assumption that the global geographic position of the United States would allow time after the declaration of an emergency to complete training; thus, the intermediate objective of basic training would meet the obligations of the Guard under the defense act. At the same time, the staff felt that the goal of providing basic training was more capable of being achieved, thereby providing greater satisfaction within the units.[25]

Starting with the 1925–26 training year, the Militia Bureau and the General Staff began to insist on the organization of both armory training and two weeks of field training around the objective of basic training. In this new program, the objective of each year's armory-training program was to prepare for the summer field-training program. In the armories enlisted men were to learn the basic elements of military behavior and discipline, weapon maintenance and marksmanship, and basic small-unit drill. Field training, then, centered on some further instruction in these areas and their application to simple field problems. It took several years of insistence on the part of Hammond and the General Staff before this new program focused on "basic training" was understood and accepted.

By 1927, Hammond reported that he was satisfied with the growing acceptance and success of the new, more limited training program and began to turn his attention to the instruction of guard officers, especially that of senior commanders and their staffs. Up to 1926, these men had focused most of their attention at field training on camp administration and the supervision of training their units. Starting that year, however, Hammond began to insist that these officers devote at least half of each day at camp to their own training.[26] This requirement ran into initial opposition from senior guard officers who were concerned with commanding their units or who feared that tactical problems would be too difficult for them. But with experience, most found the command-post exercises, tactical walks, terrain exercises, and map problems they faced at field training stimulating and professionally satisfying.[27] The professional training of more-junior officers was also given increased attention with the requirement for setting up schools for officers and NCOs in armory summer field training.[28]

By 1928, Hammond began to extend staff training to the idea of basing guard training on the division level, rather than the regiment or battalion, as had been done so far. Division training, he and others argued, would promote greater large-unit bonding and esprit while offering division commanders and staffs limited opportunities at large-unit maneuvers, which would be beneficial for junior officers and guardsmen as well.[29] The main problem here was that twelve of the eighteen existing National Guard divisions were made up of units located in two or more different states, making their assembly difficult and expensive.[30] Nevertheless, by carefully monitoring transportation costs, Hammond was actually able to hold five divisional camps in the summer of 1928, including one for a multistate division. The results were so encouraging that additional division-level training was planned for the summer of 1929.[31]

In addition to the development and implementation of this new program, Hammond sought to improve guard training in other, less noticeable ways. He created a board to draw up a general program for the development of camp-sites and target ranges.[32] In 1927 he began to press for the modernization of guard training in regard to chemical warfare, dealing with attacks by aircraft and tanks, and the motorization of units. In all these areas he pressed to make available to the Guard the ideas and doctrines being currently developed by the Regular Army.[33] Hammond was also concerned over the lack of training equipment, his annual reports increasingly given over to requests for more modern arms and equipment for training.[34]

It is fairly clear that by focusing armory training on specific goals related to field training in the summer, by orienting both armory and field training around a realizable goal, by getting senior and junior officers more involved in their own training, and by focusing field training increasingly on the division—the unit that would actually be mobilized in case of war—Hammond's training program provided an experience in the National Guard that was increasingly satisfying professionally. This increased satisfaction may have been one reason for the decline in officer attrition by the end of the decade. In addition, field training, in particular, allowed guard officers greater contact with regular officers to the extent that it was increasingly identified as a professional-mentoring process, with the regular officer transferring his up-to-date knowledge and skills to the guard officer.[35] Hence, attaining the professionalism of the regular officer became the goal of many of the more dedicated guard officers. Hammond's training program offered most of them a realistic means of getting a sense of progress toward achieving that goal. At the same time, the professional identification served to strengthen bonds between the guard and regular officers.

Along with improvements in organization and training, this period also witnessed a resolution in full or in part of two major issues that troubled the relationship of the National Guard with the Regular Army and the War Department. The first of these was the position of the Militia Bureau in relation to the General Staff. The source of the issue was a growing sense in the bureau that the staff was intruding increasingly in its affairs. Article 81 of the National Defense Act of 1920 rather explicitly limited General Staff involvement in guard affairs to matters of organization, training, and distribution of units, while the Militia Bureau was concerned with matters of administration. Over time, however, bureau officers, and especially the chief, felt that the staff was increasingly intruding into administration while limiting the bureau's capacity to communicate with corps-area commanders or other officers and organizations regarding guard matters.

The issue came into the open in 1924 with the secretary of war's decision to suspend further recognition of new guard units. Some guardsmen saw the policy as one in which their resources were being redirected to the benefit of the Regular Army. As a result, the 1924 and 1925 national conventions of the NGA passed resolutions calling for War Department affirmation of the Militia Bureau's jurisdiction over all administrative matters related to the Guard. The failure of either the department or the General Staff to respond to these resolutions exasperated the NGA. At its January 1926 convention, it voted to bring the issue to the attention of the Congress if efforts to negotiate a settlement within the War Department failed.[36] The idea of appealing to Congress for a legislative remedy had been discussed among guard leaders and in the Militia Bureau, and Hammond reluctantly had draft legislation drawn up that would amend the National Defense Act in ways to give the bureau primary jurisdiction in areas of administration, finance, and communication.

Although NGA leadership was not enthusiastic about a legislative solution, a National Guard officer serving in Congress introduced the proposed bill himself into the House, where it received a surprisingly warm reception.[37] This got the attention of the General Staff, whose officers roundly condemned it as a violation of the "one army" idea upon which the Army of the United States was based. On the other hand, staff members admitted, with some reluctance, that many complaints about their intrusion into guard affairs were justified. Greater sensitivity on the part of General Staff officers was needed to avoid having both the Guard and the Organized Reserve "form their own staffs under the Secretary of War."[38]

The issue was given to Assistant Secretary of War Hanford MacNider to resolve. After consulting with the executive committee of the NGA, MacNider sought a resolution of the situation based on a revision of the War Department's

General Order 6, the basic document governing the relations between the Militia Bureau and the Regular Army establishment. The revision, however, proved to be a major disappointment since it seemed to change little. A far better resolution appeared in midsummer, when it was announced that the new assistant secretary of war for air would also be given formal authority over matters related to both the National Guard and the Organized Reserve. The fact that the Guard now had direct access to the War Department did much to alleviate the sense of anger over the issue.[39] But the real resolution was affected without new regulations or organization. The flare-up and threat of legislative action had gotten the attention of the General Staff and demonstrated the need for its officers not only to be more sensitive to the Guard but also to treat the bureau in a more cooperative basis. By the fall of 1926, Hammond was able to report with pleasure to the annual convention of the NGA that relations between the bureau and the General Staff were now carried out cooperatively with no basis for complaint.[40]

The willingness of the Guard to settle for an informal resolution regarding the authority of the Militia Bureau in relation to the General Staff indicates that its interest in that issue was diminishing. This continued to diminish for the rest of the decade, as evidenced by the small flap generated in 1929 over the possible reappointment of Hammond to a second term as chief of the Militia Bureau. His term as chief was set to expire on June 29, 1929. By then, he had become highly regarded in both the Guard and the General Staff, and a movement developed among guard leadership to have him reappointed.[41]

This placed the General Staff in a quandary. Although the staff had come to appreciate Hammond's abilities and policies, his reappointment would conflict with a widely published policy in force since 1926 that precluded the reappointment of officers as branch chiefs. The purpose of the policy was to prevent the bureaucratization of branch offices by having their chiefs remain in Washington long enough to build entrenched power through cultivation of political and military connections. On the other hand, some in the General Staff feared that a failure to reappoint Hammond could risk a rupture in relations with the Guard, which had become cooperative during his tenure as chief. This possibility was aggravated by the fact that the National Defense Act specifically provided that the chief of the Militia Bureau could be eligible to succeed himself.[42] After considerable delay, the secretary of war announced on June 28 that, in strict conformity with the policy of rotation of officers, Hammond would not be reappointed as chief. In doing so, he emphasized that this was a matter of policy only and not a reflection on his service, since Hammond had performed his job "with distinction" and was immediately being offered the post of auditor of the Philippine Islands.[43]

The decision against reappointing Hammond generated resentment in the National Guard, though no explosion. After consultation with the executive committee of the NGA, its president, Ellard A. Walsh, announced at the 1929 convention that the issue was one in which the association had no official interest.[44] This virtual acquiescence of the NGA to an action by the General Staff that many considered almost illegal indicates the great value members of the Guard had come to place on maintaining a cooperative relationship with the Regular Army and its leadership.

The second major organizational issue facing the Guard at this time was its legal relationship to the Army of the United States as created by the National Defense Act. According to the act, the Army of the United States consisted of the Regular Army, the Organized Reserve, and the National Guard when in federal service. The problem was with the status of the Guard when not in federal service. Although this had no practical consequences, the problem was a matter of professional status and identity. Guardsmen wanted their service to have recognition as professional military activity at a national level. The idea that they would enter federal service only by being drafted was humiliating individually and seemed to accord no recognition of the status of the Guard in overall national defense.[45]

Early in the decade, the NGA proposed allowing officers to take commissions in the Organized Reserve along with their commissions in the National Guard. This would allow them to be called up without being drafted.[46] The idea proved popular and quickly spread.[47] Still, for many guardsmen, the dual commission was not a satisfactory solution to the problem in that it still failed to accord the Guard itself any professional status within the Army of the United States in peacetime. Guard officers did not want to achieve this status via a commission in the Reserve; they wanted it by virtue of their service in the Guard. Hence, pressure for another solution grew, and the issue became one of the major problems to preoccupy the Guard. Indeed, Colonel John W. Gulick, the longtime deputy to the chief of the Militia Bureau, declared, "the difficulties which have arisen over the problem of giving National Guard officers a commission in the Army of the United States have given the Militia Bureau more trouble and caused it more worry than any other subject that has come up during my experience."[48]

In response to resolutions passed at both the 1925 and 1926 NGA conventions, a committee of guardsmen drew up a report in which they proposed a solution based on federalizing the Guard and making it a permanent reserve force in the Army of the United States, but doing so without injuring state control in any way. This was legally complicated, envisioning the simultaneous existence of dual National Guards made up of the same men. The first would be the traditional

Guard raised under the militia clause of the Constitution; the second would be a federalized Guard created under the power to raise and support armed forces clause of the Constitution.[49]

The proposal was discussed for some time at all levels of the National Guard and then presented to the 1929 NGA Convention. There, after further discussion, a resolution was passed to propose to Congress amendments to the National Defense Act of 1920 to create "the National Guard of the United States as a part of the Army of the United States."[50] Although the Guard hoped for favorable congressional action in the spring, that action was delayed until passage of the 1933 National Guard Act. Nevertheless, the resolution adopted by the 1929 convention demonstrated the degree to which the Guard had become federalized in its outlook and self-image in the past four years.

The Organized Reserve

For the Organized Reserve, the second half of the 1920s was also a period apparently characterized by stability and success. But those appearances camouflaged growing internal problems and doubts that led to an increased, though largely unspoken, sense of tension and anxiety among reservists and Regular Army personnel regarding the continued viability of the entire reserve program. The success of the program continued to be seen largely in the visible and quantifiable areas of size, level of activity, and internal organization. The size of the Organized Reserve continued to grow throughout this period, with vital participation in summer training programs growing even more rapidly. In addition, reservists themselves were better organized thanks to the rapid development of the ROA. Membership grew rapidly from 17,331 in 1926 to 32,685 by the end of 1929, and it gained in organizational strength, financial stability, and level of organizational activity.[51] Subscribers to *The Reserve Officer* could see this development as their journal grew from six pages in 1926 to sixteen pages per issue in 1929. Finally, there were major, though less visible and quantifiable, improvements in the programs for ongoing professional training provided by the army for reserve officers. Participation in correspondence courses increased, as did course-completion rates, which were improved by the introduction of a conference system that allowed students to meet and discuss assignments in regular meetings, sometimes with a regular officer in attendance. Major changes in the summer training camps, including more training as units and, at the end of the period, making reserve officers responsible for much of CMTC training, were all seen as dramatic improvements.

Relations between the reservists and the regulars remained warm and positive despite growing tensions. The basic sources of strain were, on the one hand, the skepticism of many regular officers as to the military ability and professional commitment of reserve officers and, on the other, the suspicion on the part of the reservists regarding the commitment of the regulars to the reserve program as well as to the spirit of the 1920 National Defense Act itself. Still, each side saw its need for the other and found many aspects of the experience of cooperation gratifying. Reserve officers genuinely appreciated the military professionalism of the regular officers with whom they worked and valued the opportunity to train with them to build confidence in the authenticity of their own military professionalism. Regular officers, on the other hand, understood the vital role played by the Organized Reserve in mobilization for future war. The unflagging political support from the ROA was also appreciated. On a more individual level, regulars found in their contact with reservists an appreciation of their own professionalism that was rarely seen among other civilian groups.

In this period, the most significant crisis facing the reserve program came from within the ranks of the reserve officers themselves. Although there were numerous internal troubles in the program, most were part of two interrelated sets of problems slowly rising from the reservists themselves as they began to change in their character, organization, and professionally inspired self-identity.

The first of these problems was a perceived decrease in interest in military activities among reservists in general. It was initially discussed as a "deadwood" problem and focused on the issue of the low rate of reserve officer participation in correspondence-course training. Theoretically, a reserve officer was expected to carry out his training largely on his own initiative using the correspondence courses that the army had been making available since 1922. Reserve officer participation in the courses grew rapidly from around 6,000 in 1922 to over 18,000 in 1926.[52] But while many in the General Staff were satisfied with this progress, others in 1926 were appalled that less than a fifth of all reserve officers were engaged in the expected self-training, with some claiming that over a third of all reserve officers were "no more than addresses on a roster."[53]

The deadwood issue was a dynamic one in that the nature of the problem changed as the character of the reserve officers themselves changed. In 1926 the Reserve was still largely made up of officers who had fought in the war and agreed to continue their connection with the army. Many of these veterans maintained their interest in the reserves but were sufficiently confident of the military skills acquired during the war that they saw no need to participate in correspondence courses. Moreover, over time, many found their lives changing, and their interest in things military declined. This natural decline in interest was reinforced by the lack of means of maintaining interest. The units to which officers were assigned existed only on paper, and members met only if they took the initiative to do so. Hence, reserve officers rarely had the experience of being a part of something that seemed to really exist. In addition, the summer training that provided that sense of belonging and served to build interest was open to only a fraction of reserve officers. Later in the decade, as the makeup of the Reserve began to shift from veterans of the war to officers commissioned in the ROTC and CMTC programs, the problem regarding lack of interest began to shift with it. These newly minted reserve officers lacked the experience of the war to draw them into active participation in the Reserve. Instead, they often saw it as an additional burden on their time and finances, with little in the way of compensating benefits.[54]

Several initiatives were undertaken at all levels to deal with this interest problem. The conference system, which allowed reservists to meet and discuss correspondence-course assignments, was introduced locally beginning in 1924 and 1925 largely at the initiative of the regular officers assigned to duty with the Reserve as regimental executive officers. The conference system enlivened interest in the courses while serving to bring together some of the officers in a unit. In the area of summer training, the most significant change came at the end of the decade, when the War Department began using reserve officers to train the CMTC. While the change was not popular with members of the military training camp movement, it gave reserve officers leadership experience with men similar to the recruits they would be handling in a real mobilization.

The deadwood issue, however, also led to a controversy between reserve officers, as represented by the ROA, and the General Staff. Although the controversy quickly ended, it produced considerable, even if only momentary, anger between the reservists and their regular colleagues, revealing a great deal about the continuing tension in their relationship as well as problems among the Organized Reserve itself. The Regular Army's concern about deadwood in the Reserve was shared by many reservists themselves, although its basis was quite different for each group. Among regulars, and especially in the General Staff, the concern was focused on two issues: inequities in promotion and the military efficiency of the Reserve. For regular officers, promotion continued to be an emotional raw nerve, and they often tended to feel that their reserve counterparts had gotten tremendous advantages in promotion due to efforts to build up the corps rapidly. Thus, while regular officers had suffered several bouts of reduction in rank, those in the Reserve had not, even enjoying a promotion rate more rapid and assured than the regulars. This situation not only was demoralizing but also soon produced a top-heavy officer structure in the Reserve.[55]

Regarding the efficiency of the reservists, the General Staff saw the development of the ORC entering a new phase during the second half of the decade. While the major goal of the project in the first half of the decade had been to build up the Reserve as rapidly as possible to meet the quotas set by the Six-Army Plan, it began to appear in 1926 that the number of reservists had reached a midlevel optimum in terms of the capacity of the Regular Army to carry out training. Given the current limited size of the regular officer corps, it would have been difficult to expand the summer-training opportunities for reserve officers regardless of the amount of money appropriated by Congress. Moreover, the size of the ORC had reached a level that would allow the Army of the United States to carry out at least the first phase of its planned mobilization. Thus, the General Staff saw this as a time to shift the program's orientation from quantity to quality, which led to new attention being given to getting rid of deadwood.[56]

Although reserve officers shared some of these concerns, they looked at the deadwood issue primarily in terms of the existence of the reserve program and the aspect of individual self-interest. The concern here was that the deadwood officers, concentrated as they were in the middle and upper ranks, were blocking junior reserve officers from valuable summer-training opportunities, important assignments in reserve organizations, and, most importantly, promotion.[57] Hence, unit commanders and senior members of the ROA were interested in the deadwood issue primarily to provide the opportunities for training and advancement that could keep the next generation of reserve officers interested and involved.[58]

The officers in the ROA took the initiative in resolving this issue by passing a resolution at its annual convention, held in late October 1926, to allow reserve unit commanders to request the transfer of their "apathetic officers" to an unassigned status, making them ineligible for either training or promotion.[59] The War Department followed up on this by inviting senior ROA officials, including the newly elected president, Brigadier General Roy Hoffman, to Washington to discuss the principles upon which such a reform would be carried out. Then, in January 1927, after consultation with senior reserve leaders including Hoffman, the General Staff issued a set of new policies regarding promotion in the Reserve that tended to follow the ROA principles. Promotion would require active participation in correspondence courses and the devotion of a significant amount of time to reserve work and training. Officers who were up for reappointment after five years but were not meeting the requirements for promotion would be redesignated to "unassigned status" and be ineligible for training and promotion.[60]

The announcement of the new policies set off an unexpected firestorm of criticism among reserve officers, most of it reaching ROA leadership in terms of petitions, resolutions, and angry letters.[61] A panicky delegation of the National Council of the ROA met with Secretary of War Davis in March to request delaying the implementation of the new policies a year while reserve officers studied them carefully.[62] While the General Staff refused to consider this, it noted that the policies would not go into effect until January 1928, giving the ROA breathing room.

A committee of reserve officers headed by Hoffman met from mid-April until early May 1927 and developed a set of changes in the proposed policies that they hoped would mollify the disgruntled reserve officers.[63] While the General Staff initially refused to consider any changes, Chief of Staff Summerall took the more political position that maintaining good relations between the War Department and General Staff and the Reserve, as represented by the ROA, was more important than the minor dilution of the purity of the policies introduced by the staff. He, therefore, advised a more than agreeable Secretary of War Davis to accept many of the modifications proposed by Hoffman's committee.[64]

The new policy had only limited direct effect. By May 1929, only 3,135 reserve officers had failed to qualify for reappointment under it, though it is likely that many more chose not to reapply at the end of their five-year appointment. The significance of the episode was what it revealed about the fragility of relations between the Organized Reserve and the Regular Army establishment and, possibly more important, the internal divisions and insecurity that lay beneath the thin patina of success making up the outer image of the ORC.

These internal divisions and insecurities became even more apparent in a second dispute between the ROA and the General Staff. Reserve officers demanded to have bureaucratic and personal representation in the General Staff in a way similar to that of the National Guard. The resulting dispute lasted longer and became more acrimonious than the controversy regarding promotion policy for several reasons. First, reservists were frustrated in this quest both in the War Department and in Congress. Second, and more important, reservists themselves were severely and divided on the issue. This split was not so much a difference over policy or even philosophy, but rather a matter of differences in the development of a professional self-image.

The hybrid term "citizen-soldier" suggests the nature of the reservists' dilemma about identity. It was not so much a question of whether one was a "citizen" or a "soldier," but whether the hyphen joined or separated the two identities. Was the reserve officer primarily a "citizen" or a "soldier"? To Colonel Palmer and others, the answer was always clear: the hyphen split the terms. The reserve officer was a "citizen" who had also become a "soldier." And while leaders in the Regular Army might compliment the reserve officer on his patriotism and his highly developed sensitivity to his duties as a citizen, nevertheless, they still thought of him and judged him solely as a soldier. This professional military identification more than satisfied many reserve officers. They saw themselves as having both a distinct civilian and a distinct military persona and enjoyed the opportunity to put on their uniform and become a soldier, however transitory. As such, they valued military training of all sorts that might help them become better military professionals. It was this element among the reserve officers that was so contemptuous of those officers who took no interest in the military side of their citizen-soldier identity, the "deadwood."

For other reservists in the 1920s, however, the terms "citizen" and "soldier" were joined, not split, as a self-image of "soldierly citizens" began to emerge. This can be seen in an official statement of the ROA, "Object and Mission of the Reserve Officers' Association of the United States," in which it claimed its members had two sets if obligations. One set involved "military obligations," which meant "they should maintain and increase their military knowledge and skill." The second was "Civilian Obligations, such as to familiarize the nation with the need for preparedness . . . and . . . to bring home to our representatives in the Government the need for support to [*sic*] National Defense." The ROA then went on to point out, "the civilian function of the Reserve Officer is as important as the military one."[65] Indeed, many saw the civilian function as the more important one. Hoffman referred to that function alone, claiming, "As Reserve Officers you are part of that great body of patriots who foster and uphold the institutions of Government, and this is the obligation of your citizenship."[66] The influence on this internal division between reservists regarding the deadwood issue was obvious, for it meant that a significant portion of the reserve officers considered the citizenship side of their activities as relevant to their service as reservists even if their attention to their military professionalism was less than desired.

Despite these controversies, as with the case of the other civilian components, the chief aspect of duty with the Organized Reserve in the second half of the 1920s was the growing sense of stability and improvement. This, in turn, led to an increased sense of satisfaction with the program by all who were working with or in it. And while this sense of satisfaction led many to pay less attention to major underlying problems, it also provided a basis for the program's ability to weather the downturns that arose in the 1930s.

The CMTC

Of the four civilian components of the Army of the United States, the one that enjoyed the most stability in the second half of the 1920s was the CMTC. It faced no serious problems or challenges in these years. As a popular program, its relations with Congress remained good. Indeed, when the Bureau of the Budget sought to reduce appropriations for the program in 1925, congressmen quickly restored them.[67] It also received generally positive coverage in the press while attracting no hostile attention from pacifist organizations. The CMTC enjoyed generally positive support in the Regular Army, which viewed it as the last vestige of the hope of getting the American public to accept the idea of universal military training. So, even though reports showed that well less than 1 percent of CMTC graduates went on to enlist in the army, a General Staff officer noted on several occasions that the production of reserve officers was only "incidental" to the mission of the program.[68]

There were, in this period, only two significant changes made to the program. The first was to standardize the basic red course, which took up the first year of the program. The CMTCs were carried out at facilities under the jurisdiction of the various branches, each of which sought to tailor the courses to fit their own needs in producing possible reserve officers or NCOs for their branch. Yet as the basic course at almost all facilities had little military content outside of marksmanship, the General Staff decided to standardize this part of the program, a move that met with little opposition from the branches.[69] The other change was to turn the administration of the camps over to reserve units in order to give more reservist officers an opportunity for summer-camp experience. After an initial experiment with this idea in 1928, it was used throughout the program the following summer. From the point of view of camp administration, the results of this innovation were so dismal that five out of the nine corps-area commanders recommended that it be discontinued.[70] But the General Staff, and particularly Chief of Staff Summerall, remained committed to the idea of using reservists to administer the CMTCs, so efforts were made to solve the problems rather than end the practice.[71]

Finally, the army faced a racial issue as African Americans sought to attend the CMTCs. The problem was quite minor in terms of its immediate effect on the army and the program, but it was a difficult one that continued to grow in significance over the next decade. The army was aware of the issue and, in early 1923, sought to deal with it on the basis of providing what could be considered separate-but-equal opportunities for African American (then referred to as "colored") boys to attend the camps. Under this policy, the army agreed to provide a separate "colored" summer camp if applications in a corps area could be expected to result in fifty actual camp attendees. Later this policy was modified to require only fifty applications. Under these policies, "colored" camps were actually held in Arizona in 1924 and 1925. The results, however, were discouraging, with low turnouts that seemed to justify decisions against continuing them.

During the second half of the 1920s, however, there were sporadic efforts from African American communities for policy changes that might enable more members of those communities to attend the CMTCs. Surprisingly, the NAACP was not involved in the attempts to change it. Instead, such efforts came from individuals and veterans' organizations. While these individuals had no political power, their demand that African Americans be treated equally and fairly placed the army in a delicate and potentially embarrassing moral position. Finally, by 1929, a few advocates for African American participation in the camps began to reject the separate-but-equal policy followed by the War Department and to demand the right for their young men to participate in integrated camps.[72] This forced the General Staff to try to defend the policy of segregation in the CMTCs. The staff at that time took a "best interest of the boys" approach in its response. Major General Frank Parker, then assistant chief of staff for operations and training, formulated the General Staff's response, arguing: "The experience of many years has proven that segregation without prejudice is the solution to the problem most satisfactory to all concerned. . . . The morale factor in military training requires that trainees have congruent association and live in harmony with themselves. For this reason, it would be distinctly unfair to assign boys from one race to units or camps largely composed of boys from the other race."[73] The onset of the Depression seemed to end this controversy for a while, but it would reappear more vigorously in the 1930s.

CHAPTER 5

Creating Orthodoxy and Predictability

Professional Military Education in the Army, 1919–1939

E DUCATION WAS EASILY THE most important professional activity carried out by the army in the interwar period, engaging a major commitment of time from most officers. In any given year, 2,300 officers, or one-fifth of the entire officer force, was engaged in some form of professional military instruction either in the Regular Army or with the civilian components.[1] In addition, many officers who were assigned to other duties were involved during the summer with instruction of civilians in camps. Finally, all officers assigned duty with troops were also involved with the training of their men. Professional education was recognized as being virtually the only means by which officers could gain the experience needed to function in a wartime situation. Moreover, the skeletonizing of the army meant that very few officers had the opportunity to train with units anywhere close to combat strength. Hence, even before 1939, army leaders had already made the creation of professional schooling one of the military's highest priorities.

Efforts to reestablish the prewar professional-education structure began almost as soon as the war came to an end. Initiated with a mild sense of enthusiasm emerging from the experience of a war, which seemed to vindicate the army's professional training, most of the planning was completed by the fall of 1919. The system as it emerged had three main aspects. The first and most obvious one was structural. As before the war, the system was shaped around the educational needs of the officer as he advanced through his career, intended as something analogous to the systematic and progressive education seen as the educational basis of other professions. Therefore, it was built on the four tiers of formal training composing the prewar system, namely, West Point, unit schools, special service schools run by the branches, and general service schools controlled by the General Staff.

Of these four tiers, army leadership was chiefly concerned with the last two: the branch-level special service schools and the army-level general service schools. They did little to change West Point after the war. Jorg Muth, in his highly critical analysis of military education in the United States in the interwar period, gives Douglas MacArthur, who was superintendent of the Military Academy from 1919 to 1922, credit for initiating far-reaching changes in the curriculum. But Muth also notes that many of these reforms did not survive his departure.[2] Unit schools were based on the garrison schools of the prewar army and conducted as part of the on-the-job training that new officers received.[3]

The special service schools were originally designed to educate an officer newly assigned to his branch and to train him to be proficient in all duties associated with the branch up to the battalion level. These schools generally had two levels, a basic course for new officers and an advanced course, taken a few years later, aimed at acquainting officers with all the duties of their branch.[4] Later, the advanced course also took responsibility for preparing officers for the general service schools. The special service schools were under the control of the chiefs of branches and would obviously emerge as the centers for inculcating branch identity. The educational program offered by the individual special service schools will be treated at greater length in the chapters devoted to the development of the four combat branches.

Prior to the war, there had been two principal general service schools, one for majors and lieutenant colonels at Fort Leavenworth, which aimed at training for staff and command assignments within multibranch divisional structures, and the Army War College in Washington, which was to prepare officers for duty with the General Staff and for command at the highest levels. After the war, it was anticipated that there would be two schools at Fort Leavenworth: the School of the Line, which would train officers in the use of all arms and services at the divisional level, and the General Staff School, which would train officers to function as staff members at the divisional level and for higher command.[5] Both were a year in length. The entering class of the School of the Line was limited to two hundred, while the General Staff School was made up of the top one hundred graduates of the School of the Line. Under this arrangement, it was assumed that an officer headed for senior command would spend two years at the two Fort Leavenworth schools, followed by a year with troops in a unit outside his branch, and finally a year's education at the Army War College. This four-year cycle would, presumably, break an officer's primary identity with his original branch and focus it on the entire army instead.

The second aspect of the system as reinstituted was that its goal was to inculcate in the students "a uniform tactical doctrine approved by the War

Department."[6] Indeed, officer-students were also expected to learn the means of instruction so they could teach the same tactical doctrine to others. This need to ensure the unity of doctrine was considered to be extremely important and shaped much of the organization of the system. School administration was re-organized, giving the commandants complete control over the curriculum. At the same time, all schools were expected to follow General Staff directives and to submit annual reports and curriculum to the staff, which would monitor ad-herence to tactical doctrine. On the other hand, the content of that doctrine was to be worked out in the schools. All senior officers were convinced that the experience of the war would be primary in shaping all new doctrine. As a result, instructors from the army schools set up in France during the war were used as the core of the new educational system in the United States. These instructors, in turn, were encouraged to throw out old texts and to develop new ones them-selves based on the doctrines developed by the AEF in France.[7]

Finally, there were efforts made to accommodate the citizen-soldier provisions of the National Defense Act of 1920. The new mission of the educational system included the need to provide for "a reserve of trained officers qualified for organiz-ing and developing to its maximum capacity the potential military power of the nation in accordance with approved war plans."[8] At the same time, mission state-ments for special service schools included references to the need to instruct offi-cers for service connected with training National Guard and Organized Reserves.

Once the schools in the overall system were established, they rather quickly began to become competitive, with each expanding the scope of its coverage into the domains of others. By the beginning of 1921, there were complaints that the unit schools being created by corps-area commanders were moving into the educational realms claimed by the special service schools by offering specialized courses of up to four months in length.[9] At the same time, the special service schools seized on the mission to prepare graduates for the general service schools to expand their curricula into areas claimed by the Fort Leavenworth schools.[10]

Chief of Staff Pershing heard of this growing overlap and competition at the same time that he was becoming aware that Congress had no intention of supporting the army at the level of the 280,000 men promised in the National Defense Act. The increasingly apparent duplication created by this competition therefore attracted his attention both because it seemed to be leading to in-creased chaos and because it seemed to be a wasteful extravagance at a time when economy was needed.[11] Hence, in February 1922, looking for ways to reduce costs, Pershing created a politically high-powered board chaired by Major Gen-eral Edward F. McGlachlin, then the commandant of the Army War College.

He directed McGlachlin and his board to study the entire military-education system, "with a view to its simplification by such consolidation and concentration of schools," and to end the competition among schools by "delineating the exact role to be played by each school in the complete system."[12]

After some internal scuffling, the board produced a report with a number of recommendations. The two most important suggestions were, first, that the two one-year courses offered at Fort Leavenworth be condensed into a single year and, second, replacing the basic course for new officers at the branch special service schools with a course for company officers, attended several years into an officer's career. Overall, this meant reducing the years an officer spent in formal schools from five years (two in special service schools, two at the Fort Leavenworth schools, and one at the Army War College) to four.[13] Finally, the board was successful in bringing an end to the competition between schools and the unrest this caused in military education within the army. The lines of demarcation it established were accepted, and the schools began to act, as Pershing had hoped, as integrated parts of a single system.

Although no one spoke of the special service schools and the general service schools as competitors, the board's recommendations indicate that the former had already gained greater support in the army than had the latter. This may have been due, in part, to the idea that the special service schools were designed for all officers, while the general service schools were only for those selected as having the potential to become generals.[14] But in the comments by officers on the schools, it is clear that they valued the special service schools for socializing the new officer into the culture of the branch, which was, itself, increasingly becoming recognized as the primary means by which one established his professional identity within the army. As Brigadier General William D. Connor, assistant chief of staff for supply, argued, "One of the great functions of the special service schools is to set the tone and fix the esprit of officers in their own arm."[15] The members of the McGlachlin Board agreed that the special service schools were central to the creation of a branch culture, indicating that one of the major factors in their considerations was the "recognized necessity for one master school where policies can be enunciated and standardized methods of training and proficiency can be maintained."[16]

The settlement created by the board was generally accepted, becoming a kind of constitutional foundation for the army's military-educational system and stabilizing it for the remainder of the interwar period. As a result, except for working out a few of the problems within the system created by the report, the focus of attention in military education shifted to developments within the schools themselves.

Three issues continued to trouble the system, although they caused no significant controversies. The first of these was that many leaders felt that the reduction
of the program at the Command and General Staff School at Fort Leavenworth
from two years to one was wrong. This feeling persisted so that the program at
Fort Leavenworth would shift back and forth between one-and two-year courses
during the entire interwar period.

The second problem was what to do with newly minted second lieutenants
now that the basic course at the special service schools had been changed into a
company officers' course offered several years into an officer's career. The board
report recommended that the burden of providing these officers with their
basic orientation to the army and their branch would fall on the unit or "troop
schools" operated by post and tactical commanders. This decision was met with
some reservations in the General Staff, as the troop schools were seen as ad-hoc
organizations upon which one could place little confidence.[17] The army responded by having the staff organize the educational program to be followed by
the troop schools to ensure that attending officers graduated with the proficien-
cies sought in the special service schools' basic course.[18] The program was generally accepted as satisfactory, and the troop-school basic course became the new
second lieutenant's introduction to the army for the rest of the interwar period.

The third problem involved ensuring that officers attended the courses at the
special service schools at the appropriate time in their careers. The ideal set by
the board was that one be sent to the company-officer course by his fourth year in
service and to the appropriate advanced course by his twelfth year.[19] Yet almost
none of the branches were able to come even close to meeting that goal, as desirable as it seemed. A major cause of the problem was the high officer-turnover rate
during and immediately after the war. In terms of officers, there was very little
continuity between the prewar army and the army of 1920. Moreover, many of
the new men had little formal military training, having come in during the war
or immediately thereafter. Many had not been to West Point, and a surprising
number even lacked a college degree.[20]

Army leadership was anxious that this large mass of new officers be accul-
turated and socialized by means of attending the special service schools. Yet
facilities and appropriations limited average entering classes at these schools to
a number not significantly greater than the annual incoming class of new officers into the army. Hence, huge backlogs quickly built up. By 1923, the General
Staff began to keep track of the backlog by branch, but it could not find any
solution.[21] By 1929, however, one began to appear by possibly merging the company officers course with the advanced course into a single one-year offering.[22]

As the combined course would be available for a far larger number of officers, it offered a way of reducing the backlog. Moreover, many argued that the original two-year course was originally intended to deal with the mass of untrained officers in the immediate postwar period, a problem that, by 1929, had largely disappeared. Even so, nothing was done until 1932. At this time, the economic pressures generated by the Depression finally forced the army to cut the annual school quotas by 50 percent.[23] This reduction meant that the backlogs would now last for decades, with many officers facing the prospect of never getting to a service school during their entire career.[24] With this, the General Staff finally consolidated the two courses into one.[25]

Overall, in looking at the general developments within the army's professional-education system, one is struck with how stable it became after the implementation of the McGlachlin reforms. Indeed, the term "stagnant" seems more appropriate, as the system changed far less than perhaps it should have. Indeed, one of the main problems or weaknesses of the military-education system in the interwar period may have been that it lacked any machinery to ensure change when appropriate. Like all institutions, the schools had an inherent inertia that was, perhaps, aggravated by the constant turnover in administration and staff. Yet they faced no competition nor other stimulus to change. Finally, there was no other force within the army that could promote change.

One reason for this was that, despite the importance of the program for both the army and its officers, neither the army's leadership nor its officers took much interest in it once it was in place except as it concerned them personally.[26] Commandants of the various schools continued to be concerned with their own institutions, but there was little interest in the system as a whole after 1926.[27] In short, the army entered the postwar era with full confidence in its traditional system of military education and with the approach to instruction taken by the officers who taught in it. Hence, even though it was criticized by some of the officers it served, the system underwent little change during the interwar period.[28] This was due largely to the fact that the educational approach produced not only the orthodoxy and consistency desired but also a professional self-image that consistently conformed to the culture and cosmology of the army itself, leading to few internal tensions to foment any major demand for change.

In regard to what actually went on in the classrooms themselves, the foundation of the army's approach to instruction in the interwar period was referred to as the "applicatory method." Not all of the courses taught in the professional schools used this method, but most did, including the all-important courses in tactics. It had been developed before the war and was well established and well understood by the 1920s. The approach was designed to teach tactics but was quickly adopted to teach most other subjects as well.

The applicatory method was based on the belief, dominant in the U.S. military in the early twentieth century, that military activity should be treated as a science. This meant that, as in the case of other sciences, all military knowledge could be structured around a few basic principles considered universally applicable throughout all time. Success in war, therefore, depended on the correct application of these principles. While it was repeatedly claimed that the principles adopted by the U.S. Army were derived from a long and careful study of military history, they had actually been developed recently by I.F.C. Fuller, a British major general. Fuller's set of eight principles had been adopted by the British Army after the war and were then adopted by the U.S. Army, with the addition of a ninth principle, in 1921 and published in *Training Regulations 10-5*. Throughout the entire interwar period, education in the army schools was permeated by a faith that the secret to success in all military activity was based on the correct application of these principles. As General Drum, who served as first commandant of the general service schools during their reestablishment after the Great War, said, a sound course of professional military education consisted of "teaching the basic principles and illustrating their applications."[29] In addition, basing an officer's professional education on principles and applications seemed to provide the answer to the problem of teaching him the army's doctrine while providing him with the intellectual ability to respond to situations by the exercise of individual initiative. Theoretically, at least, an officer who understood how to apply the appropriate principles correctly to any situation could be counted on to do the right and expected thing.

The concept of principles and their application was the heart of the applicatory method. Yet, it tended to be used differently at the special service schools than at the Command and General Staff School. At the special service schools, a course was divided into units that were centered on learning a specific thing, such as a maneuver, or the use of a specific weapon. The unit would be introduced by linking it to what the students had already learned. The new thing would then be introduced by a demonstration, if possible. This might be live, if dealing with a weapon or an uncomplicated maneuver. Otherwise, it might be depicted on a chalkboard. This introduction would be followed by instruction in the principle involved and its appropriate application to the issue under discussion. There would then be another demonstration, after which students would attempt to perform the action themselves. Then, at the conclusion of the unit, the instructor would, again, point out the principle involved.[30]

But at the Command and General Staff School, the focal point of the applicatory method was the "map problem," which concluded each unit dealing with tactics or associated subjects. As one observer noted, "The entire scheme of military education as we have evolved rests on the map problem."[31] Most of a student's grade in a course and standing in the school—and by extension, career— rested on performance in the map problems. Each was a four-hour test involving a tactical problem linked to several of the issues covered earlier. A student was given the problem at 8:00 in the morning and was expected to have worked out on a map a suitable tactical solution and to have written the appropriate orders in the appropriate manner by noon.[32] The student's performance on the map problem would then be evaluated on the basis of whether or not his solution violated any fundamental principles.[33] This meant, in fact, that responses were scored on the basis of whether or not they conformed to a specific "school solution," which, in the words of one commandant, "properly apply the principles and doctrines upon which the art of war is founded."[34]

There were several ramifications of this approach. First, the applicatory method, especially as it was practiced by less experienced instructors, and the emphasis placed on the map problem produced some confusion in the minds of students. While Drum may have seen the purpose of the approach as teaching the principles underlying the successful conduct of war, many students saw the focus of instruction instead in the approved solutions to the map problems. Hence, they spent their time studying back files of map problems, trying to learn the approved solutions, and often emerged from the school experience feeling that the doctrine they learned resided in those official solutions.[35] In addition, the applicatory method, with the emphasis on the school solution and the need to avoid violation of principles, promoted orthodoxy in all thinking. Indeed, the primary focus in teaching and learning was to avoid errors. Instructor comments centered on pointing out errors, while class critiques of student performance were also expected to focus on such fault finding.[36] Overall, students were told that success in school was to be gained as much by a high grade point as by uniform and consistent marks, so that their chief goal became to avoid making mistakes.[37]

One recent historian, Jorg Muth, has been highly critical of the army's educational system and, especially, the Command and General Staff School. He criticizes the school's program on a host of issues, including not being transparent or even consistent in its selection system; its faculty being dominated by AEF veterans, who remained committed to the doctrines of the war and almost indifferent to modernizing trends, were often poorly informed about their subject matter, and were boring instructors to boot; and focusing on map problems rather than on outdoor tactical-command exercises using virtual units. But most of all, Muth condemns the focus on using student adherence to school solutions as the measure of ability.[38] He concludes: "The U.S. Army's professional education system produced for World War II an average officer who knew the basics of his trade in theory because he had run through a number of schools that had taught him that. He generally longed for doctrine and prepared solutions and tried to 'manage' rather than command."[39]

Indeed, in regard to the Fort Leavenworth school, this "average officer" may have actually been the desired product. As Brigadier General E. L. King, speaking as commandant to the Command and General Staff School, told incoming students in September 1926, "The purpose of the school is not to develop Alexanders, Napoleons, and Fochs, but to raise the general average of ability to produce a team that a Foch, a Napoleon or a Pershing may be able to use."[40] Such teamwork would be possible only if students were taught to set aside their own ideas and accept totally the doctrines taught by the schools. The principal role of military history as taught was to convince students that the military doctrine taught by the school was not just valid but the only possible valid doctrine.

Finally, instruction at the Army War College was quite different from that of the special service schools and the Command and General Staff School in several critical ways. The mission of the War College after 1918 was essentially twofold: to prepare officers for duty with the General Staff and to prepare them for military command at the highest level. To carry out this mission, the college's educational approach differed from that practiced in the lower schools in three major ways. First, students worked in small groups or committees rather than as individuals. These committees were given major problems related to either the planning or the conduct of a war for which they developed group solutions. The group solutions were then reported to other student groups and the faculty. Second, while the faculty provided some lectures, they acted chiefly as mentors to the groups rather than as instructors. Third, each group's solutions were discussed with faculty members and other student groups but not given formal evaluations. Nor were they critiqued on the basis of conformity to an accepted application of the principles of war—there was, in short, no school solution.[41] In addition, even though some officers finished the college's program without gaining the desired designation of "General Staff Eligible," almost no one actually failed. The distinctiveness of this program was based, apparently, on the belief that both staff work and high command were matters of teamwork rather than the exercise of genius. Also, the sense of certainty in military activity promoted by a belief in eternal principles of war and approved school solutions was significantly replaced at the War College by an acceptance of the ambiguity and contingency involved in actual warfare.[42] Thus, as an historian of the War College noted, like the Command and General Staff College, the goal of the War College was not to produce a genius or original military thought, but "to produce competent, if not necessarily brilliant, leadership that could prepare the Army for war and fight a war successfully if it came."[43]

Overall, outside of dissatisfaction with the marking system associated with the map problems, officers in the army were generally satisfied with its system of professional military education. If the experience was more comfortable than challenging, officers still left thinking they had learned a lot. The fact that the schools had produced uniformity and standardization of thinking and approaches to problem solving within the officer class was considered positive. In speaking about the army's educational system, General Hines, as deputy chief of staff, was proud to be able to point to "a growing homogeneity in the instruction methods, in the subject matter taught, and in the principles and doctrines laid down," which, he noted, was leading to a "consequent standardization of methods and ideas."[44] Even critics of the education system applauded the fact that the officers it graduated were reliably consistent in performance of their duties.[45] Finally, the vision instilled in officers that they operated in a physical and military universe governed by a few fundamental principles that remained immutable in character and promised success when followed correctly provided them not only with assurance but also a cosmology focused on authority, which was congenial with the military mindset. The fact that the applicatory method was also the approach used by the officers themselves to train their soldiers reinforced its legitimacy and made their own education part of the overall army culture.

CHAPTER 6

Building a Throne for the Queen

Infantry Branch Organization and Branch Culture in the 1920s

THE INFANTRY EMERGED FROM World War I as by far the dominant combat branch in the U.S. Army. Its centrality was the foundation of American military doctrine as later enshrined in the army's postwar governing publication on doctrine, the 1923 *Field Service Regulations*: "The coordinating principle which underlies the employment of the combined arms is that the mission of the Infantry is the general mission of the entire force. The special missions of other arms are derived from their powers to contribute to the execution of the infantry mission. . . . Infantry alone . . . possesses the power to close with the enemy and ensure the decision of battle. Its forward movement is the indispensable condition of victory."[1]

This dominating position was not just the result of the experience of that war but was also the basis of army doctrine prior to the conflict and the result of several historical forces. First, all during the nineteenth century, the army, and Americans in general, had idealized the sharpshooting individual soldier and his rifle as the heart of the American military experience. He personified the individualism, aggressiveness, and self-reliance that were seen as the basic characteristics of Americans. Second, as army officers began to professionalize during the late nineteenth century, they looked to western Europe for guidance. European armies were dominated by the ideas of the French officer Ardant du Picq, who in his classic work, *Battle Studies*, lionizes the individual soldier, seeing the man rather than the weapon as the key to victory. Du Picq was adopted by the U.S. Army and taught in all the military schools formed in the late nineteenth and early twentieth century as well as at West Point. Finally, as Mark E. Grotelueschen has pointed out, while about a third of army officers in 1917 had combat experience from service in the Spanish-American War, the Philippine War (1899–1902), or the Mexican Punitive Expedition in 1916, these conflicts involved small-group encounters dominated by rifle-carrying infantry that bore no resemblance to the war then being fought in Europe.[2]

During the relatively brief U.S. participation in World War I, this mystique of the American way of war had been translated into a tactical doctrine called "open warfare." This doctrine was not so much a detailed outline as it was a general sense of how war should be fought based on a number of shared beliefs. Its central principles were the primacy of the offensive, of the infantry, and of the human element in combat. And, as a corollary to the last, the doctrine also assumed the superiority of the American fighting man, particularly in terms of aggressiveness and ability to utilize individual initiative in combat situations. Thus, reduced to a tactical principle, open warfare envisioned an offensive assault carried out by infantry who were covered by voluminous, well-aimed rifle fire to smother enemy resistance, and who, by their aggressive spirit, determination, and individual initiative would force the enemy into the open, where the defenders would be destroyed. In this scenario artillery could be helpfully supportive, but was not considered essential.[3]

The U.S. experience in the war did almost nothing to change this view. Americans were involved in major combat for only a few months, at a time when German resistance was weakening and the war itself had, in fact, become more open. The final German capitulation in November 1918 came as a surprise to the Allies, who had expected the conflict to go on well into 1919. This success after only a limited engagement meant that U.S. military leadership saw the rapid success of their arms as a vindication of the doctrine of open warfare. While General Pershing created special boards of officers who carried out extensive studies of the American experience in the war, those concerned with the infantry quickly accepted the fundamentals of open warfare as proven. And with that, the rifle-carrying infantry "doughboy" became the icon of the American military experience in World War I.

As a result, during nearly the entire interwar period, infantry leadership saw little need to change or even examine the actual validity of its doctrine, having little incentive to modify an approach to warfare that gave the branch its dominating position in the army. Moreover, other factors during the ensuing two decades further stultified any ability to consider change. The fact that, within a few years, army budgets were reduced to near-starvation levels meant that little was left in the way of resources for technological research. Far more important, the army's commitment to training the civilian components, especially during the summer camps, proved to be an enormous distraction. Finally, the severe skeletonizing of army units, their dispersal throughout the country, and the large commitment to overseas garrisons meant that most infantry units were too small to engage in the kind of training that would lead to any sort of challenge to the existing doctrine.[4] As a result, the infantry tended to tinker with the system, especially in terms of incorporating new weapons, such as machine guns, mortars, and the tank, into its doctrine. It was not until the late 1930s, when increased funding, expansion of the army, and a growing awareness of the implications of technological changes in warfare, that any significant challenges to its doctrine began to appear. Even so, as William Odom has observed, the 1939 edition of *Field Service Regulations* was still almost totally committed to the basic principles of open warfare as described in the post–World War I 1923 edition.[5]

Instead, in the interwar period, there was more interest in the infantry in building up the internal organization of the branch. The infantry's development as a branch had made substantial progress before and during the world war. Branch consciousness among officers around the turn of the century had developed to the point that the Infantry Society, which formed in 1893, had become the Infantry Association. In 1904 it began publication of *The Journal of the United States Infantry Association*, with the title being shortened to *Infantry Journal* in 1910. By then, the editorial policy of the *Journal* began to reflect the "Queen of Battles" self-vision developing within the branch. Although the *Journal* experienced some bleak days during its first decade, it went on to flourish during the war. The explosive buildup in the army in 1917–18 led to a rapid increase in subscriptions, allowing the *Journal* to continue publication during those years without interruption, a luxury unavailable to other branch journals.[6]

This progress toward branch development accelerated during the war, as combat experience in divisions and larger units broke down traditional regimental identifications, leading officers to look increasingly to the branch as their source for organizational identity. Led by the *Journal*, the infantry took the leadership in the quest to establish chiefs of branches after the war, with discussion leading to widespread agreement on the desired role of the chief of infantry in the postwar development of the branch. Overall, therefore, the infantry emerged from the world war and subsequent army reorganization with its branch organization already well structured as well as the centrality of its mission in warfare all but universally accepted.

Therefore, having its agenda largely completed and its position as the Queen of Battles acknowledged, the infantry had, understandably, far greater incentive to celebrate and preserve the status quo than to change it. During the rest of the decade, it was chiefly concerned with three, essentially internal, issues. The first was the creation of the Office of the Chief of Infantry, which would direct the development of the branch, oversee its administration, and represent it organizationally and politically in relations with the War Department and the General Staff. The second, and far more important, issue was the development of the Infantry School at Fort Benning, Georgia. The third was the development of a branch culture that would bond officers to the infantry and out of which they could develop a common and attractive professional self-image.

The creation of the Office of the Chief of Infantry had been an important issue for officers before and during the war. The primary reason for this was an awareness of the advantages, real and imaginary, that the coast artillery was seen to enjoy, since it had branch chiefs serving on the General Staff since the turn of the century. Hence, the inclusion of a provision for a chief of infantry in the National Defense Act of 1920 was received with enthusiasm. As with the case of other branch chiefs, the chief of infantry had an imposing list of responsibilities but somewhat limited means for carrying them out. He was to advise on all matters related to his branch, to direct all the special service schools and boards within his branch, to formulate tactical doctrine within the branch, and to supervise training related to infantry. In addition, he had control over the assignment, transfer, and examination of all officers within his branch.[7] Yet the office was a small one. Outside of the chief, it was staffed by just six to eight other officers and limited clerical help. Moreover, the chief controlled little outside the Infantry School. All infantry units were under the tactical and administrative authority of corps-area commanders. In Washington the chief had no direct access to the chief of staff or to the General Staff. He could often effectively oppose policies seen as harmful to his branch but was far less able to serve as advocate for desirable policies. Still, the fact that the chief of infantry was a major general who had behind him a distinguished career gave the office considerable visibility and reinforced the vision that the infantry was a coherent organization headed by a powerful officer.

While the infantry had done a great deal to develop its branch structure even before the war, it lagged the other branches in building a program of professional education. The School of Musketry had been formed at the Presidio of Monterey, California, in 1907. Beginning as primarily a school to teach marksmanship, it rather quickly began to offer training in the use of other weapons as well as some tactics.[8] The school was moved to Fort Sill, Oklahoma, in 1913, but its further development was repeatedly disrupted by the demands for military forces on the Mexican border.[9]

American entrance into the world war then accelerated the development of infantry schooling. In 1918 a board was created to find a location where all infantry training could be combined in a modern facility with enough land to conduct large-scale training with modern weapons. The board finally selected a large site about nine miles south and east of Columbus, Georgia. Although the end of the war cooled some of the government's enthusiasm for the project, the first portion of an expanse that would soon extend over 97,000 acres was purchased on March 11, 1919.[10] To gain local support, the post was named Camp Benning after Confederate brigadier general Henry L. Benning, a native of Columbus. That Benning had been a citizen-soldier linked the post to the spirit of the new Army of the United States that would emerge from the National Defense Act of 1920.[11]

The first instructors arrived at Camp Benning on October 3, 1918, even before the land had been purchased. They had a bit over a year to plan the school that opened on November 1 the following year. Like the others, the Infantry School emerged as a blend of the two general forces that went into the special service schools' creation. The first of these was the growing professionalization of infantry as a branch, reflected in a focus on weapons and their handling.[12] It was the weapons that gave infantry its unique character and mission. The other force was the world war. The AEF had created a major school system in Langres, France, during its deployment. The system's purpose was not only to teach hastily recruited citizen-officers the rudiments of war but also to instill in the rapidly expanding army a common American doctrine.[13] Hence, this educational system was doctrine centered rather than weapons centered, and its focus was on the entire army rather than on the branch.

In the early phase of planning for the new postwar educational system, the Langres school tradition seems to have been the dominant force in Washington. Early planning called for large, multibranch educational centers that would "secure still better mutual understanding and cooperation between arms, to insure one doctrine being taught."[14] But branch influence quickly reasserted itself, so such plans, which would have ended the mission of Camp Benning even before it began, quickly died. By September 1919, General Order 112, which established the army's school system, was barely able to avoid using the term "branch" when it specified that the mission of the special service schools was "to develop and standardize the instruction and training of officers in the techniques and tactics of their respective arms or services."[15]

Although a basic course for fresh second lieutenants was offered at Benning starting in the fall of 1919, the full program opened in November 1920. After that, the history of the Infantry School at Fort Benning falls into three periods. The first of these lasted until the middle of 1922 and was characterized then and later as a pioneering period. The most notable characteristic of Benning at that time was its primitive conditions. Housing for officers, both students and instructors, was scarce, with much of the on-post quarters made up of abandoned and dilapidated structures used far earlier by tenant farmers.[16] Most officers lived in rented quarters in Columbus and commuted to Benning either by special trains or by automobile in a half-hour drive over a bumpy nine-mile dirt road affectionately called the "Daily Risk."[17] Finally, most facilities within the post were reached by such primitive dirt roads. The soil was poorly drained, so mud tended to dominate the memories of officers assigned to Benning in this period.

During those two years, the Infantry School offered three different programs: the basic course for newly minted second lieutenants, the company officers' course, and the field officers' course. Each of the three courses was nine-months long and followed roughly the same curriculum, although the basic course tended to stress weapons, while the emphasis shifted more and more to tactical doctrine in the company officers' and field officers' courses.[18] Together, they served nearly seven hundred officers, severely straining Benning's primitive facilities, while the similarity in curriculum meant that there was considerable overlap in the educational program. This was acceptable in the first years of the school, since the rapid turnover in officers during the war and afterward required that as many of the new and uninstructed officers as possible be funneled through the school system as rapidly as possible to ensure the homogenization needed to create a cohesive officer corps committed to following a common doctrine.

By 1922, these pressures were receding while Congress, in demanding constrictions in the military budgets, put new pressure on the army to economize. In this environment the duplication inherent in the earlier curriculum was no longer tenable. In reforms that followed the recommendations of the McGlachlin Board, the basic course disappeared, with responsibility for the initial indoctrination of officers now falling on unit schools. At the same time, the field officers' course differentiated itself from that for company officers, focusing more on tactics and in preparing students for the Command and General Staff School.

During the dozen years that followed the McGlachlin reforms, the worst of the conditions characterizing early Benning were ameliorated, and special amenities appeared that, in the face of smaller classes, created an ambience recalled later by student officers with considerable pleasure. As a result, the period between 1922 and 1934 stands out as a kind of "golden age" for the base and the school. The housing situation remained grim but was ameliorated by a careful organization of the search for rental units in Columbus and by efforts of members of the permanent garrison to build their own units, using the lumber from the vast stands of yellow pine on the base grounds. In addition, major buildings were gradually rebuilt in brick.[19]

Outside of housing, army personnel stationed at Benning began to build a set of amenities for the post, using funds raised locally and from contributions coming in from infantry officers elsewhere. These included Doughboy Stadium, a major facility seating 12,000 spectators and ranking among the top football fields in the Southeast. Funds donated for its construction were so generous that Benning personnel were also able to build Dowdy Field for baseball. With these, Benning soon became a major focal point for athletics in the Southeast with Major League baseball games played at Dowdy Field and major college football teams taking on the Benning team at Doughboy Stadium. Later, local funds were raised to build a massive 50,000-square-foot swimming pool, a major recreation center, a commodious officers club, and a separate hunting club. At the same time, the road between Benning and Columbus was paved, and regular bus service was established. The main roads inside Benning were paved as well. Finally, local efforts provided the base with a large post exchange, a commissary, a sizable hospital, a large laundry, and a school.[20] As a result, even though living quarters remained somewhat grim, officers at Benning had access to amenities and activities that were superior to those on almost any other post in the army, providing a quality of life that might otherwise not have been available to families in the social strata occupied by most officers. During this period, the curricular program at the special service schools changed relatively little. The schools attracted an excellent faculty, and officers attending between the years 1922 and 1934 recalled the instruction there with pride and pleasure.[21]

In 1934 the Infantry School entered the third phase of its development. Due to pressures created by the Depression to reduce costs and an awareness that its courses could not accommodate the enrollment necessary to allow all the officers who needed them the opportunity to attend, the company officers' course and field officers' course were merged into a single one-year course to allow for a far larger enrollment.[22] At the same time, Depression-related public-works money became available. As a result, Benning saw major construction of houses and other buildings as well as the further paving of roads. Thus, in the period between 1934 and 1940, much of what might be called the modern Benning emerged.[23]

The reason most officers considered their experience at the Infantry School as highly positive was that the school and the base together were increasingly successful in endowing them with a highly satisfactory new and complex sense of professional identity. Officers emerged from their experience at Fort Benning with a sense of pride in their membership in the infantry, with a confidence that they had acquired a professional expertise worthy of respect, and with an enhanced sense of self-assurance generated by association with athletic masculinity that had traditionally been seen as the hallmark of a military leader of men.

As Steven T. Barry points out, one of the main reasons that the Infantry School, and, indeed, all of the special service schools, were successful was that student officers already had many years of experience in the army. They had been rotated through a variety of positions and duties, had served in several posts, were already more than familiar with current army weapons and equipment, and had already had significant leadership experience. So, they understood the army and how it worked, having also already gained confidence in themselves as officers.[24] The most important element in this was the educational program offered by the school, which provided students with a learning experience that they saw as challenging and professional but that never threatened them with the possibility of failure. Student officers arriving at Benning immediately sensed they were entering an academic setting like that of a university. The classroom buildings, once they had been rebuilt in brick in the mid-1920s, were impressively academic in appearance. The curriculum looked collegiate, with attention given to several different subjects during the day. And, while students spent between 60 percent and 75 percent of their time in practical outdoor work, there was enough classroom time to give Benning the feeling of being a university.[25] Others compared the school to universities based on the reputation and quality of the faculty and the professional interests and enthusiasm of the students.[26]

The student officers at Fort Benning also had enormous respect for their instructors, who were admired not only for their military expertise but also for their teaching ability. As one observer put it: "We were soon impressed with the abilities of the instructors. They knew their subjects and they knew how to teach them."[27] The school early on acquired the reputation as being able to bring the best officers available as instructors.[28] In addition, that same observer noted, in regard to the teaching: "Authority was hardly perceptible, but cooperation was plainly in evidence. The spirit of wanting to do rather than having to do was everywhere apparent."[29] Students found classes remarkably open in terms of discussion and freedom, while the teachers maintained their authority much more on the basis of personality than authority.[30] As a result of this, one observer noted: "Benning is bound to be more than efficient. Benning is human. The result is the revival of a good deal of the charm that went with the army life years ago."[31]

Much of this was due to George C. Marshall, then a lieutenant colonel, who was the assistant commandant at the Infantry School from 1927 to 1932. In these years Marshall modernized the educational program. He upgraded the faculty, giving great attention to teaching ability. He sought, when possible, to replace map problems with field exercises and was noticeably skeptical of "school solutions" to problems. Instead, Marshall made a special effort to recognize imaginative student solutions to problems that differed from those approved by the school.[32]

Student officers also respected the Infantry School at Fort Benning because it clearly tried to remain up to date in matters of warfare, associating the infantry professionally with modernity in warfare. That innovation was chiefly with weapons, and the school attempted to introduce new weapons into its teaching as soon as practicable, with tanks and aircraft being part of the curriculum almost from the beginning.[33] But the most visible association with modernity in warfare was found in two organizations located in the Infantry School, although technically not part of it—the Infantry Board and the Department of Experiment. The Infantry Board was created in 1919 as the branch structure was developing. During the interwar period, it was located at Fort Benning and comprised the commandant and assistant commandant of the school along with three to five other officers. The function of the board was to "consider such subjects pertaining to infantry as may be referred to the Board by the War Department and to originate and submit to the War Department recommendations looking to the improvement of Infantry service."[34] Although the board tended to be rather passive, spending most of its time responding to items sent to it rather than initiating projects on its own, its close association with the Infantry School, both in location and in leadership, lent an aura of modernity to the school itself.

But the organization far more on the cutting edge of modernization was the Department of Experiment. The department was nominally headed by the commandant of the Infantry School and included around nine other officers and twenty enlisted men.[35] Its function was to test weapons and other military equipment submitted to it by the Infantry Board and to make recommendations regarding their utility in the infantry. The department was, initially, fairly conservative. It restricted itself largely to projects submitted to it by the Infantry Board and acting largely, as one member put it, as "a barrier to fantastic projects."[36] Still, its existence symbolized the openness of the infantry to new ideas from any source.[37] Moreover, in the 1930s the department began to take on a more initiating role in the development of weapons. Several imaginative and charismatic young officers began to develop projects on their own, making the department a force in the development of new weapons.[38]

In addition, as Barry notes, to keep its graduates up to date and, to some degree, to continue their education, the school also published the *Infantry School Mailing List*, with information about new weapons, tactical issues, and other developments in the branch.[39] Finally, as Barry also points out, given that a company commander's primary responsibility was training his soldiers, there was at the Infantry School, just as there was at all of the special service schools, a heavy emphasis on teaching officers how to train. The curriculum included major training-management modules with detailed instructions on different types of training, how to carry out each, and how to plan and evaluate training exercises.[40]

But while the educational program at Fort Benning maintained from the beginning an impressive aura of professional credibility and rigor, it was nevertheless highly accessible to the students assigned to it so that success for all students was all but guaranteed. Despite the professional aura surrounding the Infantry School, its academic program was far more technical than theoretical. This was especially true in the company officers' course, in which only about one-third of the classes were devoted to the study of tactics, while about the same amount was devoted to easily mastered, hands-on instruction regarding the use and maintenance of weapons. And even in the field officers' course, weapons instruction took up a quarter of the time, tactics only a half.[41] Other courses such as military history and psychology, which had an academic and theoretical appearance, were taught as practical matters related to leadership.[42]

The technical nature of the education was reinforced by the applicatory system, which was aimed at developing competency in technique rather than theory. Lectures or conferences first introduced students to both weapons and tactics, followed by seeing the weapon or tactic demonstrated. Students were then called upon to try out the weapon or tactical operation themselves.[43] While the Infantry School, like the Command and General Staff School, saw itself as teaching principles to be applied in given situations rather than techniques to be memorized, that distinction was largely lost on students, who happily found the learning of technique easier and more relevant to their professional needs than learning theory.[44]

Finally, it became clear to all student officers early on that the goal of the school was to graduate them. The work involved was neither taxing nor exhaustive. One student characterized his year at Benning as "unhurried and unworried."[45] Another noted, "The school takes up every subject from the beginning, so that even the least experienced officer has just as good a chance to cope as well as others who start with a good deal more knowledge."[46] Nor was the outside workload burdensome. The same officer indicated that an hour to an hour and a half of work each evening would easily get a student through the program.[47] Examinations were at a minimum and often of the "county fair" variety, in which officers observed an activity that was purposely being done incorrectly and were called upon to point out errors.[48] Moreover, sensing that competition among the students was distracting, the school sought to discourage it by replacing letter grades on all written work with a simple S or U.[49] It did maintain more discriminating records on student performance so that it could issue final efficiency reports and a class rank, but this information was not published.

While the Infantry School offered students the highly satisfactory feeling that they were undertaking a professionally demanding and respectable educational program, the facility itself also provided the officers and their families with the sense of belonging to a self-contained military community. Since Fort Benning was the virtual home of infantry, this sense of the base as a military community gave the branch a human dimension. The most notable aspect of the Benning experience for most officers, especially in the early years, was the poor housing. Officers also lived in Columbus in rental units notable for their discomfort. Omar Bradley recalled trying to study at night during the winter in a small, unheated kitchen.[50] While the school was unable to do much about the quality of housing, it did organize a Reception and Housing Committee to help with the hassle of trying to find a house.[51] At the same time, the leadership of the school expressed concern about the ability of junior officers to meet the expenses of living off post.[52] All this attention was appreciated by the officers and their families, who saw the base administration as a caring and paternalistic body.[53]

Efforts were also made as soon as possible to make Fort Benning as much of a self-contained community as possible. One way was by providing a full social life, especially for officers' wives. Among these activities were dances, including the weekly hop at the officers's club. There was a glee club and a dramatic club that presented plays at the theater every month. A women's club was active, often inviting notable authors and poets for readings or raising money for local projects.[54]

In this regard, base officials also made an effort to give social life there a sense of status. Many of the dances were highly formal; the weekly hop required a tuxedo.[55] But central to this was an effort to cultivate activities oriented around horses. Trails were developed around the post, and riding was encouraged as an appropriate leisure activity.[56] Fort Benning had a polo team and a polo club as an annex to the officers' club.[57] But the most significant activity in this regard was fox hunting. These events were held once or twice a week, with most of the formalities observed, including a nonalcoholic hunt cup and a huge post-hunt breakfast.[58]

Along with creating the Office of the Chief of Infantry, to guide the development of the branch and to represent it, and the Infantry School, to train officers as well as socialize them into the branch, the third concern of the infantry was to create a branch culture that would bond officers to the infantry and provide officers with a professional self-image to shape the character of their performance of duty along lines desired by the army and the branch. During the early and middle 1920s, this aspect of branch building seemed to have been considered to be as important as the other two.

For much of the interwar period, army officers remained convinced of the du Picquian axiom that, in warfare, it was the moral quality of the soldier rather than the weapon that brought military success. Indeed, open warfare, the foundation of American tactical doctrine in the interwar period, was based on the belief that bold and aggressive action on the part of soldiers was the key to military success. As one officer stated in *Infantry Journal*, "man remains the fundamental instrument in battle and, as such, cannot be replaced by any imaginable instrument short of one more perfect than the human body including the human mind."[59] And, in glancing through the tables of contents in *Infantry Journal* issues throughout the 1920s, one is struck by a seeming lack of interest in weapons. Hence, building an appropriate self-image in officers committed to exercising the qualities of character needed for leadership in such warfare was a major priority in the army, especially in the infantry—the branch most likely to see combat as human struggle.

In developing that self-image, the infantry initially drew heavily on the iconic doughboy of the world war. As one author claimed: "It has become the fashion these days in certain circles to call any uniformed Tom, Dick and Harry a doughboy. . . . Doughboy means an infantryman—the dust kicking, mud-slinging, sweating guy, who has nothing but his two legs and his grit to get him and his fighting paraphernalia from one busy spot to another."[60] Others would add tough and aggressive masculinity along with dogged determination to the list of desirable qualities to be possessed by the ideal infantryman. This became the heart of the professional self-image in infantry culture in the 1920s.

While the elements of this doughboy culture were already established at the end of the war, the concern was how to preserve it and, more importantly, how to socialize new officers into it. The Infantry School, as well as the atmosphere at Fort Benning, was to play a large role in this. But there were other efforts as well. One representative aspect of the effort to establish this culture was the campaign sponsored by the Infantry Association and the *Infantry Journal* to find an infantry song. In 1924 an editorial in the *Journal* declared, "The Infantry should have a bugle march which will be accepted by our arm as distinctive."[61] By October, it was announced that the Infantry Association was sponsoring a contest for an infantry song.[62] It was clear from the beginning that the song was expected to be a means of socialization of soldiers and officers within the branch.[63] The contest managers also had a fairly clear vision of the ideas they expected the winning entry to convey about the spirit and the character of the infantry.

In one of the many articles about the contest, they indicated that the key idea it was to convey was that "the Infantry is recognized as the basis of the Army. Its stated fundamental doctrine is that it is never exhausted, that it can always advance one more step and shoot one more shot.... [T]he spectacular is not for the Infantry. The Infantry's lot is exhaustive marches, unlimited hardships and extreme physical danger."[64]

But by far the most important effort to create and inculcate the doughboy culture in officers lay in athletics. During the war, competitive sport came to be seen as not only a valuable supplement to mass calisthenics in physical training but also as a means of training officers in leadership and in the development of teamwork.[65] As a result, army leaders emerged from the war as enthusiastic supporters of organized athletics within the military.[66]

The infantry followed this overall pattern regarding participation in athletic competitions. Initially, however, it was far more interested in participation in sports that were more easily identified with the martial character associated with the doughboy image. A course in coaching was begun in 1919 at the Infantry School and in a few years expanded into a two-year program.[67] But it was also the ambition of school leaders that Fort Benning should develop its own array of athletic teams, "which could compete successfully with the best in this broad land."[68] By 1921, the school had created football, basketball, and baseball teams and had been admitted into the Southern Intercollegiate Athletic Association. The school then created an intramural-sports program as a feeder for the varsity teams. It also developed a boxing program that ran matches all year long and built a swimming pool with a one-hundred-meter straightway for races.[69]

Despite this variety, the king of sports for the infantry in the early and middle 1920s was football, which would show that the branch was made up of "real 'hemen' in whose being flows the red blood of courage."[70] The enthusiasm for football at Fort Benning reached its peak in the middle of the decade with the building of Doughboy Stadium. Conceived initially as a monument to the infantry dead in the world war, the stadium emerged as an effort to put into concrete form the vision of what was seen to be the essential spirit of the infantryman. As one officer put it, the stadium would provide "an opportunity to Infantrymen today to express in fullest terms the virility and sportsmanship of doughboy personnel.... [T]he Infantry and athletics should move hand in hand,... a strong virile body is more necessary to an Infantryman than, perhaps, to any other soldier."[71]

The Fort Benning sports program was partially successful. Football spread throughout the infantry, with one regiment after another creating a team. Some of these teams played at the collegiate level, others in largely military circuits.[72]

Several regimental teams were able to play to crowds that were big enough to make the athletic programs self-financing.[73] Outside of football, infantry basketball, baseball, track, and boxing teams were active and often successful in military or intramural circuits.[74]

Nevertheless, by the end of the decade, the initial enthusiasm propelled by infantry sports program in the 1920s seemed to dissipate, as polo and other equestrian sports associated with the upper reaches of American society became more popular among the officers. By the end of the decade, one officer observed, "there are few posts where polo, horse shows, . . . and pleasure riding do not form part of garrison life."[75]

On the surface, the 1920s appeared to be largely static years for the infantry. Outside of an interest in tanks that began to grow rapidly toward the end of the decade, one searches in vain for any sense of direction of development in the military character of the infantry in this decade. Yet there were two major developments of significance. The first was the establishment of the Infantry School at Fort Benning. By the end of the decade, the school had provided its students with the confidence that they had the necessary knowledge to perform the tasks essential to infantry leadership and an adherence to a common tactical doctrine. In addition, it also provided them with a common experience bonding them to the branch.

The second development was in fostering the infantry officer's professional self-image. Two somewhat minor developments in the infantry in the later years of the 1920s, the effort—and failure—to find an infantry marching song based on the image of the doughboy, and the rise of polo, point to what might be seen as a decline in the attempt to shape infantry officers' self-image around the characteristics of the World War I doughboy. Indeed, the doughboy himself began to disappear from the *Infantry Journal* later in the decade. While this was not noted or discussed in the professional journals or service press, three developments may account for this. First, the educational program of the Infantry School was sufficiently successful that it provided its graduates with a self-image modeled on academic professionalism. Second, the appearance in 1927 of the fast tank and the excitement it began to cause in the infantry branch, as well as in the army as a whole, challenged the prevailing vision of warfare as essentially human combat. Finally, the rise of interest in polo in all of the combat branches may have indicated that officers increasingly felt that being seen as an integral part of society as a whole, and also as occupying a status level that corresponded to their vision of themselves as professionals, was an increasingly critical part of army officers' emerging professional self-image.

Both developments may have had a growing influence on the readiness of the infantry to undergo major modernization. First, the Infantry School, with the associated Infantry Board and Department of Experiment, provided the branch with a professionally accepted means of considering change, adopting it, and transmitting it to the rest of the branch. The *Infantry Journal* reinforced all of this. Second, replacing the doughboy image of tough and athletic masculinity as the basis for the professional self-image of the infantry officer with an image based more on the attainment of the professional expertise taught in the schools, combined with the attainment of an appropriate social standing in American society, may have begun the removal of earlier ideological barriers to major change in the infantry.

CHAPTER 7

Branch Stagnation

American Field Artillery, 1919–1939

I N HIS BRANCH HISTORY of the U.S. Field Artillery, Boyd L. Dastrup concludes his chapter dealing with the interwar period with the following assessment:

Consequently, with the exception of adoption of the M2 105-mm. howit-zer and M1 155-mm. gun in 1940, the development of improved fuses, and the creation of the fire direction center during the 1930s, the field artillery had not changed much since 1918. On the eve of World War II, antiquated weapons and thinking characterized the field artillery. Some progressive officers had tried to move the field artillery forward, but conservatism, lim-ited funds, and pacifism overwhelmed them, limited serious reform and rearmament, and left the field artillery poorly prepared, technologically and tactically, to fight armies that were adopting the latest weapons and innovative tactics.[1]

Low budgets and the demoralizing return of the apathy and even disdain toward the military that had become traditional in American culture were problems with which all the combat branches in the army were familiar. None, however, seemed so enervated by conservatism as the field artillery. Some causes of this are obvious. Unlike the coast artillery or the cavalry, the field artillery emerged from the world war with its mission vindicated and intact. Nor was its future significantly threatened by either of the two technological *wunderkinder* of the war, the airplane or the tank.

Another, less apparent, but still significant factor shaping the mentality of the field artillery was its particular position between two major and almost rev-olutionary developments within it as a combatant force. The first of these was a technological revolution that transformed both the weapons and tactics of field artillery to a degree that had not been seen in the past three centuries. The second was a transformation of the service into a modern military profession. Both developments began in the United States in the early 1880s and were radically accelerated by participation in the world war. But, at the end of the war, the technological revolution had virtually come to an end, represented by a stabilized weapon system, while the professional revolution was still in midflight. As a result, much of the dynamic and creative energies of the field artillery in the interwar period were directed toward shaping its development as a corporate body along lines dictated by American military professionalism at this time.

Of the two revolutions transforming artillery worldwide, the more significant was in weapons technology. This was not only precipitated by the desire of military leaders to have artillery capable of greater ranges and more rapid fire but was also heavily stimulated by technological developments. The most significant of these included new steels and new propellants that led to weapons with far greater range, breech loading, and fixed ammunition that allowed for a vastly increased rate of fire.[2]

The experience of the world war demonstrated that, taken together, these new developments created an artillery arm of fearsome power and lethality. This, in turn, led to a revolution in tactics. Deserting a battlefield that had now become too lethal for crews, guns were now located in fire pits well back from the front lines. And since the guns were now well behind the infantry and their targets were also dug in, there was a movement away from direct fire from standard guns, with their horizontal trajectories, to indirect fire from howitzers, with their arching trajectories.[3] More important, animal traction as the means of moving artillery began to give way to motor traction, principally in the form of tracked vehicles. The impetus for this later change came from the fact that the new, larger artillery weapons were too heavy for animal traction. But as motor vehicles began to prove themselves more reliable, there was a move to motorize light artillery as well.[4] By the end of the war, the technological revolution was all but completed, and artillery technology stabilized for the remainder of the century.

The United States was not far behind Europe in the technological revolutions. One reason for this was the leadership given by the Ordnance Department in the development of new weapons. By 1902, the department had developed a 3-inch rapid-fire gun to rival the French 75-mm gun. Other guns and howitzers soon followed.[5] In 1913 the army bought its first tractor to experiment with motorization. Americans were also quick to follow European leads in developing tactical responses to the technology revolution.[6] And they continued to adapt quickly to European patterns during the world war. The army gave up the 3-inch gun in

1916 and accepted not only the French 75-mm gun but also the idea of designing guns on the metric system. Many artillerymen also became enthusiastic about motorization during the war, with some arguing in favor of a full transition as soon as possible.[7] Finally, American artillerymen in France adopted the tactics of trench warfare and unobserved fire.[8] By the end of the war, American artillery officers had such confidence in the basic weapons used in the war that they saw no reason to do any more in the future than tinker with them.

On the other hand, while U.S. field artillery was as advanced as any in the world by 1919, American artillery officers lagged significantly behind their European counterparts in terms of developing a branch structure. Although recognized as a combat arm for much of the nineteenth century, it was not an organized branch. "Artillery" itself was an undifferentiated term that applied to both heavy coastal guns defending harbors and light terrestrial guns supporting mobile field units, with officers rotating between service in the field and service in coastal forts.

In the final decades of the nineteenth century, however, this situation began to change, and conditions emerged favorable to the development of field artillery as a distinct branch. This was due, in part, to the technological revolution. Serving the new artillery guns was increasingly seen as a science calling for a high degree of specialized knowledge. These currents were felt much more strongly among artillerymen in the coastal fortresses than among their brethren in the field. Hence, the coast artillery led an effort to divide U.S. artillery into two branches, a movement that reached its conclusion with the Artillery Act of 1907, which split artillery into coast artillery and field artillery. In doing so this law provided all the institutions needed to form a branch to the coast artillery. The chief of artillery (renamed the chief of coast artillery), the Artillery School, and the *Journal of the United States Artillery* all went with the coast artillery, leaving the remaining six field-artillery regiments as virtual orphans. Leadership within the six soon surfaced, however, to begin efforts to create a branch organization based on current professional models. By 1911, both a professional school, the School of Fire at Fort Sill, and a professional publication, the *Field Artillery Journal*, had appeared.[9]

Nevertheless, the branch organization of the field artillery and the professional development of its officers was still weak as the United States entered the world war. The mobilization for the conflict, then, quickly tore apart whatever organization that existed, making the war a virtual born-again experience for the field artillery. By the spring of 1917, there were only 275 officers in the field-artillery service with more than one year of experience. At the end of the war nineteen months later, that number had expanded by nearly 10,000 percent.

The School of Fire was radically expanded to turn out artillery officers in three months. The result was a rapid expansion of the field artillery's officer corps at the cost of a severe dilution of its quality and original identity.

A major step toward dealing with this confusion was made in February 1918 with the appointment of Major General William J. Snow as chief of field artillery. Snow, who had created and rapidly expanded the wartime School of Fire to train field-artillery officers, was able to bring some order out of the confusion, although he also had difficulties getting his authority accepted. Thus, at the end of the war, the field artillery emerged with a well-developed and well-accepted weapons system, which seemed to need little more than fine-tuning, and with a branch structure that lacked acceptance and organization, which was filled with a mass of hastily educated officers and had little in the way of tradition on which to build unity.

Almost as soon as the world war was over, the field artillery, along with the rest of the army, began planning for its own postwar reconstruction. As with other branches and services, the field artillery sought to base this on the lessons learned in the war. This search for lessons, in turn, spawned the creation of special boards that solicited testimony from many officers regarding their combat experiences. From that evidence, the panels developed recommendations for future development. The recommendations of four of these boards provided the basis for much of the agenda for the field artillery in the interwar period. The most important of these were, first, that the chief tactical mission of field artillery was to work in close cooperation with the infantry; second, that field artillery should be considered a system of "mutually dependent, light, medium, and heavy pieces;" and, finally, that future weapons development be seen in terms of both "ideal" weapons to be designed and deployed in the future and "practical" alternatives that could be had immediately by modifying existing armament.[10] Hence, as it entered the postwar period, the field artillery had a rather clear three-part agenda before it. It sought to create an ideal armament mix, to develop further its overall tactical doctrine, and to rebuild and strengthen the cohesion of the branch as an organization.

During the first six postwar years, however, the field artillery was unable to give its attention to any of these objectives, as its leadership had to deal with the instability within the branch caused by demobilization and developments within the army in the first half of the 1920s. The demobilization process was particularly disruptive. In addition, reorganization efforts in the early 1920s led to frequent transfers of artillery officers, so few stayed long in command of units. As late as 1925, only sixty-nine captains in the field artillery had been with their units for as long as two years.[11]

Until the middle of the 1920s inadequate personnel levels among both officers and enlisted men was seen as the most serious problem facing the branch. Of the two, the shortage of officers was the source of greatest concern. After the 1922 reduction, the authorized officer strength of the branch was 1,499. This strength level, however, was finally achieved only in 1931, although the most serious deficiencies were overcome by 1926. Moreover, the field artillery also suffered from a shortage of enlisted men until 1925, as field artillery was considered to be more work than service in other branches. As a result, soldiers in field artillery often reenlisted in other branches at the end of their term. By the middle of 1923, the field artillery had only 14,504 of its authorized 16,771 enlisted men, the largest deficiency of any branch in the army.[12] By 1925, however, these personnel problems seemed to be coming to an end.

Field artillery in the first half of the 1920s was also very much involved with the development of the civilian components. Having seen its experience with citizen-soldiers in the world war as generally positive, the field artillery generally took its role in training the civilian components seriously. During the early 1920s, it was quite positive toward the National Guard. The chief of field artillery took pains to select officers to serve as instructors in guard units who were noted for tact and patience.[13] By the late 1920s, however, he was concerned that the high rate of turnover in guard units severely lowered their military value.[14] Later, the chief's office seemed to lose interest in the Guard, possibly feeling that the Militia Bureau had shut it out of any role in training that component.[15]

The field artillery was also aware of the value of the Organized Reserve in terms of a wartime mobilization and lavished attention on it. With the passage of the National Defense Act of 1920, leadership quickly estimated that the branch would need 20,000 field-artillery officers in the Organized Reserve to meet the mobilization goals set forth in the legislation.[16] After that, the major focus of field artillery in regard to the Reserve was numbers, with progress measured by nearing the 20,000 goal.

Yet for the field artillery, the darling among the civilian components was the ROTC. The branch took an active interest in the ROTC almost as soon as the world war was over. One of the few officers in the Office of the Chief of Field Artillery was assigned almost exclusively to ROTC work. This officer worked assiduously to establish field-artillery ROTC units so that, by the time of the passage of the National Defense Act, twenty-two had already been created.[17] After this, the chief of field artillery continued to maintain great interest in them, with the designated officer still devoting most of his time to the ROTC units, inspecting many of them annually. The chief also worked to standardize the curriculum and summer camps. His greatest concern was lack of control, since ROTC units operated under the direct control of corps-area commanders.[18]

Although these issues were significant distractions for the field artillery in the first half of the 1920s, they did not halt the pursuit of an agenda created by wartime experience and by the several boards convened afterward. As noted earlier, this agenda had three parts: developing the tactical doctrine worked out during the world war, developing weapons to incorporate the ideas set by wartime experience, and continuing the development of the branch organization, which was disrupted first by the war and then by postwar demobilization.

Of these three objectives, the easiest by far was the further development of tactical doctrine since field-artillery officers emerged from the war largely satisfied with the doctrine developed there. Afterward, little happened in the army or in the nation that challenged it, so little change occurred in the interwar period. The essence of field-artillery doctrine was that the chief, if not sole, mission of artillery was to support the infantry. The centrality of this was acknowledged repeatedly in the reports of the postwar boards as well as in the professional literature in the subsequent two decades.[19] Infantry support was the basis upon which the tactical organization of field artillery at the division, corps, and army-headquarters levels was based. Although the concept remained unexamined and unchallenged during the interwar period, there was a major initial controversy as to how it was to be carried out.

The issue was whether American artillery doctrine was to be based on the observed fire of open warfare or the unobserved fire of trench warfare. Prior to the American entrance into the world war, the doctrine had been based on observed fire. Then, as noted earlier, exigencies of the war led to American adoption of unobserved fire as taught by the French. As Richard Faulkner points out, since the training of artillery officers in the United States was so sparce, most American officers were trained by the French.[20] Thus, many came to see the French system, with its strong base in science and mathematics, as more advanced and superior to the older American system, which some now even saw as obsolete.[21] General Snow, however, who remained the chief of field artillery after the war, believed otherwise, and by the end of 1919, he dictated that American field-artillery doctrine would remain based on observed fire.[22] The directive caused a major uproar in the branch, as many officers considered it a major step backward, and protests appeared in the *Field Artillery Journal*.[23] Snow defended his position in an article appearing in the *Journal* at the end of 1919 by tying it to the basic American tactical doctrine of open warfare, which the army itself was developing as the basis for its conduct in any future war.[24] And since Snow, as chief, controlled the Field Artillery School and the *Field Artillery Journal*, his view prevailed. The opposition fell off within a year as the branch united around observed fire.

Of the three long-term goals of the field artillery, the one that was the focus of greatest attention was the development of modern materiel. For a number of years after the world war, there was nothing that united the officers in the branch as much as the vision of finally completing the revolution in weaponry that had begun twenty years earlier. Field-artillery officers before and during the war had come to see this as the hallmark of a modern professional artillery. Yet despite this attention, little actual progress was made in the modernization of weapons.

During the entire interwar period two major factors frustrated the efforts to modernize artillery weapons development. One was severe budget restraints. The other was the huge inventory of artillery materiel left over from the war. This surplus impeded the effort to develop new weapons in a variety of ways. While the surplus inventory was not as well balanced between light, medium, and heavy ordnance as the field artillery would have liked, it was still available in a quantity necessary to supply a large-sized army.[25] Thus, as far as the chief of field artillery was concerned, this meant that resources could be directed toward research and development of new weapons rather than the acquisition of more materiel, however current.[26] The surplus also provided a means for at least a moderate modernization by tinkering with existing materiel. On the other hand, and more ominously, the surplus reduced any sense of urgency in the government regarding funding weapons development.

Following the model recommended by the postwar boards, with specifications for both practical and ideal weapons, development efforts proceeded along two lines. One was a pragmatic modification of existing weapons to make them suitable to deal with short-term emergencies in the immediate future. The other was to begin working on the ideal weapons specified by the boards under the assumption that these would come into use in the event of a major long-term emergency.[27] The latter trend got the most attention in the branch, leading to a tendency to equate progress in materiel development with progress toward realizing the ideals.

In its efforts to modernize its weapons, the field artillery moved in two general directions: updating the guns and howitzers themselves and motorizing their transportation, which initially meant replacing horses with trucks and tractors but later also referred to the development of self-propelled artillery. Of the two, the effort to modernize current weapons was of far greater interest in the branch. Field-artillery weapons were generally classified as either heavy, medium, or light. Heavy and medium guns and howitzers were usually assigned to

either corps or army units and were meant to attack fortifications or to inter-
dict lines of communications behind enemy lines. Light artillery was assigned
to divisions and was used primarily for close support of infantry. In general, the
branch devoted most of its attention to the development of light artillery as it
faced increasing competition from the air service over missions of interdiction
and bombardment of strongholds.[28]

During the world war, divisional artillery had been made up of 75-mm guns
with straight-trajectory fire and 155-mm howitzers with arching-trajectory fire.
After the war, in line with the army's overall focus on open, mobile warfare, the
field artillery decided to replace the 155-mm howitzer with a 105-mm howitzer,
as soon as a satisfactory model could be developed, and to modernize the 75-mm
gun. By 1926, the branch had adopted the far improved M1 75-mm gun to replace
its wartime predecessor. Yet the large supply of surplus weapons and budget constraints meant that the M1 gun was never procured, and the branch was left with
remodeling existing weapons. In the early 1930s the branch was able to mount
the wartime 75-mm gun on a new carriage. After several tests, the field artillery
found this remodeled gun acceptable, and it was put into limited production in
1936 as the M2; it remained in use well into World War II. After considerable
effort, the Ordnance Department developed the long-sought 105-mm howitzer,
which was to be the companion to the 75-mm gun in the division. But by then,
funds were so limited that few could be produced, forcing the field artillery to
fall back on the existing heavier 155-mm howitzer as the companion piece. By the
late 1930s, when funds were more generally available, the Ordnance Department
began developing a 105-mm howitzer that would be motor drawn. By 1940, it
had developed an experimental model that went into production in 1941. Until
then, however, the World War I mix of the 75-mm gun and 155-mm howitzer
remained the standard for the army's divisional artillery. Due to lack of funds,
there was no greater success in the development of new medium and heavy artillery in the interwar period.

The branch was a bit more successful in its efforts to motorize traction for
artillery, but, again, its progress was not nearly as great as had been hoped by the
postwar boards. While lack of funds was, again, the major cause, the effort to
motorize also faced considerable conservative opposition in the branch. Nearly
all the controversy over motorization involved light artillery. Initially, there were
concerns that tractor-type vehicles were still too unreliable and required logistic
support that further complicated artillery action. In addition, the mission of
light artillery was to provide close support of the infantry, which required flexible mobility, and many thought that horses were more likely to provide that than

the motorized vehicles then existing. Hence, there was a widespread feeling that the motorization of light artillery should be postponed until more reliable motor vehicles could be developed. The budget cuts of 1922 then brought all such efforts to an end for the rest of the decade.

Efforts were revived in the early 1930s chiefly due to the leadership of the new chief of field artillery, Major General Harry G. Bishop. Bishop noted that American automotive companies had made great progress in designing four-and six-wheel trucks and track-equipped tractors with cross-country abilities and highly improved reliability. At the same time, it was becoming clear that America's horse population was declining. In 1933 Major General MacArthur, as chief of staff, committed the army to motorizing 50 percent of its field artillery. Progress in this direction was still slowed by lack of funds and the need to develop a gun carriage suitable for motorized traction. By 1936, such a carriage was developed, and the War Department began to motorize light artillery despite some continued opposition. By 1940, fifty-six of the eighty-one 75-mm gun batteries had been motorized, as were the batteries of the newly developed M2 105-mm howitzer.

As important as both the development of doctrine and the modernization of weapons were for the field artillery, it was the third goal of the branch—the creation of both a branch structure and a sense of branch identity and self-image—that was the area of greatest activity and greatest advancement. The structure of the field artillery was similar to that of other branches. Organizationally, it was headed by a branch chief, in this case the chief of field artillery and his office. The two main institutions responsible for socialization into the branch and maintaining cohesion and unity were its special service school, the Field Artillery School at Fort Sill, and the *Field Artillery Journal*. A Field Artillery Association also existed as the professional organ of the branch. Outside of organizations and institutions, efforts were made to build a cohesive social life and culture, which in the case of the field artillery were centered heavily on polo and other horse-related activities as well as on the cultivation of the cult of Saint Barbara discussed later.

The Office of the Chief of Field Artillery was similar to other branch chief offices. It was headed by a major general and contained nine to ten other officers. The duties of the office included responsibility for officer assignments within the branch, research into material and tactical developments in field artillery, all training related specifically to field artillery, development of new materials, and participation in war planning. The responsibilities of the office and his rank and position meant that the chief of field artillery was able to exercise an almost dominating influence within the branch. This was especially true in the early and middle years of the 1920s when General Snow was the chief. Snow had been a colonel when the United States entered the world war. During the war he took charge of reestablishing the School of Fire at Fort Sill and expanded it rapidly. His success led to his being named chief of field artillery, an emergency office created at the beginning of 1918 to deal with the confusion in matters related to artillery prevailing in the War Department and General Staff.[29] Snow was a proud and dominating figure who had no tolerance for either incompetence or dissent. He was a superb organizer and a tenacious combatant in interbranch struggles. Snow also tended to regard the field artillery as a personal domain and was seen within the branch as the virtual father of the service.[30]

Along with the other major combat branches, the field artillery had a professional journal, the *Field Artillery Journal*. It was begun in 1910 as part of the efforts of officers to create a branch structure after the split with the coast artillery in 1907. The first few years of the *Journal*'s life were precarious, but with America's entry into the world war and the explosive expansion of the field artillery, the *Journal* began to thrive.[31] Like the other service periodicals, the *Field Artillery Journal* published articles related to technical and tactical developments and issues of professional interest to artillery officers. But it tried to widen its appeal by including pictures, articles of broader interest, and news items of interest to those officers, including a significant amount of coverage of polo activities within the branch. The *Journal* was published by the United States Field Artillery Association, a voluntary professional organization with its own set of officers.[32] The chief of field artillery, to be sure, had some control over its contents, but a knowledgeable foreign observer was impressed with the openness of the *Journal* and its willingness to publish contrasting opinions on current and controversial topics.[33] The efforts made to solicit articles and its willingness to publish contrasting views indicates that, within limits, it tried to serve as a venue in which professional dialogues within the branch could take place.[34] Overall, the *Journal* enjoyed widespread influence and support within the branch and among National Guard and Organized Reserve officers.

Yet as was also the case with the other combat branches, the most important institution within the field artillery in terms of socializing officers into the branch and developing and maintaining cohesion and unity was its special service school, the Field Artillery School at Fort Sill.[35] At the beginning of the twentieth century, as field artillery began to professionalize, Fort Sill, which offered a large area for firing and maneuver, began to become a center of activity. In 1905, a field-artillery regiment was stationed there to carry out experiments with newly developed guns and to develop tactics. In 1908, after the separation of the field artillery from the coast artillery, officials decided that to unify doctrine and practice, field-artillery officers should be trained in a single school rather than in the various regiments. An officer was sent to France to study artillery training there, and with the advice of several French officers, he helped establish the School of Fire at Fort Sill in 1911.

The School of Fire, along with most other army schools, was closed during the troubles on the Mexican border in 1916. It reopened in July 1917 after U.S. entry into the world war. Under the command of the energetic Colonel Snow, the school rapidly expanded until it was pushing two hundred prospective battery officers and one hundred prospective artillery observers through a twelve-week course, with a new class starting every week. Snow also initiated a building boom at Fort Sill, including a main classroom building modestly named Snow Hall. Even these structures, most characterized by cheap frame construction, failed to alleviate the crowded conditions characteristic of Fort Sill for a long period of time. The wartime School of Fire was continued after the armistice for several more months, although with a rapidly dwindling number of students.[36]

By 1919, plans were almost complete for the creation of a new artillery school based on the perceived needs of the field artillery in the postwar era. And even though it opened less than three weeks after the wartime School of Fire had graduated its last students, the educational program adopted was vastly different. From the beginning, it was clear that the major objective of the school would be to build a new corps of field-artillery officers who would be united by adherence to a common tactical doctrine, a common professional self-image, and a common vision of field artillery as a technically complex and highly professional organization.[37] In developing its program to achieve this objective, the field artillery was happy to follow the army's overall original educational program, in which new officers were introduced to the military profession in the basic course and later in their careers taught the more complex tactical and material techniques of their branch in two more advanced courses.

Initially, the most important of the courses taught at the new Field Artillery School was the basic course. Snow also saw it as the major opportunity for him to shape the development of the branch and its officers. He valued the basic course chiefly because it would replace older garrison schools, which he saw as inefficient and fragmented in their educational programs, since each was controlled by the regimental commander. The basic course, in contrast, was to be under the control of the chief of field artillery and would follow a curriculum developed by his office.[38] The initial cohesion created in the basic course would then be reinforced in the battery officers' course, which was to "disseminate throughout the service a unified doctrine for the handling of small units and the best methods for the instruction of such units."[39] A captain's year in this course was followed by a year with troops to allow him to assimilate the common doctrines through practice to the degree that he "learned to become an expert in his . . . profession."[40] All of this was followed later with the advanced course.

The two years after the opening of the Field Artillery School was a hectic formative period in which the principal features of its educational program were established and the major problems facing it manifested in sometimes severe forms. One of these was that the three courses carrying out the branch program were physically separated. The one-year basic course was offered at Camp Knox, Kentucky; the battery officers' course was offered at Fort Sill; while the advanced course was offered at Fort Bragg, North Carolina.

The school was also plagued with infrastructure problems, the most crucial of which was buildings for housing and classroom instruction. In each of the school areas these were inadequate in size, of poor and deteriorating quality, and scattered so that none of the separate courses had a real campus of any sort. At Fort Sill many buildings deemed "Unsuitable for Officer Housing" were still used for student officer housing for years.[41]

During this period, both the curriculum and the school year were defined. It was initially decided that the basic and the battery officers' courses would run for a year, from January to December. But within a year this was changed to a ten-month program running from September to June. This new schedule not only conformed to the rhythms of army life, with summers devoted to training civilian components, but also allowed for the more theoretical portions of the program to be offered in the fall and winter, leaving the warmer spring months open for field applications.[42] At the same time, the basic curriculum for the courses was established. While this underwent modification during the next two decades, the basic concept and forms never changed. All programs and faculties were divided into four sections—tactics, materiel, gunnery, and equitation—with equitation given only half the attention devoted to each of the others.[43] And, as was true in other branch schools, a balance was maintained between theoretical instruction and hands-on training, favoring the latter as much as possible.[44]

At the same time, the curriculum reflected some of the current strains and developments within field artillery. The initial division between the "trench warfare" school and its "open warfare" counterpart was reflected in the first few years of the school as well, with instruction provided reflecting both views. Over a relatively short time, however, open-warfare doctrines were given increasingly greater exposure until they became the established orthodoxy.[45] At the same time, the inclusion of a subsection of eighty-six hours on motors within the materiel section was indicative of early interest in motorization in the field artillery.[46] On the other hand, while equitation was given a more modern gloss by being renamed "animal transportation," it still represented the degree to which horsemanship was seen as one of the primary qualities of officer professionalism in the field artillery.[47]

Along with the curriculum, the Field Artillery School quickly developed its own style and approach to teaching. While its program was grueling in terms of material to be covered and demands for precision, overall, the focus was on maximizing officer psychic comfort with the program and graduating candidates. Instructors were cautioned to base their courses on the "the slowest, not the quickest thinker."[48] Only 2 of the 140 student officers enrolled in the basic course in 1921 actually failed.[49] As in the case of other branch schools, officer students were graded on how closely their solutions to problems conformed to the school solution. On the other hand, everything possible was done to relieve anxiety caused by grades. To avoid the competitive stress seen at some other schools, where a point or letter-grade system encouraged "fighting for tenths," work at Fort Sill was graded only as satisfactory or unsatisfactory. The only final grades in a course were "graduate" or "non-graduate." Instructors were well respected for both the depth of their knowledge and the consideration given to students. Despite this, the curriculum was so packed with material that students often came away impressed more with a sense of their own ignorance rather than a sense of accomplishment.[50] Perhaps for this reason, along with others such as the incredible inadequacy of housing, the Fort Sill experience may not have generated the same degree of enthusiasm among students and graduates that was seen at Fort Benning or even at the Cavalry School at Fort Riley, Kansas.[51]

As was the case with the other special service schools, the formative period for the Field Artillery School came to an end in 1922, with the reforms undertaken as a result of the McGlachlin Board. For the field artillery, these wrought two unwelcome changes: the elimination of the basic course and the consolidation of all courses at Fort Sill. Snow opposed both vigorously.[52] The end of the basic course meant that the training of new officers was left to troop schools, which were seen as reincarnations of the old garrison schools. Snow also deduced that consolidation of the Field Artillery School at Fort Sill would mean a contraction of school activities, whereas he was seeking an expansion.[53]

At the same time, the Field Artillery School sought to make itself the educational and even intellectual center for the branch. Its staff members developed correspondence courses for National Guard and Organized Reserve officers. The school later published a "mailing list," providing graduates with additional problems as refreshers, and developed training regulations for the branch. All this activity was carried out by officer instructors without the benefit of extra resources or even clerical support, leading to severe problems of overwork.[54] On the other hand, there was little change in the curriculum, especially in regard to issues of modernization, although some tinkering did occur. More interest in radio communication entered into instruction over time, while an advanced course in motors was set up in 1929 to create qualified instructors for corps-area schools, though it attracted few students.[55]

During the rest of the 1920s, the school also worked to develop a sense of its own institutional identity and its role and position within the branch. A patch was designed linking it with the cult of Saint Barbara, which was becoming more deeply imbedded in the organizational culture within the field artillery.[56] The school was also firmly committed to the horse culture so dominant in the branch. A riding hall was built, containing an audience gallery that could seat two hundred.[57] Fort Sill also sponsored a fox hunt.[58] At the same time, the school created an advanced equitation course to improve the level of horsemanship within the branch.[59]

Finally, the issue of highly inadequate facilities for officer quarters and for instruction continued to worsen during the 1920s. Most of the facilities available were wartime emergency wood-and-beaverboard construction. Woefully inadequate to begin with, they rapidly deteriorated further over time. More important, they were highly susceptible to fire. Between 1921 and 1929, nineteen major fires occurred at Fort Sill. These seriously aggravated the already severe problems with facilities to the point that, in 1930, a board was convened to study the possibility of moving the school to another post, such as Fort Bragg. Ultimately, it recommended against a move and suggested instead that a major building program be instituted to put the school in more-modern and more-fireproof facilities. In this way, and others, the school was poised in 1930 to enter a new era in its history.[60]

During the first five years of the 1930s, there was a growing sense that the Field Artillery School was entering a more positive and progressive chapter in its development. The most visible evidence of this was an accelerated building boom. But it was also seen in the leading role the school was taking in the modernization of the field artillery, which accelerated during the first half of the decade, and in the increased authority it enjoyed within the branch. An ambitious $11 million building program was drawn up and gradually implemented, in part with an infusion of Public Works Administration money. As a result, by 1935, much of the housing crisis at Fort Sill had been alleviated. The school also increased its interest and influence within the branch. It played an active role in the motorization program that Major General Bishop had prioritized, carrying out tests on other equipment as well, including radios, self-propelled guns, antitank guns, and other weapons.[61] Finally, through its work in developing correspondence courses, texts for regular school courses, and the *Field Artillery Manual*, the school began to establish itself as the source and authority on field-artillery doctrine.[62] At the same time, the onset of the Depression was responsible for several major disruptions of routine. In 1933 Fort Sill was made a regional headquarters for the Civilian Conservation Corps, and its demands on the school's officer personnel became so severe that the school had to close early in 1933. Moreover, budget constrictions forced all branches to curtail school activities by reducing enrollments by one-half, which meant merging the battery officers' course and the advanced courses beginning with the fall term of 1934.

The trends established at the Field Artillery School in the first half of the 1930s continued into the decade's second half, although the turbulence that marked the earlier years subsided. The only significant shift during this period was that the school became a major force in the motorization of the branch. It not only carried out research on motors but also increasingly became an advocate of more thorough motorization.[63]

Overall, in the interwar period the Field Artillery School had the twin objective of building the field artillery into a cohesive branch and to imbue its officers with a common doctrine reflecting the state of military art at the time. The school was, apparently, quite successful in achieving both goals. Like the other branch schools, it sought to weld the officers of the field artillery into a cohesive corporate body by providing a set of common experiences and teaching not only a single unified doctrine but also that success resided only within that system. Over time the school expanded its influence by means of its texts and extension courses, which brought the doctrine to officers beyond the school, including those in the National Guard and Organized Reserve. Finally, it represented the branch to the outside world, especially in the polo games and horse shows that remained central to American elites in the 1920s and 1930s. At the same time, the school remained highly aware of developments in field artillery throughout the world even if the branch was limited in its ability to keep U.S. field artillery in line with those advances.

On the other hand, the Field Artillery School, like the other U.S. special and general service schools, created a conservative outlook among the attending officers. By teaching orthodoxy, it inhibited imaginative or original thought, a tendency reinforced by the emphasis given to practical training and application of theory. Unlike the infantry and the cavalry, which had to deal with a revolutionary weapons system in the tank and with a revolutionary doctrine in the mechanized force, the field artillery and its school faced no such challenges to its comfortably evolutionary vision of change. But if it is true that the revolution in artillery weapons had already occurred and that its critical mission was in building a cohesive branch out of the agglomeration of officers in the field artillery at the end of the world war, then the school's focus on orthodoxy and its evolutionary approach to change may have been the best policy.

Branch building went on in the field artillery outside of its official organizations as well. Some of this extracurricular activity was encouraged and guided by branch leadership, but much of it came as a grassroots effort from among the officers themselves. All of it was aimed chiefly at creating a distinct branch culture that would not only provide a near-tangible sense of existence for the branch but also define for officers what it meant to be a "good field artilleryman." The strictly professional side of this effort came, in part, from the Field Artillery Association, a voluntary organization made up chiefly of field-artillery officers in the Regular Army, National Guard, and Organized Reserve. Created in 1910 in the wake of the Artillery Act of 1907, it not only provided the recently orphaned field-artillery units with a sense of their own branch existence but also was a deliberate effort to replace the prevailing "battery spirit" with a more professional branch spirit.[64] It was modeled along lines of a professional association, with its major function being the publication of the *Field Artillery Journal*. During the interwar period, the Field Artillery Association held annual meetings at which it sponsored professional research.[65]

The effort to create a branch culture also included well-developed informal elements. One part of this was an expanding collection of songs. Branch songs were an important element in defining a sense of professional identity and character for the field artillery as well as providing officers and enlisted men with a sense of community. The songs were chiefly devoted to describing work and life in the field artillery, characterizing the battery officer, and providing a branch ethos. The "Caisson Song," by far the best known of these, was composed in 1908, the year after field artillery came into existence, and extolled the toil and perseverance of artillerymen in keeping the caissons "rolling along."[66] Overall, field-artillery officers described themselves in their songs as vigorously masculine, fun loving as well as martial, and tightly knit comrades.[67]

While all the other combat branches also had their professional organizations and songs, the field artillery was unique in its possession of a patron saint.

The cult of Saint Barbara was not just an oddity but a tradition that played an increasingly important role in the development of the professional self-image of the field artillery. The association of Saint Barbara with artillery developed in Europe after the fifteenth century. American field artillery officers picked it up in France during the world war and brought it back to the United States, where the tradition spread quickly among field-artillery officers. Her position became officially recognized by the branch with the inclusion of bolts of lightning in the new seal created for the Field Artillery School. In 1934 a miniature replica of a fifteenth-century print of Saint Barbara began to appear on the frontispiece of the *Field Artillery Journal*. By the late 1930s, December 4 was celebrated by field-artillery groups as Saint Barbara's Day. Even though the cultivation of this tradition within field artillery was only a minor activity, it had some significance. Mildly encouraged by branch leadership, it was, like the field-artillery songs, an activity that developed and spread at the grassroots level and served as a source of bonding and common professional identification.

But the basic and central element of field-artillery branch culture as it emerged in the 1920s and 1930s was the horse. The horse was at least as central to the culture and social life of the field artillery as it was to that of any other combat branch, including the cavalry. Even though horseback riding had only a small and diminishing role in anticipated combat activities, horsemanship was always clearly seen as one of the critical benchmarks of an officer's military professionalism. Horse-related activities dominated field-artillery social life. While horse shows were an important activity in the branch, the most important horse-related activity was polo. This game was highly popular among the officers and strongly encouraged by both army and branch leadership.[68] As hard pressed as it was for funds, the field artillery still poured resources into polo in order to upgrade its string of ponies and to free up its officers to practice and play polo on a semiprofessional basis.[69] There were several reasons for the sport's popularity. First, as was the case with the horse shows, polo was an upper-class activity in the United States, and participation allowed officers a chance for access to and social interaction with elements of society from which they would otherwise be closed off.[70] More important, polo was popular because of its opportunities for competition. As was the case with the cavalry, the field artillery was deeply involved in competitive polo in tournaments at the regional, national, and even international level. The results of these tournaments were reported at length in a special section in every issue of the *Field Artillery Journal*. Field-artillery teams were increasingly successful, allowing officers to take pride in their branch and in the masculine attributes of professionalism celebrated in the game.[71]

Overall, the field artillery began the interwar period amid two revolutions, one in material and tactics and the other in the professionalization of officers and its restructuring into a combat branch. Of the two revolutions, by 1919, that in material and tactics was seemingly near the end of its twenty-year trajectory, leaving field artillery around the world in an apparently stabilized situation. Much change was yet to come, especially in terms of motorization of units, yet it still seemed to amount to little more than tinkering, especially with budgetary constraints in the United States severely restricting widespread research or the procurement of more modern weapons. This tinkering created some interest in the branch, but it did not arouse such passions as created by, for example, mechanization in the cavalry and infantry or the introduction of antiaircraft artillery in the coast artillery.

On the other hand, the revolutionary professionalization of officers and the development of a branch structure and culture for field artillery was still in the middle of its trajectory at the end of the world war. By 1919, the branch was still only a dozen years removed from its separation from the coast artillery, and its institutions and means of socialization were less than ten years old. The branch lacked traditions and a cadre of officers with long experience and authority to give it identity and guide its development. Hence, many officers, both in leadership positions and in the rank and file, may have tended to see matters of branch formation as more important than further refinements in matters of material and tactics.

Hence, while field artillery saw relatively little change in weapons design and usage, it underwent major changes in branch structure, with the foundation of a school system that quickly unified the branch behind a common tactical doctrine; the rise of institutions such as the Field Artillery Association and the *Field Artillery Journal*, which gave tangibility to the existence of the branch and to the professionalism of its officers; and finally, the rise of a set of common traditions and activities that helped define the professional character of its officers. As a result, regardless of the quality of the weapons with which it entered the World War II, the field artillery entered that struggle with a solid organization made up of officers with common outlooks and the capacity to think and work together.

CHAPTER 8

End of the Big Guns

Mission and Branch Identity Crisis in the Coast Artillery, 1919–1939

O F THE FOUR MAJOR combat branches in the interwar army, the coast
artillery proved to be, by far, the best able to respond to the challenges
created by the enormous changes in warfare. It did so chiefly by all
but reinventing itself from a service devoted to the defense of harbor cities to
one devoted to antiaircraft defense. In doing so it demonstrated both the surprising degree of elasticity in the interwar army as well as the final limitations
on that elasticity.

As the United States entered the world war, the coast artillery was still the
preeminent branch in the Regular Army. Throughout the nineteenth century, its
fortifications defending major seaports were the backbone of America's defense
strategy so that its mission was well regarded by the American public. While
field and coastal units were partners in a general artillery branch during the
1800s, coastal units began to develop a sense of separate identity early in the century. This development began with the founding of a special school for coastal
artillery at Fort Monroe, Virginia, in 1824. In the post–Civil War era, in which
an interest in a new professionalism based on education was rapidly developing,
the school at Fort Monroe flourished. Under the leadership of Emory Upton, it
developed a more educationally respectable curriculum by replacing some highly
technical courses with courses on military law, history, and strategy. But it remained focused particularly on mathematics and engineering.[1]

The fact that American military policy in the nineteenth century rested on
the defense of harbors by large, rifled artillery located in major forts made service
at these posts preeminent in the army. Although those who served the big guns
did not see themselves as a special branch originally, the nature of the guns and
the forts began shaping the character of the military units that served them.
The major problem with the big guns was fire control, so those who served them

and the school that taught them soon became preoccupied with this issue. This preoccupation created the perception that serving the big guns was essentially a scientific endeavor. The soldiers who served the guns thus began to fashion the character of their growing branch identity and their professional self-image along scientific and engineering lines. This developing mentality was reflected in the *Journal of the United States Artillery*, which students at the Artillery School at Fort Monroe began to publish in 1892.

The preeminence given to harbor defense in national policy and the distinction gained by the Artillery School and by the *Journal* led those who served the big guns to develop a professional identification tied to this specialization. This, in turn, led these units to gain recognition as a separate branch, a move that was partially achieved in the Army Reorganization Act of 1901, which recognized the coast artillery as a distinct entity while creating a new office headed by a chief of artillery that was responsible for the further development of the big guns.[2] The movement toward creating the coast artillery as a distinct branch culminated in the Artillery Act of 1907.[3] The act split artillery into two branches, field artillery and coast artillery, and made the coast artillery the only branch in the army with its own chief.[4] By 1911, that chief was a member of the General Staff, giving the coast artillery a decided political advantage over the other combat arms.[5] At the same time, its preeminence was indicated by the fact that 19,321 of the 69,525 officers and men allocated to the army were assigned to coast artillery.[6]

Hence, in the years immediately prior to World War I the coast artillery had emerged as a distinct branch in the army, albeit an unusual one. It had little of a distinctly military tradition upon which it could draw to develop an identity. While technically a combat arm, it identified far more with the civilian world of the scientist and engineer than with the bloody world of battlefield combat. Finally, preeminence, and the isolated nature in the service of the guns, gave the new branch an elitist sense of aloofness from the rest of the army.

The world war, however, was a disaster for the branch. With its mission based almost solely on the defense of major U.S. harbors, the coast artillery was ill prepared to play any sort of significant role in a European land war. Instead, it participated in the conflict chiefly by taking responsibility for developing railroad-and tractor-drawn heavy artillery and antiaircraft artillery.[7] At the same time, there was a widespread feeling in both the army and the public that the war had demonstrated that the days of the fort had passed. In short, the coast artillery now faced a "mission crisis," as its very reason for existence was seriously called into question.

After the war, a widespread feeling developed in U.S. public opinion, in the army, and even in the coast artillery itself that the days of heavy artillery permanently placed within fixed fortifications had passed.[8] Coast-artillery observers were impressed with the power of the new 16-inch naval gun. The power and weight of its projectile and the nearly vertical trajectory of its fall on any target meant that all current coastal fortifications in the United States were obsolete.[9] Moreover, the fact that it could be fired by a ship from over the horizon seemed to present shore gunners with a nearly impossible fire-control problem, indicating to many that the new gun had given ships a permanent advantage over fortifications.[10] Finally, some noted that an attack on the United States could be made on almost any beach and a major port taken by the flank with just such an invasion.[11]

Moreover, as confidence in the forts and big guns was disappearing, both the navy and the new air service began to claim that they were better able to carry out the mission of coastal and harbor defense than was the coast artillery. Indeed, Brigadier General William Mitchell used the spectacular bombing of the *Ostfriesland* in 1921 to demonstrate the ability of the nascent air service to defend the nation from both seaborne and airborne threats. If accepted, this doctrine would give the air service a mission that could justify its elevation to an independent force alongside the army and navy.[12] The navy repeatedly urged its claim to sole responsibility for coastal defense all during the interwar period.[13]

The seriousness of this mission crisis was further demonstrated by the fate of the coast artillery after the war. The National Defense Act of 1920 shifted the focus of defense policy from the coastal forts to the mobile army. As a result, the size of the branch was reduced dramatically. While two of every seven soldiers in 1907 were in the coast artillery, fewer than one in ten was so assigned by the mid-1920s. Moreover, as Brian Linn notes, as a final manifestation of the of the coast artillery's mission crisis, the topic of harbor defense was not even mentioned in the army's service regulations for 1923.[14]

Finally, coast artillerymen sensed that the neglect of the branch and its mission as stated in the National Defense Act of 1920 was also reflected in public opinion and even in the army.[15] As one officer complained in 1923, "our service schools fail to emphasize the importance of Coast Artillery personnel and armament in coast defense problems."[16] As a result, there was a sense of discouragement within the ranks related to the diminished position of the branch that stood out even within the general discouragement prevailing in the army in the early 1920s. As the editor of the *Journal of the United States Artillery* claimed in 1921, "No one can deny that there is some justification for a feeling of discouragement among Coast Artillery officers."[17]

The coast artillery, however, began responding to this mission crisis immediately and continued to do so during the twenty years of the interwar period.

Its approaches were varied. First, as with the other branches, there was some degree of turning inward and building a cohesive sense of branch identity among its members. More important, however, the branch attempted to redefine its mission in ways that took advantage of its "big gun" heritage and scientific expertise. Moreover, the coast artillery also forsook completely its earlier elitist sense of aloofness from other branches of the army. Instead, it sought to define its mission in ways that stressed its integration and its cooperative relationship with other branches. Apparently feeling that its seriously exposed position made cooperation with other branches a better strategy than competing with them, officers sometimes went to great lengths to emphasize the degree to which its role lay in supporting other branches and arms.

As did most of the other major branches in the army, the coast artillery made major efforts to develop a sense of professional identity and solidarity that would lead to the creation of a cohesive branch identity. In doing so, it largely followed the approaches taken by the others. At the beginning of 1923, the name of the venerable *Journal of the United States Artillery*, a holdover from the time when both field-and coast-artillery units were part of the same branch, was changed to the more branch-specific *Coast Artillery Journal*. In addition, its officers followed the lead of those in other branches by forming their own separate professional association, the United States Coast Artillery Association, in 1930. The association, however, did very little outside of holding an annual convention; giving awards to outstanding Regular Army, National Guard, and Organized Reserve units; and promoting subscriptions to the *Journal*. Even so, the association and its local branches remained popular, possibly due to the opportunities it gave to coast artillerymen to get together.[18]

The truly important forces in developing a sense of professional branch identity in the coast artillery were the special services school at Fort Monroe and the *Coast Artillery Journal*. The *Journal* not only changed its name it also broadened its editorial policy so that while it continued to publish the highly technical articles that had characterized the older journal, it also published articles on history and issues regarding the branch itself. At the same time, it was careful to maintain its traditional policy of remaining open to all opinions so that it could be considered as the voice of the officers of the coast artillery. In the early 1930s, the chief of the coast artillery, Major General John W. Gulick, had an open letter published in the *Journal* reaffirming that it was not the official organ of the office of Chief of Coast Artillery but "the organ of the entire Coast Artillery personnel—Regular Army, National Guard, and Organized Reserve."[19]

Still, the major socialization force in the coast artillery, as in other branches, was the special service school at Fort Monroe. Although not every coast-artillery officer attended, enough did so that the school was able to provide the model of professional identity in the branch. Most graduating officers left convinced that coast-artillery activities were based on the principles of a professionally respectable science that they had successfully mastered. They also took with them a set of bonding experiences shared with colleagues from other year groups. Finally, they emerged accepting, by and large, the professional identity and self-image of the engineer-soldier amalgam that had been traditional within the coast artillery since the late nineteenth century. The school was successful in this regard for largely the same reasons that the army's other special service schools were successful: it offered what seemed to be a rigorous but still accessible educational program, an attractive lifestyle, and a sense of community that led graduates to accept the values and outlooks of the branch. Like the others, the Artillery School's main offerings were a battery officers' course for junior officers and an advanced course for more senior officers. Both were small, with forty to fifty students in the battery officers' course and twenty-five to thirty in the advanced course. With a faculty of around twenty, the school enjoyed a rich student–teacher ratio and allowed the students a chance to bond in a small community.[20]

The curriculum, with a heavy dose of mathematics and science and an unabashedly competitive grading system, gave the school the appearance of intellectual rigor. This was reinforced by an associated school for advanced engineering and the research-oriented Coast Artillery Board as adjuncts to the Artillery School. But, as with the case of other special service schools, instruction aimed at student success, with courses presupposing no advanced knowledge. And while classes moved along rapidly; most were centered on acquiring technical knowledge rather than dealing with theoretical issues. Moreover, the map problems that so bedeviled students at the Fort Leavenworth schools were not a problem at Fort Monroe.[21] Finally, as was the case in the other service schools, students were encouraged to accept the school solutions to problems rather than think for themselves.[22]

At the same time, the Artillery School offered several bonding and life experiences in a community characterized by a common set of values and outlooks. In early years, housing was inadequate and old. The most notorious was the bachelor officers' quarters, referred to with humor as Old Sherwood, which was in an old frame nineteenth-century hotel.[23] In the early 1930s, most of the older housing, including Old Sherwood, was replaced by rather spacious brick apartments with modern amenities.[24]

In addition, ample provision was made for an active social and recreational life. The curriculum did not require work on the weekends, and efforts were made to give Fort Monroe an attractive set of recreational facilities.[25] While athletics were encouraged, there was nowhere near the emphasis placed on them as was found at the Infantry School. In line with the more sedate image of the engineer-soldier, athletics at Fort Monroe were purely recreational and not part of the more macho image initially being sought at Fort Benning. Hence, while the focus of athletic interest at Benning was Doughboy Stadium, at Monroe it was the beach house, with its modern dance floor, that was most popular with officers.[26]

While the coast artillery was successful in building a branch structure, its chief concern by far was to resolve its mission crisis in a way that would ensure its continued existence. This was a difficult challenge since any redesigned mission would have to be seen as clearly relevant to the nation's defense needs in a drastically new environment while still one that depended on utilization of the traditional expertise of the coast artillery. Given these objectives, the branch's initial responses tended to be evolutionary rather than revolutionary.

The most immediate response was to propose a new tactical approach to the old problem of harbor defense. Given the fact that most coast artillerymen who had seen active service in the world war were connected with heavy artillery outside of fixed emplacements, the idea that permanent fortifications had become obsolete was already widely accepted in the branch.[27] Even Major General Frank W. Coe, the chief of coast artillery at the time, noted in 1920, "The tactical undesirability of the fixed mount has always been recognized."[28] The assumed obsolescence of masonry forts, however, did not mean that coast-artillery officers abandoned the mission of harbor defense. For a few years, the branch sought to form a collaborative relationship with the air service to develop a joint defense strategy in which aircraft would join a coastal-defense effort by both attacking incoming fleets and providing radio spotting for gunfire from shore batteries manned by the coast artillery. But this approach died out after a few years.[29]

At the same time, many officers were also captivated by the idea of the mobile defense of ports using the railway-and tractor-drawn guns with which they had become familiar in the world war. Port fortification was now to be modeled on the dispersed field fortifications seen in Europe, with the heavy artillery now being mobile rather than fixed. This mobility would be both tactical, with guns able to move from place to place as needed, and strategic, with guns from a wide area of the country able to use railroad transport to concentrate quickly at a threatened point.[30]

This idea appealed to many in the coast artillery during the first years of the 1920s but then began to fade in the face of realities. The U.S. rail system was not conducive to the strategic concepts involved. Railroad guns also had to be offloaded and mounted before they could be used, significantly limiting their mobility. Nor could one guarantee the accuracy of guns placed on hastily built platforms. More important, efforts to place a 16-inch gun on a railway mount proved unsuccessful, even though most coast artillerymen agreed that only that weapon would provide successful defense against a naval invasion force headed by battleships armed with such guns.[31]

Other officers in the branch, sensing that the future of the army lay with the mobile forces, argued that the coast artillery should abandon the forts and harbors altogether and find a place within the mobile army. Based on the experience of the world war, many coast artillerymen felt that this role lay with mobile heavy artillery. Advocates of this idea, which included General Coe, saw such a concept as the natural extension of the branch's wartime service. The basic idea was to amalgamate the coast artillery with the field artillery into a single artillery branch, with coast artillery being responsible for heavy artillery, while the field artillery retained responsibility for light divisional artillery.[32] As Coe argued, during the war "the Coast Artillery was expanded to meet the artillery needs of the army, while the Field Artillery was expanded to meet the needs of the division; both branches contributed to the artillery requirement of the corps."[33] The *Coast Artillery Journal* also expressed this idea, stating, "The Coast Artillery has become in reality the Heavy Artillery of our military establishment and coast defense, . . . is only part of its mission."[34]

After the war, General Coe took a vigorous lead in the effort to amalgamate the two artillery branches, proposing the creation of a single branch headed by a chief of artillery assisted by two deputies to head sub-branches for divisional artillery and heavy artillery. And, if amalgamation failed, Coe favored renaming and reorganizing the coast artillery as "heavy artillery."[35] He continued to pursue this idea vigorously in the early 1920s.[36] In 1921 the Coast Artillery Board published a pamphlet titled *Tactical Employment of Heavy Artillery*, which was hailed by the *Journal of the United States Artillery* as likely to become the coast artilleryman's "Bible."[37] Three years later the branch was reorganized along regimental lines since, as it was explained, in time of war it was likely that coast artillerymen would "serve with artillery that is operating in the field."[38]

While interest in this idea continued throughout the 1920s, it faded by the end of the decade. Field-artillery officers were opposed to a reunification or any reorganization of the army that left their branch with responsibility only for light artillery serving with the division. Finally, although it was never stated, officers in the coast artillery may have thought that abandoning the big coastal guns in favor of becoming the army's mobile heavy artillery would mean giving up a mission that was solidly part of their branch's tradition and for which its members had a clear expertise to adopt a role that was amorphous and for which it had no particularly legitimate claim. In any case, after 1925, the concept of mobile heavy artillery was discussed less often in the *Coast Artillery Journal*, and by the end of the decade, the chief of coast artillery assured his officers that he was "not at all convinced that seacoast artillery has passed out of the picture or even lost any of its importance."[39]

Instead, during the second half of the twenties, the coast artillery returned to the coast to redefine its mission in terms that were more traditional. A new definition of the mission, "seacoast defense," emerged, which encapsulated the branch's traditional mission into a larger strategic concept in partnership with both the navy and the mobile army. This idea had its origins in a pamphlet published in 1920, *Joint Army and Navy Action in Coast Defense*.[40] The pamphlet had been brought to the attention of members of the branch in 1923 in Captain Thomas R. Phillips's prize-winning article in the *Coast Artillery Journal*. Phillips explained: "The strategy of Coast Defense consists of a series of strong points protecting our naval bases, essential war industries and essential harbors. The naval bases are protected to insure the navy freedom for offensive action. The unfortified coast is protected by the naval coast defense forces and the mobile forces of the army."[41]

Interest in the concept of seacoast defense spread quickly among those coast-artillery officers anxious to keep their branch mission focused on harbor defense. They found the cooperative nature of the strategy appealing as a means to overcome the supposed limitations of the big-gun defense of ports as well as the perceived isolation of the branch. It also legitimized harbor defense, the traditional mission of coast artillery, by putting it into the context of an overall national strategy.[42]

By 1924, the idea had made its way into Fort Monroe, reaching both the renamed Coast Artillery School and Coast Artillery Board, where it received a favorable reception.[43] At the same time, the chief of coast artillery announced that the term "coast defense," which had traditionally been used within the branch to designate a harbor command, would no longer be used in such a narrow context.[44] For the next several years, the board and the school examined closely that part of the 1920 pamphlet that dealt with the role of the army in coastal defense, an idea then called a "Positive System of Coast Defense." By 1927, a consensus had emerged on the tactical and strategic doctrine that would govern such a system. Although this doctrine was never published officially, its essence appeared in a series of articles by Major Rodney H. Smith published in the *Coast Artillery Journal*. The key idea in Smith's exposition was that coastal defense was to be a combined-arms operation involving several branches of the army, including the air service, as well as the navy. Within that combined operation, the coast artillery was to take responsibility for harbor defense, using both mobile and fixed heavy artillery.[45] By the end of the decade, coastal defense had been unofficially adopted by the coast artillery as a guiding concept, and the debate over mission largely died out. During the 1930s, it remained the core of coast-artillery seacoast doctrine.[46] But the concept generated little interest outside the branch, either in the rest of the army or in the public, and so provided no real answer for the coast artillery's mission crisis.

The only successful answer was the development of an almost totally new mission, antiaircraft defense. At the time of the world war, antiaircraft artillery represented a virtually new form of combat. There had been a few experiences before the war with efforts to bring down aerial balloons with ground fire, but the experience of firing on moving aircraft was new. The initial mission was entirely tactical. Antiaircraft artillery was to protect military forces from both attack and observation by hostile warplanes.[47] The coast artillery attacked the problem with the scientific and technological approach that was engrained in the mentality of the branch. Therefore, coast artillerymen assigned to antiaircraft artillery saw their problem largely in terms of developing a weapons technology and an approach to fire control appropriate to the task. Since most efforts during the war were in improvising a new form of artillery from existing weapons, the newly designated antiaircraft-artillery service within the branch emerged with an understanding of the kinds of weapons needed and how to approach the fire-control problem.[48]

While the postwar demobilization initially left the antiaircraft-artillery organization in disarray, coast-artillery leadership immediately undertook efforts to organize and control a postwar antiaircraft service.[49] Final approval for its creation was given to the branch in October 1919 by the secretary of war; the creation of small antiaircraft units to be assigned to harbor defense began immediately.[50] The organization of the new service then proceeded rapidly. By 1920, the commander of the Coast Artillery School at Fort Monroe created a special battalion to test new weapons and "to act as a nucleus which can be expanded and used in service with the mobile army when called upon."[51] At the same time, the branch began the publication of its mimeographed *Bulletin*, "devoted exclusively to antiaircraft subjects."[52]

The coast artillery continued developing antiaircraft artillery in the early 1920s. Surprisingly, even though the branch was so reduced in size that it felt it could not carry out its basic tasks, there was little opposition to continuing to invest personnel and resources in antiaircraft defense.[53] As a result, the service grew rapidly in size. In 1922 it had an allowance of just over 500 men. By 1923, it had 1,325 men, amounting to over 11 percent of the diminished allowance of the branch.[54] This development, nevertheless, was plagued by expressed skepticism for the project coming from all branches of the army, even from within the coast artillery itself.[55] It also had to overcome public apathy and congressional neglect.[56]

Yet two other factors played by far the dominant role in shaping antiaircraft-artillery development during the 1920s. The first was the public reaction in 1921 to the success of the air service bombing the *Ostfriesland* as well as a simulated air raid on Philadelphia.[57] After that, the focus of the unit shifted from defending military units in the field to defending cities from bombers. The second was the almost immediate and unchallenged assumption that the best way to defend nonmilitary targets from attack by bombers was to bring down the bombers. Early in the decade alternative methods of protecting military units and cities from aerial attack, such as hampering and discouraging such strikes, were considered within the branch, especially since bringing down planes seemed to be so difficult that many were dubious of success.[58] But these alternatives were summarily rejected by the coast-artillery leadership. Why they were rejected is unclear, but it seems likely that two factors were important. First, the only way to sell the idea of antiaircraft artillery to the army and the public was by proving its effectiveness in hitting targets. Arguments in defense of antiaircraft artillery were almost invariably based on demonstrations of the ability of guns to make hits; the effectiveness of alternative strategies was hard to demonstrate in peacetime.[59] In addition, although this idea was never stated explicitly, coast artillerymen had traditionally approached their mission of protecting harbors by designing guns, fire-control systems, and training methods that would result in ships being hit and sunk, which they now sought to adapt to hitting and downing warplanes. Any other approach to dealing with aircraft would likely have been difficult to imagine and accept.[60] In any case, as a result of the acceptance of this approach, the central focus of coast-artillery activities regarding antiaircraft artillery was developing guns and fire-control mechanisms that could allow some success in bringing down hostile aircraft.

The problems facing the branch in this regard were numerous and formidable. Much progress had been made during the world war in terms of providing the basic approaches and weapons, but the equipment that emerged was still largely unsatisfactory. Guns mounted on mobile platforms tended to vibrate so much when fired that crews were shaken off, while the guns had to be continually releveled for fire-control purposes.[61] Shrapnel ammunition proved unsuitable since burst fragments were irregular in size, so new ammunition that provided a more uniform set of fragments had to be developed.[62] Finally, traditional powder fuses were found to burn unevenly at higher altitudes and had to be replaced with new mechanical fuses.[63]

But by far the most difficult problem was fire control. Antiaircraft artillery sought to bring down planes by shooting fused high-explosive ammunition that would explode close enough to the aircraft to do lethal damage to the plane. The difficulty in this was in calculating not only the range to set the fuse correctly but also, and far more important, how far the gun should lead the target. By 1926, a redesigned 3-inch antiaircraft gun was developed bearing a set of instruments that calculated range and necessary lead angles and then sent this data electronically, together with fuse settings, to the guns. Personnel then had only to aim their weapons by matching pointers with the directors and load the guns with shells containing preset fuses.[64] After that, the focus of the branch was on training to eliminate, as far as possible, human error.[65]

The focus on protecting cities from aerial attack led to another set of problems. The experience of the world war had shown that cities would most likely be attacked by air at night. Again, the coast artillery emerged from the war with the basic technology and tactics for bringing down aircraft at night already set. Targets were to be illuminated by powerful searchlights, then attacked and brought down by guns. The difficult part was getting light on the target. Searchlight crews could not find targets merely by sweeping the sky, which produced only momentary glimpses of an aircraft as the lights swept by. Instead, crews had to be directed where to look. During the war, to find incoming planes, the Allies had developed instruments called sound locators. Manned by personnel with natural acute sensitivity to sound, the locators were designed to pinpoint the sound of aircraft engines within three degrees. These would then give the probable position of aircraft to the searchlight operators.[66] By 1926, branch officers felt that they had this problem under control as well, with some claiming that the antiaircraft-artillery service was now almost more accurate at night than it was during the day.[67]

The attention given by the coast artillery to antiaircraft defense changed dramatically at the beginning of 1930, when it received a new directive from the secretary of war.

It must be the normal mission of *all* Coast Artillery to serve antiaircraft guns. While the fixed defenses constitute the first line of defenses for the harbors on the coast against naval guns, the antiaircraft armament must constitute the first line of ground defense against enemy aircraft at sensitive points and vital areas. This principle will be recognized and taught. In accordance therewith all Coast Artillery will be trained to serve, skillfully and effectively, antiaircraft armament, instruments, equipment, listening devices, searchlights, fire-control, etc., in addition to the permanent assignments that units may have to fixed defenses, railway, or tractor drawn artillery.[68]

This order came out of a growing awareness on the part of the General Staff of the rapidly increasing significance of air warfare and the vulnerability of the United States to air attack. It was carefully articulated in a secret memorandum by Assistant Chief of Staff for Operations and Training, Major General Frank Parker, in which he argued that the security of the United States from such attack required a coordinated air-corps and antiaircraft-artillery defense. But such a defense, would require a great reinforcement of the antiaircraft-artillery service, so Parker proposed an expansion of the army to provide that reinforcement.[69] That increase did not happen. Instead, the antiaircraft-artillery capability of the army was augmented by making every coast artilleryman available for such defensive service.

But even though the coast artillery had already made major strides in developing its abilities and investment in antiaircraft defense, the new order still had wide ramifications. It caused major changes in the curriculum at the school at Fort Monroe, even including dropping the venerable courses in horsemanship to make room for more instruction in antiaircraft artillery.[70] Significant reorganization occurred, as all personnel assigned to seacoast artillery had to be given wartime antiaircraft-artillery-unit assignments.[71] The order also caused morale problems that widened an already significant schism between seacoast-artillery officers and antiaircraft officers, since many of the former felt threatened by the mysterious new equipment used by the latter.[72] But the most significant consequence was that the antiaircraft-artillery service rapidly became the primary mission of the coast artillery.

The War Department order also reinforced a shift in attention from weapons and techniques to tactics.[73] Discussions of tactics had occurred during the 1920s, but the topic was rarely given focused attention, and discussions rarely achieved any degree of doctrinal sophistication.[74] This, however, was already changing in the late 1920s, as issues related to weapons and techniques began fading from sight, and tactics became the focus of attention. The Office of Chief of Coast Artillery initiated some studies of tactics regarding the defense of cities in 1928.[75] Within a few years, the issue of tactics dominated antiaircraft artillery discussion.

For much of the 1930s, on a theoretical level, the antiaircraft-artillery service tended to look to Europe, specifically to Great Britain, for its guidance in the area of tactics.[76] Although officers paid attention to all British developments, their chief source of inspiration was a book entitled *Air Defense* by E. B. Ashmore, who had played a major role in designing the air defense of London during the world war. Ashmore's book dealt with experiences not only from the war but also from the redevelopment of London's air defenses up to 1928. It came to the attention of American officers in 1930 and was cited frequently in writings throughout the decade to follow. Tactics for the air defense of cities were modeled after those described by Ashmore.[77]

Efforts to develop a specifically American tactical doctrine were based on joint tactical exercises with the air service, which began in 1925 at Fort Tilden, New Jersey. At that time, however, these and several subsequent joint exercises were directed more at testing equipment than in developing tactics.[78] The first set of exercises focused on tactics was held at Aberdeen, Maryland, in 1930, at which time fundamental ideas were tested for the first time.[79] A far more sophisticated maneuver was held at Fort Knox in 1933, in which an actual defense of the base was attempted against an attack from Dayton.[80] A final exercise was held at Fort Bragg in October 1938, during which civilian cooperation and a blackout of cities was attempted.[81]

Actual tactical developments largely centered on two major sets of problems. The first was how to get sufficient warning of an approaching air strike so that guns could be manned and defending planes sent aloft. The service resolved this by borrowing the British idea of creating an intelligence network around a city, made up of civilian volunteers. The city was to be defended by two or three concentric circles of such volunteers, with the outer circle between 100 and 150 miles from the center. The most important phases of these exercises focused on testing this intelligence network, since its development was considered one of the most important tactical issues related to city defense. Several years were spent working out the appropriate communications linkages and procedures.[82]

The less technical and more difficult tactical problem was how to coordinate the defense efforts carried out by the antiaircraft artillery and air service/corps. In the early 1920s, while antiaircraft weapons and techniques were still in their infancy, there was a consensus in the branch that a successful defense of cities from hostile aerial bombardment would require the cooperative efforts of the antiaircraft-artillery service and the air service, with the former clearly subordinate to the latter.[83] As an editor of the *Journal of the United States Artillery* wrote in 1922, "The anti-aircraft gunner will be the first to admit that the most effective

weapon of air defense is the aeroplane."[84] But by the middle of the decade, and especially by the 1930s, as confidence in the effectiveness of weapons and techniques
grew, the branch sought tactical approaches to city defense that gave antiaircraft
artillery a more dominant if not the sole role in that mission. Since it was difficult
for planes and antiaircraft artillery to work together simultaneously, officers tried
to solve the problem by setting out spheres for each arm. Early in the 1920s, it was
suggested that aircraft be responsible for defense during the day and antiaircraft
artillery take responsibility at night.[85] In the mid-thirties, air-corps supporters
began to claim that defense aircraft could fight at night. This led to the idea that
aircraft would defend zones ranging 100–150 miles outside the city while antiaircraft artillery would be responsible for dealing with aircraft close in and over the
target.[86] Finally, it was suggested repeatedly that the successful defense of a city
required subordination of all forces to a single unified command. Since the antiaircraft service controlled the intelligence network that could direct defending
aircraft to an incoming enemy raid, supporters of the branch argued that it would
make sense that antiaircraft service should provide that command.[87]

By the end of the 1930s, however, some of the confidence in the effectiveness
of antiaircraft artillery began to fade, leading to concerns and challenges to some
of the basic premises upon which the tactical structure created in the 1930s were
built. For one thing, air forces were learning how to muffle the sounds of their
warplanes, seriously eroding the effectiveness of sound detectors.[88] Pilots were
also learning more about antiaircraft artillery, its tactics, and how to maneuver
when under fire. One air-corps officer bragged that if a plane was not hit with the
first burst, the pilot would be successful in avoiding the remainder.[89] Pilots also
learned that flying during periods of moonlight or haze severely reduced the effectiveness of searchlights.[90] Finally, officers claimed that bomber tactics, including mass attacks on a single sector, would overpower any antiaircraft defense.[91]

All of this led to a degree of unraveling of confidence in the antiaircraft-artillery service, as seen by the emergence of challenges to some of the basic principles
upon which it was founded. By 1939, a few officers within the coast artillery were
challenging some of the basic elements of the service. In one article, an officer
condemned the existing fire-control system as too bulky and too fragile to stand
up to the rigors of combat, the existing regimental structure as being irrelevant
to the new forms of air attack, and the lack of an overall air-defense program
that included a civil-defense aspect.[92] Another challenged the idea of protecting
cities by shooting down or turning back all attacking planes before they reached
their target, an objective he saw as impossible. He instead suggested tactics based
on hampering attacking aircraft. The officer also condemned the branch for its

tendency to seek to solve problems by inventing new weapons or techniques and approaching tactical challenges "from a too narrow mathematical and mechanical viewpoint."[93]

With America's entrance into World War II, the transformation of the coast artillery into the antiaircraft artillery was complete. Coast artillery was dissolved as a branch, its officers placed into antiaircraft-artillery units.

During the period from 1919 to 1939, the coast artillery as a branch had transformed itself more than any other combat organization in the army. It managed to do so despite operating in an atmosphere of public apathy, congressional neglect, and professional skepticism from colleagues. It also did so without indulging in the self-pity and hysterical fascination on subversion and conspiracies that was seen in other branches. Finally, it did so on the most meager of resources. Its success in this transformation was largely due to the specific character of the professional self-image and outlook of coast-artillery officers. Their engineering background and training left them open to the introduction of new technologies and at peace with the mechanization of the society around them. The tradition of open mindedness that had been central to the coast artillery since the late nineteenth century also allowed a relatively easy acceptance of change. The branch was also fortunate that it had no object such as the horse to which it had developed an emotional attachment or played a role in its identity. Nor was it burdened with undue pride, so that all during the interwar period, it took the initiative in working with other branches. In these relationships, the coast artillery also had no problem accepting a secondary and subordinate role.

At the same time, if the coast artillery demonstrated the degree to which branches of the army could change in the interwar period, it also demonstrated the limitations of change. First, it did not so much transform itself from the big-gun defense of harbors into antiaircraft artillery as it merely lost all its other missions. Second, while coast-artillery leadership was open minded, it was not imaginative. Officers tended to work with borrowed ideas rather than develop their own innovations. They spent the interwar period tinkering with the weapons, techniques, and tactics developed in the world war, even though some of them, such as the sound locators or the huge intelligence networks with their ponderous communications systems, were clearly limited. The branch took little initiative in coming up with new ideas—including radar. In short, even amid a mission crisis, the coast artillery shared many of the conservative characteristics of other branches of the army.

In part, the coast artillery's conservatism was the product of scarce resources. It was also engaged in the most conservative of objectives—self-preservation.

And, like other branches, it lacked institutional support for innovation. The Coast Artillery Board, like the boards of the other branches, was largely a reactive body, solving relatively minor problems submitted to it rather than reflecting on larger issues.[94] In addition, despite its engineering tradition, the branch was less connected with the civilian scientific and engineering community than it had been before the world war. Finally, the coast artillery's self-image as military professionals demanded that its members' existing expertise be valued by themselves and by the public. As a result, change was difficult. This was particularly evident in the case of seacoast artillery, where the radical idea of transformation into mobile heavy artillery was finally rejected in favor of the doctrine of coastal defense—a return to the "normal mission" of the coast artillery.

III

Mechanizing the Army, 1930–1939

CHAPTER 9

The Army Besieged

The Army and the Nation in the Decade of the Depression, 1930–1939

D URING THE 1930S, THE U.S. Army slowly undertook several major
shifts in direction. Its chief focus in the 1920s had been on creating
the means to mobilize as efficiently and as rapidly as possible a massive
citizen army that could fight another world war. In the 1930s, however, army
leadership began to focus attention more on creating a smaller but more usable
mobile force as well as following the trends elsewhere in the world regarding
the mechanization of the combat arms. Both developments accelerated as the
decade wore on, and by 1939, the vision of the army as to both its purpose and
means had changed significantly from what it was when the National Defense
Act was adopted in 1920. But the actual development of a military structure
that could fulfill that original vision was severely slowed by the lack of support from both the U.S. government and the American public, both of whom
focused their attention on the crippling Depression, which they thought could
be cured only by means of financial austerity. The result for the army was a
decade of anxiety, anger, and frustration in its relationship with Congress and,
especially, the president.

The first years of the Depression were among the most difficult for the army
during the entire interwar period. Its pressures led to an immediate deterioration in the relations between the military, the president, and Congress.
Moreover, the army felt increasingly besieged not only by restrictions created
by the Depression but by other forces as well. The most significant of these was
the financial crisis created by the worsening economy. In the early 1930s, both
political parties responded to the Depression by major efforts to cut the budget
to avoid a deficit. The army suffered greatly from these cuts. Later, however, as
international crises multiplied and as the administration of President Franklin
Roosevelt moved in the direction of spending its way out of the Depression,

the perceived siege began to lift. Only after 1935 could the army begin a significant exploration of modernization.

But the initially recurring budget reductions were not the only problems facing the army in the 1930s. The convening of the Disarmament Conference in 1932 created an international atmosphere reflected in a rejuvenated wave of pacifism and antimilitarism in the United States. Antiwar books, such as the widely read sensationalist expose *Merchants of Death,* published in 1934, and the efforts of the Nye Committee in Congress between 1934 and 1936 to investigate possible connections between banks, the munitions industry, and the decision to go to war in 1917 were indicative of the prevailing sense of disillusionment and cynicism in the American public and of the strength of the antiwar sentiment in the country. David Johnson notes the claim that the American peace movement in the mid-thirties had "twelve million adherents and an audience of between forty-five and sixty million people."[1] Henry Gole observes that student officers engaged in war-planning exercises at the Army War College always paid considerable attention to the antiwar sentiments in U.S. public opinion in working out solutions to the problems posed.[2] This movement became stronger as the likelihood of war in Europe increased in the second half of the 1930s. Congress passed three consecutive Neutrality Acts in 1935, 1936, and 1937 to ensure that the United States would not be drawn into another war in Europe, while a Gallup poll taken in 1938 showed that 70 percent of American voters thought that U.S. involvement in the Great War had been a mistake.[3]

The army began to feel pressures to reduce expenditures in response to the Depression early in 1930. To combat the economic downturn, President Hoover vowed to take $175 million from the budget for the following fiscal year. Accordingly, the secretary of war called on the General Staff to draw up plans for budget reductions of between $10 million and $60 million.[4] By the fall of 1931, however, the situation began to turn from discouraging to alarming. The key development was Democratic victories in a series of congressional midterm elections that gave the party control of the House. The Democrats, in general, were in favor of a far more aggressive approach to government cost cutting, with the army as one of their primary targets. This situation was aggravated by the fact that the Democratic victory made Congressman Ross A. Collins of Mississippi chairman of the Military Appropriations Sub-Committee of the House Appropriations Committee. Even before Democrats took control of the House, Collins had announced that he favored reducing the army's officer corps by a third to eight thousand, making ROTC elective at colleges, and introducing a mechanization program that would eliminate all horses from the branches.[5]

The initial influence of the Democratic victory was an effort by Hoover and the Republicans to maintain control of the economy issue by developing their own program of spending cuts. In early December the administration unveiled a budget that included a 10.3-percent reduction in War Department appropriations. Deep slashes were made everywhere. Even the air corps, long favored by Washington and the public, was hit with a 20-percent reduction. The only bright spot was an increase in funds for housing, which was justified as a means of boosting employment.[6]

By the beginning of 1932, however, this effort by Hoover and the Republicans had failed, as Democrats in the House launched an offensive to reduce government expenditures by an additional $300 million. To achieve this, they proposed a number of drastic measures, many of which were aimed at the army, which now saw itself besieged, with attacks coming from every side. Aggravating this was the approach of the forthcoming international Disarmament Conference. Its imminent convening not only suggested that armaments and large war budgets were no longer needed but also energized pacifists in all countries, including the United States. While it is unclear whether the increased level of pacifist agitation in America had any effect on army legislation in Congress, it struck a raw nerve in the army itself, as seen by a dramatic reappearance of antipacifism in the service publications.[7]

By the spring of 1932, the army seemed to be under attack from all sides. In January, Collins introduced a bill in the House calling for a strength reduction of two thousand officers, temporary suspension of the CMTC program and ROTC summer training for a year, and the virtual elimination of the cavalry.[8] The proposal precipitated a maelstrom of protests but was reported out of committee in May.[9] The War Department responded that the cuts would virtually end its ability to support the civilian components and would all but nullify the National Defense Act of 1920.[10] Democrats also attacked the structure of the military. Congressman Joseph W. Byrns of Tennessee, who was chairman of the House Appropriations Committee, proposed combining the army and navy into a single department, a move he claimed would eliminate vast amounts of bureaucratic duplication and would save $100 million a year.[11] This idea was initially popular in Congress, gaining support even from some Republicans.[12] But the enthusiasm for the bill declined as the actual savings were investigated, and the bill failed to get out of committee.[13] Finally, Democrats also sought ways to cut army pay. The House Appropriations Committee proposed a pay freeze that would end raises based on longevity.[14] By March, it was considering an actual 11-percent pay reduction for all federal services, which it claimed would save $67 million.[15] By

May, the committee was also considering ending retirement pay for any retired officer holding a job.[16] Finally, Hoover himself proposed a furlough plan that would amount to an 8.3-percent pay cut. While none of these proposals was ever considered seriously, they contributed to the siege atmosphere felt by the army.

Despite all the attacks, the army got through this financial siege without suffering any significant damage other than reduced appropriations for fiscal year 1933.[17] The army owed its success in all this to several factors. Chief of Staff Major General Douglas MacArthur was skillful and convincing in testimony before both houses of Congress. The opposition by labor unions to personnel or pay-reduction proposals was also important. Congress was also sobered by the news of Japanese military actions in Manchuria, which dampened the ardor of pacifist idealism. But the two most important factors in the army's success were the Senate, which was still dominated by Republicans, and the support of President Hoover. Although the army had originally had problems with Hoover and his earlier economizing measures, by 1932, he was seen as the military's best friend.

The army, therefore, looked at the elections coming up in the fall of 1932 with real apprehension. Democrats campaigned on the claim that cutting the budget was the only way to end the Depression and that they would be far more aggressive in making those cuts than Hoover and the Republicans. In this regard, everyone understood that the real threat came from the top of the Democratic ticket. The Democratic candidate for president, Franklin Roosevelt, repeatedly claimed in public that the army had a billion-dollar budget that he intended to slash. Since its actual budget was less than a third of what Roosevelt claimed, this apparent grandstanding was a source of considerable worry, as was his repeated pledge that he would reduce overall national expenditures by at least 25 percent.

The Democratic victory in November 1932 was, in fact, even worse than the army had feared. Not only was Roosevelt elected, but Democrats also gained control of the Senate, with several key senators who had been strong friends of the army defeated in their bids for reelection. Moreover, once Roosevelt came into office, he intended to make his will felt and proceeded in earnest to carry out the 25-percent reduction in national expenditures pledged during his campaign. In April 1933 he told his secretary of war, George H. Dern, that he intended to cut the army's budget by 25 percent, or $90 million, which would call for dismissing 2,000–3,000 officers as well as a one-year suspension or even elimination of CMTC and ROTC programs.[18] Then, by executive order, the president reduced service pay by 15 percent.[19] After this, Roosevelt attempted to reduce the size of the army. In April he asked Congress for authority to furlough 3,000–4,000 army officers on half pay.[20] This plan, however, died in the Senate.[21]

The army, however, was less fortunate in terms of overall appropriations. Congress reduced funding for fiscal year 1934 by $33 million below the level for 1933[22]. Two weeks later Roosevelt announced that he was reducing that appropriation another $80 million by eliminating the funding for all the civilian components except ROTC. By vigorous efforts, MacArthur and Dern were able to reduce this executive cut to $52 million.[23] Still, this brought the total budget reduction for the army up to the 25 percent that the president had campaigned on and pledged since coming into office. While scrambling to see what could be saved of the seemingly besieged National Defense Act, army officers wondered what the next year of the Roosevelt administration would bring.

The army's situation continued to deteriorate in 1933. In December 1932, Congress approved appropriations of $280 million for the army for fiscal year 1934, a reduction of $65 million from the funding for 1933. Worse yet, the director of the budget proposed cutting that amount by another $80 million. With the greatest of efforts, Dern and MacArthur got this additional reduction down to only $50 million.[24] However, in September it was announced that, in response to a modernization program proposed by MacArthur and Dern, the Public Works Board was willing to allocate $25 million to the army for mechanization and development of the air arm.[25] Roosevelt, however, indicated that he would not approve the release of any of these funds until the future of the Disarmament Conference was clearer.[26] On the other hand, he did release $130 million to the army to be used chiefly for bases and housing, with only a fraction of that available for modernization.[27]

In addition, the army was asked by the president to take over the administration of the Civilian Conservation Corps (CCC) program. The CCC, which was authorized by Congress just three weeks after Roosevelt's inauguration, was a relief program designed to provide work for over 250,000 unemployed young men. After the agency formed to manage the program failed to meet its goals, the CCC was placed under War Department control. It proved to be a mixed blessing. As William Odom has pointed out, the commitment to the CCC, which during 1933 and 1934 involved nearly 25 percent of the entire officer corps, cut in half the already inadequate number of officers responsible for training the citizen components while bringing training within the Regular Army to a virtual standstill.[28] At the same time, however, the program also brought the army some significant benefits. MacArthur and other leaders felt that it made Roosevelt more generous toward the army and may have saved it from a significant cut in the strength of the officer corps.[29] Moreover, as Steven Barry points out, participation in the program provided valuable training for the officers involved.

Working with the CCC gave them leadership experience in dealing with the kind of personnel that they would later find in the conscripted ranks of the army during World War II as well as with organizing and managing projects with a diverse labor pool in difficult conditions.[30] It also provided the army with practical experience in mobilizing large bodies of men, with MacArthur reporting that the military had done a better job in 1933 than it had done in the early months of 1917.[31] Henry Gole also notes that many of the thousands of reserve officers who were brought in to administer the camps benefited from that experience and remained with the army after the outbreak of World War II.[32]

Moreover, during that year, there were also a few signs that the financial siege was beginning to lift, and the army began to fare better in Washington. Roosevelt and the Democrats were gradually being weaned from the illusion that budget cutting was the solution to the Depression and were turning instead to spending in areas that would promote employment. At the same time, the army continued to benefit from broad public support, especially from the unions, which were opposed to wage and salary reductions as means to fight the Depression. Finally, by the fall of 1933, it began to look as if the Disarmament Conference was headed toward failure, seriously dampening the enthusiasm and influence of pacifists and creating a growing sense of urgency around a rearmament program. As a result, while the White House continued to cut the army's budget, threats to reduce the size of the army or to restructure it in any major way began to dissipate.

By the spring of 1934, the situation had improved to the point that the army could begin moving away from a defensive posture and play an increasing role in setting the national-security agenda. And, as before, it was more successful in its relations with Congress than with the president. In January 1934 Roosevelt submitted his budget for fiscal year 1935 in which army appropriations were reduced slightly to $245 million, but that was more than Roosevelt had initially approved for 1934, and no further cuts were made.[33] In April, as the Disarmament Conference was entering its death throes, Democratic congressman Clark W. Thompson of Texas introduced a bill to expand the size of the army to 14,000 officers and 165,000 men. Although it was introduced as a measure to deal with unemployment, the bill was quickly and enthusiastically endorsed by MacArthur, and the War Department continued to press vigorously for its passage for the rest of the year.[34] But the central issues for the army in the spring of 1934 were restoration of the 15-percent pay reduction and promotion reform. Again, leadership in these areas was taken by Congress. When Roosevelt indicated in January that he intended to extend the pay cut another six months, he precipitated a revolt in the House, where a bill to overturn the decision was defeated by a narrow margin. The Senate, however, passed a bill ending 5 percent of the pay cut.[35] This then passed the House in March. Roosevelt vetoed it, but, in a surprising setback, his veto was overridden in both houses.[36]

By the end of 1934, the siege seemed all but over. The army was heartened in December by Roosevelt's decision to extend MacArthur's tour as chief of staff for an indefinite term, a move interpreted as meaning that even the president had become a bit more of a friend of the army.[37] This interpretation was validated by Roosevelt's proposed budget for fiscal year 1936, in which appropriations for the army were dramatically increased to $312 million, which was further increased by Congress to nearly $339 million, a figure, the *New York Times* noted with approval, that represented the largest appropriation for the army since 1921.[38] Meanwhile, a bill to increase the size of the army to 165,000 men moved easily through Congress and was signed by Roosevelt in April 1935.[39] In June the president signed into law a measure doubling the size of West Point and increasing the number of regular officers entering the army through ROTC. He also spoke and handed out diplomas at West Point's commencement that year.[40] Most important, MacArthur was able to craft a promotion plan that enjoyed widespread support within the army, sending it to Congress with Roosevelt's approval.[41] The resulting bill was finally passed in July 1935, with the president signing it the very next day.[42] This seemed to mark the end of the siege and the beginning of a new era of cooperation between Congress, the president, and the military in building a new program for national defense.

While the army was relieved in 1935 that the siege of the past five years seemed to be over, the service actually enjoyed surprisingly little improvement in its overall condition in the second half of the decade. Despite rapidly growing public concern over the possibility of war in the Pacific, Europe, or both and a growing sense of panic about the potential threat posed by air warfare, the army, and especially its ground forces, gained little in the way of additional resources or support. As before, it enjoyed far greater support in Congress, especially in the Senate, than it did from the president. All the way up to the outbreak of war in Europe in 1939, Roosevelt gave only grudging approval for increases for ground forces, while funds were lavished on the navy and the air service as well as, later, to harbor and antiaircraft defense. Elsewhere, Roosevelt still appeared to see the army as an area in which money could be saved, even in terms of niggling cuts. Congress was more generous. Although it was usually willing to follow the president's lead, it often initiated proposals for greater army spending, once threatening a rebellion over what it called the president's neglect of the military.

While Roosevelt may have had a special fondness for the navy, he was, by and large, following public opinion. Throughout this period, both the American public and its leadership were defensive in their outlooks and saw the prospect of war in terms of it being a threat to the country's security. In 1935 the principal focus of this threat was Japan, which seemed to call for a naval buildup. Later, as the threat posed by Germany gained greater attention, the concern was with the danger of an airstrike, leading to a call for an explosive expansion of the air service and antiaircraft capability along with greater attention to harbor defense. By the late 1930s, the fear centered on a possible airstrike launched from a Caribbean base seized by an enemy, with particular concern for the security of the Panama Canal. The president's shift late in the 1930s to a strategy of hemispheric defense reinforced the emphasis placed on a rapid buildup of the navy and air service, along with a major reinforcement of the Panama Canal and Hawaii. For the most part, none of these fears provided much justification for an increase in ground forces.

Nor had the army made much of a case for a more extensive expansion. Its preoccupation in the 1920s with the issue of mobilizing a massive army to fight another European-style war stirred little support from a nation unwilling to be dragged into such a conflict. In the 1930s, planning began to move slowly toward the more realizable goal of the mobilization of a far smaller striking force. MacArthur's concept of an "Immediate Response Force" that was imbedded in his Four-Army Plan was a step in this direction. His successor as chief of staff, Major General Malin Craig, carried the idea much further with the creation of the Protective Mobilization Plan in 1938, aimed at an almost immediate mobilization of a striking force of 400,000 men that could be used in the event of an enemy attempt to seize a threatening base in the Pacific or the Caribbean. The bedrock requirement for all these plans, however, was a Regular Army of 14,000 officers and 165,000 men along with a National Guard of 250,000 and an enlisted reserve of 75,000. Hence, the army's main political objectives in the late 1930s were the expansion of the Regular Army and National Guard, the creation of an Enlisted Reserve, and support for a more aggressive program of mechanizing the combat arms.[43]

Sensing an improvement in the atmosphere in Washington in 1935, MacArthur began pushing for the expansion of the army to 165,000 men. Both his annual report and that of the secretary of war made strong arguments regarding the necessity of this. Both noted that with one-third of the army on duty in overseas garrisons and a significant portion of the rest involved in overhead functions, there remained only about 50,000 men and 3,000 officers in tactical units, most of which were so scattered that realistic training was all but impossible.

MacArthur also noted that veterans of the world war were now so old that they could no longer serve as a virtual reserve, so that the creation of an Enlisted Reserve force was necessary.[44] In drawing up initial budget plans for fiscal year 1936, the General Staff included $20 million for expanding the army. But under great pressure from the White House to keep budget estimates low, the staff lost its nerve on this issue and submitted an estimate to the Bureau of the Budget for funding only the 118,750 men currently enlisted.[45]

Yet the fear of war grew significantly in the United States in 1935. The failure of the Disarmament Conference and Japan's refusal to abide by the terms of the Washington Naval Arms Limitation Treaty, induced the first of the neutrality laws. Roosevelt announced plans to increase defense spending radically, while MacArthur held a secret but highly publicized session with the House Military Affairs Committee in which he outlined the need for more airplanes, more coastal defenses, increased spending on mechanization and motorization, and an eventual expansion of the army to 400,000 men.[46] While the House was sympathetic and alarmed about the perceived threat from Japan, it voted to increase the army's budget by only $50 million, of which half was to go to new planes and a quarter to end the final 5-percent pay reduction from the early 1930s. No expansion of the army was included, although the president was authorized to add funds to initiate an expansion to 165,000 men at his discretion. At the same time, the navy was to get an increase of over $100 million in its budget.[47] The Senate, on the other hand, where concern over the threat from Japan was much greater, removed the provision leaving the expansion of the army to Roosevelt's discretion and increased the army's budget by another $20 million to fund the expansion.[48] The president signed the appropriations bill, apparently accepting the idea that the increase to 165,000 troops was needed to provide for "efficient training and reasonable readiness" in peacetime.[49]

The relative degree of success in Congress and with the president in the spring of 1935 created some optimism in the General Staff as it began developing estimates for the fiscal year 1937 budget. At the same time, it also became clear that the army's needs were escalating rapidly. An awareness of the importance of technological developments in weaponry had led to the creation in late 1934 of a separate research and development program to ensure adequate funding in that area, although only $7 million to $9 million were allocated to it. Leadership also decided that it was finally time to replace all motor vehicles that were more than fifteen years old, costing around $42 million. An acceleration in the aircraft procurement program would cost over $100, million.[50] At the same time, the General Staff was planning a recruiting campaign that hopefully would create an army of 165,000 men by June 30, 1936.[51] Aware that the president would still not accept a huge increase in the budget, the General Staff slashed its own estimates by nearly 20 percent, which still left MacArthur the task of defending an overall 20-percent increase.[52]

But by late 1935, the apparent resurgence of the Depression meant that Roosevelt was far more interested in trimming federal expenditures than in expanding them. In December the Bureau of the Budget announced that it was withholding half of the already appropriated funds designated for the increase in the size of the army.[53] Then the president, in his message to Congress regarding the budget in January 1936, indicated that he would allow funding for an increase only to 147,000 men, with a hope that the expansion to 165,000 could be achieved by 1939.[54] At the same time, his budget provided the army with a modest increase of $21 million, coupled with an executive order forbidding any officer in the army or navy from expressing any view in Congress in opposition to the views of the Bureau of the Budget.[55] In the House, the president's recommendations were accepted, although an increase in the size of the army to 150,000 was authorized. Following Roosevelt's lead, the House also refused to include funds to support the Thomason Act, which was aimed at giving one thousand reserve officers experience with active duty for a year. At the same time, funds for harbor defense were increased by nearly 700 percent to $8.5 million.[56] The Senate, however, balked at this and in March 1936, by an overwhelming margin, approved funding to increase the army to 165,000 men, paying for much of this by excising the increase in coastal-defense funds. Senators also voted to fund the increase in the number of reserve officers who could be called up for active duty under the Thomason Act.[57]

The success in getting authorization for expansion to 165,000 men and the atmosphere in Washington, where both international affairs and Depression-related unemployment seemed more severe, meant that the army became less fiscally ambitious in the later months of 1936. Yet with the expansion to 165,000 men, the General Staff turned its attention to improvements in the condition of enlisted personnel. An enlisted-promotion bill was passed in the spring of 1936 that allowed greater flexibility in the distribution of soldiers in grades and ratings, which meant there could be as many as 24,000 promotions in the ranks.[58] But the most important issue was pay, which affected not only the economic well-being of the enlisted man but also the prestige and perceived standing of the army. The salaries of the upper grades of NCOs was less than that of their counterparts in the navy. In addition, the daily pay of the average soldier was less than the starting pay for an unskilled laborer.[59] But the most aggravating aspect of enlisted pay was the reenlistment bonus. The bonus was eliminated in the 1933 economy drive when the pay of all federal workers was reduced. By the second half of the decade, while these civilian reductions gradually came to an end, the reenlistment bonus was not restored. Roosevelt argued that it was not needed since the economic situation in the country meant that no inducements for reenlistment need be offered. But the army saw the bonus as part of the soldier's pay and considered it both unfair and humiliating that the troops were the only federal employees still suffering from the pay cuts of the early 1930s.

For his part, the president was greatly concerned with the resurgence of the Depression and, again, sought to respond by paring government expenses. Yet while he called for a 10-percent cut throughout the government, his budget for the coming fiscal year actually included an increase for the army of nearly $25 million, an increase in troop levels to 165,000 men by June 30, and funds for at least five hundred Thomason Act reserve-officer trainees and fifty new Thomason Act officers.[60] Despite strong pressures to cut expenses, the House went along with Roosevelt's proposals except that it trimmed the army expansion to 160,000 men, a figure then raised by the Senate to 162,000.[61] Later, both houses also passed a bill providing over $25 million for military housing.[62]

The army's initial plans in 1937 for the upcoming legislative year continued to place emphasis on modernization and on equipment, especially antiaircraft and antitank weapons, rather than personnel.[63] The General Staff was also placing finishing touches on the initial draft of General Craig's Protective Mobilization Plan, growing increasingly concerned with the so-called war reserve. Much of the previous mobilization planning had assumed that the stocks of supplies and munitions left over from the world war could be used for any future conflict. Rapid changes in military technology along with the chemical deterioration of the munitions, however, made it increasingly obvious that this could not be the case. As a result, despite major efforts to trim initial branch estimates, Chief of Staff Craig still found himself having to defend a final War Department budget estimate that represented a more than 15-percent increase over the amount authorized by Congress the previous year.[64] Roosevelt, on the other hand, remained unsympathetic to the army's arguments and continued his policy of cutting expenditures whenever possible, even refusing to fund a small officer increase voted by Congress the previous spring.[65] But the outbreak of war between China and Japan and the signing of the Anti-Comintern Pact in November 1937 alarmed him to the point that he responded at the beginning of January 1938 with a defense-budget proposal totaling nearly $1 billion. As before, however, most of the increase was for the navy. Chief of Staff Craig's estimates were pared dramatically, resulting in an increase of barely $20 million from the previous year's budget, with half of this going for aircraft. The size of the army was limited to 162,000 enlisted men, and funds were provided for only five hundred Thomason Act Reserve officers to be called to active-duty training.[66]

Roosevelt indicated, however, that further measures would be taken and that in late January he would send a supplemental appropriations bill for national defense to Congress. Some in the army hoped that this bill would be more generous to ground forces than was the initial budget. Part of their optimism was based on signs of a growing rebellion in Congress over what was seen as Roosevelt's neglect of the army.[67] The president's new proposals, however, were a disappointment for the army, which received only negligible increases in a proposal that, again, chiefly benefited the navy.[68] The most notable feature of the supplement for the army was the creation of an Enlisted Reserve, which would allow former soldiers to put themselves on a retainer and be liable for call up, a program funded in its first year at $450,000.[69]

In 1938 the army again focused its attention on equipment, with even greater emphasis on antiaircraft and antitank weapons. In part, this reflected efforts by Craig and the General Staff to respond to the public's concern that military preparations should be solely defensive in character.[70] At the same time, the staff was becoming increasingly concerned regarding the war-materials reserve and, particularly, for "those items of equipment which industry cannot produce until long, if not fatal, periods of time have elapsed."[71] Nevertheless, the staff initially planned to offer budget estimates that were as frugal as possible, asking for only 13,000 officers and increasing the research and development budget for the Ordnance Department by only $100,000. By late 1938, however, the international situation seemed to change dramatically, giving rise to increased concern in Washington and throughout America. Events in Europe, especially those related to the Munich crisis, caused public and political attention to shift focus from Japan to Germany and from a perceived naval threat to the threat of attack from the air. The result of all this was a decision by Roosevelt to increase military spending radically, especially on aircraft and antiaircraft defenses, and finally to adopt a hemispheric defense strategy. The General Staff became optimistic that the president's increased concern with defense and public's increased concern would create an atmosphere conducive to a major expansion of the army's budget. Hence, the staff submitted ambitious budget estimates that included an expansion of the army to 180,000 men and 15,000 officers and a radical acceleration in the procurement of equipment, using the Protective Mobilization Plan as well as its overall modernization program.[72]

Initially, events seemed to fulfill the General Staff's hopes. Within two weeks of the Munich agreement, Roosevelt announced that he had ordered a thorough examination of the nation's defense needs, noting that while in the past budget concerns had played a controlling part in determining defense appropriations, such funding would now be based on the county's needs.[73] It was rumored that the president wanted a massive increase in the number of aircraft and a core army of 400,000 men, with the army and navy expected to receive funding increases of $150 million each.[74]

But soon, the army's hope for increased ground forces began to dissipate as public concern about the nation's vulnerability to an air attack rose to a pitch bordering on hysteria. As Henry Gole notes, by the late 1930s, the development of the B-17 as a bomber with transatlantic capabilities and news coverage of the devastation being caused by the bombing of cities in wars in Spain, China, and Ethiopia created an awareness among Americans of the nation's presumed vulnerability to aerial attack.[75] Roosevelt contributed to this by stating repeatedly that airstrikes were his principal concern. At his news conference on November 15, 1938, when he announced the adoption of the policy of hemisphere defense, he emphasized that the possibility of an air attack was "infinitely closer" than it had been five years ago and that one of his primary goals was to make the nation impregnable from the air.[76] By that time, the army was already being inundated by requests from towns all over the country, including many far inland, for antiaircraft protection, while the panic caused by Orson Welles's radio drama *War of the Worlds* at the end of October was testament to the level of American anxiety over a perceived vulnerability from the sky. By the middle of November, army leaders were expressing concerns that public panic would upset any rational plan for strengthening national defenses.[77]

Such anxiety initially seemed justified. In early January 1939 Roosevelt forwarded to Congress his proposal to boost defense spending by $300 million, a 30-percent increase over the previous year's budget. Again, nearly all of this went to the navy and the air corps; ground forces saw only $9 million of the increase.[78] Even the hope that this year the army would finally get the full complement of 1,000 reserve officers promised by the Thomason Act was disappointed, as the final bill allowed only for 650 such officers, an increase of only 150 over the 500 that Roosevelt had provided earlier.[79] But a week later, after a long conference with top military advisors, the president sent Congress a special message that included a request for a supplemental defense bill of $525 million. While $300 million was to go for more aircraft, nearly $150 million was to go to ground forces, including $110 million for the purchase of "items that could not be made quickly," which included antitank guns, antiaircraft artillery, gas masks, and other similar equipment.[80] While the president referred to the difficulty the United States had in mobilizing for the world war, he emphasized that he was not contemplating involvement in a new European war but, rather, wanted to ensure that the country had "armed forces strong enough to ward off a sudden attack against strategic positions and key facilities essential to insure sustained resistance and ultimate victory." He also made it clear that his major concern was the security of the Panama Canal Zone. Congress approved these sums almost without dissent.[81] Later, it passed legislation doubling the size of the air corps and augmenting the size of the garrison in the Philippines. Chief of Staff Craig was also informed that funding would be available to increase the army from 165,000 enlisted to 200,000 men, a figure inserted into the initial drafts for the army's budget estimates for fiscal year 1941.[82]

The army, in turn, began to adapt Craig's Protective Mobilization Plan into a readiness posture commensurate with the president's concerns for the security of strategic positions. In his annual report for 1939, Craig referred to a new orientation of "forward defense" in an "outpost line of security" that would center on the creation of a "small, hard-hitting division to seize or hold naval and air bases."[83] At the same time, Secretary of War Harry H. Woodring sought to "vitalize" the officer corps by calling on Congress to authorize new personnel policies for the army that would eliminate up to 2,300 officers deemed either overaged or physically unfit for their rank. While Woodring defended his policy in terms of getting rid of the "hump" that was still causing a demoralizing stagnation in promotion, he emphasized that his primary concern was getting rid of officers incapable of exercising field command in time of war. Therefore, his plan not only called for the forced retirement of general and field-grade officers above certain age levels but also intended to have all officers given a thorough medical examination to determine physical fitness for wartime duty. Nor was this program restricted to the Regular Army, as the secretary called on the states to carry out similar examinations for officers in the National Guard. Polls taken by the *Army and Navy Journal* showed that Woodring's proposal had the support of nearly two-thirds of all officers in the army.[84] Nevertheless, it got bogged down in Congress, and action on it was postponed until the following year. Thus, it was only as Europe moved into war at the end of the summer of 1939 that Congress, and especially Roosevelt, finally began to accept the army's own minimum program for national defense.

CHAPTER 10

Stability amid Crisis

The Civilian Components in the 1930s

THE CIVILIAN COMPONENTS HAD been the center of the army's attention in the first half of the 1920s as the "new army" envisioned in the National Defense Act of 1920 was being created. By the 1930s, however, this degree of interest was beginning to fade. There were several reasons for this. First, in the 1930s the army's focus was beginning to shift to the challenges of adapting to the problems and potentialities brought to warfare by the industrial revolution. In addition, the Depression exposed what appeared to be a continued, and possibly growing, lack of governmental and public interest in the concept of the citizen-soldier. At one point, in its cost-cutting zeal, Congress removed from an army appropriations bill virtually all funds to support the civilian components. On the other hand, by the early 1930s, the components had been in existence for over a decade, and most of the problems associated with them had been worked out. Finally, by the early 1930s, the AEF coterie that had dominated the General Staff in the 1920s was passing into retirement. Their experience in the world war had led them to focus on the problems of mobilizing a mass army. The leadership emerging in the 1930s was less interested in mobilization and more concerned with the new and more mobile forms of warfare seemingly made possible by motorized vehicles, ones that seemed to depend more on smaller professional forces than on the large masses of quickly trained amateurs of the world war. But while the civilian components were no longer the center of the army's attention, they continued to enjoy the growing stability that had begun during the latter half of the 1920s while being shielded from much of the turmoil created by the cost-cutting associated with the Depression.

The Reserve Officer Training Corps

Of all the civilian components, the ROTC was affected the least by the Depression. Outside of a few small funding cuts, it suffered no major damage to its program in the 1930s except for a reduction in the length of summer camp from six to four weeks in 1934, resulting from the massive cut in appropriations made in the spring of 1933. The camps were restored to six weeks the following summer.[1] The army was heartened by the fact that the program continued to grow and basked in the strong support given to it by the administrators of participating colleges and universities, especially those in the land-grant system.[2] On nearly all campuses, ROTC units were popular and well supported. Even in elite private universities, where male-student participation in the program was on a voluntary rather than compulsory basis, there was widespread involvement and strong support for the programs from the administration. At Princeton roughly 30 percent of the students participated, while the alumni at Yale provided the unit with an armory, stables, and a classroom building.[3] Overall, experience with the program gave the army the pleasure of knowing that there was one segment in society that supported the citizen-soldier concept inherent in the National Defense Act and appreciated the role of the army in developing it. As a result, the main concerns with ROTC in this period were limited to modifying the program to meet needs and to respond to critics from other areas of society.

The land-grant colleges and universities were the backbone of ROTC, and their administrations were among its strongest civilian backers. They appreciated the fact that the program meant that the army provided the resources and means to carry out the military-training mission required of them in the Morrill Act. They were also aware that the financial support given to cadets in the advanced course acted as a form of scholarship aid for a substantial number of their students. Finally, many presidents and chancellors shared the idea, still popular among educators at the time, that military training was a valuable addition to the physical and moral development of their students. Therefore, for most of this period, relations between the land-grant schools and the War Department were cordial, and the Association of Land-Grant Colleges and Universities remained a constant supporter of the ROTC in the lobbies of Congress.[4]

Given the large degree of satisfaction with the program on the campuses and in the army, there were few efforts made to change it. An ongoing problem that continued to be a source of increasing concern in the early 1930s was the imbalance among the branches. Since each combat branch had its own set of ROTC units, with infantry units being less expensive than others and cavalry units seen as having more dash, schools tended to host these units in preference to the those belonging to the field artillery and coast artillery branches. As a result, the production of reserve infantry and cavalry officers exceeded the needs of mobilization plans, while a growing deficiency continued to develop in the field-and coast-artillery arms.[5] Since the War Department could not change the branch designation of units at host institutions and did not have funds to increase enrollments in the artillery units, efforts were made to manipulate quotas in enrollments for advanced courses and for summer training in such a way as to reduce this imbalance. This tinkering alleviated the disparity but did not end it.[6]

A major review of the entire ROTC curriculum resulted only in minimal final changes, pointing to the overall stability the program had achieved by the end of the 1920s and the large degree of satisfaction with it. The major force behind the reexamination of the curriculum came from Charles Summerall in his final year as chief of staff. The general was greatly influenced by an article written by Dr. Glenn Frank, president of the University of Wisconsin, that was highly critical of the ROTC curriculum, claiming that it was mostly basic drill and dull.[7] On May 12, 1930, within days of reading this piece, Summerall called on the General Staff to conduct a thorough examination of the ROTC curriculum, with an eye to reducing routine drill and introducing more instruction that used the applicatory methods then being followed at in the special service schools.[8] Summerall gave this matter high priority and demanded quick action. While the staff was initially skeptical as to the need for major changes in the curriculum, feeling that outside critics were likely members of "anti-defense groups," it was also aware of criticism within the army that ROTC graduates lacked sufficient interest in military matters so that few seriously engaged in their obligations for further study as reserve officers.[9] As a result, by the summer of 1931, the focus of the reform effort was on inspiring student cadets "with a desire to share in the Nation's defense."[10] A curricular revision was finally unveiled at the end of December 1932. But it dealt more with problems of coordination between the program and the host institutions than with Summerall's concerns. Subject matter in the program was reorganized so that courses of study more closely resembled college courses and were sequenced in a logical progression.[11]

The major problem facing ROTC in this period was attacks on the program by pacifist groups. These were strongly reinforced in the 1930s by the growing antiwar sentiment and excitement regarding the Disarmament Conference between 1932 and 1934. All this allowed anti-military groups sufficient prominence to mount several significant challenges to the program. As in the 1920s, they realized that, although the entire ROTC program was too popular to attack with any hope of success, it had one vulnerable feature—the requirement that participation in the basic course was compulsory for all males. This aspect was unpopular with students and many faculty members and was hard to justify in public.[12] Hence, opponents focused their attention on this issue, lobbying for legislation at state and national levels to end the compulsory feature, agitating public opinion to force educational institutions themselves to drop the requirement, and assisting students' individual opposition to it.[13]

The War Department, on the other hand, had difficulty in formulating a consistent strategy to deal with these challenges. One major problem was that compulsory participation in the basic course was not supported by any national legislation, being mandated instead by either state legislation or the regulations of the land-grant schools themselves. Moreover, the department was hampered by the fact that no objections had been raised when the University of Wisconsin ended compulsory participation in the basic course in 1923, creating a precedent that haunted the department for the next two decades. As a result, it responded to cases as they arose, fashioning a defense for each issue. Still, by 1937, when the last of these challenges was raised, it had developed a roughly consistent approach.[14]

The first challenge to the compulsory issue came in 1930 with the introduction of a bill by Congressman George Welsh, a Republican from Pennsylvania, that would prohibit schools from making participation in military-training a requirement. The War Department's response was to allow the land-grant institutions to carry the fight against this legislation while aligning itself in their support and encouraging them by noting that enactment of the Welsh bill could cause the program to withdraw units from many schools.[15] At the same time, Summerall called on the General Staff to develop countermeasures against such attacks. Although no such policy was developed, opposition from the land-grant institutions was sufficient to ensure that the Welsh bill never got out of committee. A similar bill introduced in 1935 also died in committee.[16]

The issue of the basic-course requirement was raised again in 1934, when the Board of Regents at the University of Minnesota voted to make participation optional rather than compulsory. In this case the War Department was embarrassed by the 1923 Wisconsin precedent. It seriously considered withdrawing the three units training at Minnesota but finally decided against it, feeling that the public would see the withdrawal as punitive, which would play into the hands of the ROTC opponents. Instead, a compromise was negotiated in which only the infantry unit was withdrawn from the school, leaving the field-artillery and coast-artillery units on campus.[17]

The last challenge came in 1937, when the legislature of North Dakota passed a law that prohibited making participation in the basic course compulsory. The War Department found this challenge more difficult since the action had been taken by a state legislature rather than by either of the two land-grant schools in the state, North Dakota University and North Dakota Agricultural College, whose faculties and administrations were strongly in support of the compulsory provision. To remove units from the schools would seem to be punishing loyal institutions for the actions of the legislature. Thus, even though the experience with Minnesota indicated that if participation in the basic course was made optional, enrollment in the advance course would soon drop to a nonviable level, the General Staff decided to keep the units in place on a trial basis, with no further action taken.[18]

Finally, what is perhaps most surprising is not that some land-grant universities challenged the compulsory basic-course provision in the 1930s, but that so few actually did. Given the high degree of pacifist sentiment that built up in the country during the 1930s and the unpopularity of the requirement among male students, one might have expected a far greater degree of challenge. Indeed, as Michael Neiberg notes, by the mid-1930s, only twenty-one private schools not subject to legislation related to the Morrill Act had eliminated the compulsory basic-course requirement.[19] The fact that so few land-grant schools had challenged the provision is testimony to the high degree of value these institutions placed on the program.

Overall, despite these challenges and the efforts made to tinker with the structure of the program, the dominating feature of ROTC in the entire 1930s was its stability and continued overall popularity. It was, in many respects, the army's most successful civilian program. Despite the unrest in the nation at the time, challenges to the program from the outside were minimal and largely confined to Minnesota and the Dakotas. This stability and popularity were due to several factors, including the financial support given by the program to the participating institutions and many of their students. The War Department was also wise in decentralizing the ROTC program and giving host institutions a large degree of influence in developing the units on their campuses. Officers assigned duty in the ROTC were encouraged to be active campus and community citizens; in fact, most were personally popular.[20] Finally, the nation's educators at the time were favorable to military training, seeing it as a valuable addition to the programs at their schools and a symbol of prestige.

The National Guard

The chief trend in the development of the National Guard during the entire 1930s was a growing stabilization of the program, allowing for continuous improvement in both performance and satisfaction. Even at the height of the Depression, the chief of the Militia Bureau was able to report: "With the strength of the National Guard remaining practically a fixed quantity in recent years, the continued increase in both armory drill attendance and field training has enabled instruction and training to proceed and advance beyond any previous record. The result is a standard and condition of all-round effectiveness never before attained." He concluded, "the National Guard finishes the year [1931] in the best condition of its long history."[21] During much of this time, appropriations limited the Guard to around 190,000 men, nearly all of whom participated in armory drills and summer field training. Attendance at field training was remarkably steady, while turnover among officers tended to diminish during the decade. And while the Depression years provided significant strain and challenge, the morale of the Guard remained high.

The National Guard suffered relatively little from the Depression itself. In 1933 and 1934, allocations to the Guard were cut drastically, and pay reductions ordered for the Regular Army affected the Guard as well. But the Guard was still able to provide the customary forty-eight armory drills and fifteen days of field training a year by drastically curtailing all other expenditures.[22] Further reductions in appropriations in 1933 finally forced it to cut the number of paid drills from forty-eight to thirty-six. The Guard, however, managed to weather this adversity with little damage to its stability. The reduction to thirty-six drills was almost academic, as most units continued to offer forty-eight drills and most guardsmen attended all of them, even if they were only paid for thirty-six. And even drastically reduced appropriations still allowed the Guard to continue to motorize its artillery and modernize the force.

By far the most significant development for the Guard in the 1930s was passage of the National Guard Bill in 1933. The initiative for this legislation was taken five years earlier by the NGA. At the association's convention in 1926, the NGA called for amending the National Defense Act to grant the Guard federal recognition in peacetime.[23] The Militia Bureau established a committee to study the legal aspects of the proposal, and a final draft bill was sent to Congress, where it sat for five years. Under prodding from the NGA, Congress finally took up the bill and passed it in the spring of 1933, with Roosevelt signing it on June 15. The act essentially gave existing Guard units federal recognition so that they would be called up for service intact and would be released from service intact. It also officially changed the name of the Militia Bureau to the National Guard Bureau.[24]

In 1935 the National Guard began enjoying the same increases in appropriations from Congress as the Regular Army so that the second half of the 1930s was seen as a period of constructive growth. In addition to greater overall appropriation, Congress began a program of slowly expanding the size of the Guard. The General Staff had long argued that the minimum strength needed by the Guard to discharge its duties under the National Defense Act was 210,000 men. But since 1930 its size had remained fixed at only 190,000 guardsmen. In 1935 Congress embarked on a plan to increase the size to 210,000 in four yearly incremental expansions of 5,000 men each.[25]

At the same time, the cooperation between the National Guard and the Regular Army continued to grow. The number of guard officers invited to attend Regular Army schools increased annually, with the intention that there would be one guard officer with Regular Army training in every unit. The Guard also began participating in Regular Army maneuvers in 1936 and 1939.[26] All of this resulted in heightened morale in the Guard, evidenced by a rapid improvement in the retention rate among officers.

Organized Reserve

Although the Organized Reserve was, in many regards, the most critical of the four civilian components of the Army of the United States, and even though the Reserve experienced modest growth in numbers and improvement in training during the 1930s, the program was still the least successful and most frustrating of the four. All during the decade, it suffered from a variety of problems, including inadequate appropriations, internal apathy, and even confusion regarding mission and objectives. The response of the War Department and of the reservists themselves entailed a few small measures aimed at doing the best with what was available while taking advantage of opportunities as they came along.

Lurking in the background of all the other problems was some ambiguity as to the mission of the Organized Reserve. Generally, the problem was that the ORC program was meant to fulfill two different objectives that were not entirely complementary. On the one hand, it was stated officially that "the training mission of the Reserves is to maintain in every unit of the Organized Reserves an efficient cadre of officers, ... which is individually and collectively competent to perform the duties required in mobilizing and training the unit at war strength."[27] At the same time, it was also stated in the army regulations regarding the ORC, "The ultimate objective in training units of the Organized Reserve in time of peace is to provide partially trained units which may be readily expanded to war strength and completely trained in time of emergency."[28] The question of whether reserve units were to be chiefly concerned with mobilizing and training a conscripted citizen army or were to be contingents of a nearly ready combat force was never resolved in the 1930s, and reforms in training efforts often shifted between one and the other of the two objectives.

The issue of greatest concern to the army regarding the Organized Reserve was numbers. Throughout the interwar period, nearly all thinking regarding the Reserve was dominated by the memory of the 1917 mobilization, which was seen as slow and haphazard. As a result, a great deal of the army's energy and thought went into the preparation of detailed mobilization plans. The overall scheme developed in the early 1920s called for a mobilized army of fifty-four divisions, nine to be supplied by the Regular Army, eighteen by the National Guard, and twenty-seven by the Organized Reserve. The central problem for the reserve program, therefore, was to ensure that the ORC was large enough to support twenty-seven divisions. The mobilization plan developed in 1928 called for between 180,000 and 190,000 reserve officers.[29] Yet in 1930 there were only a few more than 100,000 officers holding reserve commissions, only 80,000 of whom being carried on the "active assigned" list.[30] The ORC experienced only slow growth so that by 1936 the number of active assigned officers had risen to nearly 92,000. That expansion then accelerated toward the end of the decade when it reached 104,000 reserve officers.[31]

The slowness in this increase was due to a number of factors. One was a large turnover in reserve officers coming out of the ROTC. Many had little interest in the army and did not apply for reappointment after their initial five-year commitment. At the same time, the army was constrained by limited appropriations and personnel shortages so that it was unable to cope with a larger number of officers even if they had been available. Moreover, for most of the 1930s, budgetary constraints limited the number of reservists who could engage in the fourteen days of active-duty training offered each year to around 20,000. As a result, there was concern in the General Staff that any significant expansion of the size of the ORC would lead to further dilution of a training program that was already stretched too thin.

Along with limited numbers, the other major issue with the ORC program was training. The overall concern here was that this program was inadequate to produce officers who would be nearly ready to fill wartime leadership positions.

For one thing, it was thought to be too skimpy. While reserve officers in the armies of most major military powers were given a full year of initial training supplemented by up to a month of annual training, the U.S. training program through the ROTC was calculated to be the equivalent to only four months of initial training supplemented by two weeks of active-duty training received, at best, once every three years.[32] Most of the army's attention in this regard was given to the two weeks of active-duty training. The fact that, for most of the 1930s, appropriations restricted training to only 20,000 reserve officers meant that it was available to less than one-fourth of those on the active assigned lists.[33] Limited funding, however, was not the only problem. Many reserve officers proved reluctant to give up two weeks of vacation time to take training. Thus, there were actually so few officers applying for active-duty training that a large number of those were able to take it every year while many others never received any training at all.[34] This situation was compounded by the fact that in the 1930s the character of the ORC began to change. Veterans of the world war, who had dominated the program in the 1920s, were now leaving, and the corps began filling instead with graduates of the ROTC program. By 1931, these graduates became the largest single cohort in the ORC.[35] Since none of these men had had any combat experience, the need to give them some form of active-duty training seemed imperative.

There was also concern with the inactive training in the program. In some cases, this was conducted using conferences and other forms of classes sponsored by reserve units and carried out, whenever possible, by the Regular Army officer assigned to support the unit. But the heart of the army's inactive-training efforts was made up of extension-school courses taken on a correspondence basis. The army had given great attention to developing and refining these courses in the 1920s. The assignments were submitted to and corrected by the regular officer assigned to the reserve officer's unit. Nevertheless, participation in the program was limited for most years in the 1930s to around 45,000 of the 80,000 reserve officers on the active assigned list.[36] There was, in addition to this limited participation, also considerable concern that, while the correspondence courses gave an officer some understanding about the theoretical and technical aspects of his craft, they offered no training in leadership or administration, considered to be the most important skills needed by an officer, nor any opportunity to apply the principals learned. As one officer observed, "A recent tour of duty with the C.M.T.C. at which junior officers were expected to be able to carry on the responsibilities of their grade, proved clearly that officers educated solely by book learning were useless when troops were to be handled."[37]

Behind all this was a problem of apathy or lack of interest on the part of a large portion of the reserve officers enrolled. Many joined the ROTC programs in college for reasons other than an interest in military affairs, and a significant number of them graduated without having developed that interest. Also, those who did aspire to become military officers often found little in the inactive-training program to sustain that interest. They rarely saw their fellow officers and rarely engaged in any activities that could generate or sustain motivation. Correspondence courses seemed dull, and chances for active-duty training were remote even if one had the time or interest to attend. Eventually, reserve officers' interest in military matters faded as they became absorbed in their civilian occupations, their families, and their communities. This lack of interest was seen not only in the low level of participation in extension courses but also in high attrition rates, with the majority of officers who accepted the five-year reserve appointment that came with commissioning in the ROTC program either failing to qualify for or even seek reappointment.[38]

These problems seemed so intractable that no major effort was made in the War Department in the 1930s to overcome them. Instead, especially in the first half of the decade, it tinkered with the program where possible to make small gains and sought to take advantage of any opportunity that came along to enhance reserve training. The result was a gradual improvement, with the numbers enrolled increasing slowly and the numbers engaged in extension courses rising as well. At the same time, this somewhat opportunistic approach to the problem also contributed to a continued lack of focus and coherence in the overall program. The first significant reform had come earlier, in 1928, in the effort to clear "deadwood" out of the ORC. In 1930 the rules regarding promotion were tightened further to require the satisfactory completion of all extension-course work appropriate to the new grade. In addition, the candidate had to demonstrate both knowledge and military abilities by passing examinations and practical tests.[39] Further, reserve officers were sent an outline of the military knowledge they were expected to master for promotion. The following year each one was sent a copy of the field manual appropriate for his branch. One short-term result of this was a dramatic rise in the number of officers enrolled in extension-course work.

Shortly after MacArthur became chief of staff, the General Staff engaged in a serious reconsideration of existing reserve-officer training policies. In the summer of 1931, the Operations and Training Division proposed a new approach. It pointed out that, while the long-held ideal for active-duty training for reserve officers was one period of training every three years, appropriations would not allow this. Therefore, the staff suggested a new scheme for training that "would be based upon a system of priority in which money and energy would be expended on reserve officers in direct proportion to the urgency of their employment in war and in inverse proportion to the degree in which their peacetime occupation prepares them for war-time duties."[40] Although MacArthur did not accept the scheme, he still liked its emphasis on expanding the combat readiness of those reserve units that would be involved in the first phases of mobilization. Therefore, he asked the Operations and Training Division staff to consider a training scheme that "would provide for placing all critical reserve units with commanders and key officers on active duty training every year with as much of their personnel as possible."[41]

The division responded with a modified version of its original proposal.[42] Although MacArthur also failed to accept this revision, subsequent policy changes continued to focus on the training of reserve units that would be among the first mobilized and involved in combat. While the ideal that every reserve officer should get active-duty training once every three years continued to be the stated backbone of the War Department's reserve-officer training program, actual policies increasingly favored combat units.[43]

The War Department also sought to upgrade training at reserve units while reducing dependence on thinly stretched regular officers by sending more reserve officers to the army's special service schools. Toward the end of 1930, Brigadier General Edward L. King, who headed the Operations and Training Division, suggested a program aimed at sending enough reservists to such schools to provide, over time, for one school-trained officer with each major unit of the Organized Reserve. He pointed out that, due to falling prices, the costs of sending 20,000 reserve officers to active-duty training for fourteen days had decreased to the point that the savings could be used to pay for the increased numbers sent to the schools.[44] After some discussion, the expansion was approved in 1932.[45]

Finally, as an additional alternative to the two-week summer training program during the 1930s, the Organized Reserve took over the training at the CMTCs as well as the administration of many of the CCC camps. This was controversial, based on fears that it would lead to a serious diminution in both the camp experience and the prestige of the program.[46] It was tried, therefore, in the late 1920s on an experimental basis, with only a few reserve units involved. While the initial experiments did show that there was a diminution in the quality of the camps, most of the problems were ironed out in the next few years. At the same time, reserve units involved were enthusiastic about the experience, feeling that it provided valuable training in the skills that would be needed in any early mobilization and training of a citizen army, a view shared in the War Department.[47]

Surprisingly, the ORC benefited little from the somewhat greater attention given the army after 1935. The secretary of war continued to ask dutifully each year for funds to increase to 30,000 the number of officers provided active-duty training, which would allow them to receive training once every three years, but he did so with little enthusiasm and with seemingly little hope of receiving any kind of approval.[48] Nor did the program change much in these years. Combat units involved in the earliest phases of mobilization and new ROTC graduates continued to be favored for active-duty training as were reserve officers who were actively pursuing inactive training. The emphasis on practical training was continued as well.[49]

The one exception to this was the Thomason Act, which passed Congress in 1936 and provided funds for giving one thousand reserve officers a year of active-duty training, after which fifty would receive commissions in the Regular Army. Developing a training program for these officers provided a significant problem for the army, since nearly all the Thomason Act reserve officers were recent ROTC graduates. The plan included an intense schooling program complemented by assignment to units of the Regular Army. After a year's experience, this training plan was modified to give the reserve officers less time in school and more practical experience with troops.[50] The program proved popular. As Edward Coffman notes, the extra pay was an incentive during Depression years that brought highly talented officers into the program. Steven Barry points out that the provision to give the top fifty Thomason Act reserve officers regular commissions brought into the army some of the highest-quality reserve officers available.[51]

Yet while the Thomason Act injected some life into it, during the 1930s, the Organized Reserve had hardly developed into the organization called for in the National Defense Act of 1920. It was neither the size expected nor led by officers with anywhere near the training needed. In fact, the overall training level of the Reserve probably deteriorated, as veterans of the world war were increasingly replaced by green ROTC graduates with no combat experience and only minimal experience with troops. In the spring of 1940, an officer despairingly described what he considered to be a typical reserve unit:

> This particular regiment has 104 officers. To start with it is short 2 field officers and 6 captains. Twenty seven have never had active duty, although it has been available; 21 have had one 2-week tour and 16 have had two tours. . . . Four lieutenants are 46 years of age or older. One officer is not eligible for active duty because he is drawing disability compensation as a World War veteran. Six had World War experience of one kind or

another. Forty-four are studying an Extension Course. Twenty-one first lieutenants are over time in grade, i.e. have not done the courses required for promotion. Seventy-eight are R.O.T.C. graduates, four are graduates of the C.M.T.C.[52]

It is doubtful that this is what Colonel Palmer had in mind in 1920.

Citizens' Military Training Camps

The CMTC had never been much more than an auxiliary program in the army. It had been created after the failure to include provisions for universal military training in the National Defense Act of 1920 in the hope of popularizing military training and to produce a few reserve officers and men trained to become NCOs in time of war. While the program was moderately popular in the 1920s, it never created the hoped-for groundswell of support for military training. By the beginning of the 1930s, the army had started to lose interest in it. Despite its increased popularity, the CMTC was somewhat neglected all during that decade.[53] The program was nearly cut from the budget entirely in 1934, being rescued only by Congress. In several other years it was not even mentioned in the annual reports of the secretary of war and the chief of staff, nor was it improved in any significant way. The only major change was the policy of turning over a significant portion of the training responsibilities in the camps to reserve officers, a policy designed to improve training in the Organized Reserve at the expense of the quality of training offered by the CMTCs.

The only issue of any significance facing the program in the 1930s was the matter of race, which had already surfaced in the 1920s. As was the case in the late 1920s the demands were initiated by African American leaders of local organizations, especially the American Legion, with the strong support of local African American congressmen. As before, the main objective of the army in addressing the issue was to avoid controversy. The overall approach, again as in the 1920s, was to give the appearance of fairness by following a policy of offering separate-but-equal camps. This policy was reiterated in 1930 by Assistant Secretary of War Frederick Payne: "The policy of the War Department as promulgated authorizes corps area commanders to establish a colored Citizens Military Training Camp in their respective areas; firstly, when applications are received from qualified and eligible colored applicants in a sufficient number to warrant the holding of such a camp; secondly, when sufficient funds and suitable personnel are available for training."[54]

There were significant problems, however, in following this policy that led to strains between the War Department, which generally favored holding as many camps as possible, and corps-area commanders and other unit commanders where these camps might be held. The officers there were wary of the sympathies and prejudices of local citizens as well as the impossibility of asking units of white soldiers to service camps made up of African Americans, which was responsible for the phrase "suitable personnel" in Payne's statement of policy. In most cases the opposition of local officers was sufficient to block holding a camp. But there were a few instances when CMTCs were held. In 1931 an organizer in Saint Louis, with support from three congressmen, requested a camp be held in his area. Although he was unable to recruit the minimum number of applicants needed to justify the camp, the General Staff indicated to the local corps-area commander that the minimum be regarded as "only a guide," and the camp was held.[55] In 1936 a CMTC was held at Fort Meyer, Virginia, after local opposition was overruled by the assistant chief of staff for the Operations and Training Division.[56] Finally, a highly successful camp was held on the West Coast in 1938 despite concerns of the corps-area commander regarding possible local opposition.[57]

Overall, this was not a serious problem for the army. There were only eight documented efforts to open CMTCs to African Americans in the 1930s. A few of these had the support of one or more members of Congress but little else in the way of political backing. But its reemergence was a harbinger of what was to come during and after World War II regarding race and the army. Otherwise, it was a sign of the success of the CMTC program's efforts to convince Americans that military training was good for their sons. The uncomfortable difficulties arose when African Americans understood and accepted this and sought these benefits for their youth as well.

CHAPTER 11

Modern Weapons and Traditional Tactics

The Infantry and Tanks, 1919–1939

A LTHOUGH THE NATIONAL DEFENSE Act of 1920 awarded the infantry total control over the development of tanks and tank warfare, the branch failed to develop a realistic and tested means of integrating the new weapons system into its structure during the entire interwar period. As a result, while its vision of the combat use of tanks remained fixed on the experience of the world war, the infantry had to watch with ill-concealed envy as the cavalry first won the right to develop its own tanks in the early 1930s and then went on to become the dominant mechanized force in the army.

This failure was not due to lack of interest. From 1920 onward, the *Infantry Journal* carried positive and even enthusiastic articles about tanks while reviewing technological developments in Europe and recalling the army's experience with them in the world war. Branch leadership was also positive in its interest. Nor did the infantry fail to develop a consensus regarding tank tactics. Instead, it accepted a tactical doctrine almost immediately, based on its wartime experience, which then remained virtually constant throughout the interwar period. Instead, two main problems were responsible for the infantry's failure to become the predominant tank branch. The first was an inability to develop a consensus regarding preferred models compounded by strained relations with the Ordnance Department, which was responsible for the actual procurement of tanks once the infantry had supplied specifications. The second was a lack of anywhere near adequate appropriations to support the program. Until late in the 1930s the infantry never had more than a few prototypes, which were not enough to develop and test its tactical doctrines.

Americans had used tanks during the world war and, indeed, had formed a nearly autonomous tank corps headed by Brigadier General Samuel D. Rockenbach. From this experience he, along with several other officers, became enthusiastic about the future of tanks and hoped the corps would retain its autonomous status after the war. But several factors militated against that. During the war, tanks were primarily used tactically as infantry-support weapons. Since the top speed of the two vehicles used, the light six-ton French Renault FT-17 and the heavy forty-ton British Mark VIII, was five or six miles per hour, there were few other roles they could play. More important, the army's commitment to the principles of open warfare, which subordinated all other arms to the support of the advance of the infantry, made the existence of an independent tank corps all but superfluous. As a result, the 1920 National Defense Act made tanks part of the infantry.

Based on these factors, and on its experience in the war, the infantry continued to accept what had been the army's wartime tactical doctrine for the use of tanks in combat. In an article entitled "Tank Tactics," published in June 1920, Rockenbach outlined the basic concepts that remained the foundation of the infantry's tactical doctrine for the next two decades. In his view, the tank was solely an infantry-support weapon. As was the case in the world war, the army would possess two types of tanks, heavy and light. He then elaborated on their roles: "The heavy tanks precede the light tanks and the infantry, especially in the early stage of an attack on works, in order to secure passage and to cover the infantry and light tanks while they clean up. The function of the light tanks is then to fight in immediate touch with the infantry, destroy machine guns, cut the wire, and break up other resistance retarding the infantry."[1]

By 1922, the infantry had formally adopted this concept as doctrine while providing each division with a company of tanks (on paper).[2] Outside of a few modest modifications, that doctrine remained intact for the remainder of the interwar period, successfully weathering all challenges. The published works of British tank theorists Basil Liddell Hart and J. F. C. Fuller were well known in U.S. Army circles. Indeed, articles by both men were carried in military journals. Several of the army's own tank specialists, among them Captain Sereno Brett and Major Ralph E. Jones, argued in published articles for a wider approach to tank tactics, including the use of massed formations, but to no avail.[3] Within the doctrine, however, there was one notable change. In the early 1920s the focus was on the light "accompanying tank," which was to fight in coordination with the advancing riflemen. The heavy tank was assigned to lead, though only by a few hundred yards, and clear the way by knocking out obstacles such as machine guns and wire. It was therefore considered a special weapon to be used only as conditions permitted and, as such, was the junior partner in an advance. In the teaching of the Command and General Staff School in the middle of the 1930s, on the other hand, that relationship began to change. Primary focus was increasingly given to what were now called the "leading tanks," whose objective was to break through to the enemy rear area, while "accompanying tanks" retained the traditional mission of coordinated combat with riflemen.[4] Yet while the infantry may have been evolving in the direction of using attacks by massed tank units, it balked at any idea that they would operate outside the control of an infantry unit. As the chief of infantry in 1937, Major General George A. Lynch cautioned the Infantry School: "While it is advisable to concentrate effective numbers of tanks against decisive objectives, this should not be taken as to imply that these tanks operate in one large group under separate command."[5] And as late as 1941, the chief of infantry was still arguing in his final report that "tanks can effectively lead the attack and prepare for the foot infantry advance by suppressing hostile resistance, in particular machineguns."[6]

With doctrine set, the major issue for the infantry was the design of a set of satisfactory weapons. Unlike the stability that characterized the development of the tactical use of the tank, the efforts to develop a satisfactory vehicle were turbulent and largely unsuccessful, with one pilot project after another failing to gain sufficient acceptance that would lead to the manufacture of a standard model. A part of the problem lay in the fact that responsibility for tank development was dispersed among three agencies. The first was the Office of the Chief of Infantry, which was responsible for determining tactical and strategic roles of tanks in warfare and the types of tanks needed to fulfill those missions. The second was the Tank School, whose personnel were the army's experts on the design of tanks and their abilities. The third was the Ordnance Department, which was responsible for the designing and engineering of tanks that fulfilled the infantry's strategic and tactical specifications. The boundaries of these responsibilities, however, were never clear, and each organization saw the tank from a different perspective. In addition, the views of the chief of infantry shifted with changes of personnel. Finally, tanks and the process of their design were extremely expensive, and funding was extremely limited.

The first postwar ideas regarding tank development began in the Ordnance Department, which became interested in a new, fast medium tank being designed in Great Britain. This model would be used in an independent force and serve as an all-purpose tank, replacing both the six-ton light Renault and the forty-ton heavy Mark VIII. During the summer of 1919, the department began designing two different medium tanks of its own. At the same time, it sought using arm guidance from the still existent tank corps. Rockenbach, as head of the corps, was enthusiastic about the medium tank, which figured into his overall hope of maintaining the independence of his unit. Officers who had experience with tanks in the world war were also enthusiastic about the idea of a fast, general-purpose medium tank. They considered it the only model needed by the army.[7]

The tank they sought was to carry sufficient armor to protect it from .30-caliber armor-piercing bullets, travel cross-country at a speed of twelve miles per hour, carry a light cannon and two machine guns, and have a cruising radius of at least fifty miles.[8] By August 1919, a preliminary design had been created that won Rockenbach's approval, and the Ordnance Department began to develop an actual pilot model, calling it the M1921. Later, inspired by British innovations in suspension systems, the department also began the development of a second pilot model, the M1922. By November, the M1921 was completed and ready for a shop test, which was successful.

Caught up in its own organizational issues, the infantry was slow to establish its leadership in tank design. It was not until March 1921 that the chief of infantry presented his recommendations to the War Department. He accepted the development of the medium tank, though only as a replacement for the old forty-ton heavy tank and as the junior partner in the two-tank doctrine.[9] Based on this, the secretary of war issued a directive on April 3, 1922, to guide the further development of tanks. It agreed in principle with the recommendation to develop two types, but with priority given to the medium version. But due to the limited capacities of standard railway cars, of highway bridges in the United States, and of the pontoon bridges assigned to a division, the directive specified that the medium tank should weigh no more than fifteen tons.[10] This created a serious problem. Both the M1921 and M1922 were designed to meet the tactical needs of the infantry, rather than the problem of strategic mobility raised by the War Department. The M1921 weighed twenty-three tons, while it was expected that the unfinished M1922 would weigh twenty-five tons.[11]

Somewhat reluctantly, the Ordnance Department began work in early 1923 on a design for a fifteen-ton medium tank, the M1924. The work did not go smoothly, as those working on the new plans as well as officers in the Tank School felt that the features essential for a fighting tank were being sacrificed to meet the weight limitation.[12] Finally, in the early summer of 1924, the commandant of the Tank School, in obvious frustration, wrote angrily to the chief of infantry: "I think that it is a matter of common knowledge that a Tank embodying the requirements which have been laid down by your office for a Medium Tank cannot be built within the limit of 15 tons, which has been imposed upon you by higher authority. . . . Under the present limitation of 15 tons, no Tank can be turned out that will fulfill the requirements either as to protection for crew, gun power, or performance."[13] He went on to suggest that work on the earlier M1921 and M1922 prototypes be continued. As the infantry was also developing new pontoon bridges capable of supporting eighteen tons, a compromise was suggested in the form of a medium tank that, when stripped down, would weigh only eighteen tons.[14] By then, the War Department had already agreed to support the further development of the M1921 as long as further studies would be made for the possible future development of a fifteen-ton tank. In 1927 a pilot model of the redesigned M1921, which still weighed twenty-three tons, was completed and designated the T-1 medium tank. It was accepted by the War Department for standardization.

By then, however, attitudes in the Chief of Infantry's Office had changed considerably. The major reason for this was the appointment of Major General Robert H. Allen as chief of infantry in March 1925. Allen was convinced that the tank, particularly the light version, was the weapon that could restore maneuver to warfare and thus was more in line with the army's prevailing doctrine. As he stated, "A light tank weighing approximately 5 tons and capable of being carried by truck is *the* tank for maneuver warfare under any and all conditions, and cannot be replaced by any tank that cannot be carried by a truck in the present state of mechanical development."[15] In contrast, Allen came to see the medium tank as a part of the old stabilized warfare of the world war and of no use in a war of maneuver.[16] By August, he was already calling for a study of light-tank development by the major European powers.[17]

By the beginning of 1926, Allen moved to shift the emphasis in tank development to a light tank. In a memorandum to the War Department in early January, he stated that the twenty-three-ton medium tank was a suitable replacement for the old forty-ton heavy tank and that no further work was needed on it. Nor did he see any purpose in pursuing a fifteen-ton alternative. Instead, he sought to have the Ordnance Department focus on a light tank by either developing a means to remodel the existing six-ton model or designing a new five-ton version.[18] This was followed later in the month with a set of specifications for a light tank drawn up by the Tank School and approved by Allen. Emphasis was again placed on a weight limit of six tons so that it could be transported in a standard, commercially available truck rather than in a specially designed carrier.[19] In early March the War Department agreed to Allen's proposal to study the possibilities of either remodeling the existing six-ton tank or developing a new five-ton model. But it insisted that work on both the twenty-three-ton and fifteen-ton designs continue.[20]

In the Ordnance Department, both the Rock Island Arsenal in Illinois and departmental facilities in Washington undertook the design of the new light tank. By September, both groups had developed several concepts, with the major difference being that the Rock Island design had the engine in the rear of the tank, while the Ordnance Department design placed the engine in the front, thereby making it possible for the chassis to also be used for a cargo carrier. To resolve this placement conflict, the department sought the advice of a group of twelve civilian automotive engineers. This group studied the designs, especially the issue of the location of the engine and recommended in favor of locating the engine in the front of the tank.[21] This was accepted by the department in December, and work went forward toward building a pilot model.

Ironically, while the somewhat redundant effort to design the light tank in Washington was undertaken to improve liaison between the Ordnance Department, the Office of the Chief of Infantry, and the Tank School, communications between the three bodies actually deteriorated. The fault in this breakdown lay chiefly with Chief of Staff Allen, who had made developing the light tank his own project. Captain George Rarey, the Tank School's principal authority on tank design, was concerned about placing the engine in front and confronted Allen on the issue.

The chief of staff told Rarey emphatically that, "He [Allen] did not consider it a function of the Tank Board or any concern of theirs as to the design and drawing of any of the vehicles."[22] In September 1927 a pilot model of the tank, made up of a metal chassis and a wooden tank house, turret, and guns, was shown to Allen and Rarey. The general was enthusiastic about the model, while the captain was muzzled.[23] The Ordnance Department then ordered the building of four full prototypes of the tank. Based on the successful tests of these and on Allen's enthusiastic support, the Ordnance Department recommended that the design be accepted by the War Department for standardization.

The pilot models were completed at the end of May 1928 and subjected to a number of tests. The performance of the new light tank, now labeled the T1-E1, was extremely impressive in terms of speed, range, armament, and durability, leaving most of the observers of the trials enthusiastic about it.[24] One of the tanks was then sent to Fort Meade for a test by the Tank Board at the Tank School. The board proposed several changes, one of which was to move the engine to the rear of the vehicle. The chief of infantry approved the minor changes proposed by the board but vetoed moving the engine on the grounds that it would require an entirely new design. Based on the minor changes proposed after all the trials, the chief of infantry and the Ordnance Department proposed building a new prototype, the T1-E2, in November 1928. It was completed in June 1929.

In the meantime, Allen's term as chief of infantry ended in the spring of 1929, with Major General Stephen O. Fuqua succeeding him. While Allen had largely excluded the Tank School and Tank Board from the development of the light tank, both Fuqua and the War Department were solicitous of the board's opinion and sent them the new T1-E2 for tests and evaluation.[25] After several days of trials, the board pointed out that placing the engine in front raised the temperature in the crew compartment to an unacceptable level and impaired the driver's vision and the gunner's ability to aim. Consequently, the board recommended that it not be adopted as a standard model and that no further development be undertaken of that design.[26]

The Tank Board's opinion was also influenced by the fact that it had found another tank chassis that it considered far superior to that used on the T1-E2. This alternative frame was offered by a civilian entrepreneur and inventor named J. Walter Christie, one of the most colorful personalities in the history of the army during this period. He was a largely self-taught mechanical engineer who took an early interest in automobiles. During the world war, he designed mechanized weapons for the army. Some years afterward, he set out to design a new tank and in 1928 came up with the M1928. The most attractive feature of the Christie tank chassis was its strategic mobility. Tanks used in the war had extremely limited range since their treads wore out within eighty to one hundred miles, especially when traveling on hardened roads. This meant they had to be carried to any mobilization point by truck or railcar. A force of 500 light tanks, therefore, would also need 500 carriers, and any convoy of immobilized tanks would be highly vulnerable to attack. Christie solved this problem by designing a chassis that ran on four rubber tires on each side while carrying its own treads. This meant that the M1928 could travel by road to a mobilization point without a truck and then be converted to an overland tank by having its treads put on at the last minute, an operation that took about an hour to complete. In addition, due to a new suspension system, the Christie model could travel over roads at almost unheard-of speeds of up to forty miles per hour.

The Tank Board started testing the new M1928 in October 1928. The tests uncovered several problems, however, and the chassis was returned to Christie, whose company dealt with the problems and resubmitted it to the board in June 1929. After new tests, enthusiastic board members declared, "this tank chassis is far superior to the chassis of any light tank which they have tested or of which they have any knowledge." In August they recommended to Fuqua that the Christie model be adopted and standardized.[27] For the next three years, the infantry pursued a tortuously complex effort to have the M1928 developed as its light tank and produced in such numbers that tactical tests and doctrine could be developed. These efforts were complicated by strained relations between the branch and the Ordnance Department and between the department and Christie, the difficulties of working with a civilian contractor within the framework of the army's weapons-development system, fund limitations and the year and a half lead time between submission of proposals for budget allocations and actual receipt of such funding, the rise of the cavalry as a rival in tank development, and finally, Christie's own mercurial temperament.[28]

An effort by Fuqua to use funds already appropriated by Congress to purchase five or six Ti-E2 tanks to buy fully armored Christie tanks instead was thwarted by the Ordnance Department. The department was clearly angered that the infantry had rejected the Ti-E2 and demanded that there be no large order of Christie tanks until it had tested them for reliability under service conditions. For this, it needed only one prototype vehicle, not five or six.[29] The secretary of war deferred to the department, which then dickered with Christie over the price of just one tank until June 1930. Christie then failed to deliver the prototype until January 1931. The outcome of the department's testing did result in an order for seven tanks, which were delivered between October 1931 and May 1932. Four of the tanks, designated the T-3, went to the infantry, and the other three went to the cavalry, which, to the consternation of Fuqua, was also already well into its own mechanization program. Receiving the four new tanks, Fuqua impatiently called for the T-3's standardization only to be thwarted again by the Ordnance Department, which pointed out defects in the design and called for an extensive period of further tests.[30]

From then on, the situation deteriorated rapidly. Relations between Christie and the Ordnance Department became acrimonious. Moreover, by then the inventor's attention had become focused on yet another new tank design, and he all but lost interest in the T-3. At the same time, the cavalry dropped its interest in the Christie tank, finding it too heavy, too expensive, and its fighting compartment too small. A directive from the War Department in favor of a lighter and less expensive tank then ended the infantry's efforts to standardize the T-3. But while the army's contacts with Christie all but disappeared, the infantry continued to favor the convertible-tank idea until well into the second half of the 1930s.

In the meantime, the development of the Ti-E1, along with developments in Great Britain, triggered a sudden flurry of interest in 1928 in a concept called a "mechanized force." The mechanized-force concept is discussed more fully in the next chapter, but, briefly, it involved the idea of creating a totally mechanized and largely autonomous combined-arms unit to be used for long-range missions, such as flanking movements or seizing and holding vital strategic positions for regular units to occupy later. In the United States an experimental mechanized force was created in 1928, but while it generated a degree of excitement, no funds were made available for further development until the middle of 1930. A mechanized unit was then created and stationed at Camp Knox, Kentucky, but was disbanded in May 1931 after Chief of Staff MacArthur assigned the development of mechanization to both the infantry and the cavalry.

Fuqua initially took a positive attitude toward the idea of a mechanized force. Nearly all the personnel and equipment used by the experimental unit in 1928 were loaned to the force by the infantry. Fuqua's attitude remained positive when the new mechanized force was created in 1930. Yet by early 1931, he increasingly began to see it as a rival and a competitor. Initially, his major concern was that the existence of the mechanized force would make it even harder for the infantry to get the tanks he so desperately wanted. But as his staff did further research, he began to see the force as a threat to the infantry's control of tanks and their development. Thus, beginning in March 1931, he began peppering the chief of staff with protests regarding the existence of the mechanized force as an independent organization that could gain control over tank development, stating in one communication, "It is unbelievable that a small contingent such as the mechanized force, equipped and trained for a special mission, should take over the development of types of equipment and weapons for the army at large."[31]

During all this time, Fuqua continued to press for more tanks. He was frustrated no such funding for the infantry was included in the War Department budget for fiscal year 1931. He then asked that enough money be put into the budget for fiscal year 1932 to purchase twenty-four tanks, which would be enough to begin studying tactics. His request was disallowed by the War Department. Fuqua then asked for at least five tanks, enough to outfit a platoon that could carry out some tactical exercises, pointing out that if this was denied, the infantry would be unable to carry out any tactical exercises until 1934. But instead, the War Department ordered the seven T-3 tanks noted above, with four to go to infantry but only for further tests of the design.[32] In addition, Fuqua discovered in early 1933 that the Ordnance Department pointedly did not include any provision for infantry tanks in its five-year plan for 1935–40.[33]

Things then changed dramatically. At the end of April 1933, after the War Department finally lost confidence in Christie, it ordered that all future development efforts be restricted to creating a light tank suitable for both the infantry and the cavalry.[34] This demand was enthusiastically endorsed by Major General Edward Croft, the new chief of infantry. Croft was entirely opposed to the two-tank concept that the infantry had followed during the previous thirteen years. He saw the medium tank being of possible use in a mass attack carried out by an army command but felt that his branch should focus solely on the tank as an infantry-support weapon allotted to the division. Like Fuqua, Croft was deeply concerned that the infantry was not getting any tanks. He felt that the main reason for this was a search for perfection that led to the production of one prototype after another but no production of tanks for the user arms. As he stated at one point, "The impression that I have gotten through reading volumes on tank discussion—an impression which after six months in office amounts almost virtually to a conviction—is that there has been entirely too much talk on, and too little getting of, tanks."[35] He hoped that the development of an adequate and inexpensive light tank could quickly lead to standardization and production. Croft was also aware of the developments in antitank weapons that were, to an increasing degree, shifting the balance of power on the battlefield back in the direction of defense. Feeling that it was hopeless to try to armor a tank to meet these developments, he preferred to have a large number of inexpensive tanks and accept casualties. He also opposed the Christie wheel-and-track concept. Croft, therefore, called on the Infantry Board and the Tank School to develop specifications for a light tank weighing seven and a half tons or less.[36]

The board and school complied with the chief of infantry's request, though only with the greatest reluctance. By the middle of August, the Ordnance Department had sent Croft a set of specifications for a new light tank, the T-2. This, finally, precipitated a near-confrontation between the general and his tank experts at Fort Benning. Croft had given the Infantry Board a long letter listing his reasons for focusing solely on a light tank. On August 25 the president of the board, Colonel F. L. Munson, responded with a detailed protest against both Croft's plan and the April directive from the War Department. Munson stated that the board still favored the two-tank concept, but if the budget allowed only one, they felt that it "should be the one that had been service tested and recommended for standardization by the testing and using service. That tank is the T-3 (Christie) Medium." Munson then went on to refute the arguments used by the War Department against the Christie while emphasizing the importance of a medium tank in frontal assaults.[37]

The quarrel widened in September. Croft tended to blame the Infantry Board for the fact that the development of tanks seemed to lead endlessly from one prototype to another because it continued to impose modification after modification during and after the development of a prototype. Therefore, he declared that the responsibilities of the board were limited to providing specifications to the Ordnance Department, otherwise, infantry officers were not to interfere in the work of the department.[38] The board responded with a lengthy and detailed study of the entire history of tank development in the infantry, emphasizing the debacle in 1928 when the T-1, designed without participation by infantry representatives, appeared with the engine in the front instead of in the rear. Regarding collaboration with the Ordnance Department, the report stated crisply, "It is also reasonable to assume that no designer whose point of view is primarily that of a mechanical engineer can be expected to design a satisfactory tank without constant collaboration with an associate who understands thoroughly the tactical features essential for its employment in combat." The report then went on to detail the desirable features of the Christie T-3 and refute objections to it.[39] By the end of the year, the tank experts seemed to have prevailed, and the quarrel came to an end. Croft's office issued a new policy paper regarding tanks, now embracing the two-tank concept, calling for both a light and a medium tank, and endorsing the convertible Christie model as the desired medium type.[40]

In April 1934 the situation regarding tanks for the infantry changed dramatically in two interrelated ways. First, Congress approved a War Department request for well over $2 million to provide the infantry with thirty-six tanks, eighteen light and eighteen medium, enough for two tank companies. That same month Croft and other officers from his office witnessed the test of several models at the Aberdeen Proving Grounds in Maryland. Croft was sufficiently impressed with what he saw to push for getting more of the same tanks rather than losing more time with redesigns, arguing, "If the Infantry is to get tanks it is essential to get *now* what is available *now*.[41]

There were four tank models tested at Aberdeen: a version of the older Christie medium tank, now labeled the T3-E2; the T-4, which was also a convertible medium tank; the T-5, a tracked medium tank designed chiefly for the cavalry; and the T-2, a light tank. Of the four, Croft favored the T-4 as a medium and the T-2, the only light tank tested. At the same time, the infantry was finally losing interest in convertible tanks, whose main advantage was strategic mobility. A track tank could not move great distances without wearing out treads, so that they had to be carried to combat locations on specially designed carriers. But when it began to appear that they could be transported by rail so that carriers might not be needed, the strategic issue began to fade. Greater emphasis was now given to tactical combat abilities, where, it was felt, the all-track vehicles had an advantage. Hence, by the end of the year, the infantry had come to favor the T-4, but only as an all-track vehicle.[42]

The following year, 1935, was even better for Croft and the infantry. A test model of the new light tank was delivered in November 1934 and received Croft's enthusiastic approval. Its top road speed was between thirty and forty miles an hour, which approached that of the Christie tanks, and as a tracked vehicle, it was ready for immediate combat on arrival..[43] A year later, in November 1935, the infantry was on schedule to receive fifty-four light tanks and eighteen medium tanks during 1936.[44] There were, however, troubling concerns. The branch was repeatedly reminded that tanks were expensive as was their maintenance, so units were requested to refrain from using them at maximum speed to reduce wear and tear.[45] Far more important, there was concern that the armor, especially on the light tanks, was inadequate. Croft, of course, felt that the pace of development of antitank weapons was such that tanks would never have fully adequate armor. Yet he also adhered to the traditional view that the principal mission of light tanks was to assist the infantry in the advance rather than to lead the advance. These vehicles, therefore, would work in cooperation with advancing infantry units in cleaning up pockets of resistance, meaning they would be less likely to face anything but .30-caliber rifle or machine-gun fire. For all this, tanks that were light, fast, cheap, and plentiful were needed, while taking casualties was to be expected.[46]

The first eighteen of the new light tanks arrived at Fort Benning in late March 1936. The Infantry School had already been informed by Croft that, upon their arrival, the school should give the highest priority to a study of the "organization, drill, and tactics appropriate for this weapon."[47] By the middle of May, the Department of Experiment had thoroughly tested one of the T-2s, and while several problems were uncovered, both the department and the Infantry Board considered it suitable for infantry use. At the same time, the board began a full study that would allow it to create the regulations for tank use. Croft hoped that, in doing so, the board could also start creating a body of men with significant familiarity with tanks who could later be transferred to units getting tanks. But he was still concerned that a complete set of regulations probably could not be written until the infantry had a full battalion of fifty-four tanks with which to conduct tactical training and experimental exercises. Such numbers were not expected until the end of the year.[48]

On the surface, 1937 also looked like a good year. By the end of October, the branch had 246 light tanks, either on hand or to be delivered, and eighteen of the new T-4 medium tanks.[49] It also had a new chief of infantry, Major General George A. Lynch, who adhered to the traditional view of infantry leadership regarding tanks to an almost exaggerated degree. Within months of coming into office, he told the commandant of the Infantry School that, in the instruction given in its courses, "the use of infantry tanks in close support of other infantry troops should be stressed." Lynch then went on to add: "Tanks should be kept out of action until definite resistance has been located. They should be launched against definite objectives and promptly supported by foot troops. Upon the arrival of such foot troops the tanks should be withdrawn and assembled in the rear." He also made it clear that infantry tanks were to be considered organic to infantry units and not be used for massed assault by a special organization.[50]

But 1937 became most notable for the setbacks confronting the infantry's tank program. The first of these was continued and growing concern about the vulnerability of light tanks to evolving antitank weapons, a matter of critical concern since infantry doctrine was based on light tanks. The initial concern was that the 5/8-inch armor of the T-2 was sufficient against .30-caliber rifle fire but not against the .50-caliber machine guns increasingly being used as an antitank weapon. Moreover, by 1937, it was clear that newer and even more powerful weapons were emerging to the point that the Ordnance Department estimated that three inches of armor would be necessary to offer protection against these arms.[51]

Along the same line, the continuing experience of the Spanish Civil War (1936–39) produced disquieting concerns about the viability of the entire concept of light tanks. In a major "restudy" of the role of tanks in warfare, called for by Chief of Staff Craig, his assistant chief of staff for operations and training, Brigadier General George P. Tyner, reported:

> From the viewpoint of material, the light tank . . . armed only with a machinegun has been found to be not adapted to the attack of an organized defense position. In the contest between gun and armor, the antitank gun, for the present at least, has gained the upper hand. The lesson which has been drawn from the operations in Spain is to increase the armor and armament of the tank rather than its speed. . . . The offensive power of an armored unit lies in the firepower, speed, and armor protection of its vehicles. . . . [O]f the three, fire power is the most important, for it is firepower that determines the outcome of combat not only against ground troops but also against other mechanized forces.[52]

The Infantry Board was also coming to the same conclusion. While it believed that there were still uses for the light tank, by the fall of 1937, the board began to see the medium tank as infantry's main armored weapon. Yet far earlier, in February, the board, after considerable tests, determined that it could not endorse the new T-4 for standardization or for any use other than training. Fortunately, the Ordnance Department had already begun the design of a new medium tank, the T-5, in 1936, and a wooden prototype was available in the summer of 1937. But after successful tests, that model did not reach production until 1939. So, at the same time that development of newer antitank weapons seemed to make the infantry's T-2s obsolete, the fact that the T-4 was considered unsatisfactory meant that the infantry did not have a medium tank either.

Finally, the infantry began to face the threat of losing control of tanks altogether with the major revival of the mechanized-force concept among the top leaders in the General Staff. This arose in 1935 when Craig, as chief of staff, showed considerable interest in the idea. Army maneuvers in 1936 tended to reinforce this, prompting Craig's assignment to Assistant Chief of Staff Tyner to provide him with the "comprehensive restudy" of the role of tanks in warfare mentioned earlier. Tyner's lengthy and wide-ranging report covered a variety of issues related to both tanks and aviation, including the mechanized force. Of that, Tyner observed: "The concept of a mechanized force is generally accepted by all European Armies. . . . All foreign armies have organized separate tank units under General Headquarters reserve for allotment to larger units to be employed on fronts where strongly organized resistance must be overcome in order to regain the momentum of the attack." He then went on to argue, "Experience has shown that the older arms will fight in their traditional way and that except for the mechanized reconnaissance detachments of the Cavalry, mechanization can be carried on only through what is, in effect if not in name, a new arm." Tyner also noted that some felt that the chief reason MacArthur had abandoned the concept in 1931 was conflict between the branches and, especially, the opposition of the infantry to assignment of tanks to the new force.[53]

Despite Tyner's rather obvious enthusiasm for the concept of a mechanized force, he did not go so far as to advocate creating one. He cited several problems the attempt would entail noting, also, that such an action would require legislating an amendment to the National Defense Act, which could cause conflicts and open opposition from the "interested arms." Yet he did recommend several policy changes that would amount to a gradual move in the direction of a mechanized force. In particular, he proposed eliminating the tank companies assigned to infantry divisions and assigning them to a single infantry regiment, which would become a mechanized unit to eventually be equipped with medium tanks. In doing so, Tyner also expressed the growing lack of confidence within the General Staff in the light tank and the idea of it as an effective support for the infantry in its advance, which was the heart of the infantry tank doctrine. He also advocated the creation of a self-contained "mechanized division" comprised entirely of mechanized cavalry units. This signaled the growing feeling in the staff that the tank was a cavalry rather than an infantry weapon.[54] Few of Tyner's recommendations were acted upon, but his "restudy" was a strong indication of the direction in which the wind was blowing.

During 1938 and 1939, the infantry, along with the rest of the army's leadership, watched developments in Europe closely. Earlier, *Infantry Journal* had published two translated articles by German general Heinz Guderian on tanks and mechanized warfare.[55] But most of the attention continued to be focused on the civil war in Spain. Given the small numbers of tanks employed there, observers found it hard to draw definite conclusions, which meant that existing doctrines still went largely unchallenged. It was reported in *Infantry Journal*, that massed tank attacks, an idea getting greater attention among U.S. military leaders, were not undertaken in Spain, while "on the rare occasions when tanks had to go it alone against machine-guns and heavy weapons . . . they have usually met with disaster."[56] Thus, General Lynch continued to adhere to the traditional doctrine of tanks and infantry advancing cooperatively in two waves, with medium tanks leading to neutralize or destroy antitank weapons and light tanks following with the foot soldiers to knock out machine-gun emplacements, a position that still had expressed War Department approval.[57]

There was, instead, far greater interest shown in modifying tank design to cope with the increasing effectiveness of antitank weapons and with combat against other mechanized units. By early 1939, Lynch, responding to developments in Europe, began pressing the Ordnance Department to replace the .50-cal. machine gun that was the principal armament on the light tank with a 37-mm gun with armor-piercing capability. At the same time, the department had already begun developing a new version of the T-5, the T5-E1, that would carry a 75-mm gun. At Lynch's request, the Infantry Board studied the preliminary plans of the department and approved them with the stipulation that, following developments in Germany, the tank's gun be mounted in a turret.[58]

During these last several years, the infantry also began giving more attention to the development of its own antitank weapons. Experiments were carried out with mines and guns as early as 1926.[59] In 1928 General Allen, as chief of infantry, responded to the development of the fast tank by ordering tests of existing weapons for antitank defense. At that time, it was assumed that the 37-mm gun would be the army's principle antitank weapon. With the assumption that warfare would be carried out by fast light tanks, the lightness and flexibility of an antitank gun and the training of men to hit a moving target rather than the armor-piercing capacity of weapons was the main concern.[60]

Interest in antitank warfare increased considerably in the second half of the 1930s, with articles appearing on the use of mines and overall tactics.[61] Only in

1937, however, was attention given to developing new weapons. By that time, the army was far behind other armies in the development of specifically designed antitank guns. Within a few months, the Ordnance Department had developed its first specifically designed antitank weapon, a modified 37-mm gun mounted on a carriage designed to facilitate shooting at a moving target.[62] Although there was growing recognition that something more powerful was needed, given tank developments elsewhere in the world, the 37-mm gun remained the army's main antitank weapon through 1939.[63]

By the end of the 1930s, the leadership of the General Staff was rapidly losing patience with the seeming lack of progress in the development of tanks within both the cavalry and the infantry. With everyone's gaze fixed on Europe and the impressive development of armored divisions in countries there and elsewhere, it seemed increasingly imperative that the development of mechanized warfare in America be rapidly accelerated. The creation of a specific armored arm seemed more promising than allowing the existing branches free reign to develop tanks and doctrines themselves. In his final report as chief of staff, written in the early summer of 1939, General Craig lamented what he saw as the disparate development of mechanized forces in the United States, calling for a focus on a "powerful mechanized organization to be used when opportunity offers a decisive attack element." This endorsement of using tanks in a massed attack was contrary to the infantry's central doctrines.[64] Lynch sensed this movement toward the creation of an armored force as virtually a separate combat arm. In an article written for *Infantry Journal* just before the German invasion of Poland, the chief of infantry attacked the idea of a separate armored force: "There is much evidence to support the belief that in most cases tank corps had their origin in personnel difficulties. There was difficulty in adapting officers and men trained in non-mechanized infantry and cavalry operation to the needs of mechanized units. This difficulty certainly no longer exists in our services."[65]

But time ran out. The impressive performance of German armored divisions in Poland in the fall of 1939, then again in the invasion of France in the spring of 1940, as well as the performance of mechanized units in maneuvers in America convinced army leadership that armored development in the United States needed to be centralized in a single armored force. This force was created in the spring of 1940, thereby ending infantry's independent involvement with mechanization.

The arguments in favor of creating the armored force tended to blame the infantry and the cavalry for the slow development of American tanks and mechanized warfare. In particular, branch rivalry and bickering, coupled with the tendency of traditional services to continue to fight in their traditional ways, were blamed for this slow development. There is some substance to these charges.

But while branch rivalry existed, it actually had little influence on the issue of mechanization except that infantry and cavalry opposed the development of the mechanized force in 1930 and 1931. Otherwise, the bickering between branches occurred mostly in the early 1930s and was occasioned chiefly by the extreme lack of financial resources.

The charge that the infantry clung to its traditional doctrines viewing tanks only as an accompanying weapon that assisted troops in their advance is closer to the mark. Infantry leaders were aware of the idea of using tanks in mass attacks to break through enemy positions but paid little attention to them. This meant that if the army wanted to develop armored divisions, it would have to do so outside the infantry. There were several causes for this conservatism on the part of the branch. The concept of an armored division severely challenged infantry's self-image as the Queen of Battles and the highly masculine self-image of its officers, for whom the weapon was always subordinate to the man. The conservatism of the army's schools, with their heavy emphasis on adherence to orthodoxy rather than innovation, was also likely a contributing factor. But the infantry was not alone in its adherence to traditional doctrine. Even in 1938 and 1939, the sessions at the Command and General Staff School dedicated to mechanized warfare taught infantry doctrine and were only beginning to adopt the principle of massed attack.[66]

On the other hand, it must be kept in mind that the introduction of mechanized weapons was a highly ambiguous development for which there was little experience to act as a guide. The experience of the world war was examined carefully but was of little value after the development of the fast tank. And it was highly unclear to U.S. military leaders what kind of war they might face in the future and the doctrines and weapons they would need to fight it. For most European powers, this was not a problem. While the American focus on a war of movement led to the emphasis on the development of light tanks, which proved to be a dead end by the late 1930s, most European countries also looked to developing light tanks. The medium tank, which would be the principal weapon of an armored division, did not begin to appear until after the Spanish Civil War had proved the vulnerability of the light version. And while the infantry may have been conservative in its adherence to traditional doctrine, it made every effort to acquire tanks and incorporate them. Finally, the principal hindrance to tank development in the United States was the highly limited appropriations allocated to the army during the entire interwar period. It was not until very late in the 1930s that the infantry began to have enough tanks on hand that it could finally begin a realistic development of doctrine.

CHAPTER 12

Mounts or Motors?

The Cavalry and Its Response to Mechanization, 1919–1939

ORLD WAR I CAUGHT American cavalry at an early stage of a major transformation. Although the branch had identified itself in a general way with the traditions of European cavalry, it nevertheless took pride in its own distinctiveness. From the U.S. point of view, European horse soldiery was a product of feudalism, which shaped it along the lines of heavy cavalry in the cuirassier tradition.[1] American cavalry, on the other hand, was seen as having grown out of democracy and the needs of the frontier so that it emerged within the dragoon tradition of mounted infantry. As such, its missions were focused on scouting, reconnaissance, and police work, and it was characterized militarily by mobility rather than shock. This vision of cavalry was reinforced by the experience of the American Civil War. Then, during the late nineteenth century, American cavalry was largely stationed on the western frontier. While there, the horsemen functioned mainly as a frontier constabulary, their military activities continuing to stress mobility rather than firepower or shock.

With the end of westward expansion at the end of the nineteenth century, cavalry began a rather dramatic change in character. These changes came slowly at first, but as the army in general shifted its orientation from constabulary duties to national defense against a possible invasion by European powers, the cavalry sought to change its role and character along the same lines. The revised branch was to be a combat force, capable of delivering a decisive blow in battle. To do this, the cavalry began giving up its western orientation and outlooks and, instead, began remodeling itself along European lines. Officers went to Europe, and especially to France, to study European techniques and bring them back to America.[2] The Cavalry School at Fort Riley was reorganized and renamed the Mounted Service School, with classes heavily devoted to European equitation and modern methods of horse care.[3] At the same time, there was a move to balance the emphasis on mobility with a new stress on firepower. After some discussion, the traditional light carbine was replaced with a rifle that would make the dismounted cavalryman the equivalent of the infantry soldier in terms of fire effectiveness. Later, during the world war, the machine gun was introduced, further increasing firepower and reinforcing a growing tendency within the branch toward fighting dismounted.[4]

The world war, however, was a disaster for cavalry, both in the United States and in western Europe. Although there were a few notable cavalry encounters in 1914 and later in peripheral areas in the Middle East, horse soldiers saw little action in the war on the western front. As William Odom points out, only one of the seventeen cavalry regiments in the United States in 1917 was actually sent to France, and it saw relatively little action.[5] With the widespread feeling that the trench warfare of the western front represented modern industrial warfare and the pattern for future conflicts, this inactivity further contributed to a growing military and public perception that cavalry's day was passing. The Superior Board, which met after the war to evaluate the lessons learned during the conflict, concluded that "the mounted combat of large bodies of Cavalry is probably a thing of the past."[6] The army's commitment to the doctrine of open warfare, as expressed in *Field Service Regulations* of 1923, clearly relegated the cavalry to subordinate roles: "Cavalry executes the missions of reconnaissance, counter reconnaissance, and security in the service of large units and delivers combat in the execution of these missions."[7]

Cavalrymen were very much aware of the prevailing sentiment against their branch, which led to considerable demoralization and despair, especially in the years immediately following the world war. The cavalry was reduced from seventeen regiments to fourteen, with just 20,000 men, by the National Defense Act of 1920 and then reduced again over the next several years to less than 10,000.[8] Yet there was also a sense that it had greater problems and causes for concern than did other branches. In 1926 the chief of cavalry told the graduating class at the Cavalry School: "There is no doubt that Cavalry is on the defensive at the present time. . . . [W]e are fighting for our lives."[9] The branch's chief problem was the widespread public view that the last war had rendered it obsolete. The opening line in a poem published in *Cavalry Journal* in 1922 put it succinctly, "'Tis said that Cavalry is dead."[10]

Much of cavalry development in the 1920s and 1930s was shaped by responses to, or at least an awareness of, this crisis. One path was for cavalrymen to ignore the reality around them and withdraw into their own professionally prescribed world. A major part of this effort lay in reconstructing the experience of the world war in a way that either placed emphasis on the few areas in which cavalrymen had been significant contributors or to argue that the combat, especially on the western front, had been an anomaly and was not really representative of modern warfare.[11] In addition, as David Johnson has pointed out, the branch stressed its service in patrolling the Mexican border, a mission for which horse soldiers were particularly suited.[12]

Surprisingly, the cavalry made little effort to recapture public support or rebuild its own morale with an enthusiastic embrace of the citizen army created by the National Defense Act. It did not ignore the citizen components. The branch maintained eleven ROTC units and ten CMTC units, while around a hundred cavalry officers served with Organized Reserve units and another fifty with National Guard units.[13] But these activities attracted little attention within the branch. Part of the reason for this was the sense that personnel reductions of the early 1920s had made a focus anywhere difficult.[14] Perhaps the most important reason for its relative indifference to the citizen army was that, early on, the branch sought to be seen as the nation's readiness force. As the editor of *Cavalry Journal* put it, "Practically alone, among all the land forces available at the outbreak of hostilities, the cavalry need not await an augmentation of her force to be effective."[15]

Yet despite this persistent tendency by some cavalrymen to look inward and to deny outside reality, the major responses of the branch to the perceived existential threats were constructive and professional. Of these, two were most significant in terms of shaping the organizational development of the cavalry and creating a more consistent outlook to build cohesion among its officers. The first of these, following the trends in the other services, was to build a new cohesive sense of branch identity oriented around both the concepts of the new academic military professionalism as well as a new set of tangible branch institutions. Cavalry had several of the latter which were, for the most part, similar in form and function to those of other branches but contributed to giving cavalry identity a particular character.

One of these institutions was *Cavalry Journal.* This publication was the oldest by far of the military branch journals in the United States, having been established in 1885. It was created by the Cavalry Association to be a "professional and scientific magazine" that was to support the overall objectives of the association, which were "to disseminate knowledge of the military art and science, to promote the professional improvement of its members, and to preserve and foster the spirit, the traditions, and soldiery of the cavalry of the Army of the United

States."[16] The mild—and largely unseen—internal contradiction in this commitment to modernizing the cavalry profession while preserving the character of its traditions continued to dominate the *Journal* all during the interwar years. It also illustrated what may have been the greatest challenge facing the branch in that period. The *Journal* was published in the office of the chief of cavalry. Although the chief felt free to suggest directions for it to develop and read over the articles selected for publication, the *Journal* remained reasonably open to diverse views, particularly in the sensitive area of mechanization.[17] Yet it was also committed to building branch unity by disseminating among the faithful an optimistic vision of the present and future worth of the cavalry.

The organization seen as most responsible for giving the branch its identity and direction of development was the Office of the Chief of Cavalry. There had been a growing demand within the branch for the creation of such an office for nearly ten years, and the achievement of that goal in 1920 in a period of overall despair was greeted as a virtual deliverance.[18] The chief had a lengthy and imposing list of responsibilities but only limited abilities to carry them out. He was to advise on all matters related to his branch, to direct all of its special service schools and boards, to formulate tactical doctrine, and to supervise training. In addition, he had control over the assignment, transfer, and examination of all officers within the cavalry.[19] Yet the office was a small one. Outside of the chief himself, it was staffed by just eight or nine other officers and limited clerical help.[20] Moreover, the chief controlled little outside the special service schools. Cavalry troops were under the tactical and administrative command of corps-area commanders. In Washington the chief had no direct access to the chief of staff or to the General Staff. He could often effectively oppose policies seen as harmful to his branch but was far less able to serve as advocate for those desired. Still, the fact that the chief of cavalry was a major general with a distinguished career as a soldier and a horseman gave the office great visibility and promoted the idea that the cavalry was a coherent organization headed by a powerful officer. As such, the office was the source of much hope within the branch.

Outside of the Office of the Chief of Cavalry, there were two other commands that were distinctly cavalry and served as focal points of activity related to the development of the branch. One of these was the First Cavalry Division at Fort Bliss, Texas. During the interwar period, the First Cavalry Division was the manifestation of the new commitment of the branch to an active and decisive combat role. The heart of this doctrine was that cavalry should act in large bodies such as divisions and even corps. The role of the First Cavalry Division was to develop through experiment and application new tactical ideas of how to act in this new concept. As such, it was the focal point for much attention within the cavalry, with its maneuvers attracting observers from all over the branch. Moreover, since the division dealt with experimental ideas and equipment, it had its own panel, the First Cavalry Division Board, to organize such tests and report on results.[21] Yet the division was also a tactical organization, which meant it was under the control of the Eighth Corps Area commander, so that the chief of cavalry had no command authority over it. Correspondence between the division and the chief traveled a long and circuitous route through the corps-area commander's headquarters and the Adjutant General's Office. As a result, cavalry activities at Fort Bliss, though highly visible, were not always well coordinated with those elsewhere in the branch.[22]

Despite the importance of the chief of cavalry and the First Cavalry Division in giving both direction and a sense of branch tangibility, the other command and the principal force shaping cavalry identity and fostering a common professional outlook among its officers was the Cavalry School at Fort Riley in Kansas. Like most of the other special service schools, it was successful in terms of imbuing its graduates with respect for a common doctrine and with an enthusiasm to spread what they learned throughout the branch.[23] The reasons for the Cavalry School's success were the same as at its army counterparts. The academic program appeared to be rigorous but was quite accessible, Fort Riley offered students the support of a largely self-contained military community with an active social life, and the school guided student officers in the development of an attractive professional self-image linked to the cavalry. Where the Cavalry School differed from the others was that the horse was central to all aspects of that education.

Fort Riley was a western post, and its association with control of Native Americans gave it a distinct identification with cavalry. In 1887, with the rise of the new professionalism in the army, General Philip Sheridan, as commanding general of the U.S. Army, ordered the creation of a School of Application for Cavalry and Light Artillery at Fort Riley. The school opened in 1893, and its subsequent history reflected the developments within the cavalry as a whole. In 1901, as part of a movement to reorganize and professionalize the military-education system, it underwent a major transformation that made it clearly more professional. As a school of application, it had been responsible for giving junior officers a basic orientation to their duties. This responsibility was now rapidly transferred to garrison schools, and the Fort Riley institution was mandated to teach the new ideas regarding equitation prevailing in the armies of Europe. This adjustment took several years, as graduates of the school were sent to Europe, particularly to the Cavalry School at Saumur, France, to learn the new European techniques. These officers then returned to teach these methods at Fort Riley. To recognize this change, the school was renamed the Mounted Service School in 1907 and acquired its motto, *Mobilitate Vigemus* (we thrive by mobility). By then, its entire curriculum was focused on equitation and the various arts and crafts associated with caring for horses. In 1916, under the pressure of the Mexican campaign, the school was closed and remained shuttered for the world war. But by this time, it had earned an enviable reputation as a center for the most modern ideas about military riding and the care of horses in the country.[24]

When the school reopened in the fall of 1919 it underwent a second radical transformation, introducing a major academic component similar to that found in the other special service schools. It also underwent another name change, from the Mounted Service School to the Cavalry School. Administrators and faculty had to start from scratch in building the new curriculum, making the first several years rather hectic.[25] As was the case with the other special services schools, the Cavalry School was mandated to teach three major courses: a basic course for entering second lieutenants, a troop officers' course for captains, and an advanced course for field-grade officers. This resulted in a student population many times larger than before the war.[26] In addition, the students came from a variety of backgrounds, including recently promoted enlisted war veterans, many of whom were not convinced of the value or credibility of the school and did not take their academic work seriously.[27] By 1922, however, most of these problems were resolved, and the Cavalry School had established an organization and curriculum that lasted the rest of the interwar period.

The academic part of the program was rigorous, and the approach taken was more like that at the Command and General Staff School at Fort Leavenworth than was the case in the other special service schools. It was dominated by the applicatory method.[28] Grades were based on performance on map and terrain problems, and that performance was measured according to an approved school solution.[29] At the same time, however, the courses were still taught in a way that made them readily accessible to students.[30]

And as was the case with the other special service schools, there was a Cavalry Board attached to the school associating the latter with progress in the branch. The board was made up of the commandant of the school, the assistant commandant, and three other officers. It was the official clearinghouse for all new ideas regarding cavalry, especially equipment.[31] In addition, the board, working with members of the faculty at the school, wrote dozens of training pamphlets and made recommendations on doctrine and organization. And even though it rejected four out of five ideas presented to it, the panel was still seen as a modernizing force.[32] On the other hand, while the board and the school sought to be progressive forces within the cavalry, they were also committed temperamentally and by their way of operations to an evolutionary vision of change.[33] The Cavalry School and the Cavalry Board may have been eager sponsors of modernization, but they were generally not proponents of anything like a revolution.

Furthermore, despite the commitment of the school to a modernization of the branch, the most dominating force at Fort Riley in terms of both the academic training and the professional ideals promulgated was the horse. Nearly half of the hours in the academic program were devoted to equitation and other issues related to riding or care of horses. A student officer could expect to be in the saddle for at least two or more hours each day and in stables for several more. In addition, on entering the school, students were given an unbroken horse that they were expected to turn into a trained cavalry mount by the time of graduation. Finally, graduation itself was preceded by a series of equestrian exercises and competitions called June Week.[34]

The horse also dominated social life at Fort Riley. Unlike the situation at other schools, Riley had adequate quarters for officers so that poor housing was not a common bonding experience as it was at Fort Benning, Fort Sill, or Fort Monroe. Instead, the student-officer community there bonded around horses. They also enjoyed an active social life, with weekly dances, bridge games, and frequent dinner parties, most of which were formal.[35] Even here, the horse was nearly always present. At parties, conversations were likely to be about horses.[36] In addition, wives were given riding lessons, and on weekends families would often be found riding together.[37] The school itself was also active in promoting this horse-centered social life, sponsoring several foxhunts each week. Finally, the cavalry more than shared the same obsession with polo as the other combat branches. Indeed, the sport was a passion that united and defined most American cavalrymen.[38] The *Cavalry Journal* devoted a separate section in each issue to polo. All major posts had teams, and games were followed with great intensity.[39] Yet it seems clear that, for most cavalrymen, polo was associated much more with horsemanship as an attribute of military professionalism than it was with horses. Many cavalry officers who were leaders in the move to mechanize their branch were also passionate polo players.[40]

While providing cavalry officers with a common sense of branch identity and perspective was important in building the branch, the most significant response to charges of obsolescence was the development of a new strategic and tactical doctrine to make cavalry clearly relevant to the conduct of modern warfare. This was a difficult task. There had been little cavalry action in the world war that could give guidance in developing doctrine, while America's cavalry tradition embraced an ambiguously wide range of missions. As a result, some discussion of alternative missions appeared in *Cavalry Journal* in the early 1920s, including ideas regarding deep raids, wide flanking movements, and others. But cavalry officers with wartime experience in France had developed their own recommendations regarding doctrine, and these soon prevailed.[41] Their basic idea, and the idea that would come to dominate branch doctrine for the entire interwar period, was that the cavalry should form the arm of decision in combat. This did not mean that cavalrymen would be giving up any of their old roles, but it did mean, as one influential cavalry leader put it in 1920, "to assist the infantry and other arms to gain a favorable decision in battle is *the most important use of cavalry.*"[42] This reflected not only the branch's movement in the direction of the heavy-cavalry tradition that was already well underway even before the world war but also the cavalry's inability to find anything in the experience of the war itself to suggest a change in direction.[43]

The Chief of Cavalry's Office took the lead in developing these new roles, some of which were at variance with the army's prevailing infantry-based doctrine of open warfare. In drafting *Training Regulations 425-105*, the basic guide to cavalry tactics published in 1922, the office provided cavalrymen with far more central combat roles. As the regulations stated, "Modern war emphasizes the fact that a mounted attack, exactly timed, is almost always successful and is less costly than a prolonged fire fight."[44] Cavalry officers in general felt that the trenches in France were an anomaly to rather than the harbinger of modern war, especially any defensive war fought in the United States. Hence, as was the case with most in the army, much of their discussion of tactics assumed a fluid and open combat situation. Nevertheless, the frontal assaults described in the *Training Regulations*, including "mounted attacks with extended order formations across fire swept areas," indicated that the cavalry sought a decisive role in warfare involving extended fronts.[45] A warning that commanders ought not fritter away their cavalry resources on numerous reconnaissance missions but save them for decisive opportunities showed that the branch was giving priority to its combat mission.[46]

The combat mission envisioned, however, required not only a significant augmentation of firepower but also the introduction of shock tactics, which had been almost foreign to the nineteenth-century American cavalry tradition. Much of the reforms of the 1920s and 1930s revolved around building up the firepower and shock capacity of cavalry units. The growing interest in shock quickly led cavalry officers to an interest in tanks. Although the National Defense Act relegated tanks to the infantry and the 1923 *Field Service Regulations* did not list them as a cavalry weapon, the 1922 *Training Regulations* included a special chapter on tanks. Although that chapter was careful to point out the limitations of tanks, the authors were clearly fascinated with their capacity to augment cavalry units: "Tanks are essentially offensive weapons, acting by shock and short-range fire." They then noted several times the utility of tanks in clearing away wire, machine guns, and other obstacles to cavalry charges.[47] Hence, given their ability to endow cavalry with the firepower and shock capacity to carry out the decisive combat missions desired, tanks became of deep interest to the branch from almost the beginning of the 1920s.

Inherent in this concept that the cavalry's chief role was to act as an arm of decision were three other ideas. The first was that cavalry was to operate as a mass unit at the corps, or at least at the division, level. Leadership resisted any efforts to make cavalry units organic components of divisions or corps, hoping instead that mounted units could operate as a separate corps organic to an army command. Second, the effectiveness of cavalry units would be enhanced by significantly increasing their firepower, even at the cost of some reduction in treasured mobility.[48] Third, cavalry should be prepared to fight both mounted and dismounted as well as in combined actions.[49]

Efforts by branch leadership to introduce the organization and weapons necessary to make cavalry an arm of decision were paralleled by efforts to translate the concept into strategic and, especially, tactical principles. This was difficult, since, again, the cavalry had played no such role in the world war. Nor did cavalry experience in the American Civil War provide much guidance, since it had rarely acted as a decisive force in combat. Hence, the branch had little experiential base other than that gained from maneuvers out of which new tactical principles could be drawn. Still, the cavalry did begin to develop at least an initial conceptual basis for developing tactics for the new doctrine. The key was that horsemen had the ability to carry out mounted combat, dismounted combat, or a combination of the two.[50]

This flexibility was attractive but difficult to translate into principles. For instance, the idea of cavalry units able to ride quickly to a point, dismount, engage in fire action, remount, and then move quickly to another point seemed to provide a means of restoring tactical mobility to the battlefield. Yet the branch was unable to solve the problem of where to place the horses during dismounted action. Keeping them close to dismounted troops could expose them to fire, while removing them a safe distance seriously reduced any advantages in tactical mobility.[51] The difficulties with mounted combat were even greater. While on a theoretical level mounted action seemed synonymous with decision, it was a concept with which American cavalry had little experience and was hard to translate into viable tactical principles in modern warfare. The mounted charge was a European shock tactic, and Americans had had little experience or previous interest in emulating it.[52] Moreover, while officers were willing to argue that a man on a horse could cross an area under fire more rapidly and, therefore, more safely than a man on foot, it was still hard to translate this into tactical principles. Instead, proponents had to admit that, under modern conditions, the frontal assault could be made only in dispersed formations, which then would rob the assault of most of its shock value. Moreover, horses would still be unable to deal with barbed wire.[53]

Finally, while fighting combined mounted/dismounted actions seemed to give cavalry tactical versatility, it was, again, hard to translate this idea of combining stability with mobility into tactical principles beyond the idea of dismounted troops providing covering fire for a mounted assault.[54] On a larger scale, advocates foresaw combined action in terms of dismounted troops engaging and fixing an enemy force while mounted units engaged in a flanking action. This approach was incorporated in the Cavalry Board's publication *Tactical Principles and Logistics for Cavalry* and widely accepted in the branch.[55]

Overall, it began to become clear that it was the vulnerability of the horse that stood in the way of developing any realistic tactical approach to remodeling cavalry as the arm of decision. This led a number of officers to the idea of giving cavalry a capacity for shock action by using tanks to make the frontal assaults carried out earlier by heavy cavalry units. Tanks would be impervious to fire, allowing them to form in the compact masses needed for shock; nor would they be impeded by wire.[56] Yet this idea, which meant substituting machines for horses in carrying out what was meant to be cavalry's major mission, would finally force the branch to face its long-brewing identity crisis linked to the horse.

Although the idea of its being the arm of decision was included in the teaching at the Cavalry School almost from the beginning, it took some time to get the cavalry itself organized and armed for such a role. Original hopes to create a separate corps were dashed by the limited personnel allowed by the National Defense Act. Even then, it was thought that the cavalry would be able to create two divisions as the basis for an independent corps.[57] But the personnel reductions that followed in 1921 and 1922 dashed those hopes as well, leaving the cavalry with horsemen enough for only one division. Thus, the First Cavalry Division became the laboratory within the branch for creating a mounted force that could be decisive in combat. In addition, efforts at modernizing the cavalry began to center more and more on transforming the division into a prototype of a unit that would make the cavalry an arm of decision. These efforts with the First Cavalry Division came to dominate the development of the branch for the rest of the interwar period.

The effort to transform the First Cavalry Division into a more self-contained unit, possessing greatly increased firepower and shock capacity with the capability of independent action, began in the second half of the 1920s under the leadership of a new chief of cavalry, Major General Herbert B. Crosby. This project fit in with the vision of the development of warfare held by Crosby, who became chief of cavalry in 1926, and his staff in which the central combat role would be played by units such as the division he was designing. This concept was stated most succinctly by one member of his staff:

> All the principal countries of the world are deeply concerned in reorganizing their armies with the purpose of restoring to them that mobility of warfare which was largely lost during the World War on the western front, due to the fact that the development of all kinds of rapid firing arms outstripped measures to counteract them. Armored fighting vehicles seem at the moment to be one of the means of breaking through strongly entrenched positions and, once a break is made, the war of maneuver is restored with full play for all the existing arms.[58]

Crosby's interest in tanks was reinforced by the radical changes in design that the infantry and Ordnance Department had introduced in 1927. Observing these vehicles demonstrated, Crosby immediately saw their potential as cavalry weapons. He also attended the First Cavalry Division's maneuvers in 1927 in Texas, where armored-car units were employed for the first time, and he found them impressive as well.[59] Hence, in 1928 Crosby formed the First Armored Car Troop and recommended inclusion of a light tank company as well as an armored-car troop and antitank weapons into the First Cavalry Division.[60] His goal was to develop it into a division that would be "highly mobile" yet "powerful in battle."[61] And, while Crosby and others in the branch could see a number of ways of doing this, it was clear that the primary change would be to introduce armored fighting vehicles into the cavalry division.

Crosby was aided in all this by the determination of Major General Summerall, who began his tenure as chief of staff in 1926. In 1928 Summerall expressed his dissatisfaction with what he considered the mere tinkering going on in the branches in the face of more radical changes elsewhere in the world. Given the possibilities offered by advances in science and industry, he called for an aggressive and thorough modernization of the army.[62]

With Summerall's interest in modernization already apparent in Washington, Crosby moved quickly to take advantage of it. To do so, he worked in close partnership with Major General George Van Horn Moseley, commander of the First Cavalry Division and an officer with significant personal influence in the General Staff. By April 1927, a year before Summerall's blanket call for modernization, and responding to directives sent to other branch chiefs, Crosby offered the chief of staff a program for modernizing the First Cavalry Division. It included the replacement of the carbine with a semiautomatic rifle, the creation of an air-observation squadron, and, most important, the adoption of both an armored-car and a tank unit in the division. Within the year, he received War Department approval for funding in the 1929 budget to put a tank unit in the division [63] Crosby's work during the remainder of his tenure as chief of cavalry was focused on carrying out this major reorganization of the division. He reorganized his own staff, creating a Tactical Development Section, which would be responsible for "developments in mechanization, particularly in regard to tanks, armored cars, and in the motorization of artillery." And, even without the vehicles being assigned, he revised the division's tables of organization to include them.[64]

Crosby's program then faced a serious challenge with the rapid rise in the late 1920s of army leadership's interest in a new concept called the "mechanized force," which was to be developed as an independent combined-arms organization outside of the traditional combat arms. This interest was the product of two factors: the development of the fast tank in 1927 and experimental maneuvers by the British Army with its own recently created mechanized force at Aldershot later that year. Secretary of War Davis had attended the British maneuvers and was sufficiently impressed to call on the General Staff to develop an American mechanized force for experimental purposes.[65] The staff proceeded to do so by first undertaking a major study of the concept, which was completed in March 1928.[66] This echoed the cavalry's concept of a combat arm that would prove decisive on the battlefield by the use of shock and firepower to break through an enemy front.

Almost every major offensive operation studied in the light of the power of the defense in modern war, brings out some situation somewhere on the front of a large unit, corps or army, which could best be solved by a self-contained, highly mobile mechanized unit of great striking power and of limited holding power.... Viewed as a corps unit such a force must have sufficient size and penetrating power to strike, in an appropriate situation, the most important blow which is to be struck on the front of that army corps. It must be able to go through to a region beyond the placements of hostile corps artillery, to disorganize and deny action to the hostile corps reserve. Its penetration must be of a depth and frontage which shall, as a result, facilitate and lead to the decided advance of the corps as a whole.

While declaring that a mechanized force would be a unique entity not tied to a branch, the study also noted: "The employment of the force more nearly parallels that of cavalry than of any of the existing branches. . . . The cavalry viewpoint and characteristics of mind is essential to the proper development of such a force."[67]

At the same time, the development of the new tank and the British experiment inspired considerable excitement throughout the army. By the middle of 1928, a flurry of articles appeared in service journals enthusiastically discussing aspects of the mechanized force and the potential uses of the new weapons. There were several reasons for this excitement, some personal and some institutional. Regarding the latter, some officers recognized that the United States had entered the machine age, and in the words of one officer, the "army must cut its cloth accordingly."[68] The enthusiasm of the American press and public opinion reinforced this view. But what was most attractive about the idea of a mechanized force built around the new fast tank was the seeming promise that it would restore mobility to warfare.

The General Staff study and the discussions in the service journals covered the major issues associated with the use of fast tanks and a mechanized force, and there was consensus on most points. Nearly all agreed that the major asset of the new tank, its speed and mobility, would be wasted if it served merely as an accompanying weapon in infantry divisions. There was also agreement that a mechanized force should be organized as an independent and self-contained unit capable of using its mobility to seize and temporarily hold targets of opportunity or in flanking movements to harass an enemy's rear areas. There was also general agreement that, for a mechanized forced to be an independent and self-contained unit, it had to be a combined-arms command with its own infantry, cavalry, artillery, and support units, all of which being completely mechanized. The only area in which there was less discussion and consensus was the issue of how such a force would fit into the overall structure of the army. While there was considerable agreement that in operational terms the unit would best be assigned to a corps or even army command, the question of whether it would be a new force such as the air corps or instead would be developed under the auspices of one of the traditional combat branches was largely ignored. Only the General Staff study dealt with this, noting gingerly that, while the National Defense Act of 1920 had given the control of tanks to the infantry, the tactical and strategic missions for which a mechanized force would be best suited were those of the cavalry.[69]

The Experimental Mechanized Force called for by the secretary of war came into official existence on July 1, 1928, at Fort George Meade, Maryland. It was a combined-arms force made up of infantry foot units and two infantry tank battalions, an armored-car platoon lent by the cavalry, a field-artillery battery pulled by trucks, an air-observation squadron, and units from the Signal Corps, the Medical Corps, and the engineers. While tasked with carrying out a variety of tests related to both minor tactics and performance of weapons, it had no budget support. At the time that Summerall ordered the creation of this force, he also ordered the creation of a board made up of representatives from all the combat branches that would "look at the creation of a mechanized force within the current budget." The board eventually concluded, "At the present time the development of tank and weapons has not progressed to the point where we could be justified in asking Congress for funds to procure the number of modern tanks and weapons necessary for a test as extreme as the one contemplated." The report was shown to President Hoover with a request that funds be put in the 1930 fiscal-year budget, but the request was turned down. The General Staff was finally able to include a small sum in the 1931 fiscal-year budget.[70] The delay in getting budget support meant that the development of any permanent mechanized force was put on hold for over a year. Then, in the fall of 1930, a new unit was assembled at Fort Eustis, Virginia. The life of this force was short, however, as opposition to it built up in the branches. The infantry initially had supported the idea, but coming to see the mechanized force as a challenge to its monopoly on tanks and, like the air corps, as another competitor for scarce resources, it began to oppose the concept vigorously. Crosby, also, initially expressed support for the idea of a mechanized force but wanted to channel its development along lines parallel to his own efforts to develop the First Cavalry Division as a force of decision. In doing so, he sought to identify the mechanized force with cavalry and to minimize its threat as a rival. When possible, Crosby also drew attention to the parallels between the Experimental Mechanized Force and the cavalry, cautioning against a radical mechanization.[71]

Crosby's tenure as chief of cavalry came to an end in 1930. Like many other cavalry officers in the 1920s, he felt that the future survival of the branch was dependent on its transformation into a hard-hitting force that could be decisive in essentially fluid and mobile forms of warfare. His objective was to begin the transformation of the First Cavalry Division into such a force chiefly by initiating the process of mechanization. But mindful as well of the institutional needs of the cavalry, he sought to carry out this initial makeover in a cautiously methodical and evolutionary manner that would leave the branch and the traditions holding it together intact.

Within the context of cavalry as a branch, Crosby's evolutionary approach had much to commend it. But within larger contexts, the rapid mechanization of American and other Western societies and the military transformations elsewhere made the pace of change generated by his efforts to contain the process of mechanization within the cavalry too slow. This had already become a source of frustration to many in the General Staff in the late 1920s, and consequently, they began to consider means of mechanizing the army, such as the mechanized force, outside the constraints of existing branches. The inherent tension between the imperatives to carry out mechanization in a timely fashion and the need to carry it out in a manner that would not be dangerously disruptive to branch organizations would come to a head in the ensuing decade.

Crosby was succeeded as chief of cavalry by Major General Guy V. Henry Jr. Henry initially planned to continue the main lines of Crosby's efforts to make the cavalry an arm of decision by reinforcing traditional horse units with mechanized forces. He also followed his predecessor's policy of assuring an impatient General Staff of the branch's commitment to mechanization while pointing out the similarities between cavalry and the proposed mechanized force. In a personal letter to Chief of Staff MacArthur, Henry stated, "The general role of cavalry as conceived in America and that of an independent mechanized force is essentially the same, but for open warfare conditions neither arm can take the place of the other." He then mentioned his intention to continue the development of the branch in this direction by adding more armored cars and even greater firepower to cavalry units.[72]

Henry also carried out several practical measures aimed at mechanization. He experimented with substituting trucks for horse-and mule-drawn wagons to speed up transport. He also continued the development of radio communications as introduced by Crosby.[73] Most importantly, Henry sought to increase further the shock and firepower of cavalry units. He continued to push the development of an armored, tracked cross-country vehicle with a high degree of mobility that could serve with cavalry units.[74] The chief also began giving attention to the need for cavalry units to develop an antitank capacity, looking to a pack-mounted.50-cal. machine gun with armor-piercing bullets and new 37-mm. guns in the division pool as answers.[75]

But Henry soon realized that his hope that the cavalry and a mechanized force could coexist in some form of symbiotic relationship was unrealistic. More and more cavalry officers were coming to see a separate mechanized fore as a dangerous rival that could threaten the very existence of their branch. Fears that cavalry would be seen as obsolete had existed since the end of the world war, but President Hoover's effort in 1929 to reduce the federal budget by means of a drastic reform of the army in which, among other things, he suggested that "armored cars and motorization" could replace the horsemen caused many to link mechanization with the extinction of the cavalry.[76] With the personnel losses occasioned in the mid-1920s to support the rise of a nearly independent air service still a recent memory, it was not hard for officers to see the new mechanized force as a threat to the very existence of cavalry as a branch.[77]

Henry explained all this to MacArthur in March of 1931.[78] Although the chief of staff was anxious to accelerate the army's fledgling mechanization program, he also became increasingly aware of the danger to the morale and coherence of the branches if that program were to be carried out by an independent force. Hence, on May 1, a month after receiving Henry's letter, MacArthur announced his policy in which the fledgling mechanized force was dissolved and the infantry and the cavalry were each given control of mechanization efforts within their respective branch.[79] While the dissolution of the force was seen by many as a step backward, the emphasis in MacArthur's policy statement was on accelerating mechanization, among other things, specifically calling for the creation of a fully mechanized cavalry regiment. And, even though he spoke reassuringly of the cavalry in the future being made up of both horse and mechanized units, it was clear that the emphasis was to be on the latter.[80]

To many, the mechanized force, like the new air service, seemed to offer a revolutionary new and more mobile form of warfare based on rapid wide, sweeping flank movements that would replace the war of attrition seen in the world war. One of the leading proponents of this view was Lieutenant Colonel Adna R. Chaffee, Jr. The son of a highly respected cavalry officer, Chaffee was brought up in western frontier posts, where he became an expert and enthusiastic horseman. He had joined the General Staff in 1927 just as the project of creating the Experimental Mechanized Force had been assigned. He became fascinated with the project, and for the next thirteen years, Chaffee was the leading advocate of creating some kind of mechanized force. As a result, historians tend to portray him as a military revolutionary. He was, in fact, rather conservative. Like others in the cavalry, he feared for the future of his branch, especially after Hoover's call in 1929 that suggested its eventual elimination. Chaffee saw the mechanized-force concept as a way to preserve the branch, even if horses might no longer be part of it. Thus, he supported Henry in his efforts to persuade MacArthur to terminate the independent mechanized force and to assign the tasks of mechanization to both the infantry and the cavalry.[81] With the end of the mechanized force, Chaffee became a leader in the effort to mechanize cavalry. However, in doing so he sought to give mechanized cavalry the character of traditional American light cavalry, emphasizing those missions that depended on long-range marches and surprise. In that regard he was in opposition to the efforts of successive chiefs of cavalry to remodel the branch as the arm of decision. Some other officers in the branch agreed with him so that, as Steven Barry points out, "a lively debate existed in the branch between the eyes-and-ears traditionalists and the fighters."[82]

Finally, while MacArthur's May 1 directive ended the mechanized force and placed responsibility for future such efforts in the hands of the branches, it was still unclear how much control Henry, as chief of cavalry, would actually be allowed in regard to carrying out the mechanization of cavalry units. As soon as it was decided that a mechanized regiment would be located at Camp (later Fort) Knox, the General Staff also directed that the responsibility for carrying out the mechanization program within the regiment would rest with the commanding general of the Fifth Corps Area, who reported directly to the staff. The role of the chief of cavalry would be limited to "the initiation of recommendations to the War Department . . . and with such inspections . . . as may be directed by the War Department."[83]

Henry understood that MacArthur sought the complete mechanization of the cavalry and was appalled at the immensity of the project.[84] Nevertheless, he accepted the challenge with genuine enthusiasm.[85] Still, he was also aware that an accelerated mechanization policy posed two serious threats to the branch. First, a mechanized cavalry unit could easily be transformed into a new version of the mechanized force that would supersede the cavalry, especially since Henry had little control over the project. At the same time, the policy also threatened the integrity of the cavalry as a branch by aggravating a growing partisan struggle between advocates of mechanization and defenders of the horse, thereby threatening the cohesiveness of the branch and its culture. Hence, in responding to MacArthur's policy, Henry sought to gain control of the mechanization program by supporting it so actively that he could regain authority over it while also acting in ways that would reassure traditional cavalrymen that the horse still had a central role to play in the branch.

Cavalry mechanization began with the transfer of a regiment from Texas to Fort Knox, where it was to become the First Cavalry Regiment (Mech.) While the regiment was under the control of the Fifth Corps-Area Commander, Henry used every means possible to stay in direct communication with the regiment and exploited his own personal relationships with its officers to reinforce that contact. At the same time, he directed the Cavalry School to include a large number of hours of instruction on mechanized units and associated tactics, even at the expense of instruction in horsemanship. In addition, Henry called for an experimental reorganization of the Second Cavalry Regiment, stationed at the Cavalry School, that would make it a creditable force to counter mechanized units by including more armored cars,.50-cal. machine guns, and motorized transport.[86]

Most important, however, Henry and others in leadership positions in the branch continued to develop the new mechanized regiment into the kind of heavy firepower shock force that Crosby and other cavalry leaders sought in the 1920s. In describing mechanized units and weapons, the textbook on mechanized cavalry developed at the Cavalry School in 1932 stated: "Mechanization, as applied to cavalry, seeks to transplant the cavalry characteristics of mobility, firepower and shock to completely motor-propelled fighting units largely equipped with armored vehicles."[87] This emphasis on shock was repeated throughout the text, frequently in the context of the use of tanks in helping cavalry units break through established positions.[88] Elsewhere, Henry and others stressed the idea that mechanized cavalry was to be seen as cavalry mounted on machines instead of horses rather than as a new form of the mechanized force.[89]

At the same time, General Henry and others sought to placate those officers who viewed mechanization as a threat to the cavalry as they knew it, trying to convince them that there would always by a place for the horse. In doing this they followed the concept of "two cavalries"—one horsed, the other mechanized—as initiated by MacArthur in his policy statement on mechanization.[90] Although in his vision MacArthur clearly relegated horsed cavalry to a minor role, Henry and other branch leaders talked about the two as complementary equals, each with its own sphere of operations but with many opportunities to work together. It is unclear whether Henry really believed that "two cavalries" was anything more than a brief transitional phase leading to the eventual complete mechanization of the cavalry.[91] Regardless, the concept did help soothe the anxieties of traditional cavalrymen who feared the disappearance of the horse, so Henry defended it as if it were permanent. The concept remained the official doctrine of his office for the remainder of the 1930s.[92]

Overall, during his term in office, Henry had succeeded in initiating the mechanization of cavalry without having it tear the branch apart. He did this by regaining as much control as possible of the project, then shaping the development of mechanized cavalry along the lines of a shock force to act as an arm of decision, which was similar to Crosby's goal in the 1920s. At the same time, the "two cavalries" concept helped prevent a schism in the branch and a crisis in its culture. His efforts to hold the branch together were also aided by his genial personality and personal ties with many officers on both sides of the mechanization issue. All this masked the fact that the stability of the cavalry during the mechanization of the 1930s was more fragile than it appeared. It was dependent on mechanization proceeding at an evolutionary pace within the apparent context of fulfilling the long-term plans of becoming the arm of decision on the battlefield. Any significant acceleration of the pace of mechanization or indication that the project was no longer a cavalry program could threaten the branch with breakdown.

Henry was succeeded in 1934 by Major General Leon B. Kromer, who also sought to carry out the plan to make cavalry the arm of decision by increasing its firepower and shock potential. Like Crosby and Henry, Kromer tended to see the value of the mechanization program in terms of its ability to transform the cavalry division into a force with shock, firepower, and mobility. By the end of his first year in office, he had announced that the cavalry's top priority was placing a mechanized regiment in every cavalry division.[93] As he explained to the General Staff, "The Cavalry Division undoubtedly has a need for mechanized shock vehicles and this fact was fully realized within the present table of organization for the Cavalry Division drawn up in 1920."[94] Moreover, Kromer sought to reorganize the mechanized regiment by increasing the number of tanks in it from thirty-six to fifty-six in order to increase its shock power while pushing the development of a combat car, or tank, especially designed for cavalry and more heavily armed.[95] In addition, he added a battalion of self-propelled artillery to the mechanized regiment to further augment its firepower. Kromer also redefined the mission of cavalry in the *Cavalry Field Manual*, published in 1938: "Cavalry is that combatant arm of the Army organized primarily to perform those missions of ground warfare that require great strategic or tactical mobility combined with fire power and shock."[96] Much of the *Manual* was devoted to tactical discussions emphasizing mechanized-unit engagements meant to be tactically decisive.[97]

But Kromer ran into difficulties with his program from two directions. The first came from officers with the First Cavalry Regiment (Mech) being developed at Fort Knox who, like Chaffee, sought to develop mechanize cavalry along the lines of traditional cavalry, focused on reconnaissance and deep raids.[98] The other was from the General Staff, which had never accepted the cavalry's vision of itself as the arm of decision. Instead, it tended to limit that branch to auxiliary roles principally associated with reconnaissance.[99] Moreover, interest in the concept of an independent mechanized force outside the strictures of the branches was again rising in the General Staff. By 1935, the staff was beginning to see a mechanized force as a shock group serving as a reserve to be used at a critical moment. Thus, it was increasingly suspicious of and opposed to Kromer's efforts to increase the shock capacity of cavalry units.

Kromer also found his ability to control the process of mechanization within the cavalry challenged by other forces. For one thing, mechanization had created a momentum of its own that sometimes forced him into unpalatable situations regarding his branch. In 1936, for instance, he was ready to begin the mechanization of a second regiment, but political opposition made transferring a cavalry regiment from a current base to Fort Knox all but insuperable. The only solution was to mechanize the Thirteenth Cavalry Regiment, which was one of the two units stationed at the Cavalry School and thus under the direct control of the chief of cavalry. General Henry, who was now commandant of the school, protested vigorously that the loss of the regiment would cripple the school.[100]

But the most significant problem faced by Kromer was maintaining cavalry control of mechanization. In this his challenge came from two directions. The first was from officers in the First Cavalry Regiment (Mech.) at Fort Knox. A number of leaders in the mechanization movement felt strongly that the process would proceed faster and better outside of branch control. Among them was Brigadier General Daniel Van Voorhis, commander of the First Cavalry Regiment (Mech.), who had been deeply disappointed with the 1931 decision to place mechanization under branch control.[101] As a result, there was always a degree of tension between Fort Knox and the chief of cavalry.[102]

As these tensions grew in mid-1937, Kromer attempted to tighten his control over Fort Knox by creating a mechanization board there that would be subordinate to the Cavalry Board at Fort Riley.[103] Van Voorhis objected strongly to the idea, setting off a controversy with Kromer's office that lasted nearly two years.[104] Aggravating the issue was the fact that Van Voorhis claimed a monopoly on mechanization and refused to cooperate with the Cavalry School to expand the mechanization instruction offered there.[105] These disputes dragged on for nearly two years and into the first year of Major General John K. Herr's term as chief of Cavalry. Although most of them were resolved by compromises favorable to the chief of cavalry, the difficulties still served to increase Herr's suspicions that any more-rapid mechanization would take place at the expense of the horse cavalry.[106]

However, the greatest challenge to the chief's control over the mechanization of cavalry came from the General Staff, elements of which sought to exercise that authority themselves. The critical idea here was the old concept of the mechanized force as a combat unit made up of elements from a number of branches but operating outside the control of any of them. This would also be a force whose development would be controlled by the General Staff rather than by the branches. Although MacArthur's 1931 policy of mechanization development throughout and within all arms negated the mechanized-force idea, it did not die. It emerged again in 1935. By then, the Seventh Cavalry Brigade (Mech.) had been formed with the mechanization of a second cavalry regiment. An attempt to add a mechanized field-artillery unit to the brigade led to the suggestion from the General Staff that this would then make the Seventh Brigade a mechanized force.[107] Shortly afterward, reacting to a request by Kromer to increase the combat-car strength of the mechanized regiments from thirty-six to fifty-six, Major General John H. Hughes, the assistant chief of staff for operations and training, registered his dissent, saying that "the organizational trend of the cavalry seems to be toward emphasizing shock and firepower rather than the performance of truly Cavalry functions."[108]

But the main effort to revive the concept of a mechanized force came in the middle of 1937. In a terse but angry memorandum, MacArthur's successor as chief of staff, Major General Craig, called for a complete reconsideration of the army's program of mechanization. MacArthur's preferred path, he claimed, had led to duplication of effort and did not allow for the development of a coherent policy. Noting that all the major nations in Europe were following a program based on the concept of a mechanized force, he argued that the U.S. Army should follow suit.[109]

The result was a major policy memorandum from the Operations and Training Division focused on mechanization. It was clear in the paper that Craig's main target was the infantry rather than the cavalry, as one of his main goals was to redirect tank development from light tanks toward medium tanks. Still, the memorandum fairly dripped with contempt for branches in general.[110] In response, Kromer disagreed with the claim that mechanization could take place only outside the branches. In fact, he made his bid to stay in control of mechanization by expressing a determination to outdistance even the General Staff in regard to the pace of such modernization by recommending mechanizing a third cavalry regiment in order to form a mechanized division.[111]

Kromer's gambit seems to have been successful. Craig's policy thrust tended to dissipate in the effort to translate it into specific directives, especially regarding the cavalry. Moreover, while Van Voorhis was able to block the branch chief's effort to create a mechanized cavalry division by the mechanization of a third regiment, Kromer found himself receiving General Staff support in other areas.

In particular, the staff accepted a tacit agreement allowing the chief of cavalry to circumvent the subordination of the Seventh Cavalry Brigade (Mech.) to the Fifth Corps Area commander.[112]

Finally, there was also the problem of opposition to mechanization from traditionalists within the cavalry. Although these active opponents were highly vocal and left behind an impressive trail of paper, they were not organized and were never strong. Most were found among older officers and those stationed with regiments in the Southwest. Officers who had been through the Cavalry School and/or who had any contact with mechanization were usually supportive of this modernization effort.[113] Still, the sentiments of the opposition resonated well among many cavalry officers. The arguments regarding the limitations of mechanized vehicles and the advantages of the horse were logical and convincing to those with little contact with the former. The fact that mechanization seemed to be based on imagination and theory, none of which had ever been tested in combat conditions, troubled those whose culture was based on an empirical pragmatism and evolutionary change.[114]

Although opponents to mechanization based their arguments on analyses of the comparative suitability of horses and machines in carrying out the cavalry's many functions, the issue that really united them was the horse. As noted earlier, for many, the horse was central to the identity of cavalry as well as to the professional identity of its officers. It was what made the cavalry a distinctive and attractive way of life and provided the branch with a sense of elitism within the army and society. For many, cavalry without the horse was all but unthinkable. Thus, in a period in which the cavalry was undergoing slow mechanization and most cavalrymen still rode horses, both General Henry and General Kromer had to be careful to avoid taking positions that could cost them the confidence of many of the officers in their branch.

Despite the success of both chiefs in maintaining control of mechanization, the situation in 1939 from the standpoint of the cavalry was rapidly deteriorating and moving into crisis. One factor in this was General John K. Herr, who replaced Kromer as chief of cavalry in March 1938. Like his predecessors, Herr accepted and actively sought to promote the doctrine of the arm of decision.[115] But he lacked the flexibility of mind of his two predecessors and was too much committed to the horse to make the sacrifices that might have allowed cavalry to continue to control mechanization as a new world war started in Europe.[116]

This situation was aggravated by the growing rift between horse and mechanized cavalry. Kromer's plans for accelerated mechanization angered many horsemen.[117] At the same time, belief in the principle of "complementarity" as a guarantee of a continued place for the horse was breaking down.[118] Advocates of the horse became ever more shrill in their denunciation of mechanization as both sides saw themselves entering into an "either/or" situation. And while the cavalry had been successful in fending off Craig's efforts in 1937 to revive the idea of an independent mechanized force, the episode left behind a residue of suspicion and hostility against the General Staff that approached paranoia.[119]

As a result of all this, although Herr entered office willing to continue a mechanization program, including the creation of the mechanized division Kromer had suggested, he soon fell into the trap of seeing himself as the savior of the beleaguered horse cavalry.[120] At the same time, the quick destruction of Poland in 1939, followed by France in 1940, created a new atmosphere in the army in which support for the mechanized-force concept skyrocketed. Herr, on the other hand, could do no better than move grudgingly from one compromise to another, rapidly destroying confidence in the ability of the cavalry to guide mechanization. On July 10, 1940, the creation of the Armored Force was announced, the name indicating that not only had the "force" concept been victorious but also that all connection of the cavalry with the history of "mechanization" had been repudiated.[121]

It has been argued that the cavalry lost control of mechanization, and with it survival in the industrial age, basically due to Herr's unwillingness and even inability to deal with the crisis created by the perceived need for an accelerated mechanization of the army.[122] There is something to be said for this. Yet there were larger structural issues involved that may have made the dilemma facing Herr all but irresolvable. First, there was an almost unbridgeable gap between the cavalry and the General Staff in terms of understanding the mission of the cavalry. The branch's effort to reinvent itself as the "arm of decision" went largely unnoticed elsewhere. In a long eulogy to the cavalry published in 1929, General Summerall made no mention of its role as the arm of decision, while the General Staff in 1937 ridiculed the idea of smashing through an enemy line.[123] Finally, William Odom points out that the 1939 regulations, as the final word in the development of doctrine in the interwar period, did suggest that mechanized cavalry had the ability "to intervene rapidly at a decisive point in battle" and stressed its firepower and armored protection as much as mobility. Nevertheless, like the *Field Service Regulations* of 1923, its vision of doctrine was still dominated by the principles behind open warfare, basically limiting modern cavalry to the traditional functions of light cavalry.[124]

More important, there was a larger problem inherent in the nature of the branch as an organization. In the interwar period the branch was called on to socialize its officers into the military, not only educating them into their duties but also creating a cohesive corps held together by common outlooks, values, and allegiances. At the same time, branches were also responsible for modernizing their weapons, tactics, and doctrines. The first task called for traditions to be venerated; the second, for them to be abandoned. The task of modernizing a force in the face of such a contradiction called for both flexibility and patience. To some degree the cavalry had the necessary flexibility so that its progress in mechanization accelerated during the 1930s while the traditionalist opposition to it, while becoming increasingly more shrill, declined. But such a transition took time. In 1939, as the war that had once been only imminent now became present, a sense of crisis developed that led the army's leadership to lose patience with the branches and succumb to the siren call of the independent mechanized force that would centralize control of this modernization process in the hands of the General Staff. Nevertheless, the new Armored Force proved ephemeral, and tanks entered World War II as the main armament of armored divisions, a military organization strikingly similar to what the cavalry had been trying to create during the interwar period.

Conclusion

D URING A CONFERENCE SESSION in 1994 regarding the National Defense Act of 1920, one historian offered the opinion that the act was a project based on an almost stunning naïveté. In many ways he was right. Both the 1916 and the 1920 defense acts came at a highly unusual time in American history. In the years immediately prior to World War I and for a very short time afterwards, the rapidly growing popularity of universal military training as an act of positive progressive social engineering, together with the near-panic of the preparedness movement, gave the army a golden moment when it could get congressional approval of a military policy at least somewhat along the lines it desired. It was, however, a very short-lived moment. Indeed, the window was already rapidly closing just as the National Defense Act of 1920 was finally legislatively approved and signed. Nevertheless, provisions that the army had managed to have included in the act indicate that its leadership may have mistakenly seen this temporary euphoria as a "new normal." Three major assumptions along this line seem implicit both in the act and in the army's actions afterward. First, it was apparently assumed that the nation would embrace and support the citizen army enthusiastically. The importance given in the early 1920s to ensure that its units were spread throughout the country suggests an expectation that they would be popular. Also, the sudden spurt of articles in service journals later blaming its lack of popularity on various subversive or pacifist agencies implies this same expectation. Second, the provisions for the CMTC in the act indicate that it was felt that the nation's young men would generally come to like military training. Third, the provisions for the Organized Reserve seem to have been based on the belief that a large number of more mature men would find military activity so attractive that they would be willing to dedicate a significant portion of their leisure to a rigorous self-training program to make themselves nearly as proficient as their professional colleagues in the Regular Army.

Within a few years, each of these three basic assumptions was shown to be illusory, leading to such discouragement that, during the budget crisis of 1925, the General Staff gave serious consideration to abandoning the citizen army. Nevertheless, the leaders at that time and afterward chose to continue to develop the program to the extent that allocated resources would allow, even in the face of public and government antipathy. By 1939, they had much to show for their efforts. Despite setbacks, the need to scale down unrealistic expectations, and ever diminishing budget allocations, especially in the early 1930s, the citizen components of the Army of the United States were organized and gradually grew while gaining in competence and stability. The combat branch organizations were also organized, and each became increasingly successful in terms of socializing and training its officers, in creating a common branch culture, and in developing agencies to promote a modernization of weapons and equipment. Finally, the new army school system provided a rationally organized program of progressive military education to guide officers through their careers and to promote homogeneity in thought as well as adherence to a common doctrine. That all of this was accomplished despite extremely limited support and resources within a society that had become increasingly antipathetic was a truly impressive achievement.

Still, the citizen army created by the 1920 National Defense Act was significantly flawed, as has been noted by its critics. The most frequent fault cited both during the interwar period and since then was the conservative character of the Regular Army. While William Odom has analyzed what he identifies as doctrinal stagnation in the period, David Johnson has focused on the systemic features of the interwar army that hindered technological development, especially regarding tanks. While there is no need to restate all their arguments. In brief, both claim that the army placed a higher priority on maintaining the maximum possible number of officers that appropriations would allow, at the cost of limiting funds for technological development.[1] Since the main reason the army needed as many officers as possible was to support the training of the citizen components, they argue that the more limited degree of technological innovation, especially in the 1930s, was due in part to the commitment to the citizen components. To some extent, this is true, although Johnson tends to overlook the frantic efforts made by the chiefs of infantry and the cavalry to get tanks. Yet it is also true that mechanization was very expensive, and given the extremely limited funds appropriated for the army in the 1930s, it is hard to see how the relatively meager savings that might have been made available by abandoning the training of the citizen components would have made any significant difference with the mechanization program. To have tried to keep pace with advances of the major European powers would likely have called for vastly greater appropriations than Congress, the president, and the American people would have been willing to make.

Another problem with the citizen army was its cost in terms of the Regular Army's own training. During the summers, the best time of the year for outdoor training, every available regular officer was involved in training the civilian components. Moreover, the summer training program was exhausting. Finally, in order to save as many officer slots as possible to provide for guard and reserve training, officials decided early in the 1920s to carry out the personnel reductions required by smaller budgets by radically skeletonizing existing units rather than eliminating some of them. This all but eliminated opportunities for training of any but small units. The army was not able to hold major training maneuvers until the summer of 1939.[2] That August, two sets of maneuvers were held, one in Manassas, Virginia, and the other in Plattsburgh, New York. Both demonstrated a surprising lack of readiness on the part of the Regular Army and, especially, the National Guard. Hanson Baldwin, military correspondent for the *New York Times*, wrote a highly critical report of the maneuvers, pointing out numerous deficiencies, including the fact that more than half of the participating men had never fired their weapons in any type of combat training. An article that appeared later in the *Baltimore Sun* quoted the opinion of unnamed army sources that the military was less prepared for war than it had been in 1917.[3]

Finally, all during the interwar period, it was reasonably clear that the citizen components were not receiving the training necessary to be able to carry out their assigned functions should war occur. This was especially true for the Organized Reserve. According to the Six-Army Plan, the Reserve was responsible for training selective-service inductees in twenty-seven divisions during a mobilization. Yet in 1939 only 100,000 reserve officers were available to do this, which was far too few for that purpose. Moreover, the reservists were essentially self-trained by completing correspondence courses. As regular officers who worked with them pointed out, correspondence courses cannot teach leadership. A relatively few reserve officers were able to attend the two-week summer camps, but only a portion of this meager experience had anything to do with carrying out training related to mobilization. Many individual reserve officers did derive some benefit from their leadership roles in summer CMTCs and later with CCC camps, but their units did not. Although reserve officers were assigned to locally organized units that could meet and might even have a small office, training as a unit did not occur. Outside of the "Defense Test" of 1924, which was ostensibly meant to test the ability to carry out the mobilization plans but had far more to do with public relations, the army carried out no mobilization exercises. Fortunately, the actual mobilization that began after the German invasion of Poland on September 1, 1939, was carried out slowly, keeping deliberate pace with public opinion, and was carried out by the Regular Army. As a result, the original plan for the ORC to carry out the mobilization role assigned to it was never implemented.

Yet these deficiencies were only partly due to flaws in the reserve system. The main problem with this system in the interwar period was that it was seriously lacking in support from the government and the Regular Army, both in terms of finances and personnel. Palmer and others were naïve in their expectation that a large body of civilian men would take such a keen interest in military activity that they would willingly invest significant portions of their leisure time in a self-training program to make themselves competent officers in the event of war. This was especially true in the 1930s, when the world war veterans in the Reserve were increasingly replaced by graduates of ROTC programs, young men who had not had any wartime experience to motivate interest in serving in the Reserve. In addition, most reserve officers found self-training through correspondence courses time consuming and uninteresting. To stimulate their interest in remaining in the program and actively pursue their training, reserve officers needed far more opportunities for interaction with regular officers and with each other in order to feel part of a real program achieving recognizable results. The early controversy over dedicated office space with military accoutrements, the creation of the ROA, and the enthusiasm with which reserve officers participated in the CMTCs and, later, supported the CCC program repeatedly demonstrated this. The army, however, had nowhere near the number of officers nor was it given the budgetary resources to supply this kind of support. On the other hand, the program did provide around 100,000 reserve officers in 1939 who, while clearly nowhere near as competent as their counterparts in the Regular Army, still aided the military considerably in mobilizing and training the forces being raised in this period, a fact recognized repeatedly by the wartime chief of staff, General George Marshall.[4]

Compared to the ORC, the National Guard appeared to have been somewhat better prepared for war, though it, too, had serious deficiencies. According to the Six-Army Plan, on mobilization the Guard was to provide eighteen combat-ready divisions in thirty days. The National Defense Act allowed it an enrollment of 424,800 to meet this goal. Soon, however, in the social environment of 1920s America, raising the Guard to that level through voluntary enlistments was not possible nor would the army's consistently diminished annual budgets support it. Therefore, for most of the interwar period, the strength of the Guard was less than 200,000 men. This number was then increased in the late 1930s so that by the time of Roosevelt's piecemeal mobilization, it had reached 280,000 guardsmen. On August 27, 1940, Congress authorized the mobilization of the Guard units, which began to be called up from time to time for a years' service. By June 1941, the entire Guard had been mobilized. On December 31, 1941, the call-up was extended for the duration of the war plus six months. Three months later eighteen of the twenty-nine divisions mobilized in the U.S. Army by that time had come from the National Guard.[5]

Yet while the Guard had met the quotas set by the Six-Army Plan, the mobilization exposed major deficiencies in its training. Senior regular officers, such as Lieutenant General Leslie McNair, who, as chief of staff for General Headquarters, U.S. Army was responsible for mobilization and training, were openly contemptuous of the Guard. Critics of its performance in the Manassas and Plattsburg maneuvers directed the bulk of their reproach at its officers.[6] Finally, after a major set of maneuvers in Louisiana in the fall of 1941, McNair undertook a massive purge of senior officers, which fell hardest on the Guard and the Reserve. His major complaint was the "comparatively low training ceiling of the officers which left them unable to maintain discipline."[7] Some of this antipathy may have reflected remnants of earlier prejudices against the Guard held by older regular officers. The charge that guard officers were unable to maintain discipline reflected a longstanding belief on the part of regulars that the local recruitment of these units meant that officers and men knew each other, leaving officers less able to treat their men with rigorous authority. Richard Faulkner notes that this attitude was quite observable among regular officers during World War I.[8] But McNair's opinion was also shared by Hanson Baldwin, the highly respected military reporter, who had observed the maneuvers.[9] So there was a major deficiency in the training of National Guard officers that was clearly manifested in the maneuvers and elsewhere.

But, as the performance of the guard divisions in the ensuing war demonstrated, these deficiencies were not due so much to the nature of the Guard as an organization as they were to the conditions under which it was developed during the interwar period. As was the case with the Organized Reserve, Palmer and others basically saw the Guard as a citizen component that would largely train itself. While the Regular Army was committed to assist both the Guard and the Reserve in their training, the drastic personnel reductions in the opening years of the 1920s and the subsequent budget reductions severely curtailed its ability to do so. As many observers pointed out, all this put a heavy burden on guard officers, who had to plan and execute the training programs for their own units and complete the correspondence courses needed for their advancement, leaving little time for their own training. Nor did the army's limited budget allow guard officers much opportunity for the kind of field exercises and maneuvers that would have given them both practical experience and training in leadership. The result was the brutal crash course in leadership training during the mobilization of 1939–41 that many in the Guard failed to survive.

EARLY IN JUNE 2020 my wife and I had a special private dinner in our apartment graced by one of the best bottles in my small cellar. It was June 4, and we were celebrating the 100th anniversary of the passage of the National Defense Act of 1920. It is quite possible that our dinner may have been the only observance of that centennial anniversary held in the country. If so, that is too bad, since even though that act has been followed by many more defense acts, the basic organization of the army it created has remained largely unchanged. The army is still a citizen military that includes the Regular Army and the three main civilian components—the National Guard, the Officer Reserve Corps, and the Reserve Officers Training Corps—that were given their formal place in the overall structure by the 1920 National Defense Act. The act also formalized the branch structure of the Regular Army. While the branches play less of a role in the organization of the army now than they did in the interwar period, they still very much exist and remain critical in orienting and socializing new officers into the army. Indeed, most officers will spend their entire careers within their branch. And while many new schools have been developed, the basic educational program set up in the 1920s under the act is still operating.

Moreover, the two-year period following the end of World War I was the first and only moment since the writing of the Constitution that the nation actually had the opportunity to choose the type of military organization responsible for providing its security. Two very different options were clearly available. One, the March-Baker plan, would have given that responsibility to an entirely professional Regular Army, which would be augmented in time of major emergency using a draft. The other option was the citizen army proposed by Palmer and the reformers in the General Staff. Brian Linn states this dichotomy succinctly, observing that the issue "was [would] the U.S. Army . . . be a small, highly trained, technologically sophisticated mobile elite or would it serve as the cadre for a large mass army such as the American Expeditionary Force in World War I."[10] From a strictly military point of view, the March-Baker plan may have been the superior policy. But Congress and the nation chose the citizen army, doing so because, regardless of its drawbacks, it was based on the nation's traditions and values. As Palmer warned in the *Report on the Organization of the Land Forces* in 1912, "The practical military statesman . . . does not propose impracticable or foreign institutions but seeks to develop the necessary vigor and energy within the familiar institutions that have grown with the national life."[11]

During the first five years of the 1920s, the Regular Army worked diligently to make a success of the new citizen army, but with discouraging results. The United States had not embraced the new citizen army as its own, as the skepticism toward the military that had long been part of the American tradition returned. At the same time, the efforts to create the citizen components were discouragingly less than successful to the point that leaders in 1925 were questioning whether to give up on the project. Moreover, alternatives to the citizen army soon began to look more attractive. The first of these was the cavalry's effort to remake the First Cavalry Division into a new force that could be the arm of decision on the battlefield by restoring mobility to warfare. This was followed by the introduction of the fast tank and, with it, the idea of a mechanized force that could carry out a new form of ground warfare that would replace the bloody and senseless attrition of the western front with open-war maneuvering and replace the mass armies of the world war with small, mobile, professional armies possessing highly sophisticated arms. The subsequent experiments with the mechanized force raised enthusiasm among some officers in part because it seemed to make the return of maneuver to warfare a real possibility. This vision, and its accompanying enthusiasms, did not die with General MacArthur's disbanding of the mechanized force before it was even established. The cavalry under Generals Henry and Kromer continued in the effort to create a mechanized cavalry force that would act as an arm of decision that would restore movement to warfare. At the same time, the General Staff revived the idea of the mechanized force and finally adopted it in 1940 with the creation of the Armored Force.

The dream then seemed to have been realized in 1939 and 1940, as the spectacular initial successes of Germany's panzer forces appeared to prove that highly armored and mobile forces based on combined arms could restore movement and maneuver to warfare. But the development of antitank weapons soon erased the momentary offensive advantage of tanks. By 1943, even in the vast plains of Russia, warfare had again become a slugging match, and the armored division that was supposed to open up the battlefield was largely relegated to the role of exploiting breakthroughs created by the infantry. The American army that fought World War II was clearly a citizen army whose leadership was largely trained within the framework of the institutions created by the National Defense Act of 1920. The way it fought that war may have been less decisive and more costly in terms of lives and treasures than it should have been. But that army won the conflict and thereby validated the citizen army as the American way of war.

ABBREVIATIONS USED IN CITATIONS

ANJ	*Army and Navy Journal*
AO	*Army Ordnance*
CAJ	*Coast Artillery Journal*
CJ	*Cavalry Journal*
CW	*Chemical Warfare*
FAJ	*Field Artillery Journal*
FSR	United States War Department, General Staff, *FM100-5: Field Service Regulations* (Washington, DC, 1923)
IJ	*Infantry Journal*
JUSA	*Journal of the United States Artillery*
LOC	Library of Congress, Washington, DC
ME	*Military Engineer*
NA	National Archives, Washington, DC
NYT	*New York Times*
RG	Record Group
RO	*Reserve Officer*
SHSW	State Historical Society of Wisconsin, Madison
USAMHI	United States Army Military History Institute.

NOTES

Introduction

1. Michael S. Neiberg describes the development of this volunteer system in *Making Citizen-Soldiers: ROTC and the Ideology of American Military Service* (Cambridge, MA: Harvard University Press, 2000), 25–18.

2. J. P. Clark, *Preparing for War: The Emergence of the Modern U.S. Army, 1815–1917* (Cambridge, MA: Harvard University Press, 2017), 129–35.

3. James E. Hewes Jr., *From Root to McNamara: Army Organization and Administration, 1900–1963* (Washington: Center for Military History, 1975), 5.

4. Unless otherwise noted, this discussion of the work of Emory Upton is based on Clark, *Preparing for War,* 64–125.

5. Emory Upton, *The Armies of Asia and Europe* (New York: Appleton, 1878; reprint, Westport, CT: Greenwood, 1968).

6. The manuscript was edited and published posthumously in 1904. Emory Upton, *The Military Policy of the United States* (Washington, DC: Government Printing Office, 1904).

7. Neiberg, *Making Citizen-Soldiers,* 18.

8. Root's political struggles to secure the passage of his reform legislation are described at length in Clark, *Preparing for War,* 187–96.

9. While the new professionals rallied around the *Journal of the Military Service Institute,* the young professionals rallied around the new *Infantry Journal.*

10. James L. Abrahamson, *America Arms for a New Century: The Making of a Great Military Power* (New York: Free Press, 1981), 106–7.

11. Wood outlined this idea in considerable detail in his diary. Wood Diary, Jan. 24, 1911, LOC, Leonard Wood Diary and Papers, Box 6.

12. Wood Diary, Dec. 17, 1910, LOC, Wood Diary and Papers, Box 11.

13. Wood Diary, Jan. 12, 1911, LOC, Wood Diary and Papers, Box 11.

14. Editorial, "Some National Guard Tendencies," *IJ* 8, no. 1 (July/Aug. 1911): 93–104. A meeting between Wood and guard leaders in April became acrimonious. Wood Diary, Apr. 10, 1911, LOC, Wood Diary and Papers, Box 6.

15. In an editorial published in the *Infantry Journal* in the summer of 1911, the editor claimed that this debate was going on "in our quarters and in our clubs." "Where Does

the Army Stand?" *IJ* 8, no. 1 (July/Aug. 1911): 83–93. Articles on the subject began to appear in the service journals early in 1912.

16. By early 1912, the *Infantry Journal* commented editorially on what it saw as a wide-spread feeling of severe disorientation and alienation in the army. Editorial, *IJ* 8, no. 6 (May/June 1912): 874.

17. "Army Legislation Proposed," *ANJ* 48, no. 34 (Apr. 22, 1911): 1017.

18. James W. Pohl, "The General Staff and American Military Policy: The Formative Years, 1898–1917 (PhD diss., University of Texas, 1967), 1157–58.

19. Wood Diary, Nov. 21, 1911, LOC, Wood Diary and Papers, Box 6.

20. "Brigade and Division Posts," *ANJ* 49, no. 8 (Oct. 21, 1911): 221.

21. Irving B. Holley Jr, *General John M. Palmer, Citizen Soldiers, and the Army of a Democracy* (Westport, CT: Greenwood, 1982), 204–5.

22. *Report of the Organization of the Land Forces of the United States* (Washington, DC: Government Printing Office, 1912), NA, RG 165, 7280, 61.

23. Ibid., 12.

24. Clark, *Preparing for War*, 186–87, 232–34; Hewes, *From Root to McNamara*, 15.

25. "Army Appropriation Bill," *ANJ* 49, no. 39 (May 25, 1912): 1222.

26. Wood to Theodore Roosevelt, Sept. 27, 1913, LOC, Wood Diary and Papers, Box 65. J. P. Clark claims that Wood was more interested in the social benefits of universal military training than in the military ones. Clark, *Preparing for War*, 250.

27. Wood to Paul Morton, Dec. 23, 1910, LOC, Wood Diary and Papers, Box 49.

28. *Organization, Training, and Mobilization of Volunteers under the Act of April 1914* (Government Printing Office, Washington, 1916). A copy can be found in the National Archives in Record Group 165, file number 8160, document 25. Hereafter, documents from the National Archives will be cited in terms of their record group, file number, and document number. In this case, RG 165, 8160–25.

29. William Mitchell, Memorandum, July 7, 1913, NA, RG 195, 8222–1; Mitchell, "Military Organization," *IJ* 10, no. 3 (Nov./Dec. 1913): 390–92.

30. Chief, Division of Militia Affairs to the Chief of Staff, Nov. 28, 1914; William H. Johnson, Memorandum, Dec. 17, 1914; Hugh Scott, Memorandum for the Secretary of War, Jan. 19, 1915, NA, RG 165, 8222–2.

31. "Proposed Increase in the Army," *ANJ* 51, no. 36 (May 9, 1914): 1145.

32. *Chief of Staff, Annual Report for 1914* printed in *Secretary of War Annual Report for 1914* (Washington, D. C. Government Printing Office, 1914), 130–34.

33. "The Sixty-Third Congress," *ANJ* 52, no. 16 (Dec. 19, 1914): 506.

34. Lindley Garrison, Memorandum, Feb. 25, 1915, LOC, Tasker H. Bliss Papers, vol. 189; Tasker Bliss, Memorandum for the War College Division, Mar. 11, 1915, NA, RG 165, 9053–1.

35. Draft of a Bill for the Reorganization of the U.S. Army, Apr. 5, 1915, NA, RG 165, 8481–17; "Plans for Army Legislation," *ANJ* 52, no. 30 (Mar. 27, 1915): 935; "Plans for Army Legislation," *ANJ* 52, no. 31 (Apr. 3, 1915): 982.

36. Woodrow Wilson, "Annual Message to Congress," Dec. 8, 1915, *The Papers of Woodrow Wilson*, ed. Arthur S. Link et al., 69 vols. (Princeton, NJ: Princeton University

Press, 1966–94), 31:421–23; Montgomery Macomb, Memorandum, Apr. 13, 1915, NA, RG 165, 9053-18; Macomb, Memorandum for the Adjutant General, Apr. 26, 1915, NA, RG 165, 9053-12.

37. "The War Department's Military Policy," *ANJ* 52, no. 51 (Aug. 24, 1915): 1624.

38. Wilson to Garrison, July 21, 1915, *Papers of Woodrow Wilson*, 34:4.

39. Enoch Crowder, Memorandum for the Secretary of War, July 31, 1915, NA, RG 165, 9053-26. Almost all of Wilson's correspondence on this issue stressed cost. See, for example, Garrison to Wilson, Sept. 17, 1915, NA, RG 165, 9053-39.

40. The *Army and Navy Journal* made the Continental Army the focus for its attack especially because it was based on voluntarism. See, for instance, "Secretary Garrison's Plan," *ANJ* 52, no. 10 (Nov. 6, 1915): 304.

41. Statement of Capt. S. J. Bayard Schindel, Jan. 26, 1916, U.S. Senate, Committee on Military Affairs, *Preparedness for National Defense: Hearings before the Committee for Military Affairs, U.S. Senate, 64th Congress, 1st Session* (Washington, DC: Government Printing Office, 1916), 505.

42. Statement of Maj. P. D. Lockridge, Jan. 28, 1916, U.S. House, Committee on Military Affairs, *To Increase the Efficiency of the Military Establishment of the United States: Hearings before the House Committee on Military Affairs* (Washington, DC: Government Printing Office, 1916), 832–34; statement of Maj. George Van Horn Moseley, Jan. 26, 916, Senate, *Preparedness for National Defense*, 490–92; Tasker Bliss to W. G. Haan, Jan. 19, 1916, LOC, Tasker Bliss Papers, vol. 197; Editorial, "Military Legislation," *IJ* 12, no. 1 (Jan. 1916): 633–34.

43. Garrison to Wilson, Feb. 12, 1916, LOC, Henry Breckinridge Papers, Box 521; "Resignation of Secretary Garrison," *ANJ* 53, no. 25 (Feb. 19, 1916): 783.

44. "The Mobilization of the National Guard," *IJ* 13, no. 1 (July/Aug. 1916): 76.

45. "The Militia Muddle," *NYT* (Aug. 2, 1916): 2.

46. "Statement of Major-General Hugh Scott," n.d., NA, RG 165, 9317-14.

47. *Secretary of War Annual Report for 1916* (Washington, D. C. Government Printing Office, 1916), 12; "Federalization of the National Guard Called a Failure," *NYT* (Dec. 5, 1916): 10.

48. Chief of Staff, Memorandum for the War College Division, Oct. 31, 1916, NA, RG 165, 9832-1; Chief of Staff, Memorandum for the War College Division, Dec. 11, 1916, NA, RG165, 9832-5.

49. John T. Pratt to Palmer, Nov. 21, 1916; Pratt to Palmer, Nov. 30, 1916, LOC, Palmer Papers, Box 2

50. War College Division, Memorandum for the Chief of Staff, Dec. 9, 1916, NA, RG 165, 9832-4.

51. "Testimony on 18–19 Dec. 1916 before the Senate," NA, RG 165, 9317-14; "Universal Training Bill," *NYT* (Dec. 22, 1916): 8.

52. Joseph Kuhn, Memorandum for the Chief of Staff, Feb. 14, 1917, NA, RG 165, 9876-20.

53. , *Secretary of War Annual Report for 1916* (Washington, D. C. Government Printing Office, 1916) 16; Baker to Wilson, Mar. 26, 1917, *Papers of Woodrow Wilson*, 41:1933.

54. Baker to William Howard Taft, Feb. 7, 1917, *Papers of Woodrow Wilson*, 41:1983.

55. "Bill to Organize Big Citizen Army," *NYT* (Feb. 24, 1917): 1.

56. "Secretary Baker on Military Policy," *ANJ* 54, no. 7 (Oct. 14, 1916): 210.

57. Kuhn, Memorandum for the Chief of Staff, Feb. 20, 1917, NA, RG 165, 943.

58. John W. Chambers, *To Raise an Army: The Draft Comes to Modern America* (New York: Free Press, 1987), 133.

59. *Secretary of War Annual Report for 1917* (Washington, D. C. Government Printing Office, 1917), 42. 42.

60. *Secretary of War Annual Report for 1918* (Washington, D. C. Government Printing Office, 1918), 66; Edward M. Coffman, *The Hilt of the Sword: The Career of Peyton C. March* (Madison: University of Wisconsin Press, 1966): 198.

61. Henry Jervey, Jr. to Lytle Brown, Oct. 17, 1918, NA, RG 165, 7942–2(h) (emphasis in the original document).

62. War Plans Division, Memorandum, Nov. 19, 1919, NA, RG 165, 7942–2(c).

63. March to Pershing, Dec. 18, 1919, LOC John J. Pershing Papers, Box 123; E. S. Hartshorn, "Plan for the Reorganization of the War Department," n. d., NA, RG 165, 7942–2(o).

64. The bill was introduced by Congressman Stanley Dent, Democrat of Alabama, on January 16, 1919.

65. Lytle Brown to Chief of Staff, Jan. 28, 1919, NA, RG 165, 9625–148.

66. "The Army Reorganization Bill," *ANJ* 56, no. 20 (Jan. 18, 1919): 713.

67. Editorial, *ANJ* 56, no. 55 (May 3, 1919): 932.

68. "Confusion in Military Legislation," *ANJ* 57, no. 4 (Sept. 17, 1919): 115; "General Officers Testify," *ANJ* 57, no. 6 (Oct. 11, 1919): 176.

69. "Army Reorganization Postponed," *ANJ* 57, no. 11 (Nov. 15, 1919): 337.

70. Holley, *General John M. Palmer*, 436–38.

71. "The Tentative Army Bills," *ANJ* 57, no. 17 (Dec. 27, 1919): 521.

72. "House to Amend National Defense Act," *ANJ* 57, no. 19 (Dec. 19, 1919): 458.

73. Palmer, "Inner History of the National Defense Act of 1920," LOC, Palmer Papers, Box 4; William Lacey, "Report by the Committee of the War Plans Division on S 3632," NA, RG 165, 8481–132.

74. Baker to Wilson, Feb. 9, 1920, *Papers of Woodrow Wilson*, 65:576–77.

75. Palmer to H. B. Clark, Apr. 9, 1920, LOC, Palmer Papers, Box 4.

Chapter 1

1. "Army Appropriations Act," *ANJ* 57, no. 40 (June 5, 1921): 233.

2. "Secretary Baker Explains Large Army," *ANJ* 56, no. 15 (Dec. 11, 1920): 420.

3. "Mr. Baker before House Committee," *ANJ* 56, no.16 (Dec. 18, 1920): 458.

4. "Reducing the Army to 175,000," *ANJ* 58, no. 20 (Jan. 15,1921): 531.

5. "Army Appropriations Bill Passed," *ANJ* 58, no. 44 (July 2, 1921): 1152.

6. "Fight Expected on Appropriation [*sic*] Bill," *ANJ* 59, no. 29 (Apr. 18, 1922): 947.

7. *Army and Navy Journal* reported that one committee member thought that the Coast Guard was a branch of the army. "Changes in Military Legislation," *ANJ* 59, no. 5 (Oct. 1, 1921): 102.

8. *Annual Report of the Secretary of War, 1923* (Washington, D. C., Government Printing office, 1923), 12–15; *Annual Report of the Chief of Staff, 1923,* published in *Annual Report of the Secretary of War, 1923,* 112.

9. "National Defense vs Politics," *ANJ* 59, no. 38 (May 20, 1922): 899; "The *Army and Navy Journal* Opens the Fight for Repeal of the Elimination Act," *ANJ* 59, no. 51 (Aug. 19, 1922): 1253; James Harbord, Memorandum for the Chief of Staff, Mar. 21, 1922, LOC, James Harbord Papers, Box 11.

10. William O. Odom, *After the Trenches: The Transformation of the U.S. Army, 1918– 1939* (College Station: Texas A&M University Press, 2008), 82.

11. As quoted in Michael R. Matheny, *Carrying the War to the Enemy: American Operational Art to 1945* (Norman: University of Oklahoma Press, 2011), 25.

12. Richard Spaulding, "Creation of a Single List," *ANJ* 57, no. 2 (Aug. 13, 1920): 132–37.

13. "An Anonymous Promotion List Circulating," *ANJ* 58, no. 33 (Apr. 16, 1921): 901.

14. "Court to Uphold Law on Promotion List," *ANJ* 58, no. 40 (June 11, 1921): 1082.

15. Alfred Boynham to Palmer, Feb. 12, 1924, LOC, John McAuley Palmer Papers, Box 5.

16. The General Staff saw a perceived hostile press as so serious a problem that the War Department News Bureau was transferred to the Morale Bureau of the War Plans Division and given the assignment of countering unfriendly articles. General Staff, War Plans Division, *Annual Report,* 1920, 51.

17. John Pershing, "The Citizen Army," *IJ* 27, no. 6 (Dec. 1925): 621–23, quoted in *CW* (Aug. 1923): 16.

18. Most of the preparedness articles appeared in *Infantry Journal,* which was less narrowly professional in its outlook, but some appeared in *Cavalry Journal* and *Coastal Artillery Journal* as well. For an example of these, see James Harbord, "National Defense," *IJ* 22, no. 3 (Mar. 1923): 274–77. For the last article to appear in *Cavalry Journal* on how the act would ease the army's social isolation, see "Creating a Citizen Army: Our Principal Mission," *CJ* 32, no. 133 (Oct. 1923): 114–15.

19. See, for instance, Elbridge Colby, "Get It to the Press," *IJ* 23, no. 4 (Oct. 1923): 373–75.

20. Henry Almond, "Training for Citizenship," *IJ* 23, no. 2 (Aug. 1923): 125.

21. "Bolsheviki Sedition," *IJ* 18, no. 5 (May 1921): 534.

22. See, for instance, Editorial, "Clear Thinking and Peace," *JUSA* 55, no. 5 (Nov. 1921): 471–73.

23. Pershing, Memorandum on Training, Jan. 18, 1923, NA, RG 407, 353.

24. For instance, Editorial, "Out of the Doldrums," *CJ* 31, no. 129 (Oct. 1922): 405–6.

25. E. T. Johns, "Weekly Washington Letter," *ANJ* 60, no. 8 (Oct. 21, 1922): 176.

26. Hugh Drum, Memorandum for the Chief of Staff, Dec. 20, 1923, LOC, Pershing Papers, Box 62.

27. "Army Defense Test Is to Be Held on September 12," *ANJ* 61, no. 38 (May 17, 1924): 906.

28. "Defense Test Plans Progress Despite Political Opposition," *ANJ* 61, no. 49 (Aug. 3, 1924): 1173.

29. War Department, "Summary of the Results of the Defense Test," Sept. 14, 1924, LOC, Pershing Papers, Box 62.

30. Pershing to March, Sept 29, 1924, LOC, Pershing Papers, Box 124.

31. *Annual Report of the Chief of Staff, 1926,* published in *Annual Report of the Secretary of War, 1926* (Washington, D. C., Government Printing office, 1926), 51.

32. *Annual Report of the Secretary of War, 1925* (Washington, D. C., Government Printing office, 1925), 26.

33. Illegible to Hines, Dec. 16, 1925, LOC, John L. Hines Papers, Box 31.

34. "Lighten the Soldiers' Burdens," *ANJ* 61, no. 9 (Oct. 27, 1923): 204.

35. "Army Officer Leaves to Be Few This Summer," *ANJ* 61, no. 29 (Mar. 15, 1924): 690.

36. "Headed for CCC," *CJ* 32, no. 142 (Dec. 1925): 522.

37. *Annual Report of the Secretary of War, 1924* (Washington, D.C., Government Printing office, 1924), 3.

38. E. T. Johns, "Special Washington Services Newsletter," *ANJ* 62, no. 13 (Nov. 19, 1924): 1585.

39. "Throttles Navy Probe to Hide Truth Concerning U.S. Fleet," *ANJ* 61, no. 16 (Dec. 20, 1924): 1653.

40. Nolan to Hines, May 5, 1925, LOC, Hines Papers, Box 31.

41. E. T. Johns, "Special Washington Services Newsletter and Commentary," *ANJ* 62, no. 39 (May 31, 1925): 2209.

42. E. T. Johns, "Special Washington Services Newsletter and Commentary," *ANJ* 62, no. 40 (Jun. 6, 1925): 2235.

43. The Legislative Committee was made up of the deputy chief of staff; the five assistant chiefs of staff, G-1 through G-4; the head of the War Plans Division; and a representative from the Judge Advocate General's Office.

44. "Special Washington Services Newsletter and Commentary," *ANJ* 62, no. 41 (June 13, 1925): 2235.

45. "Special Washington Services Newsletter and Commentary," *ANJ* 62, no. 46 (July 18, 1925): 2377.

46. "Special Washington Services Newsletter and Commentary," *ANJ* 62, no. 52 (Aug. 29, 1925): 2521.

47. Editorial, "Reducing the Budget," *IJ* 25, no. 5 (Nov. 1925): 675.

48. This anger was expressed in a spate of service journal articles. See, for instance, Pershing, "Citizen Army," 621–23; and Editorial, "Economy," *CAJ* 53, no. 6 (Dec. 1925): 511–12.

49. There were only three such articles in the major service journals in the first half of 1925, while there could have been as many as three in a single issue of any of them in the first half of 1923.

50. The first example of an article taking this new approach is Robert W. Corrigan, "The Case for Disarmament," *IJ* 24, no. 3 (Mar. 1924): 298–99.

51. Thomas Hammond, "The ABC of National Defense," *IJ* 26, no. 5 (Nov. 1925): 535.

52. "Address of Major General John L. Hines to the Annual Convention of the National Guard Association in Philadelphia, Dec. 1, 1924," LOC, Hines Papers, Box. 40.

53. See, for instance, "Encourage National Defense," *ANJ* 62, no. 9 (Jan. 10, 1925): 1734.

54. See, for instance, P. S. Bond, "Our Military Policy," *ME* 14, no. 76 (July/Aug. 1922): 195–98, 252; 24, no. 77 (Sept./Oct. 1922): 283–86, 346.

55. See, for instance, Editorial, "The Development of a Military Policy," *CAJ* 62, no. 6 (June 1925): 514–21; and Charles Dobbs, "Problems of the New Army," *FAJ* 25, no. 6 (Nov./Dec. 1925): 534–37. These two journals rarely published articles with any sort of political overtones.

Chapter 2

1. As quoted in William O. Odom, *After the Trenches: The Transformation of the U.S. Army, 1918–1939* (College Station: Texas A&M University Press, 2008), 84.

2. *Chief of Staff Annual Report, 1920* as published in *Annual Report of the Secretary of War, 1920* (Washington, D.C., Government Printing Office, 1920), 158, 159.

3. Ibid., 5.

4. "The New Army of the United States," *ANJ* 58, no. 2 (Sept. 11, 1920): 30.

5. War Department, General Order 48, Aug. 12, 1920, NA, RG 407, 321.11.

6. War Department, General Order 24, June 17, 1921, NA, RG 407, 321.11.

7. War Department, Special Order 155–0, July 7, 1921, NA, RG 407, 321.11.

8. G-1, Personnel; G-2, Intelligence; G-3, Operations; G-4, Supply, and War Plans Division.

9. Adjutant General to Commanding Generals of all Corps Areas, Sept. 27, 1921, NA, RG 407, 320.

10. Adjutant General to Commanding Generals of all Corps Areas, Sept. 27, 1921 (emphasis on "brief" in original).

11. John M. Hines to Harbord, Feb. 5, 1922, LOC, Hines Papers, Box 2.

12. L. D. Gasser, Memorandum for the Chief of Staff, Nov. 14, 1921, NA, RG 407, 321.1.

13. Pershing, Memorandum for General Lassiter, June 21, 1922, LOC, Pershing Papers, Box 134.

14. Pershing to Sydney G. McKay, May 31, 1921, LOC, Pershing Papers, Box 146.

15. Adjutant General to the Chiefs of Branches, Aug. 3, 1921, LOC, Pershing Papers, Box 134; Pershing to Guy S. Presler, May 16, 1922, Ibid., Box 165.

16. Pershing to Palmer, Apr. 15, 1921; Pershing to Palmer Aug. 15, 1921, LOC, Palmer Papers, Box 4.

17. Palmer's major effort in this regard was a lecture he delivered at the Army War College on September 23, 1921, which was later distributed to all officers. See War Department Bulletin #16, Oct. 3, 1921, LOC, Palmer Papers, Box. 4.

18. "Officers Expected to Support War Department Policy," *ANJ* 59, no. 44 (July 1, 1922): 1059.

19. "Military Discussion," *CJ* 31, no. 129 (Oct. 22, 1922): 403–4.

20. Robert Whitfield, Memorandum for the Director, Operations Division, Mar. 25, 1921, LOC, Pershing Papers, Box 134; William Wright, Memorandum to the Director, War Plans Division, Apr. 28, 1921, LOC, Hines Papers, Box 5.

21. Whitfield, Memorandum for General Jervey, June 25, 1921, LOC, Pershing Papers, Box 134.

22. *Annual Report of the Secretary of War, 1922* (Washington, D.C., Government Printing Office, 1922), 19.

23. War Department, General Order 31, July 18, 1921, LOC, Hines Papers, Box 7.

24. See, for instance, Odom, *After the Trenches*, 93–94.

25. *Annual Report, Chief of the Militia Bureau, 1918* (Washington, D.C. Government Printing Office, 1918), 10, 11.

26. Many senior regular officers felt that the Guard had been shabbily treated in the world war. Haan, in particular, stated, "We will have many things to explain when we get home as to what was done to so many of the National Guard divisions." Haan to William Lassiter, Feb. 15, 1919, WSHS, William G. Haan Papers, Box 4. Richard S. Faulkner provides a number of examples of what he calls an almost Prussian attitude taken by regular officers toward their counterparts in the Guard during the war. Faulkner, *The School of Hard Knocks: Combat Leadership in the American Expeditionary Forces* (College Station: Texas A&M University Press, 2012), 221.

27. *Annual Report, Chief of the Militia Bureau, 1919* (Washington, D.C., Government Printing Office, 1919), 5.

28. John K. Mahon, *History of the Militia and the National* Guard (New York: Macmillan, 1983), 174.

29. "Prospects of the National Guard," *ANJ* 56, no. 37 (May 17, 1919): 1297.

30. Carter, Memorandum for the Chief of Staff, June 12, 1919, NA, RG 325.4.

31. John D. Rove, Chairman, Organizing Committee, National Guard Association of the United States, to the Adjutants General Association, Aug. 17, 1919, NA, RG 407, 325.4.

32. The numbers dropped from 36,012 on June 30, 1919, to 35,827 on November 30, 1919. *Annual Report of the Secretary of War, 1919* (Washington, D.C., Government Printing Office, 1919), 89; "The National Guard in Theory and Practice," *ANJ* 57, no. 15 (Dec. 13, 1919): 456.

33. By the end of 1920, the numbers were up to 54,017. *Annual Report, Chief of the Militia Bureau, 1920* (Washington, D.C., Government Printing Office, 1920), 7.

34. "The New National Guard Bill," *ANJ* 57, no. 11 (Nov. 15, 1919): 332.

35. *Annual Report, Chief of the Militia Bureau, 1921* (Washington, D.C., Government Printing Office, 1921), 6; *Annual Report, Chief of the Militia Bureau, 1922* (Washington, D.C., Government Printing Office, 1922), 5.

36. Ibid., 6.

37. George C. Rickards, Memorandum for the Chief of Staff, July 6, 1921, NA, RG 407, 325.44.

38. Rickards, Memorandum for the Chief of Staff, Sept. 20, 1922, NA, RG 407, 325.44.

39. *Annual Report, Chief of the Militia Bureau, 1922*, 9

40. James Harbord, Memorandum for the Chief of the Militia Bureau, Dec. 22, 1921, NA, RG 407, 325.43.

41. Palmer to Pershing, Feb. 18, 1922, LOC, Pershing Papers, Box 134.

42. "Report of a Committee of the War Department General Staff Convened in the War Department," Jan. 15, 1923, NA, RG 407, 325.4.

43. This problem was mentioned in *Infantry Journal* only once. "The End of the Year," *IJ* 23, no. 2 (Aug. 1923): 214.

44. Ibid., 212.

45. "National Guard Prospects," *IJ* 24, no. 4 (Aug.1924): 499–500.

46. Many earlier armories had special galleries from which the public could watch drills.

47. The Guard expanded by only ninety-seven in the entire year. *Annual Report, Chief of the Militia Bureau, 1924* (Washington, D.C. Government Printing Office, 1924), 17.

48. General Staff, Operations and Training Division, G-3. *Annual Reports, 1924-25*. 9.

49. William G. Haan, Memorandum for the Chief of Staff, July 13, 1920, WSHS, William G. Haan Papers, Box 8.

50. "National Guard Troops in the Reorganization," *ANJ 58*, no. 9 (Oct. 3, 1920): 226; "Designation of War Units by States," *ANJ* 58, no. 15 (Dec. 11, 1920): 417.

51. *Annual Report of the Secretary of War, 1921* (Washington, D.C., Government Printing Office, 1921), 12; "Corps Area Commanders vs. the Militia Bureau," *ANJ* 59, no. 3 (Sept. 17, 1921): 187.

52. "National Guard Policies to be Revised," *ANJ* 59, no. 6 (Oct. 8, 1921): 229; Rickards, Memorandum for Col. Hunt, Mar. 20, 1922, LOC, Pershing Papers, Box 134; George C. Marshall to General Pershing, Apr. 28, 1922, Ibid.

53. L. D. Gasser, Memorandum for the Director of Operations Division, July 8, 1921; Pershing to Director of Operations Division, July 22, 1921, NA, RG 407, 321.15.

54. "The Militia Bureau," *IJ* 27, no. 1 (July 1925): 87–97.

55. "Mobilization Defense Test," *IJ* 25, no. 2 (Aug. 1924): 208–9.

56. *Annual Report of the Secretary of War, 1921*, 24.

57. The Militia Bureau conceded that a typical guardsman received only about 150 hours of training a year. *Annual Report, Chief of the Militia Bureau, 1925* (Washington, D.C., Government Printing Office, 1925), 23.

58. "Place of the National Guard in the National Position of Readiness," Nov. 1, 1922, LOC, Palmer Papers, Box 5.

59. "A School for Instructors," *IJ* 24, no. 2 (Feb. 1924): 214.

60. *Annual Report of the Secretary of War, 1921*, 24; General Staff, Operations and Training Division, G-3. *Annual Reports, 1922*. 6.

61. General Staff, Operations and Training Division, G-3. *Annual Reports, 1923*, 15.

62. Hugh D. Drum, Memorandum for the Chief of Staff, May 31, 1924, NA, RG 407, 353.

63. General Staff, Operations and Training Division, G-3. *Annual Reports, 1924-25*, 56–57.

64. *Annual Report, Chief of the Militia Bureau, 1924* (Washington, D.C., Government Printing Office, 1924), 18.

65. "General Hammond Addresses the MOWW," *IJ* 27, no. 5 (Nov. 1925): 632.

66. Ibid.

67. Adjutant General to Corp Area Commanders, Apr. 26, 1921, NA, RG 407, 354.1.

68. Ibid.

69. Haan, Memorandum to the Adjutant General, May 17, 1921, NA, RG 407, 354.1.

70. "Citizens' Military Training Camps" (brochure), n.d., LOC, Pershing Papers, Box 39.

71. Haan, Memorandum for the Adjutant General, Jan. 12, 1921, NA, RG 407, 341.1.

72. Haan, Memorandum for the Adjutant General, Mar. 17, 1921, NA, RG 407, 354.1.

73. Ibid.

74. Adjutant General to Corps Area Commanders, Apr. 26, 1921, NA, RG 407, 354.1.

75. General Staff, Operations and Training Division, G-3. *Annual Reports, 1922*, 13.

76. C. H. Martin, Memorandum for the Chief of Staff, Sept. 13, 1921, NA, RG 407, 354.1.

77. Palmer, Memorandum for General Pershing, Nov. 16, 1921, LOC, Pershing Papers, Box 39. The dissenter was the governor of North Dakota, who denounced the camps for teaching militarism.

78. Palmer, Memorandum for General Pershing, Nov. 16, 1921.

79. General Staff, Operations and Training Division, G-3. *Annual Reports, 1922*, 14.

80. Lassiter, Memorandum for the Adjutant General, Feb. 7, 1922, NA, RG 407, 354.1.

81. William Cruikshank, Memorandum for the Chief of Staff, May 1, 1922, NA, RG 407, 354.1.

82. Horace Stebbins to Pershing, May 3, 1922, LOC, Hines Papers, Box 5.

83. H. W. Caygill, "C.M.T.C. Recruiting," *IJ*, 21, no. 5 (Nov. 1922): 535–40; Stebbins to Pershing, May 3, 1922.

84. Pershing to Stebbins, May 19, 1922, LOC, Pershing Papers. Box 137.

85. William Cruickshank, Memorandum for the Adjutant General, Jan. 3, 1923, NA, RG 407, 354.1.

86. "Selling the Army to the American People," *ANJ* 60, no. 17 (Dec. 23, 1922): 397.

87. Henry C. Jewell, Memorandum for the Adjutant General, Nov. 28, 1922, NA, RG 407, 354.1.

88. T. Q. Donaldson, Memorandum for the Chief of Staff, Mar. 19, 1924; C. H. Martin, Memorandum for the Chief of Staff, June 7, 1924, NA, RG 407, 354.1.

89. "General March's Weekly Interview," *ANJ* 56, no. 23 (Feb. 8, 1919): 815.

90. *Chief of Staff Annual Report, 1919* as published in *Annual Report of the Secretary of War, 1919* (Washington, D.C., Government Printing Office, 1919), 283.

91. Henry Jervey, Memorandum for the Adjutant General, May 24, 1920, NA, RG 165, 9153–229; "Building up the ORC," *ANJ* 57, no. 21 (Jan. 24, 1920): 641.

92. *Chief of Staff Annual Report, 1919*, 281.

93. "Reserve Officers' Associations," *ANJ* 57, no. 12 (Nov. 22, 1919): 336.

94. "Reserve Corps Notes," *ANJ* 57, no. 34 (Apr. 24, 1920): 792.

95. "Officers' Reserve Corps Losses," *ANJ* 58, no. 29 (Mar. 19, 1921): 1091.

96. "Officers' Reserve Corps," *ANJ* 57, no. 44 (July 3, 1920): 1357.

97. General Staff, Operations and Training Division, G-3. *Annual Reports 1920–21*, 18.

98. Haan, Memorandum for the Adjutant General, Dec. 1, 1920, NA, RG 407, OR 326.1.

99. Special Regulations 46, "General Policies and Regulations of the Organized Reserve," Feb. 16, 1921, NA, RG 407, OR 326.1.

100. John W. Weeks to State Governors, June 3, 1921, NA, RG 407, OR 326.1.

101. Lassiter, Memorandum for the Chief of Staff, Sept. 12, 1921, NA, RG 407, OR 320.

102. Adjutant General to Corps Area Commanders, Apr. 5, 1921, NA, RG 407, OR 326.1.

103. "Minutes of a Conference of Organized Reserve Boards Held at Governors Island, May 20, 1921," NA, RG 407, OR 326.1.

104. Adjutant General to the Commanding General of the Fifth Corps Area, June 24, 1921, NA, RG 407, OR 326.1.

105. William Lassiter, Memorandum for the Adjutant General, July 17, 1921, LOC, Pershing Papers, Box 134.

106. See, for instance, Jonathan A. Straat to Commanding General, Seventh Corps Area, Dec. 9, 1921; T. J. Powers to Commanding General, Sixth Corps Area, Dec. 14, 1921, NA, RG 407, OR 320.

107. Lassiter, Memorandum for the Chief of Staff, Sept. 12, 1921.

108. Lassiter, Memorandum for the Chief of Staff, Oct. 22, 1921, NA, RG 407, OR 320.

109. Lassiter to Adjutant General, Apr. 1, 1922, NA, RG 407, OR 320.

110. "Officers' Reserve Corps of 100,000," *ANJ* 58, no. 26 (Feb. 26, 1921): 724.

111. "O.R.C. Notes," *ANJ* 58, no. 20 (Jan. 15, 1921): 558.

112. Palmer pleaded with Pershing that the number of regular officers assigned to duty with the Reserve not be cut further. Palmer to Pershing, Jan. 31, 1921, LOC, Pershing Papers, Box 134.

113. W. D. Connor, Memorandum for the Assistant Chief of Staff, G-3, Sept. 9, 1922; Pershing, Memorandum for General Lassiter, Oct. 3, 1922, NA, RG 407, OR 400.35.

114. Stuart Heintzelman, Memorandum for the Adjutant General, Nov. 22, 1922; M. B. Stewart, Memorandum for the Assistant Chief of Staff, G-3, Oct. 7, 1922, NA, RG 407, OR 400.345; Harrison Hall to Commanding Generals of Corp Areas, Mar. 3, 1922, NA, RG 407, OR 680.341.

115. Editorial, "More Training for Reserve Officers," *IJ* 18, no. 6 (June 1921): 622.

116. Lassiter to Adjutant General, Jan. 19, 1922, NA, RG 407, OR. 354.1.

117. Lassiter, Memorandum for the Adjutant General, NA, RG 407, OR 354.1.

118. Hines to Pershing, Apr. 23, 1922, LOC, Pershing Papers, Box 94.

119. Ibid.

120. "Reserve Officer Department," *IJ* 20, no. 5 (May 1922): 581; General Staff, Operations and Training Division, G-3. *Annual Reports 1922,* 9.

121. "Reserve Officer Conference Instills Sense of Responsibility," *ANJ* 59, no. 39 (May 27, 1922): 925.

122. "'R' Removed from Collars," *ANJ* 59, no. 19 (Jan. 7, 1922): 415.

123. "Reserve Officer Department," *IJ* 58, no. 6 (Dec. 1921): 705.

124. This vision is summarized in Palmer, "Remarks of Col. J. M. Palmer before a Board of Review of Reserve Officer Regulations, January 8, 1923," LOC, Palmer Papers, Box 5.

125. E. B. John, "Washington Newsletter," *ANJ* 60, no. 37 (May 12, 1923): 889.

126. F. C. Boggs to Adjutant General, Oct. 10, 1922, NA, RG 407, OR 322.

127. Robert F. McMillan to Commanding General, Fourth Corps Area, Oct. 3, 1923, NA, RG 407, OR 322.

128. Robert L. Collins to all Corps Area Commanders, Apr. 7, 1923, NA, RG 407, OR 322.

129. J. B. Wilson to Adjutant General, Oct. 20, 1924, NA, RG 407, OR 322.

130. S. D. Sturgis to Adjutant General, Dec. 2, 1924, NA, RG 407, OR 322.

131. "Reserve Officer Department," *IJ* 22, no. 2 (Feb. 1923), 232–33; 23, no. 4 (Oct. 1923): 472–74; 23, no. 6 (Dec. 1923): 729–32.

132. "Reserve Officer Convention Asks for Six Full FAs and War Department Representation," *ANJ* 62, no. 9 (Nov. 1, 1924): 88.

133. John R. Delafield to John B. Weeks, Mar. 2, 1925, NA, RG 407, OR 300.

134. Drum, Memorandum for the Chief of Staff, Apr. 23, 1925, NA, RG 407, OR 300.

135. Ibid.

136. James K. Reaves, Memorandum for the Assistant Chief of Staff, G-3, May 1, 1925, NA, RG 407, OR 300.

137. Reserve Officer Committee #3, Memorandum for the Assistant Chief of Staff, n.d., NA, RG 407, OR 300.

138. Davis to Delafield, Sept. 14, 1925, NA, RG 407, OR 300.

139. Arthur J. Klein, "The "Army Correspondence Courses," *IJ* 26, no. 1 (Jan. 1925): 1–12.

140. J. C. Carsten to the Adjutant General, Aug. 16, 1923, NA, RG 407, OR 353.

141. Drum to the Adjutant General, Apr. 30, 1924, NA, RG 407, OR 353.

142. An Instructor, "How Good Is the Reserve Corps?," *IJ* 27, no. 3 (Sept. 1925): 280–83.

143. Quoted in "Reserve Officer Department," *IJ* 27, no. 3 (Sept. 1925): 340.

144. "Address of Major General John L. Hines before the Annual Convention of the Reserve Officers Association," Oct. 9, 1925, LOC, Hines Papers, Box 41.

145. Drum, Memorandum for the Chief of Staff, Nov. 5, 1925, NA, RG 407, OR 322.

146. This early history of the ROTC program is taken from Victor B. Hirshauer, "The History of the Army Reserve Officers Training Corps, 1916–1973" (PhD diss., Johns Hopkins University, 1975), 1–44; and Gene M. Lyons and John W. Masland, "The Origins of ROTC," *Military Affairs* 23, no. 1 (Spring 1959): 1–4.

147. "Statement on Educational Institutions Giving Military Training," NA, RG 165, 9053–121.

148. Montgomery Macomb, Memorandum for the Chief of Staff, July 3, 1916; Macomb, Memorandum for the Chief of Staff, Sept. 19, 1916, NA, RG 165, 9282–22. By this time, there were 36,000 students enrolled in courses in 102 schools. *Annual Report of the Secretary of War, 1916* (Washington, D.C., Government Printing Office, 1916), 17.

149. D. W. Ketchum, Memorandum for the Chief of Staff, Aug. 22, 1918, NA, RG 165, 9089 40.

150. "Slash Student Army Training Corps," *ANJ* 56, no. 5 (Oct. 18, 1918): 175.

151. Lytle Brown, Memorandum for the Chief of Staff, Nov. [?], 1918, NA, RG 407, ROTC 000.862.

152. COEST to District Inspection Officer, Third District, Dec. 7, 1918, NA, RG 407, ROTC 000.862.

153. "Plans for Training Reserve Officers," *ANJ* 56, no. 21 (Jan. 25, 1919): 741.

154. Michael S. Neiberg, *Making Citizen-Soldiers: ROTC and the Ideology of American Military Service* (Cambridge, MA: Harvard University Press, 2000), 27.

155. Robert E. Wyllie, Memorandum for the Chief of Staff, Apr. 19, 1919, NA, RG 407, ROTC 425.

156. *Annual Report of the Secretary of War, 1919* (Washington, D.C., Government Printing Office, 1919), 21.

157. Enrollments reached over 100,000 in September 1919.

158. Editorial, "The R.O.T.C. and the Coast Artillery," *JUSA* 93, no. 3 (Sept. 1920): 293.

159. "Annual Report, ROTC," General Staff, Operations and Training Division, G-3. *Annual Reports 1922,* 12.

160. Brown, Nov. 1, 1919, NA, RG 407, ROTC 000.862.

161. Wyllie, Memorandum for the Chief of Staff, Apr. 11, 1919, NA, RG 407, ROTC 475; Lytle Brown, Memorandum for the Chief of Staff, Mar. 17, 1919, NA, RG 407, ROTC 246.85.

162. Brown, Memorandum, Mar. 17, 1919.

163. P. G. Harris, Memorandum for the Assistant Chief of Staff, Operations and Training Division, Jan. 23, 1922, NA, RG 407, ROTC 245.845.

164. Drum, Aug. 26, 1924, NA, RG 407, OR 322.

165. *Chief of Staff Annual Report, 1924* as published in *Annual Report of the Secretary of War, 1924* (Washington, D.C., Government Printing Office, 1924), 206.

166. Ibid.; Adjutant General to Commanding General Northeastern Department, June 7, 1920 NA, RG 407, ROTC 403.401.

167. H. A. White to Director, War Plans Division, Mar. 24, 1920, NA, RG 407, ROTC 400.35.

168. At a conference held by Morrow at the War Department in 1920, college presidents cited uniforms and the bonding requirement as the two most critical issues related to ROTC. "ROTC Conference at the War Department," *ANJ* 57, no. 27 (Mar. 6, 1920): 817.

169. Albert B. Dockery, "R.O.T.C. at an Essentially Military College," *CJ* 30, no. 124 (July 1921): 290.

170. Ollin B. Ellis, "The Future of the R.O.T.C." *IJ* 16, no. 9 (Mar. 1920): 755.

171. Instructor, "Military Training at Colleges," *IJ* 16, no. 5 (Nov. 1919): 406.

172. Ibid.

173. In 1922 the ROTC Branch of the Operations and Training Division listed the problem of rapid rotation of officers as the second-most-important problem facing the program. Instructor, "Military Training at Colleges," 406.

174. Lassiter, Memorandum for the Adjutant General, Nov. 9, 1921, NA, RG 407, ROTC 000.862; Harold E. Briggs, "A Look at the R.O.T.C.," *JUSA* 53, no. 3 (Sept. 1920): 249.

175. As was the case with the CMTC, officers in charge of summer camps took pride in publishing figures on gains in average weight and chest expansion obtained attendees experienced. See, for instance, General Staff, Operations and Training Division, G-3. *Annual Reports, 1920–21,* 34.

176. Robert C. Grow, "The Reserve Officer Training Course at a Large University," *CJ* 30, no. 125 (Oct. 1921): 373–77.

177. Robert C. Davis, Memorandum for the Chief of Staff, June 1, 1922, NA, RG 407, ROTC 312.3.

178. Brown, Memorandum for the Chief of Staff, Mar. 17, 1919, NA, RG 407, ROTC 333.9.

179. R. M. Beck, Memorandum for the Adjutant General, Nov. 19, 1919, NA, RG 407, ROTC 210.4; "Inspection of ROTC Units," *ANJ* 57, no. 7 (Oct. 18, 1919): 201.

180. Training regulations governing the camps were issued in May 1918. Seven camps, limited mostly to students in the advanced course, were scheduled for June. Special Regulations 44a; H. P. McCain, Memorandum for the Chief of Staff, May 22, 1918, NA, RG 407, ROTC 354.14

181. William M. Cruikshank, Memorandum for the Chief of Staff, Mar. 1, 1922, NA, RG 407, ROTC 354.17.

182. For instance, see A. Donaldson to Chief of Cavalry, Feb. 1, 1922, NA, RG 407, ROTC 354.17.

183. For instance, see Lassiter, Memorandum for the Chief of Staff, Dec. 30, 1921, NA, RG 407, ROTC 354.1.

184. For instance, see Farnsworth, Memorandum for the Chief of Staff, Jan. 12, 1922, NA, RG 407, ROTC 354.17.

185. Enrollments in camps were 3,363 in 1919; 6,228 in 1920; 6,300 in 1921; and 8,000 in 1922. General Staff, Operations and Training Division, G-3. *Annual Reports, 1922,* 14.

186. Adjutant General, Memorandum for the Chief of Staff, May 6, 1921, NA, RG 407, ROTC 111.02.

187. Pershing Memorandum for General Lassiter, Feb. 7, 1922, LOC, Pershing Papers, Box 134.

188. Don Gilman, "The R.O.T.C. and the C.M.T.C.," *IJ* 24, no. 6 (June 1924): 749; General Staff, Operations and Training Division, G-3. *Annual Reports, 1923*, 25; General Staff, Operations and Training Division, G-3; *Annual Reports, 1924-25*, 34.

189. Archibald Campbell to Adjutant General, Jan. 12, 1924; Robert L. Collins to Corps Areas Commanders, Apr. 9, 1924; Rudolf Springer to A. P. Echols, July 9, 1924; D. E. Nolan, Memorandum for the Assistant Chief of Staff, G-3, June 27, 1924, NA, RG 407, ROTC 421.

190. Gilman, "R.O.T.C. and the C.M.T.C., " 776; Drum, Memorandum for the Chief of Staff, June 3, 1924, NA, RG 407, ROTC 000.863; Drum, Memorandum for the Adjutant General, Dec. 24, 1924, NA, RG 407, ROTC 121.62.

191. Editorial, *IJ* 25, no. 5 (Nov. 1924): 569.

192. Lassiter, Memorandum for the Adjutant General, Apr. 12, 1923, NA, RG 407, ROTC 354.17; General Staff, Operations and Training Division, G-3. *Annual Reports 1923*, 24; General Staff, Operations and Training Division, G-3. *Annual Reports, 1924–25*, 39.

193. Gilman, "R.O.T.C. . and the C.M.T.C.," 776; General Staff, Operations and Training Division, G-3, *Annual Report of the G-3 Division, 1923*, 13; General Staff, Operations and Training Division, G-3. *Annual Reports 1924-25*, 25–26.

194. Drum, Memorandum for the Chief of Staff, June 18, 1924, NA, RG 407, ROTC 000.862; Edgar T. Collins, Memorandum for the Assistant Chief of Staff, G-3, May 20, 1924, ibid.

195. Drum, Memorandum for the Chief of Staff, June 3, 1924; Drum, Memorandum for the Adjutant General, Dec. 24, 1924.

196. Drum, Memorandum for the Chief of Staff, June 19, 1924, NA, RG 407, ROTC 000.862.

197. Livingston Farrell to the Secretary of War, Sept. 15, 1925; Wm. Snow, Memorandum for the Chief of Staff, Aug. 26, 1925, NA, RG 407, ROTC 000.862.

198. Drum, Memorandum for the Adjutant General, Sept. 16, 1925, NA, RG 407, ROTC 000.862.

199. Drum, Memorandum for the Adjutant General, June 29, 1925; E. J. Conley to All Professors of Military Science and Tactics, July 30, 1925, NA, RG 407, ROTC 000.862.

200. F. W. Coe to the Adjutant General, Aug. 25, 1925; Snow to the Adjutant General, Aug. 26, 1925, NA, RG 407, ROTC 000.862.

201. Farrell to the Secretary of War, Sept. 15, 1925; Kenyon Rutherford to the Secretary of War, Sept. 25, 1925; Drum, Memorandum for the Adjutant General, Sept. 10, 1925, NA, RG 407, ROTC 000.862.

202. Drum, Memorandum for the Adjutant General, Nov. 6, 1925; "Report of the Committee on Military Organization and Policy Adopted at the Meeting of the Association of Land Grant Colleges at Chicago, Ill, Nov. 19, 1925," NA, RG 407, ROTC 000.862.

Chapter 3

1. *Annual Report of the Secretary of War, 1928* (Washington, D.C., Government Printing Office, *1928*), 1.

2. Editorial, *ANJ* 66, no. 27 (Mar. 2, 1929): 528.

3. *Annual Report of the Secretary of War, 1926* (Washington, D.C., Government Printing Office, *1926*), 32; "House Makes Record in Passing Military Bills," *ANJ* 63, no. 37 (May 15, 1926): 883.

4. E. B. Johns, "Impressions of Army Legislation," *IJ* 28, no. 1 (Jan. 1926): 3.

5. *Annual Report of the Secretary of War, 1926,* 30–31; "War Department Saved $5,433,000 in Year," *ANJ* 64, no. 1 (Sept. 4, 1926): 1.

6. Campbell King, Memorandum for the Chief of Staff, Nov. 11, 1925; Dwight F. Davis to John M. Morin, May 5, 1926, NA, RG 407, 320.2.

7. "Reserves Fight for National Defense Looms," *ANJ* 63, no. 2 (Sept. 12, 1925): 25–26; "Special Service News, Comment, and Gossip," *ANJ* 63, no. 5 (Oct. 3, 1925): 101.

8. John C. O'Laughlin, "No Army or Navy Officer Personnel Cut Contemplated," *ANJ* 63, no. 6 (Oct. 10, 1925): 121.

9. O'Laughlin, "No Army or Navy Officer Personnel Cut Contemplated," 121; "Army Budget Estimates," *ANJ* 63, no. 16 (Dec. 19, 1925): 243.

10. Editorial, "Congress in Session," *IJ* 28, no. 1 (Jan. 1926): 73; E. B. Johns, "Impressions of Army Legislation," ibid., 3–6.

11. "War Department Appropriations Bill," *ANJ* 63, no. 23 (Feb. 6, 1926), 613; "Army Appropriations Bill Passed," *ANJ* 63, no. 28 (Mar. 13, 1926): 659; E. B. Johns, "The Senate and National Defense," *IJ* 28, no. 4 (Apr. 1926): 381–87.

12. Fox Connor, Memorandum for the Chief of Staff, Feb. 19, 1926, NA, RG 407, 111.

13. B. H. Wells, Memorandum for the Chief of Staff, June 24, 1926; Calvin Coolidge to Dwight F. Davis, June 18, 1925, NA, RG 407, 111.

14. Walker, Memorandum for the Chief of Staff, Sept. 16, 1926; Walker, Memorandum for the Chief of Staff, Nov. 27, 1926, NA, RG 407, 320.02.

15. M. H. McIntyre, "Army Forced to Cut Its Strength to 110,900," *ANJ* 64, no. 5 (Oct. 2, 1926): 97; Editorial, "The Spirit of the Army," *IJ* 29, no. 5 (Nov. 1926): 548–49.

16. E. S. Hartshorn, Memorandum for the Assistant Chief of Staff, G-4, Dec. 24, 1926, NA, RG 407, 320.22; "President in Favor of Adequate Defense," *ANJ* 64, no. 11 (Nov. 13, 1926): 341; Wells, Memorandum for the Chief of Staff, Jan. 7, 1927, NA, RG 407, 320.22; "Coolidge Moves to Find Funds," *ANJ* 64, no. 28 (Mar. 12, 1927): 652.

17. "What the Services May Expect from Congress," *ANJ* 64, no. 13 (Nov. 27, 1926): 291; "Army Estimates Are Probed by Committee," *ANJ* 64, no. 19 (Jan. 8, 1927): 337, 358; W. Frank James, "Handling Military Legislation in the House of Representatives," *IJ* 31, no. 2 (Aug. 1927): 115–30.

18. Editorial, *ANJ* 66, no. 9 (Oct. 27, 1928): 117.

19. "New Congress Faces Personnel Problems," *ANJ* 66, no. 33 (Apr. 13, 1929): 645, 647.

20. "Defense in Spotlight after Hoover's Moves," *ANJ* 66, no. 48 (July 27, 1929): 977. The text of Hoover's speech appears on page 979.

21. Robert K. Griffith Jr., *Men Wanted for the U.S. Army: America's Experience with an All-Volunteer Army between the World Wars* (Westview, CT: Greenwood, 1982), 114, 115.

22. Dwight F. Davis, "War Department Program, Military: Directive for Fiscal Year 1931," NA, RG 407, 111.

23. Editorial, *ANJ* 67, no. 45 (July 12, 1930): 1057; *Annual Report of the Chief of Staff, 1930,* as published in *Annual Report of the Secretary of War, 1930* (Washington, D.C., Government Printing Office, 1930), 137–39.

Chapter 4

1. The best sources on the CME campaign are Ronald Schaffer, "The War Department Defense of ROTC, 1920–1940," *Wisconsin Magazine of History* 53, no. 2 (Winter 1969–70): 108–20; Gene M. Lyons and John W. Masland, *Education and Military Leadership: A Study of the R.O.T.C.* (Princeton, NJ: Princeton University Press, 1959), 46–48; James H. Hawkes, "Antimilitarism at State Universities: The Campaign against Compulsory ROTC, 1920–1940," *Wisconsin Magazine of History* 49, no. 1 (Autumn): 1965: 41–54; and Victor B. Hirshauer, "The History of the Army Reserve Officers Training Corps, 1916–1973" (PhD diss., Johns Hopkins University, 1975), 177–209.

2. Winthrop D. Lane, *Military Training in Schools and Colleges of the United States: The Facts and an Interpretation* ([New York]: Committee on Military Training, 1926).

3. "Congress Asked to Stop Compulsory Drills," *ANJ* 63, no. 34 (Apr. 24, 1926): 811; "Compulsory Training Hearings," *ANJ* 63, no. 35 (May 1, 1926): 835.

4. Drum, Memorandum for the Chief of Staff, Nov. 12, 1925, NA, RG 407, ROTC 000.862.

5. Malin Craig, Memorandum for the Chief of Staff, Jan. 11, 1927, NA, RG 407, ROTC 000.862.

6. Drum, Memorandum for the Chief of Staff, Nov. 12, 1925.

7. Frank Parker, Memorandum for the Chief of Staff, Dec. 7, 1927, NA, RG 407, ROTC 000.862.

8. James H. Hawkes, "Antimilitarism at State Universities," 41–54.

9. Hirshauer, "History of the Army Reserve Officers Training Corps," 127, 161, 172, 173.

10. "War Department Drops R.O.T.C. Bayonet Practice," *ANJ* 63, no. 43 (June 26, 1926): 1025.

11. In a representative article in *Infantry Journal*, the author notes opposition to ROTC on campus but reassures his fellow officers that the "level-headed" students would prevail and defend the program. Garrett Drummond, "Military Training in the Universities and Colleges," *IJ* 32, no. 1 (Jan. 1928): 60.

12. Jim D. Hill, *The Minute Man in Peace and War: A History of the National Guard* (Mechanicsburg, PA: Stackpole, 1964), 317–46.

13. Speech by Creed C. Hammond, *Official Proceedings of the National Guard Association of the United States General Conference, 1928,* Washington, D.C. National Guard Association, 1928), 50–53; *Annual Report of the Secretary of War, 1928* (Washington, D.C., Government Printing Office, 1928), 7, 8.

14. Ibid., 8.

15. Creed Hammond to Adjutant General, May 26, 1926, NA, RG 407, 325.4.

16. Ibid.

17. Parker, Memorandum for the Chief of Staff, May 23, 1927; Wells, Memorandum for Assistant Chief of Staff, G-3, Apr. 29, 1927; Secretary of War to Herbert H. Lord, June 10, 1927, NA, RG 407, 325.4; *Annual Report of the Chief of the Militia Bureau, 1928* (Washington, D.C. Government Printing Office, 1928), 55.

18. *Official Proceedings of the National Guard Association of the United States General Conference, 1929* Washington, D.C. National Guard Association, 1929), 31–32.

19. Hammond to the Assistant Chief of Staff, G-3, Nov. 21, 1925, NA, RG 407, 111.

20. *Annual Report of the Chief of the Militia Bureau, 1929* (Washington, D.C. Government Printing Office, 1929), 50.

21. "Speech by Creed C. Hammond," 1928, 56.

22. *Annual Report of the Chief of the Militia Bureau, 1929,* 1.

23. Ibid., 3.

24. Lecture by Fred B Shaw, Infantry Training Section, Militia Bureau, Mar. 3, 1926, quoted in "Items on the National Guard," *IJ* 29, no.1 (July 1926) 100–101; Frank Lockhead, "National Guard Training Objectives," *IJ* 30, no. 2 (Feb. 1927): 169–75.

25. Lockhead, 169-75; R. M. Chesaldine, "Progress of the National Guard," *IJ* 30, no. 3 (Mar. 1927): 319–21.

26. Hammond to Adjutant General, Oct. 20, 1926, NA RG 407, 353.

27. Ibid.

28. See, for instance, "National Guard Training Directive, Training Year 1928–1929" Oct. 15, 1927, NA, RG 407, 353.

29. Parker, Memorandum for the Chief of Staff, Aug. 15, 1928, NA, RG 407, 353.

30. Ibid.

31. General Staff, Operations and Training Division, G-3. *Annual Reports, 1928–29,* 10.

32. "Speech by Creed Hammond," 1928, 56.

33. "National Guard Training Directive, Training Year, 1928–1929," Oct. 15, 1927, NA, RG 407, 353.

34. *Annual Report of the Chief of the Militia Bureau, 1929,* 23.

35. "Items on the National Guard," *IJ* 28, no. 6 (June 1926): 652.

36. "Militia Bureau Independence Favored," *ANJ* 63, no. 33 (Apr. 17, 1926): 787.

37. Hammond to the Adjutant General, Feb. 26, 1926, NA, RG 407, 353. "New G.O. to Widen Mil. Bureau Powers," *ANJ* 63, no. 29 (Mar. 20, 1926): 689; "Militia Bureau Independence Favored," *ANJ* 63, no. 33 (Apr. 17, 1926): 787.

38. Harry A Smith, Memorandum for General King, Feb. 27, 1926; Fox Connor, Memorandum for the Assistant Chief of Staff, G-1, Mar. 4, 1926, NA, RG 407, 321.15.

39. "Law Creates New ASW," *ANJ* 63, no. 44 (July 3, 1926): 1049.

40. Hammond, Report, *Official Proceedings of the National Guard Association of the United States General Conference, 1926* (Washington, D.C. National Guard Association, 1926), 42.

41. "Reappointment of Militia Chief Discussed," *ANJ* 66, no. 10 (Nov. 3, 1928): 135.

42. Ibid.

43. "Vacancy as Chief of Militia Bureau," *ANJ* 66, no. 45 (July 6, 1929): 960.

44. *Official Proceedings of the National Guard Association of the United States General Conference, 1929*, 41–42.

45. Milton Reckord, "Guard as Component of U.S. Army Studied," *ANJ* 66, no. 45 (July 6, 1929): 905–6.

46. John D. Markey, "Why a Dual Commission in for National Guard Officers," *IJ* 30, no. 3 (Mar. 1927): 262.

47. "The National Guard," *IJ* 33, no. 6 (Dec. 1928): 656–57.

48. *Official Proceedings of the National Guard Association of the United States General Conference, 1926*, 80.

49. "Report of Special Committee on the Status of the National Guard," *Official Proceedings of the National Guard Association of the United States General Conference, 1929*, 64–69.

50. *Official Proceedings of the National Guard Association of the United States General Conference, 1929*, 142; "Plan Moves to Better Federal Status," *ANJ* 67, no. 10 (Nov. 9, 1929): 216.

51. "Report of Brigadier General Roy Hoffman," *RO* 6, no. 5 (May 1929): 12.

52. General Staff, Operations and Training Division, G-3. *Annual Reports, 1925-1926*, App. G.

53. H. A. Finch, "Not So Good," *IJ* 28, no. 1 (Jan. 1926): 45.

54. William R. Jamieson, "Reserve Corps Problems—Present and Future," *RO* 5, no. 2 (Mar. 1928): 12; A. H. Bowley, Memorandum for the Chief of Staff, May 9, 1930, NA, RG 319, 343.

55. Henry P. Fry, "Stabilizing Our National Defense System," *IJ* 33, no. 1 (July 1928): 37.

56. "Major General Summerall Discusses War Department's Attitudes towards Reserves," *RO* 4, no. 7 (Sept. 1927): 4; "Convention Urges Reforms for Reserves," *ANJ* 44, no. 9 (Nov. 3, 1926): 204.

57. J. H. Tatsch, "Keeping Fit as a Reserve Officer," *RO* 3, no. 8 (Sept. 1926): 63.

58. "Now It Must Be Told," *RO* 2, no. 6 (July 1926): 47.

59. "Convention Urges Reform for Reserves," *ANJ* 54, no. 9 (Nov. 3, 1926): 192.

60. "A Sweeping Change of Policy," *IJ* 30, no. 2 (Feb. 1927): 215–16.

61. "Promotion in the Reserves," *IJ* 30, no. 3 (Mar. 1927): 204.

62. "New Policies Considered," *RO* 4, no. 2 (Mar. 1927): 2, 3.

63. "New Policies Study Committee," *RO* 4, no. 3 (Apr. 1927): 2; "Secretary of War Will Take Direct Action on Reserves," *ANJ* 64, no. 35 (Apr. 30, 1927): 797.

64. "Reserve Decision Made," *ANJ* 64, no. 41 (June 11, 1927): 917; "Reserve Regulations Approved by the W. D.," *ANJ* 64, no. 1 (July 2, 1927): 977.

65. "Object and Mission of the Reserve Officers' Association of the United States," *RO* 3, no. 7 (Aug. 1926): 53.

66. "General Hoffman's Annual Report," *RO* 3, no. 9 (Oct. 1926): 76.

67. R. S. Kimball to Commanding Generals, Corps Areas, Nov. 27, 1925, NA, RG 407, 354.1.

68. Parker, Memorandum for the Chief of Staff, Nov. 7, 1928; Lutz Wahl, Memorandum for the Deputy Chief of Staff, Dec. 30, 1927; Parker, Memorandum for the Chief of Staff, Nov. 8, 1928, NA, RG 407, 354.1.

69. Edward L. King, Memorandum for the Chief of Staff, Oct. 31, 1929, NA, RG 407, 354.1. An exception was made for the Signal Corps.

70. King, Memorandum for the Chief of Staff, Oct. 5, 1929; Harry Hawes to Dwight Davis, Feb. 23, 1929, NA, RG 407, 354.1; Parker, Memorandum for the Chief of Staff, Feb. 23, 1929.

71. King, Memorandum for the Chief of Staff, Oct. 5, 1929.

72. One writer, Floyd Logan, pointed out to President Hoover that the National Defense Act of 1920 contained no reference to holding segregated camps. Logan to the President of the United States, Mar. 13, 1929, NA, RG 407, 354.1.

73. Parker, Memorandum for the Chief of Staff, Mar. 27, 1929, NA, RG 407, 354.1.

Chapter 5

1. Parker, Memorandum for Chief of Staff, Feb. 24, 1928, NA, RG 407, 353.

2. Jorg Muth, *Command Culture: Officer Education in the U.S. Army and the German Armed Forces, 1901–1940, and the Consequences for World War II* (Denton: University of North Texas Press, 2011), 45–47.

3. War Department, General Order 112, Sept. 25, 1919, NA, RG 407, 353.

4. Ibid.

5. Ibid.

6. Ibid.

7. Office of the Chief of Staff, Memorandum, Mar. 8, 1919, NA, RG 407, 353.

8. War Department, General Order 36, Sept. 14, 1920, NA, RG 407, 353.

9. Adjutant General to Department and Corps Area Commanders, Feb. 26, 1921, NA, RG 407, 353.

10. Pershing to James Harbord, July 23, 1921, LOC, Pershing Papers, Box 134.

11. Pershing to Chief of the War Plans Division, Sept. 6, 1921; Pershing to Harbord, Dec. 8, 1921, LOC, Pershing Papers, Box 134.

12. Chief of Staff to Edward F. McGlachlin, Feb. 4, 1922, NA, RG 407, 353.

13. "Proceedings of a Board of Officers Convened at Washington, D.C., pursuant to para. 44 S. O. 175 WD," July 28, 1922, Combined Arms Library, Command and General Staff College, Fort Leavenworth.

14. All during the early twenties, officers suggested that Leavenworth be made accessible to all officers, indicating that the schools may have suggested an exclusivity that was resented. C. S. Farnsworth, Memorandum for the Adjutant General, May 4, 1922, NA, RG 407, 353.

15. Connor, Memorandum for the Chief of Staff, Apr. 5, 1922, NA, RG 407, 353.

16. "Proceedings of a Board of Officers."

17. Lassiter, Memorandum for the Chief of Staff, Apr. 17, 1922, NA, RG 407, 350.

18. Drum, Memorandum for the Adjutant General, May 16, 1924, NA, RG 407, 350.

19. Parker, Memorandum for the Chief of Staff, Jan. 3, 1929, NA, RG 407, 353.

20. One colonel remarked that one of his officers was called "the Professor" since he was the only officer in the regiment with a college degree. Archie M. Palmer, "Details of Officers to Educational Institutions," *IJ*, 20, no. 2 (Feb. 1920). 180.

21. Lassiter to Adjutant General, Apr. 25, 1923, NA, RG 407, 353. In most branches it was estimated that it would take between ten and thirteen years to overcome the backlog for the company officers course and over thirty years to get through the backlog for the advanced course. Parker, Memorandum for the Chief of Staff, Jan. 3, 1929, NA, RG 407, 350.

22. Ibid.

23. John H. Hughes, Memorandum for the Chief of Staff, July 17, 1933, NA, RG 407, 353.

24. Edward Croft, Memorandum for the Chief of Staff, July 13, 1933, NA, RG 407, 353.

25. Drum, Memorandum for the Assistant Chief of Staff, G-3, Aug. 23, 1933, NA, RG 407, 353.

26. There were hardly any articles in the service journals about the military-education system apart for those advising officers regarding what to expect there.

27. One can see a similar falloff in interest in professional education in the professional journals during the second half of the 1920s.

28. Bernard Lentz, "The Applicatory Method," *IJ* 20, no. 6 (June 1926): 608–9; Harris Pendleton, "The Business of Going to School," *IJ* 25, no. 2 (Aug. 1924): 129; W. H. Wilson, "General Principles of Military Pedagogy," CAJ 66, no. 5 (Nov. 1926): 405–22. Jorg Muth describes at length the number of officers who were dissatisfied with their education at Fort Leavenworth. Muth, *Command Culture*, 115–47.

29. Drum, "Address to the Graduates of the General Services Schools, June 28, 1921," *FAJ* 11, no. 6 (Nov./Dec. 1927): 577.

30. W. A. Dumas, "Instructional Methods," *IJ* 27, no.4 (Oct. 1925): 383–84; Francis G. Bonham, "The Military Instructor," *IJ* 29, no. 4 (Oct. 1926): 361.

31. John H. Burns, "Vitalize the Map Problem," *IJ* 44, no. 5 (Sept./Oct. 1937): 412.

32. Pendleton, "Business of Going to School," 129–34.

33. Ibid., 131.

34. Hanson E. Ely, *Address at the Opening of the General Service Schools* (Fort Leavenworth, KS: General Service Schools Press, 1922).

35. Pendleton, "Business of Going to School," 130.

36. Dumas, "Instructional Methods," 383.

37. Pendleton, "Business of Going to School," 131.

38. Muth, *Command Culture,* 124–46, 190–95.

39. Ibid., 194.

40. "Gen. E. L. King Talks at Opening of the General Service Schools," *ANJ* 44, no. 2 (Sept. 11, 1926): 25. The comment was republished in several other venues.

41. Michael R. Matheny summed up the difference between the Command and General Staff School and the War College by saying that Fort Leavenworth was about training, the War College about education. Matheny, *Carrying the War to the Enemy: American Operational Art to 1945* (Norman: University of Oklahoma Press, 2011), 57.

42. George S. Pappas, *Prudens Futuri: The US Army War College, 1901–1967* (Carlisle Barracks, PA: Alumni Association of the US Army War College, 1967), 89–134; Edward M. Coffman, *The Regulars: The American Army, 1898–1941* (Cambridge, MA: Belknap Press of Harvard University Press, 2004). 245.

43. Harry P. Ball, *Of Responsible Command: A History of the U.S. Army War College,* rev. ed. (Carlisle Barracks, PA: Alumni Association of the US Army War College, 1994), 253.

44. John L. Hines, "Address at the Army War College Graduation Exercises," June 28, 1924, LOC, Hines Papers, Box 40.

45. Bernard Lentz, "A Decade of Army Schools," *IJ* 39, no. 5 (Sept./Oct. 1932): 360.

Chapter 6

1. *FSR,* 11.

2. Mark E. Grotelueschen, *The AEF Way of War: The American Army and Combat in World War I* (New York: Cambridge University Press, 2007), 12.

3. Kenneth Finlayson, *An Uncertain Trumpet: The Evolution of U.S. Army Infantry Doctrine, 1919–1941* (Westport, CT: Greenwood, 2001), 29–69; Grotelueschen, *AEF Way of War,* 30–36.

4. In a letter to Senator David Walsh, Democrat of Massachusetts, Frederick H. Payne, the assistant secretary of war, pointed out that, due to the need to staff administrative positions, to carry out the military education programs, to service the citizen components, and other requirements, only 5,031 of the 12,133 officers then in the army were actually on duty with troops; of that number, 1,836 were assigned overseas, leaving only 3,155 serving with troops in the country. And, of course, many of these were detailed to the air corps. F. H. Payne to Sen. David Walsh, May 27, 1932, in *Eisenhower: The Prewar Diaries and Selected Papers, 1905–1941,* ed. Daniel O. Holt and James Leyerzapf (Baltimore: Johns Hopkins University Press, 1998), 222–23.

5. Odom, *After the Trenches,* 133–38.

6. "The *Infantry Journal,*" *IJ* 15, no. 6 (Dec. 1918): 529; "The Infantry Association," *IJ* 16, no. 4 (Apr. 1919): 542.

7. War Plans Division, Memorandum for the Adjutant General, Aug. 27, 1920, NA, RG 177, Entry 39.

8. T. W. Brown, "The Infantry School at Camp Benning," *IJ* 15, no. 11 (May 1919): 861–62.

9. James P. Wharton, "The Infantry School," *ME* 27, no. 152 (Mar./Apr. 1935): 36–37.

10. Brown, "Infantry School at Camp Benning," 861, 863. The money needed to purchase the remainder was allocated in 1920. "Camp Benning Project Wins in House," *IJ* 16, no. 1 (Jan. 1920): 595.

11. Wharton, "Infantry School," 38.

12. Ibid., 37.

13. Paul B. Malone, "The Need for an Infantry School," *IJ* 16, no. 5 (Nov. 1919): 438.

14. Office of the Chief of Staff, War Plans Division, Training and Instruction Branch, Memorandum, Mar. 8, 1919, NA, RG 407, 350.

15. War Department, General Order 112, Sept. 25, 1919, NA, RG 407, 353.

16. Ralph B. Lovett, "Up from the Primitive," *IJ* 42, no. 3 (May/June 1935): 219.

17. Ibid.

18. "The Infantry School Course," *IJ* 17, no. 4 (Oct. 1920): 330–31.

19. A. B. Warfield, "Fort Benning: The Home of the Infantry," *IJ* 32, no. 6 (June 1928): 575–78.

20. Ibid., 573–80.

21. Alfred McHenry, "The New Benning," *IJ* 48, no. 1 (Jan. 1941): 6–7.

22. Edward Croft, Memorandum for the Chief of Staff, July 13, 1933, NA, RG 94, 352.01; "Infantry School," *IJ* 41, no. 1 (Jan./Feb. 1934): 14.

23. Lovett, "Up from the Primitive," 219–21.

24. Steven Thomas Barry, *Battalion Commanders at War: U.S. Army Tactical Leadership in the Mediterranean Theater, 1942–1943* (Lawrence: University Press of Kansas, 2013), 49.

25. J. M. Moore, "Notes from the Infantry School," *IJ* 16, no. 10 (Apr. 1920): 884; "Infantry School Programs," *IJ* 23, no. 3 (Sept. 1923): 275.

26. Elbridge Colby, "Teaching Methods at the Infantry School," *IJ* 20, no. 3 (Mar. 1922): 284–89.

27. Bernard Lentz, "Refreshing at the Infantry School," *IJ* 36, no. 1 (Jan. 1936): 57.

28. Omar Bradley, when he was detailed to the Infantry School as an instructor in 1929, was impressed by the fact that George C. Marshall, who was then the assistant commandant, was able to bring to Benning virtually anyone he wished to serve as instructor. Omar N. Bradley, *A Soldier's Story* (New York: Henry Holt, 1951), 64.

29. Lentz, "Refreshing at the Infantry School," 57.

30. Ibid., 58; Colby, "Teaching Methods," 284–89.

31. Lentz, "Refreshing at the Infantry School," 57.

32. Jorg Muth, *Command Culture: Officer Education in the U.S. Army and the German Armed Forces, 1901–1940, and the Consequences for World War II* (Denton: University of North Texas, 2011), 137–46.

33. School leaders in 1920 announced the intention of having tanks and aircraft on base for instruction purposes. "Infantry School Notes," *IJ* 16, no. 2 (Feb. 1920): 676.

34. James B. Gowan, "The Infantry Board," *IJ* 24, no. 3 (Mar. 1924): 290.

35. J. B. Switzer, "Department of Experiment: The Infantry School," *IJ* 18, no. 3 (Mar. 1921): 221.

36. Leonard Boyd, "The Department of Experiment," *IJ* 27, no. 4 (Oct. 1925): 399.

37. Switzer, "Department of Experiment," 221.

38. One officer, Captain George Rarey, spent several years searching for a way to protect tank drivers from bullet splash. His efforts involved the development of a relationship with private industry in the search for a transparent material for windows in tanks or for use in tanker goggles. A second officer, Captain Sydney Negrotto, spent several years developing a cradle for the .50-caliber machine gun that would make it adaptable for use as an antiaircraft weapon for infantry units on the march. R. H. Kelly, "Department of Experiment," *IJ* 41, no. 4 (July/Aug. 1934): 249–53.

39. Barry, *Battalion Commanders at War,* 47.

40. Ibid., 49.

41. "The Infantry School," *IJ* 21, no. 6 (Dec. 1922): 635–37.

42. The heart of the military-history course was an assignment to prepare a monograph on an operation in the world war that would be the basis of a fifteen-minute classroom presentation; this aimed at teaching student officers public speaking. Sterling A. Wood Jr., "Life of a Student Officer," *IJ* 27, no. 4 (Oct. 1925): 388. Psychology was adopted to giving an academic basis for teaching leadership. "Infantry School Notes," *IJ* 16, no. 8 (Feb. 1920): 675.

43. Ibid., 672.

44. Edgar T. Collins, "Forward," *IJ* 32, no. 6 (June 1928): 531; Colby, "Teaching Methods," 284–89.

45. Joseph J. Bollenbeck, "Ordered to Benning," *IJ* 32, no. 4 (Apr. 1928): 403.

46. Ibid.

47. Ibid.

48. Ibid.

49. Wood, "Life of a Student Officer," 388.

50. Bradley, *Soldier's Story,* 54.

51. Robert A. McClure, "Housing Student Officers," *IJ* 32, no. 6 (June 1928): 616.

52. "Living Conditions in the Infantry School," *IJ* 36, no. 1 (Jan. 1930): 74–75.

53. A Lieutenant of Infantry, "Student Impressions at the Infantry School," *IJ* 18, no. 1 (Jan.1921): 23.

54. Madge Peyton, "The Army Woman in Fort Benning," *IJ* 32, no. 6 (June 1928): 581–87.

55. Ibid.

56. Pleas B. Rogers, "Boots and Saddles at Fort Benning," *IJ* 27, no. 4 (Oct. 1925): 392–97.

57. E. E. Walker, "The Officers' Club," *IJ* 32, no. 6 (June 1928): 643.

58. W. Collier, "The Infantry School Hunt," *IJ* 32, no. 6 (June 1928): 608–13.

59. Elbridge Colby, "Our Arm of the Service," *IJ* 24, no. 1 (Jan. 1924): 5. Brian Linn has discussed the dominant role that focus on "the human element" played in American military thinking in the interwar period. Brian McAllister Linn, *The Echo of Battle: The Army's Way of War* (Cambridge, MA: Harvard University Press, 2007), 129–32.

60. "The Doughboy," *IJ* 17, no. 2 (Sept. 1920): 292.

61. "An Infantry March for Field Music," *IJ* 25, no. 2 (Aug. 1924): 127.

62. "Competition for an Infantry Song," *IJ* 25, no. 4 (Oct. 1924): 387.

63. "Symbolic Song for the Infantry," *IJ* 30, no. 5 (May 1927): 536.

64. "The Infantry Song," *IJ* 29, no. 6 (Dec. 1926): 648.

65. H. J. Koehler, "Athletic Life at West Point," *IJ* 24, no. 5 (May 1924): 547.

66. Even mass calisthenics were reorganized to make them a form of athletic contest. Alfred G. Hill, "Athletics on a Large Scale," *IJ* 15, no. 11 (May 1919): 872–77.

67. Walt C. Johnson, "Athletic History of the Infantry School," *IJ* 27, no. 4 (Oct. 1925): 375.

68. Ibid., 375.

69. Ibid., 376–79.

70. Ibid., 381.

71. Brook Lemon, "Doughboy Memorial Stadium," *IJ* 24, no. 4 (Oct. 1925): 366.

72. "Football in the Infantry," *IJ* 28, no. 1 (Jan. 1928): 82–85.

73. "Football Now Leading Organized Athletics," *IJ* 29, no. 4 (Oct. 1926): 443; "Financing Regimental Athletics," *IJ* 30, no. 5 (May, 1927): 544–45.

74. "Infantry Athletics at the Field Artillery School," *IJ* 31, no. 1 (July 1927): 85.

75. Emons B. Whisner, "Polo and Horse Shows," *IJ* 32, no. 6 (June 1928): 629.

Chapter 7

1. Boyd L. Dastrup, *King of Battle: A Branch History of the U.S. Army's Field Artillery* (Fort Monroe, VA: US Army Training and Doctrine Command, 1992), 201.

2. Dastrup, *King of Battle*, 126–29.

3. Ibid., 148–55; Ian V. Hogg, *A History of Artillery* (London: Hamlyn, 1974), 156–57.

4. United States Field Artillery School, *History of the Development of Field Artillery Material* (Fort Sill, OK: Field Artillery School, 1941), 59.

5. Dastrup, *King of Battle*, 129–31, 145–59.

6. Vincent Meyer, "Evolution of Field Artillery Tactics during and as a Result of the World War, Part II," *FAJ* 22, no. 3 (May/June 1932): 321.

7. Ibid.

8. Dastrup, *King of Battle*, 167, 174; Roger D. Swain, "The Field Artillery: Progress or Retrograde," *FAJ* 9, no. 2 (Apr./June 1919): 218–21.

9. Dastrup, *King of Battle*, 152–55.

10. "An Artillery Study Made in the AEF," *FAJ* 10, no. 1 (Jan./Feb. 1920): 53–57; Dastrup, *King of Battle*, 180, 182–85.

11. "Annual Report of the Chief of Field Artillery, 1926," *FAJ* 16, no. 6 (Nov./Dec. 1926): 559.

12. "Annual Report of the Chief of Field Artillery, 1923," *FAJ* 14, no. 1 (Jan./Feb. 1924): 47.

13. "Annual Report of the Chief of Field Artillery, 1928," *FAJ* 18, no. 6 (Nov./Dec.1928): 576.

14. "Annual Report of the Chief of Field Artillery, 1925," *FAJ* 16, no. 1 (Jan./Feb. 1926): 70.

15. In his report for 1928, the chief of field artillery completed a set of brief comments regarding the National Guard with this enigmatic statement: "War Department policies not contemplating any supervision or inspection of National Guard activities by this office, no contact was had with that important component of the National Defense, except as was brought about by the attendance of officers and enlisted men of the National Guard at courses in the Field Artillery School." "Annual Report . . . , 1928", 576. This statement was then repeated in all subsequent annual reports as the only comment concerning the National Guard.

16. "Annual Report.1923," 41.

17. Edwin P. Parker Jr., "The Development of the Field Artillery ROTC," *FAJ* 25, no. 4 (July/Aug. 1935): 334–42. Two units were lost later.

18. "Annual Report . . . ,1925," 64.

19. For instance, see "Artillery Study Made in the AEF," 53; Wm. B. Meloney, "The Spirit of Artillery," *FAJ* 14, no. 5 (Sept./Oct. 1924): 423; and George D. Wahl, "The Direct Support of Infantry in an Attack," *FAJ* 34, no. 5 (Sept./Oct. 1934): 429.

20. Richard S. Faulkner, *The School of Hard Knocks: Combat Leadership in the American Expeditionary Forces* (College Station: Texas A&M University Press, 2012), 154.

21. William J. Snow, "Field Artillery—A Retrospect," *FAJ* 8, no. 4 (Oct./Dec. 1919): 478.

22. William J. Snow, Training Directive #6, Dec. 1919, as noted in *FAJ* 9, no. 4 (Oct./Dec.1919): 613.

23. Swaim."The Field Artillery—Progress...," 218–21.

24. Ibid., 218.

25. *Annual Report of the Chief of Field Artillery, 1920* (Washington, DC: Government Printing Office, 1920), 6.

26. Ibid.

27. "Annual Report of the Chief of Field Artillery, 1924," *FAJ* 15, no. 1 (Jan./Feb. 1925): 135.

28. The following discussion of weapons modernization was largely taken from Dastrup, *King of Battle*, 172–202.

29. William J. Snow, "The First Chief of Field Artillery," *FAJ* 30, no. 1 (Jan./Feb. 1940): 4–6.

30. This position is suggested by the reverence with which Snow was treated in the *Field Artillery Journal*, including the publishing of portions of his memoirs in two major articles. See Snow, "The First Chief of Field Artillery," *FAJ* 30, no. 1 (Jan./Feb. 1940): 2–14; 30, no. 2 (Mar./Apr. 1940): 97–106.

31. Charles S. West, "The Early Years of the Journal," *FAJ* 27, no. 6 (Nov./Dec. 1936): 448–49.

32. One subscribed to the *Journal* by joining the United States Field Artillery Association. Editorial, *FAJ* 10, no. 5 (Sept./Oct. 1920): 652.

33. Sir J. G. W. Headlum, "The Regimental Journals of the United States Artillery," *FAJ* 11, no. 6 (Nov./Dec. 1921): 537–38.

34. The United States Field Artillery Association offered an annual prize to essays on set topics, with the top entries being published annually. Editorial, *FAJ* 10, no. 5 (Sept./Oct. 1920): 652.

35. The main source for the early history of the Field Artillery School is Riley Sunderland, *History of the Field Artillery School*, vol. 1, *1911–1942* (Fort Sill, OK: Field Artillery School, 1942). Other sources used here include "A Brief History of Fort Sill and the Field Artillery School," *FAJ* 23, no. 6 (Nov./Dec. 1933): 528–41; E. Durette, "Fort Sill in Wartime," *FAJ* 23, no. 3 (May/June 1933): 239–45; William J. Snow, "Origins of the Field Artillery School," *FAJ* 31, no. 2 (Feb. 1941): 100–109; and Morris Swett, "The Forerunners of Sill," *FAJ* 23, no. 6 (Nov./Dec. 1933): 453–63.

36. Sunderland, *History of the Field Artillery School*, 73.

37. The fundamental ideas behind the field artillery's initial educational plans were spelled out in an article written by the Training Section of the Office of the Chief of Field Artillery. "A Proposed Scheme of Officers' Schools for the Field Artillery," *FAJ* 9, no. 2 (Apr./June 1919): 207–17. The commitment to this new professional model of military education rather than one based on mere technical training was symbolized by changing the name of the school at Fort Sill from the "School of Fire" to the "Field Artillery School." Sunderland, *History of the Field Artillery School*, 74.

38. " Proposed Scheme of Officers' Schools," 208, 212; William Bryden, "The Field Artillery of the Army of the United States," FAJ 11 no. 3 (May/June 1921): 265. Snow also argued that the highly technical nature of field artillery made control of the lower schools by the Training Section of the General Staff inappropriate. "Proposed Scheme of Officers' Schools," 207.

39. Ibid., 211.

40. Ibid., 213.

41. Sunderland, *History of the Field Artillery School*, 75, 76.

42. Ibid., 79–80.

43. At the basic school at Camp Zachary Taylor in 1920, the division of class hours between the four areas were Tactics, 428 hours; Materiel, 413; Gunnery, 508; and Equitation, 215. *Annual Report of the Chief of Field Artillery, 1920*, 15.

44. Lassiter to Adjutant General, Dec. 3, 1920, NA, RG 177, Entry 34, 319.1.

45. Sunderland, *History of the Field Artillery School*, 78–79.

46. Ibid., 75.

47. An effort was made in 1920 to reduce the number of hours given to animal transport at the battery officers course at Fort Sill. But this was squashed by the commandant, Major General Ernest Hinds, who expressed disappointment with the quality of horsemanship displayed by students in riding and in horse shows. Sunderland, *History of the Field Artillery School*, 82–83. Hinds's successor actually increased the hours devoted to equitation. Ibid., 89.

48. Ernest Hinds, "Graduation Address to the Classes at the Field Artillery School, June 14, 1924," *FAJ* 14, no. 5 (Sept./Oct. 1924): 472.

49. Dwight E. Aultman to the Chief of Field Artillery, July 19, 1922, NA, RG 177, Entry 34, 319.1.

50. "A Reserve Officer's Impression of the Field Artillery School," FAJ 16, no. 5 (Sept./Oct. 1926): 545–46.

51. There is a real dearth of firsthand accounts of the student experience at Fort Sill, so the degree of officer-graduate satisfaction is almost impossible to gauge. But one sees little evidence of the same enthusiasm at Fort Sill that generated major volunteer building programs at Fort Benning. Even the lack of articles in *Field Artillery Journal* regarding the Fort Sill experience might be telling.

52. Sunderland, *History of the Field Artillery School*, 86–87.

53. Ibid, 83.

54. "Annual Report . . . 1924," 197; "Annual Report . . . 1925," 503; Sunderland, *History of the Field Artillery School*, 95–96.

55. "Annual Report of the Chief of Field Artillery, 1929," *FAJ* 18, no. 6 (Nov./Dec. 1929): 581.

56. Sunderland, *History of the Field Artillery School*, 113.

57. "Annual Report . . . 1924," 194.

58. M. Beck, "The Artillery Hunt," *FAJ* 20, no. 1 (Jan./Feb. 1930): 53–59.

59. "Annual Report . . . , 1928," 581.

60. Sunderland, *History of the Field Artillery School*, 116–18; "Fort Sill to be Permanent Home of the Field Artillery School," *FAJ* 20, no. 6 (Nov./Dec. 1930): 96–97.

61. Sunderland, *History of the Field Artillery School*, 123, 132.

62. Ibid.; "Annual Report of the Chief of Field Artillery for 1931," *FAJ* 21, no. 6 (Nov./Dec. 1931): 582, 584.

63. Sunderland, *History of the Field Artillery School*, 152–54.

64. Wm. J. Snow, "Sketch of the Origins of the Field Artillery Association," *FAJ* 22, no. 4 (July/Aug. 1932): 412.

65. "The United States Field Artillery Association," *FAJ* 23, no. 1 (Jan./Feb. 1933): 53–55.

66. "The Field Artillery Song," *FAJ* 16, no. 4 (July/Aug. 1926): 443.

67. "The Songs of the Field Artillery," FAJ 28 no. 3 (May/June 1928): 240–45.

68. In 1932, 409 field-artillery officers were participating members of the Army Polo Association. "Polo: The Army Polo Association," *FAJ* 22, no. 3 (May/June 1932): 315.

69. By 1928, an officer was assigned on a fulltime basis to be army polo-team manager. The army had also built Mitchell Field on Long Island, New York, which was home of the Army Polo Center and was considered one of the finest polo facilities anywhere on the East Coast. "Plans of the Central Polo Commission," *FAJ* 18, no. 2 (Mar./Apr. 1928): 173–75.

70. As one officer of modest means remarked, "By the grace of a benevolent government, I, though a lowly second lieutenant in the first pay period, was enabled to live as horsey an existence as though I had been born to the Elysian Fields of Meadowbrook or Pinehurst." He also noted the large amount of work associated with maintaining animals, indicating that it was the social mobility rather than any love of horses that had gotten him involved in polo. "Confessions of an Ex-Horseman," *FAJ* 35, no. 4 (July/Aug. 1935): 343.

71. Interest in playing competitive polo was army-wide and enjoyed considerable support from within the General Staff. See, for example, "Army Polo Plans for the 1927 Season," *FAJ* 17, no. 3 (May/June 1927). 323. By 1928, army teams, made up chiefly of officers from the cavalry and field artillery, were winning championships with great frequency. "Plans of the Central Polo Commission," *FAJ* 18, no. 2 (Mar./Apr. 1928): 173.

Chapter 8

1. "Establishment of the Coast Artillery School and its Operations until the War," *CAJ* 60, no. 6 (June 1924): 479. Upton's efforts to elevate the curriculum at Fort Monroe are noted in J. P. Clark, *Preparing for War: The Emergence of the Modern U.S. Army, 1815–1917* (Cambridge, MA: Harvard University Press, 2017), 108. Clark also notes that it was after his experience at Fort Monroe that Upton began his career as a military reformer. Ibid., 109.

2. 31. Stat. 748, Feb. 2, 1901; Leon B. Kromer, Memorandum for the Assistant Secretary of War, Aug. 26, 1937, NA, RG 177, Entry 39, 322.02.

3. Johnson Hagood, "A Reunited Artillery," *CAJ* 61, no. 6 (Dec. 1924): 470–73.

4. 34 Stat. 861 Jan. 25, 1907. The split was scarcely equal. The coast artillery emerged with nearly 14,000 men in 126 companies, while the field artillery emerged with only 4,800 men in 30 companies. Larry H. Addington, "The U.S. Coast Artillery and the Problem of Artillery Organization, 1907–1954," *Military Affairs* 40, no. 1 (Feb. 1976): 1.

5. The Chief of Artillery, Major General Arthur Murray, was also a highly influential lobbying force with Congress and the administration. Addington, "U.S. Coast Artillery," 1.

6. "Extracts from the *Annual Report of the Chief of Coast Artillery, 1924*," *CAJ* 61, no. 6 (Dec. 1924): 484.

7. Gaining these missions was largely the product of the lobbying efforts of another energetic Chief of Coast Artillery, Major General Erasmus Weaver. Addington, "U.S. Coast Artillery," 2.

8. The Superior Board, convened to study the lessons of the world war, recommended shifting responsibility for seacoast fortifications to the navy, which would effectively end the coast artillery branch. Brian McAllister Linn, *The Echo of Battle: The Army's Way of War* (Cambridge, MA: Harvard University Press, 2007), 121–22.

9. James P. Prentice, "The Effect of Air Service on the Tactics of Coast Defense," *JUSA* 52, no. 2 (Feb. 1920): 101; Homer Oldfield, "The Passing of Permanently Placed Artillery," *JUSA* 52, no. 4 (Apr. 1920): 317.

10. Sanderford Jarman, "Future Seacoast Defense Artillery: Its Mission and Influence," *JUSA* 52, no. 3 (Mar. 1920): 206.

11. Prentice, "Effect of Air Service on the Tactics of Coast Defense," 101, 105.

12. David E. Johnson, *Fast Tanks and Heavy Bombers: Innovation in the U.S. Army, 1917–1945* (Ithaca, NY: Cornell University Press, 1998), 84.

13. Kenneth E. Hamburger, "The Technology, Doctrine, and Politics of U.S. Coast Defense, 1880–1945" (PhD diss., Duke University, 1986), 257, 265–76; Linn, *Echo of Battle*, 127.

14. Linn, *Echo of Battle*, 122.

15. "Publicity," *CAJ* 60, no. 3 (Mar. 1924): 220.

16. Richard R. Welshmen, "The Importance of Coast Artillery in Our National Defense," *CAJ* 59, no. 1 (July 1923): 57.

17. "Making the Grade on High," *JUSA* 55, no. 2 (Aug. 1921): 180.

18. "Notes of the Coast Artillery Association," *CAJ* 76, no. 1 (Jan./Feb. 1935): 47. Over 300 members attended the 1937 national convention of the association. The two-day program offered little except a few speeches and a large number of receptions. The convention was touted as promoting fellowship. "The Convention," *CAJ* 80, no. 6 (Nov./Dec. 1937): 497.

19. "The Coast Artillery Journal—the Organ of the Coast Artillery Corps," *CAJ* 72, no. 6 (June 1930): 523.

20. William H. Wilson, "The Coast Artillery School Today," *CAJ* 60, no. 6 (June 1924): 501–8; "*Annual Report of the Chief of Coast Artillery, 1926,* Extracts," *CAJ* 66, no. 1 (Jan. 1927): 10.

21. Wilson, "Coast Artillery School Today," 503–7; "I See That You Are Ordered to School," *CAJ* 72, no. 4 (Apr. 1930): 342.

22. "I See That You Are Ordered To School" 342.

23. "The Coast Artillery School," *CAJ* 72, no. 5 (Nov. 1930): 468–70; "The Coast Artillery School," *CAJ* 75, no. 1 (Jan./Feb. 1931): 67.

24. "In Conference," *CAJ* 74, no. 3 (Mar./Apr. 1931): 229.

25. "I See That You Are Ordered to School," 342.

26. "The Coast Artillery School," *CAJ* 74, no. 4 (July/Aug. 1932): 73.

27. One officer claimed that the prevailing feeling within the corps was that permanent forts were now obsolete. J. C. Matheson, "The Future of Permanent Fortifications," *JUSA* 52, no. 2 (Feb. 1920): 181. Another agreed, asserting that this view was held by "a very large majority of coast artillery officers." F. E. McCammon, "The Future of Seacoast Artillery," *JUSA* 59, no. 2 (Feb. 1921): 137.

28. Frank W. Coe, "The Chief of Coast Artillery and the Corps," *JUSA* 52, no. 3 (Mar. 1920): 199. In fact, Coe was a major force in the effort to shift the mission of the coast artillery away from fixed gun emplacements to control of mobile heavy artillery. Addington, "U.S. Coast Artillery," 2.

29. Hamburger, "Technology, Doctrine, and Politics of U.S. Coast Defense," 265; Linn, *Echo of Battle*, 121–23.

30. This idea was discussed in a number of articles in *Coast Artillery Journal*, but the seminal explication was in Jarmon, "Future Seacoast Defense Artillery," 201–26. This article was the winner of the gold medal in the *Journal*'s 1919 essay contest. It was cited later as being the center of a debate, with most officers in the coast artillery in agreement with its position. McCammon, "Future of Seacoast Artillery," 132. Coe also endorsed the idea. Coe, "Chief of Coast Artillery and the Corps," 199–200. The idea was also attractive since the United States had fallen heir to a large amount of mobile ordnance at the end of the world war. Emanuel R. Lewis, *Seacoast Fortifications of the United States. An Introductory History* (Washington, DC. Smithsonian Institution Press, 1970), 102.

31. Lewis, *Seacoast Fortifications*, 103–4.

32. Coe, "Chief of Coast Artillery and the Corps," 401.

33. Ibid.

34. "The Coast Artillery Corps," *CAJ* 65, no. 5 (Nov. 1926): 455.

35. No copy of the Coe letter could be found, but the basic ideas were discussed in the many responses to it. For instance, R. H. C. Kelton to Coe, Dec. 8, 1919, NA, RG 177, Entry 9, 322.2.

36. Coe to the Adjutant General, Sept. 29, 1924, NA, RG 177, Entry 9, 322.2.

37. "The Mission and Tactical Doctrine of Coast Artillery," *JUSA* 59, no. 4 (Apr. 1921): 387.

38. "Reason to Rejoice," *CAJ* 60, no. 4 (Apr. 1924): 312; C. H. McNeill, Memorandum for the Chief of Staff, Oct. 15, 1920, NA, RG 177, Entry 9, 320.7.

39. "Seacoast vs Antiaircraft Artillery," *CAJ* 73, no. 3 (Sept. 1930): 163.

40. *Joint Army and Navy Action in Coast Defense* (Washington, DC: War Department and Navy Department, 1920).

41. Thomas R. Phillips, "Some Phases of the Office to Aircraft on the Future Mission, Organization, Equipment and Tactics of the Coast Artillery Corps," *CAJ* 58, no. 3 (Mar. 1923): 210.

42. Henry J. Hatch and Joseph F. Stiles, "Coast Defense—Logical and Visionary," *CAJ* 60, no. 1 (Jan. 1924): 1–21; E. J. Callan, "The Function of Coast Artillery in the Positive System of Coast Defense," *CAJ* 61, no. 3 (Sept. 1924): 212–19. Hatch and Stiles were both members of the Coast Artillery Board.

43. The commandant of the school gave a presentation on coast defense to a corps-area commander's staff in 1925. H. D. Todd Jr., "The Coast Artillery and Its Relation to Other Branches," *CAJ* 63, no. 1 (July 1925): 57–59.

44. The term "Harbor Defense" would be used instead. *"Annual Report of the Chief of Coast Artillery for 1925*—Extracts," *CAJ* 63, no. 6 (Dec. 1925): 567.

45. Rodney H. Smith, "The Combined Arms in Coast Defense," *CAJ* 66, no. 3 (Mar. 1927): 197–217; "Seacoast Defense," *CAJ* 67, no. 4 (Oct. 1928): 279–89; "Command of Land and Air Forces in Coast Artillery," *CAJ* 78, no. 4 (July/Aug. 1935): 245–48.

46. The 1938 prize essay was largely a recapitulation of the coast-defense doctrine, the author stating, "The defense of a coastal frontier is an Army problem which requires the direct cooperation of troops of all arms and services." E. M. Benitez, "The Backbone of Sea Power," *CAJ* 82, no. 1 (Jan./Feb. 1939): 9.

47. O. L. Spiller, "The Service of Anti-Aircraft Artillery," *JUSA* 57, no. 4 (Sept./Oct. 1919): 392. The new assignment generated a series of articles in *Journal of the United States Artillery*, suggesting some enthusiasm for it.

48. Spiller, "Service of Anti-Aircraft Artillery," 396–406.

49. D. W. Collins to John B. Murphy, Aug. 7, 1919, NA, RG 177, Entry 9, 322.76.

50. Coe, Memorandum for the Chief of Staff, Oct. 21, 1919, NA, RG 177, Entry 9, 322.76; Adjutant General to CG North Atlantic Coast Artillery District, Oct. 30, 1919, ibid.

51. John B. Murphy to Commanding General, Training Center, Fort Monroe, Mar. 2, 1920, NA, RG 177, Entry 9, 322.2.

52. Bulletin A. A. 1.001, n.d. [although the first Bulletin indicated that the publication was established on Nov. 25, 1922], NA, RG 177, Entry 9, 300.53.

53. Some coast-artillery officers did question the branch's continued interest in the area, suggesting that it might be better to turn the job over to the air service, but this was a distinctly minority position. H. J. Knerr, "Anti-Aircraft?," *JUSA* 52, no. 2 (Feb. 1920): 152–59.

54. C. H. McNeill, Memorandum for the Chief of Staff, Oct. 15, 1920, NA, RG 177, Entry 9, 320.7; "Extracts from the *Annual Report of the Chief of Coast Artillery for 1923*," *CAJ* 61, no. 1 (Jan. 1924): 24.

55. G. M. Barnes, "A New Antiaircraft Weapon," *AO* 12, no. 68 (Sept./Oct. 1931): 93. An officer writing in 1922 mentioned the "Coast Artillery officers who have hitherto fought shy of Anti-Aircraft work, feeling it was still too inchoate and undeveloped to warrant their attention." "Harmony in Anti-Aircraft Doctrine," *JUSA* 56, no. 6 (June 1922): 564. On the other hand, the artillery journal actively encouraged the development of antiaircraft artillery, calling on officers to submit articles on the subject. Ibid. 551.

56. Many officers were also discouraged by the fact that the air service was getting so much press attention, while the antiaircraft service was ignored. Ben F. Harmon, "The Past and Future of Defense against Aircraft," *CAJ* 63, no. 5 (Nov. 1925): 449; R. R. Welshman, "A Discussion of Sky and Coast Defense," *CAJ* 65, no. 1 (July 1926): 15–30.

57. R. L. Goetzenberger, "Anti-Aircraft Defense," *AO* 2, no. 8 (Sept./Oct. 1921): 75.

58. Knerr, "Anti-Aircraft?," 152–59.

59. Coe, when he was chief of coast artillery, pointed to the success of his guns in hitting practice targets as the main reason for dismissing alternative strategies. F. W. Coe, "The Coast Artillery and the Engineers," *ME* 15, no. 3 (Sept./Oct. 1923): 402.

60. In rejecting alternative tactical approaches, Coe characterized them as "negative." Coe, "Coast Artillery and the Engineers," 402. Many writers justified the legitimacy of coast artillery taking over the mission of antiaircraft artillery on the idea that it was similar to the branch's traditional mission of shooting at moving targets. Andrew Hero Jr., "Present Status and Development of Coast Artillery," *CAJ* 69, no. 6 (Dec. 1928): 463.

61. G. M. Barns, "The New Antiaircraft Weapons," *AO* 12, no. 68 (Sept./Oct. 1931): 94.

62. C. L. W. Ruggles, "Antiaircraft Defense," *AO* 6, no. 35 (Mar./Apr. 1926): 351.

63. Glenn P. Anderson, "Defense against Aircraft," *JUSA* 55, no. 3 (Sept. 1921): 261.

64. Ruggles, "Antiaircraft Defense," 352–53.

65. Ibid., 353

66. W. P. Boatwright, "Major Boatwright Comments on Captain Phillips' Article," *CAJ* 58, no. 4 (Apr. 1923): 374–75.

67. Ruggles, "Antiaircraft Defense," 353.

68. Quoted in Andrew Hero, "New Year Greetings from the Chief of Coast Artillery," *CAJ* 72, no. 1 (Jan. 1930): 1.

69. Parker, Memorandum for the Chief of Staff, Apr. 3, 1929, NA, RG 177, Entry 9, 320.10. The origin of the memorandum is uncertain. There is evidence that it was initially drafted by a member of the coast artillery on service in Parker's office, even though the memorandum clearly was not initiated by the coast artillery.

70. H. T. Burgin to the President of the Coast Artillery Board, Oct. 19, 1929, NA, RG 177, Entry 9, 352.5; "Coast Artillery School," *CAJ* 72, no. 6 (June 1930): 531; "Coast Artillery School," *CAJ* 74, no. 7 (Nov./Dec. 1931): 541; "Coast Artillery School," *CAJ* 75, no. 1 (Jan./Feb. 1932): 61.

71. "The Reorganization and New Training Objectives of the Coast Artillery Corps," *CAJ* 72, no. 1 (Jan. 1930): 9.

72. Sanderford Jarman, "Future Coast Artillery," *CAJ* 73, no. 5 (Nov. 1930): 414.

73. The shift was already noticed by the editors of *Coast Artillery Journal* by 1930. "Air Defense," *CAJ* 72, no. 2 (Feb. 1930): 108.

74. The earliest discussion in JUSA was Anderson, "Defense against Aircraft," 256–62.

75. "*Annual Report of the Chief of Coastal Artillery,* Extracts," *CAJ* 70, no. 1 (Jan. 1929): 17.

76. "Air Defense," 108; A. F. Englehart, "Antiaircraft Defenses: Their Development during the World War—Part II," *CAJ* 77, no. 4 (July/Aug. 1934): 270.

77. "Air Defense," 108; Arthur B. Nicholson, "Defense against Night Bombardment," *CAJ* 82, no. 5 (Sept./Oct. 1939): 388.

78. "*Annual Report of the Chief of Coast Artillery, 1925*—Excerpts," *CAJ* 62, no. 6 (June 1925): 568.

79. "Comments on the Joint Antiaircraft–Air Corps Exercises at Aberdeen," *CAJ* 73, no. 3 (Sept. 1931): 451.

80. "The Air Corps–Antiaircraft Exercises at Fort Knox," *CAJ* 76, no. 1 (Jan./Feb. 1933): 71–72.

81. J. Bennet, "Joint Antiaircraft–Air Corps Exercises," *CAJ* 81, no. 6 (Nov./Dec. 1938): 442–46.

82. By 1936, it was estimated that an antiaircraft regiment would be issued 232 miles of wire (weighing over sixteen tons) to link this network. A new unit, the Antiaircraft Intelligence Service, was created to be attached to each antiaircraft artillery regiment to create and maintain this network. Robert W. Berry, and John A. Sawyer, "Antiaircraft Intelligence Service," *CAJ* 79, no. 1 (Jan./Feb. 1936): 50–52; L. W. Bartlett, "Antiaircraft Communications," *CAJ* 81, no. 3 (May 1938): 209–11.

83. "Harmony in Anti-Aircraft Doctrine," *JUSA* 56, no. 6 (June 1922): 563.

84. Ibid.

85. This idea was already in circulation in 1921. Anderson, "Defense against Aircraft," 256.

86. Robert N. Mackin, "Airplanes Can Be Stopped," *CAJ* 80, no. 5 (Sept./Oct. 1937): 400; Muir S. Fairchild, "Anti-Aircraft Defense," *Military Review* 19, no. 74 (Sept. 1939): 13.

87. Edward W. Timberlake, "The Effect of Antiaircraft Artillery on the Employment of Aviation," *CAJ* 75, no. 3 (May/June 1932): 178; H. R. Oldfield, "Antiaircraft Artillery—Its Function, Organization, and Present Development," *CAJ* 75, no. 1 (Jan./Feb. 1932): 5.

88. Pilots were also learning to fly in dispersed formations to confuse sound detectors. H. A. Dargue, "Bombardment Aviation and Its Relation to Anti-Aircraft Defense," *CAJ* 77, no. 5 (Sept./Oct. 1934): 334.

89. Dargue, "Bombardment Aviation," 334.

90. Arthur B. Nicholson, "Defense against Night Bombardment," *CAJ* 82, no. 5 (Sept./Oct. 1939): 391.

91. Nicholson, "Defense against Night Bombardment," 386.

92. John R. Lovell, "Aircraft Preparedness," *CAJ* 82, no. 4 (July/Aug. 1939): 339–49.

93. Nicholson, "Defense against Night Bombardment," 386–97.

94. The annual reports of the chief of coast artillery broke down the issues the board considered into those it raised itself and those brought to it from others. The ratio was normally about ten to one in favor of the latter.

Chapter 9

1. David E. Johnson, *Fast Tanks and Heavy Bombers: Innovation in the U.S. Army, 1917–1945* (Ithaca, NY: Cornell University Press, 1998), 108.

2. Henry G. Gole, *The Road to Rainbow: Army Planning for Global War, 1934–1940* (Annapolis, MD: Naval Institute Press, 2003), 50–52.

3. Paul Dickson, *The Rise of the G.I. Army, 1940–1941* (New York: Atlantic Monthly Press, 2020), 43.

4. E. E. Booth, Memorandum for the Adjutant General, Aug. 5, 1930, NA, RG 407, III.

5. "Congressman Collins Planning Army Cuts," *ANJ* 69, no. 5 (Oct. 3, 1931): 97. Collins also argued that ridding the army of 4,000 older officers would ease the promotion problem.

6. "Air Corps and Militia Hurt by Money Cuts," *ANJ* 69, no. 16 (Dec. 19, 1931): 337, 358; "Efficiency of Militia at Stake in Budget," *ANJ* 69, no. 15 (Dec. 12, 1931): 327.

7. An editorial in the influential *Army and Navy Journal* claimed, "Penuriousness and Pacifism have combined in the House Appropriations Committee to strike at the services." Editorial, *ANJ* 69, no. 33 (Apr. 26, 1932): 800.

8. "Wide Cuts Planned for Army and Navy," *NYT* (Apr. 12, 1933): 7.

9. "Army Bill in House Cut to $386,983,452," *NYT* (May 6, 1932): 9.

10. "2,000 Army Officer Cut Recommended to House," *ANJ* 69, no. 36 (May 7, 1932): 841.

11. "House Leader Urges Combining of Services," *ANJ* 69, no. 21 (Jan. 23, 1932): 481.

12. "House Clears Way for Unified Defense Bill," *ANJ* 69, no. 25 (Feb. 20, 1932): 577.

13. "Vote down Consolidation," *ANJ* 69, no. 32 (Apr. 19, 1932): 745.

14. "Appropriations Committee Moves to Stop Pay Increases Based on Length of Service," *ANJ* 69, no. 25 (Feb. 20, 1932): 577–79.

15. "Showdown on Plan for Pay Slash Near," *ANJ* 69, no. 30 (Mar. 10, 1932): 697–98.

16. "Threatened Pay Cuts," *ANJ* 69, no. 36 (May 7, 1932): 843.

17. C. C. McCormack, Memorandum for the Chief of Staff, Aug. 15, 1932, NA, RG 407, 111.

18. "Wide Cuts Planned for Army and Navy," *NYT* (Apr. 12, 1933): 7.

19. "President Asks Power to Make Pay Slashes," *ANJ* 70, no. 28 (Mar. 1933): 549; "New Pay Cut System Effective on April 1," *ANJ* 70, no. 29 (Mar 18, 1933): 569; "Pay Cut of 15% Decreed by President," *ANJ* 70, no. 31 (Apr. 1, 1933): 609, 619.

20. "Seeks to Cut Strength of Army by Furlough," *ANJ* 70, no. 34 (Apr. 22, 1933): 669, 670, 689.

21. "May Defeat Furloughs for Services in Senate," *ANJ* 70, no. 39 (May 27, 1933): 776; "Army Personnel Saved; Senate Kills Furlough," *ANJ* 70, no. 40 (Jun. 3, 1933): 789. The fact that the furlough plan would end the capacity of the army to support the CCC camps was a factor in Roosevelt's decision to abandon it. "Army Officer Cut Is Not Abandoned," *NYT* (May 30, 1933): 1.

22. "Army Training Suffers in Slash of $52,500,000," *ANJ* 70, no. 43 (June 24, 1933): 849. Appropriations approved by Congress were for fiscal year 1932, $339,517,017; for fiscal year 1933, $309,739,924; and for fiscal year 1934, $276,550,381. The president's confidential executive order reduced the 1934 figure to $225,000,000.

23. *Annual Report of the Secretary of War for 1933* (Washington, D.C. Government Printing Office, 1933), 16–18.

24. "The Army in 1933," *ANJ* 71, no. 18 (Dec. 30, 1933): 348.

25. "$25,000,000 Award Made for Defense" *NYT* (Oct. 22, 1933): 15. "Editorial, *ANJ*, 71, no. 2 (Sept. 9, 1933): 29.

26. "Modernization of the Army," *ANJ* 71, no. 1 (Sept. 2, 1933): 1.

27. Ibid.

28. William O. Odom, *After the Trenches: The Transformation of the U.S. Army, 1918–1939* (College Station: Texas A&M University Press, 2008), 100.

29. Dickson, *Rise of the G.I. Army,* 29.

30. Steven Thomas Barry, *Battalion Commanders at War: U.S. Tactical Leadership in the Mediterranean Theater, 1942–1943* (Lawrence: University Press of Kansas, 2013), 39–43.

31. Edward M. Coffman, *The Regulars: The American Army, 1898–1941* (Cambridge, MA: Belknap Press of Harvard University Press, 2004), 243.

32. Gole, *Road to Rainbow,* 5.

33. "Estimates for Army," *ANJ,* 71, no. 19 (Jan. 6, 1934): 77.

34. "M'Arthur Urges Adequate Army," *NYT* (Apr. 21, 1934): 5; "Larger Army Endorsed by General MacArthur," *ANJ* 71, no. 34 (Apr. 21, 1934): 665, 683; "179,000 Army Urged by Dern and Baker," *NYT* (May 30, 1934): 4.

35. "Senate Votes to Drop 15% Pay Cut on July 1," *ANJ* 71, no. 26 (Feb. 24, 1934): 505.

36. "Departments Propose to Effect New Pay Act," *ANJ* 71, no. 31 (Mar. 31, 1934): 605.

37. "President Retains General Douglas MacArthur as Chief of Staff to Aid Program in Congress," *ANJ* 72, no. 16 (Dec. 15, 1934): 319.

38. "Estimates for Defense Show Marked Increase," *ANJ* 72, no. 20 (Jan. 12, 1935): 400, 402.

39. "Increase in Regular Army and National Guard Approved," *ANJ* 72, no. 33 (Apr. 13, 1935): 675. The legislation originally allowed Roosevelt to increase the size of the army at his discretion. In the final legislation this discretionary authority was removed. "Army Rise Favored by Senate Group," *NYT* (Mar. 2, 1935): 13; "Signs Army Increase Bill," *NYT* (Apr. 10, 1935): 4.

40. "Pass West Point Bill," *ANJ* 72, no. 39 (May 25, 1935): 807; "Increase in West Point," *ANJ,* 72, no. 42 (June 15, 1935): 880, 888.

41. "White House Approves Army Promotion Bill," *ANJ* 72, no. 22 (Jun. 24, 1935): 437.

42. "Army Promotion Bill Signed, Effective August 1," *ANJ* 72, no. 45 (Aug. 3, 1935): 1045.

43. An overview of the development of U.S. military policy and mobilizations plans between 1935 and 1939 can be found in Russell F. Weigley, *History of the United States Army* (1967; reprint, Bloomington: Indiana University Press, 1984), 415–19; Marvin A. Kriedburg and Merton G. Henry, *History of Military Mobilization in the United States Army, 1775–1945* (Washington, DC: Department of the Army, 1955), 474–79; and Richard W. Stewart, *American Military History,* vol. 2, *The United States Army in a Global Era, 1917–2008* (Washington, DC: Center of Military History, U.S. Army, 2016), 66–68.

44. *Annual Report of the Secretary of War for 1934* (Washington, D.C. Government Printing Office, 1934), 3; *Annual Report of the Chief of Staff, 1934,* as published in *Annual Report of the Secretary of War for 1934* (Washington, D.C. Government Printing Office, 1934), 54–56.

45. George H. Dern to D. W. Bell, Sept. 17, 1934, NA, RG 407, 111.

46. "Increase in Army Funds," *NYT* (Jan. 1, 1935): 11; "Army Chiefs and House Group in Secret Talks," *NYT* (Feb. 9, 1935): 7.

47. "House Group Votes a $50,000,000 Rise in Funds for Army," *NYT* (Feb. 20, 1935): 1.

48. "Big Army Bill Wins in Senate," *NYT* (Mar. 9, 1935): 1.

49. "Increase in Army Long Recommended," *NYT* (Apr. 14, 1935): IV, 10.

50. William T. Carpenter, Memorandum for the Chief of Staff, Jan. 30, 1935; R. E. Callan, Memorandum for the Deputy Chief of Staff, Nov. 2, 1934, NA, RG 407, 111.

51. *Annual Report of the Secretary of War for 1935* (Washington, D.C. Government Printing Office, 1935), 4.

52. Initial service estimates called for appropriations of $513 million. The General Staff reduced this to $428 million. The army's budget for fiscal year 1936 was $356 million. Douglas MacArthur to D. W. Bell, Sep. 14, 1935, NA, RG 407, 111.

53. "Budget Bureau Seeks Reduction in Army's Authorized Strength," *ANJ* 73, no. 16 (Dec. 21, 1935): 305.

54. "Defense Budgets Give Services More Funds," *ANJ* 73, no. 19 (Jan. 11, 1936): 365.

55. Malin Craig, Testimony before the House Military Affairs Committee, Dec. 1935, NA, RG 407, 111; Editorial, *ANJ* 73, no. 21 (Jan. 25, 1936): 403.

56. "Record Army Fund for 150,000 Troops is Voted by House," *NYT* (Feb. 15, 1936): 1.

57. "Record Army Bill Voted by Senate," *NYT* (Mar. 24, 1936): 1. Most of the debate on this legislation was focused on a canal project in Florida.

58. "Advancement of Enlisted Men Approved," *ANJ* 73, no. 42 (June 20, 1936): 937.

59. "Press for Enlisted Pay Heavy This Congress," *ANJ* 75, no. 34 (Apr. 23, 1938): 745.

60. "Provisions of War Department Estimates," *ANJ* 74, no. 19 (Jan. 9, 1937): 390.

61. "House Puts Check on Economy Slash; Passes Army Bill," *NYT* (May 1, 1937): 7.

62. "Pass Army Housing Bill," *ANJ* 74, no. 47 (July 24, 1937): 1084.

63. "Army-Navy Increase on Congress Program," *ANJ* 75, no. 7 (Oct. 16, 1937): 121.

64. The army's estimates for fiscal year 1938 were $481 million as compared to the $409 million authorized by Congress the previous year. Statement of the Chief of Staff before the Director of the Bureau of the Budget on Estimates for the Fiscal Year 1938, NA, RG 407, 111.

65. Editorial, *ANJ* 75, no. 9 (Oct. 30, 1937): 168.

66. "Defense Budget Outlays Raised to $990,000,000," *NYT* (Jan. 6, 1938): 1; Editorial, *ANJ* 75, no. 19 (Jan. 7, 1938): 384.

67. "$25,000,000 More Sought for Army," *NYT* (Jan. 24, 1938): 1. Roosevelt was surprised by the charges that he was neglecting the army. He had a conversation with Secretary of War Harry H. Woodring, who suggested a list of items totaling around $30 million that the president might include in new legislation. Roosevelt included all of those items. Harry H. Woodring to the President, Jan. 24, 1938, NA, RG 407, 111.

68. "Budget Action on Army," *NYT* (Feb. 2, 1938): 2.

69. "Senate Votes Bill Raising Army Fund," *NYT* (Apr. 4, 1938): 14; "Army Appropriations," *ANJ* 75, no. 40 (June 4, 1938): 877.

70. *Chief of Staff Annual Report, 1938*, as published in *Annual Report of the Secretary of War for 1938* (Washington, D.C. Government Printing Office, 1938), 29–30.

71. *Annual Report of the Secretary of War for 1938*, 2.

72. "New Budget to Speed Up Rearmament of Army," *ANJ* 76, no. 2 (Sept. 10, 1938): 21, 24.

73. "President Lays Plans for Defense Increase," *ANJ* 76, no. 9 (Oct. 29, 1938): 169.

74. "Roosevelt Moves to Rush Expansion of Army and Navy," *NYT* (Oct. 15, 1938): 1; "Roosevelt to Ask for Vast Air Fleet," *NYT* (Nov. 6, 1938): 1, 24.

75. Gole, *Road to Rainbow*, 83.

76. "Roosevelt to Arm All Americas," *NYT* (Nov. 16, 1938): 1.

77. "Army Is Perturbed over Fear of War," *NYT* (Nov. 16, 1938): 29.

78. "$309,351,000 added to Defense Outlay," *NYT* (Jan. 6, 1939): 13.

79. Editorial, *ANJ* 76, no. 27 (Mar. 4, 1939): 607.

80. "President Urges Needs of Defense," *NYT* (Mar. 5, 1939): 40.

81. "Roosevelt's Message on Defense," *NYT* (Jan. 13, 1939): 8; "Congress Adopts Big Defense Bill," *NYT* (Mar. 23, 1939): 10.

82. *Annual Report of the Chief of Staff, 1939* as published in *Annual Report of the Secretary of War for 1939* (Washington, D.C. Government Printing Office, 1939), 26; "Directive—War Department Military Program for the Fiscal Year, 1941," n.d. NA, RG 407, 111.

83. *Annual Report of the Chief of Staff, 1939*, 35.

84. Woodring to Sen. Morris Sheppard, Apr. 23, 1939; Harry H. Woodring to Albert L. Cox, May 9, 1939, NA, RG 407, 320.2; "Service Views on Age-in-Grade Proposal," *ANJ* 76, no. 42 (June 17, 1939): 977; "Action on Age-in-Grade Delayed 'til Next Year," *ANJ* 76, no. 48 (July 29, 1939): 1127.

Chapter 10

1. *Annual Report of the Chief of Staff, 1935* as published in *Annual Report of the Secretary of War, 1935* (Washington, D.C., Government Printing Office, 1935), 52.

2. The trends in enrollments in ROTC in this period can be seen in the following tables.

Year	Enrollments in the Basic Course	Enrollments in the Advanced Course
1930	60,545	12,485
1931	62,692	13,194
1932	60,188	13,801
1933	55,676	14,056

Figures are from General Staff, Operations and Training Division, G-3. *Annual Reports 1931*, 6; General Staff, Operations and Training Division, G-3. *Annual Reports, 1932*, App. A.; and General Staff, Operations and Training Division, G-3. *Annual Reports, 1933*, 5.

3. Alfred E. Kasten, "The R.O.T.C. at Princeton University," *FAJ* 33, no. 2 (Mar./Apr. 1933): 179; Anonymous, "The R.O.T.C. at Yale," *FAJ* 32, no. 5 (Sept./Oct 1932): 471.

4. A. G. Crane to the Secretary of War, Oct. 14, 1933, NA, RG 407, ROTC 000.862.

5. King, Memorandum for the Chief of Staff, Mar. 27, 1930, NA, RG 407, ROTC 000.862.

6. King, Memorandum for the Chief of Staff, Mar. 27, 1930; Edgar T Collins, Memorandum for the Chief of Staff, July 13, 1932, NA, RG 407, ROTC 000.862; John H. Hughes, Memorandum for the Chief of Staff, Dec. 7, 1933, NA, RG 407, ROTC 320.2.

7. Charles P. Summerall, Memorandum for the Assistant Chief of Staff, G-3, May 12, 1930, NA, RG 407, ROTC 000.862.

8. Ibid.

9. King, Memorandum for the Chief of Staff, Apr. 2, 1931, NA RG 407, ROTC 000.862; Johnson Hagood, "R.O.T.C., the Key to National Defense," *IJ* 38, no. 5 (Sept./Oct. 1931): 403–7; Ralph A. Palmer, "The College Trained Army," *CAJ* 74, no. 1 (Jan. 1931): 46 47.

10. King, Memorandum for the Adjutant General, June 30, 1931, NA, RG 407, ROTC 000.862.

11. Duncan K. Major Jr., Memorandum for the Chief of Staff, Dec. 27, 1932, NA, RG 407, ROTC 000.862.

12. Both the National Educational Association and the American Federation of Teachers supported legislation ending the compulsory feature of ROTC, even though both organizations supported the ROTC program in general. The American Student Union and the National Student Federation of America also supported legislation ending the compulsory feature. Victor B. Hirshauer, "The History of the Reserve Officers Training Corps, 1916–1973" (PhD diss., Johns Hopkins University, 1975), 171–72.

13. Hirshauer discusses these opponents in detail. "History of the Reserve Officers Training Corps," 175–208.

14. The efforts by the War Department to defend ROTC are carefully analyzed in Ronald Schaffer, "The War Department's Defense of ROTC, 1920–1940," *Wisconsin Magazine of History* 53, no. 2 (Winter 1969–70): 108–20.

15. Patrick J. Hurley to W. Frank James, Dec. 31, 1930, NA, RG 407, ROTC 000.862.

16. Hirshauer, "History of the Reserve Officers Training Corps," 142.

17. Hughes, Memorandum for the Chief of Staff, Mar. 30, 1937, NA, RG 407, 000.862.

18. Brown, Memorandum for the Assistant Chief of Staff, G-3, Oct. 10, 1934, NA, RG 407, 00.862; Hughes, Memorandum for the Chief of Staff, Mar. 30, 1937.

19. Michael S. Neiberg, *Making Citizen-Soldiers: ROTC and the Ideology of American Military Service* (Cambridge, MA: Harvard University Press, 2000), 30.

20. Bower Davis, "On the Reserve Officer Training Corps," *IJ* 37, no. 3 (Sept. 1930): 292.

21. *Annual Report of the Chief of the Militia Bureau, 1931* (Washington, D.C., Government Printing Office, 1931) 1, 37.

22. "The National Guard Convention," *CAJ* 75, no. 6 (Nov./Dec. 1932): 455.

23. House of Representatives, 73rd Cong., 1st sess., 1933, H. Rep. 141, 2.

24. Herold J. Werther, "The Act of June 15, 1933," *CAJ* 73, no. 3 (May/June 1934): 226–29.

25. *Annual Report of the Chief of the Militia Bureau, 1935* (Washington, D.C., Government Printing Office, 1935), 1.

26. *Annual Report of the Chief of the Militia Bureau, 1936* (Washington, D.C., Government Printing Office, 1936) 1; *Annual Report of the Chief of the Militia Bureau, 1937* (Washington, D.C., Government Printing Office, 1937) 12; *Annual Report of the Chief of the Militia Bureau, 1939* (Washington, D.C., Government Printing Office, 1939), 16.

27. Quoted from U.S. Army, TR 10-5, *Basic Military Training*, in King, Memorandum for the Chief of Staff, Aug. 8, 1931, NA, RG 407, OR 353.

28. Quoted from War Department, *Officers' Reserve Corps*, A.R. 140-5 (1931), in King, Memorandum for the Chief of Staff, Aug. 8, 1931.

29. Charles P. Summerall, "The Officers' Reserve Corps," *IJ* 37, no. 5 (Nov. 1930): 463.

30. H. A. Finch, "Nothing Is Wrong with the Reserves," *IJ* 38, no. 7 (July/Aug. 1931): 357.

31. Richard B. Crossland and James T. Currie, *Twice the Citizen: A History of the United States Army Reserve, 1908–1983* (Washington, DC: Office of the Chief, Army Reserve, 1984), 49.

32. *Annual Report of the Chief of the Militia Bureau, 1930* (Washington, D.C., Government Printing Office, 1930), 93.

33. During the lean years of the Depression budgets, 1934 and 1935, appropriations allowed only around 12,000 and 17,000 reserve officers, respectively, to take active-duty training. After 1937, appropriations began to increase, allowing nearly 32,000 to take active-duty training in 1940. Crossland and Currie, *Twice the Citizen*, 49.

34. Over 5,000 of the reserve officers taking active-duty training in the summer of 1931 were repeaters. Irving J. Phillipson, Memorandum for the Chief of Staff, Oct. 24, 1931, NA, RG 407, OR 353.

35. L. L. Stewart, "The Officers' Reserve Corps," *CAJ* 74, no. 3 (May/June 1931): 281.

36. The number of officers involved rose dramatically, from around 38,000 in 1930 to around 46,000 in 1932, possibly because of the tightening of standards needed for promotion. It leveled off there. General Staff, Operations and Training Division, G-3. *Annual Reports,1931*, 5.

37. Charles I. Clark, "An Organized Reserve," *CAJ* 80, no. 1 (Jan./Feb. 1932): 53.

38. The interest problem is discussed well in F. J. Baum, "What's the Matter with the Reserve?," *CAJ* 74, no. 2 (Feb. 1931): 116–18.

39. *Annual Report of the Chief of Staff, 1931*, as published in *Annual Report of the Secretary of War, 1931* (Washington, D.C., Government Printing Office, 1931), 44.

40. King, Memorandum for the Chief of Staff, Aug. 8, 1931.

41. Ibid.

42. King, Memorandum for the Chief of Staff, Oct. 3, 1931, NA, RG 407, OR 353.

43. See, for instance, "Reserve Training Policies, 1934," Mar. 6, 1934, NA, RG 407, OR 353.

44. King, Memorandum for the Chief of Staff, Dec. 29, 1930, NA, RG 407, OR 353.

45. Edgar T. Collins, Memorandum for the Chief of Staff, July 20, 1932, NA, RG 407, OR 353.

46. R. A. Hill, "Reserve Policies and National Defense," *CAJ* 78, no. 1 (Jan./Feb. 1935): 56.

47. LeRoy F. Smith, "The Reserve Regiment with the C.M.T.C.: An Experiment That Worked," *IJ* 37, no. 3 (Sept. 1930): 325–30; *Annual Report, G-3 Division, 1933*, 4.

48. *Annual Report of the Secretary of War, 1934* (Washington, D.C., Government Printing Office, 1934), 8; *Annual Report of the Secretary of War, 1935* (Washington, D.C., Government Printing Office, 1935), 12; *Annual Report of the Secretary of War, 1936* (Washington, D.C., Government Printing Office, 1936), 6.

49. General Staff, Operations and Training Division, G-3. *Annual Reports 1936*, 3.

50. General Staff, Operations and Training Division, G-3. *Annual Reports 1937*, 4.

51. Edward M. Coffman, *The Regulars: The American Army, 1898–1941* (Cambridge, MA: Belknap Press of Harvard University Press, 2004), 244; Steven Thomas Barry, *Battalion Commanders at War: U.S. Tactical Leadership in the Mediterranean Theater, 1942–1943* (Lawrence: University Press of Kansas, 2013), 8.

52. M. C. Shea "Our Reserves: Prepared or Potential," *CJ* 49, no. 218 (Mar./Apr. 1940): 156.

53. Applications rose from 58,695 in 1929 to 82,959 in 1931. But after the program was reduced by budget cuts in 1934 and 1935, interest dwindled, and applications in 1938 were back down to 57,673. General Staff, Operations and Training Division, G-3. *Annual Reports, 1931*, 3; King, Memorandum for the Chief of Staff, Nov. 20, 1931, NA, RG 407, 354.1; General Staff, Operations and Training Division, G-3. *Annual Reports, 1938*, 2.

54. Payne, Assistant Secretary of War, to L. C. Dyer, Dec. 15, 1930, NA, RG 407, 354.1.

55. Hagood Johnson to Adjutant General, Apr. 23, 1931; C. J. Bridges to Commanding General, 7th Corps Area, Apr. 29, 1931, NA, RG 407, 354.1.

56. Hughes, Memorandum for the Chief of Staff, Mar. 7, 1936, NA, RG 407, 354.1.

57. George P. Tyner, Memorandum for the Chief of Staff, Oct. 22, 1937, NA, RG 407, 354.1.

Chapter 11

1. S. D. Rockenbach, "Tank Tactics," *ME* 12, no. 63 (May/June 1920): 273.

2. "The Tactical Employment of Tanks in Battle," *General Service Schools Mailing List* 3, no. 11 (Oct. 1923): 29.

3. Sereno Brett, "Tank Combat Principles," *IJ* 25, no.2, (Feb. 1926): 132–41; Ralph E. Jones, "Our Tanks," *IJ* 35, no. 6 (Dec. 1929): 594–600.

4. "Academic Notes," *Command and General Staff School Mailing List*, 14, no. 53 (June 1934): 146–47.

5. George A. Lynch to Commandant, the Infantry School, July 12, 1937, NA, RG 177, Entry 40, 470.8.

6. Chief of Infantry to Adjutant General, Final Report, Apr. [?], 1941, NA, RG 177, Entry 40, 319.1.

7. Ordnance Department, "History of the Development of the Light Tank," NA, RG 177, Entry 40, 470.8.

8. John Leonard, "The Development of Tanks," *IJ* 27, no. 5 (Nov. 1925): 488.

9. Ibid.

10. Adjutant General to the Chief of Ordnance, Apr. 3, 1922, NA, RG 177, Entry 40, 470.8. Tanks larger than fifteen tons could still be carried on railroad cars but required the design of special cars. S. D. Rockenbach, "Weight and Dimensions of Tanks," *IJ* 21, no. 1 (July 1922): 13.

11. Leonard, "Development of Tanks," 489.

12. H. L. Cooper to Chief of Infantry, July 22, 1925, NA, RG 177, Entry 40, 470.8.

13. O. S. Eskridge to Chief of Infantry, June 2, 1924, NA, RG 177, Entry 40, 470.8.

14. Adjutant General to the Chief of Infantry, Sept. 3, 1924, NA, RG 177, Entry 40, 470.8.

15. R. H. Allen to Adjutant General, June 6, 1926, NA, RG 177, Entry 40, 470.8 (emphasis in original).

16. Allen to Hanson Ely, Jan. 19, 1927, NA, RG 177, Entry 40, 470.8.

17. Willey Howell to Oliver S. Eskridge, Aug. 27, 1925, NA, RG 177, Entry 40, 470.8.

18. Allen to Adjutant General, Jan. 6, 1926, NA, RG 177, Entry 40, 470.8.

19. Howell to Chief of Ordnance, Jan. 23, 1926, NA, RG 177, Entry 40, 470.8.

20. Adjutant General to the Chief of Infantry, Mar. 11, 1926, NA, RG 177, Entry 40, 470.8.

21. Along with certain combat advantages that placing the engine in front provided, that design also made it possible to use the same chassis for building a tank-carrying truck, which would not have been available if the engine were placed in the rear.

22. Cooper to the Chief of Infantry, July 24, 1929, NA, RG 177, Entry 40, 470.8.

23. Ibid.

24. During the tests, the tank maintained an average speed of twelve miles per hour, as opposed to six for the world-war tank. It was able to run for two thousand miles without an overhaul, while the older tank could only go around eighty miles. Its maintenance costs were only a fifth of the world-war tank. Finally, it was armed with both a 37-mm cannon and a .30-caliber machine gun, while the older tank had only one weapon or the other.

25. Allen was, apparently, admonished by the secretary of war for failure to include the Tank Board in tank-development projects. Adjutant General to the Chief of Infantry, Jan. 4, 1929, NA, RG 177, Entry 40, 470.8. Fuqua expressed his personal respect for the officers of the board. Stephen O. Fuqua to James K. Parsons, Dec. 4, 1929, NA, RG 177, Entry 407, 470.8.

26. James K. Parsons to Chief of Infantry, Dec. 18, 1929, NA, RG 177, Entry 40, 470.8.

27. Parsons to Chief of Infantry, Aug. 22, 1929, NA, RG 177, Entry 40, 470.8.

28. George F. Hoffmann has disentangled the story of these three years. Hoffmann, "A Yankee Inventor and the Military Establishment: The Christie Tank Controversy," *Military Affairs* 39, no. 1 (Feb. 1975): 12–18. Unless otherwise noted, Hoffmann is the basic source for this description of the Christie period in the infantry's efforts to get a tank.

29. David Johnson claims that the Ordnance Department felt that the Christie tanks were unreliable and poorly engineered, while the infantry, which preferred fast tanks that could avoid gunfire, felt the Ordnance tanks were too slow. David E. Johnson, *Fast Tanks and Heavy Bombers: Innovation in the U.S. Army, 1917–1945* (Ithaca, NY: Cornell University Press, 1998), 118–19.

30. Fuqua, Memorandum for the Deputy Chief of Staff, Mar. 27, 1933, NA, RG 177, Entry 40, 470.8.

31. Fuqua to the Adjutant General, Mar. 24, 1931, NA, RG 177, Entry 40, 537.3.

32. Fuqua, Memorandum for the Deputy Chief of Staff, June 23, 1931, NA, RG 177, Entry 40, 470.3.

33. Fuqua to the Deputy Chief of Staff, Mar. 27, 1933.

34. Wm. F. Pearson, 12th Endorsement, To the Chief of Ordnance, Apr. 29, 1933, NA, RG 177, Entry 40, 470.8.

35. Edw. Croft to W. B. Wallace, Oct. 31, 1933, NA, RG 177, Entry 40, 470.8.

36. Croft to the President of the Infantry Board, Aug. 8, 1933, NA, RG 177, Entry 40, 470.8.

37. F. L. Munson to the Chief of Infantry, Aug. 25, 1933, NA, RG 177, Entry 40, 470.8.

38. Croft to the President of the Infantry Board, Sept. 5, 1933, NA, RG 177, Entry 40, 470.8; Johnson, *Fast Tanks and Heavy Bombers*, 119.

39. W. D. Wallace to the Chief of Infantry, Oct. 12, 1933, NA, RG 177, Entry 40, 470.8.

40. Policy Governing Tanks and Combat Cars, Dec. 22, 1933, NA, RG 177, Entry 40, 470.8.

41. Wm. C. Young, Memorandum for the Chief of Infantry, Apr. 26, 1934; Croft to the Adjutant General, May 7, 1934, NA, RG 177, Entry 40, 470.8.

42. Jesse A. Ladd to the President of the Infantry Board, June 2, 1935, NA, RG 177, Entry 40, 470.8.

43. "New Army Tank," *AO* 15, no. 88 (Jan./Feb. 1935): 240.

44. J. B. Woolnough to the President of the Infantry Board, Nov. 18, 1935, NA, RG 177, Entry 40, 470.8.

45. Charles A. Walker to the Chief of Infantry, Dec. 13, 1935, NA, RG 177, Entry 40, 470.8.

46. Croft, Memorandum for the Chief of Staff, Dec. 14, 1935, NA, RG 177, Entry 40, 470.8.

47. Woolnough to the Commandant of the Infantry School, Dec. 4, 1935, NA, RG 177, Entry 40, 470.8.

48. Woolnough to the Adjutant General, Mar. 24, 1936, NA, RG 177, Entry 40, 470.8.

49. George P. Tyner, Memorandum for the Chief of Staff, Oct. 25, 1937, NA, RG 177, Entry 40, 470.8.

50. Lynch to the Commandant of the Infantry School, July 12, 1937, NA, RG 177, Entry 40, 470.8.

51. Woolnough to the Commandant of the Infantry School, Sept. 24, 1937, NA, RG 177, Entry 40, 470.8.

52. Tyner, Memorandum for the Chief of Staff, Oct. 25, 1937.

53. Ibid.

54. Ibid.

55. Heinz Guderian, "Armored Forces, Part One," *IJ* 44, no. 5 (Sept./Oct. 1937): 418–21; Guderian, "Armored Forces, Part Two," *IJ* 44, no. 6 (Nov./Dec. 1937): 522–28.

56. "International Military Survey: Spain," *IJ* 45, no. 1 (Jan./Feb. 1938): 77.

57. Johnson, *Fast Tanks and Heavy Bombers*, 120–21. Indeed, Lynch was still advocating this approach to the use of tanks with infantry in his "Final Report," written before he resigned as chief of infantry in April 1941. Chief of Infantry to Adjutant General, Final Report, Apr. [?], 1941.

58. "International Military Situation: Tanks," *IJ* 46, no. 2 (Mar./Apr. 1939): 195; Edwin Butcher to the Chief of Infantry, Mar. 9, 1939, NA, RG 177, Entry 40, 470.8.

59. "Experiments with Explosives for Anti-tank Defense," *IJ* 29, no. 5 (Nov. 1926): 541.

60. "Anti-Tank Defense," *IJ* 32, no. 5 (May 1928): 534–35; "Armor Piercing Shell for the 37 mm Gun," *IJ* 34, no. 5 (May 1929): 534; Caspar A. Crim, "Training for Anti-Tank Firing of the 37 mm Gun," *IJ* 36, no. 6 (June 1930): 601.

61. W. L. Roberts, "Antitank Mines," *IJ* 42, no. 3 (May/June 1936): 217–21.

62. "The New Antitank Gun," *IJ* 46, no. 1 (Jan./Feb. 1938): 72–73; "The Antitank Gun," *AO* 20, no. 115 (July/Aug. 1938): 25–28.

63. Joseph Greene, "The Case for Antitank," *IJ* 45, no. 3 (May/June 1938): 213–22.

64. *Annual Report of the Chief of Staff, 1939,* as published in *Annual Report of the Secretary of War, 1939* (Washington, D.C., Government Printing Office, 1939), 81.

65. George Lynch, "Firepower, Manpower, Maneuver," *IJ* 46, no. 6 (Nov./Dec. 1939): 503.

66. Even after the invasion of Poland in September 1939, the school still taught that "mechanization is not a new arm of the service: . . . it is a new weapon for assisting combatant arms in the accomplishment of their mission" "Mechanized Cavalry—Armament, Organization, and Characteristics," lecture given at the Command and General Staff School, Sept. 29, 1939, Curricular Materials, Command and General Staff College, Fort Leavenworth, KS.

Chapter 12

1. George W. Grunert, "Cavalry in Future Wars," Lecture, Mar. 13, 1933, U.S. Army War College Curricular Files, USAMHI; Guy V. Henry, "The Trend of Organization

and Equipment of Cavalry in the Principal World Powers and Its Probable Role in Wars of the Near Future," *CJ* 41, no. 170 (Mar./Apr. 1932): 5. Henry was chief of cavalry at the time he wrote this article.

2. Henry was one of these officers and played a large role in this modernization, which he discusses at length in his memoirs. Guy V. Henry, Jr., "A Brief Narrative of the Life of Guy V. Henry, Jr." Guy V. Henry Papers, USAMHI, 29–56.

3. George H. Cameron, "The Cavalry School and Its Main Functions," *CJ* 29, no. 119 (Apr. 1920): 7–10.

4. Lucian K. Truscott, Jr., *The Twilight of the U.S. Cavalry: Life in the Old Army, 1917–1942* (Lawrence: University Press of Kansas, 1989), 16–18.

5. William O. Odom, *After the Trenches: The Transformation of the U.S. Army, 1918–1939* (College Station: Texas A&M University Press, 2008), 63.

6. As quoted in Odom, *After the Trenches,* 63.

7. *FSR,1923,* para. 80.

8. "A Story in Figures," *CJ* 48, no. 116 (Nov./Dec. 1939). 518. The cavalry adjusted to the second reduction by skeletonizing its regiments.

9. Truscott, *Twilight of the U.S. Cavalry,* 102.

10. Jack Wade, "Lest We Forget," *CJ* 31, no. 128 (July 1922): 312.

11. This tendency generated a whole host of articles. Elbridge Colby, "Cavalry in the Recent War," *IJ* 16/ (July 1919): 26–37; Anonymous, "Cavalry: The Constant Factor Present in Decisive Operations of the World War," *CJ* 47, no. 202 (May/June 1938): 209–12; 47, no. 208 (July/Aug. 1938): 302–6.

12. David E. Johnson, *Fast Tanks and Heavy Bombers: Innovation in the U.S. Army, 1917–1945* (Ithaca, NY: Cornell University Press, 1998), 124.

13. "Extracts from the *Annual Report of the Chief of Cavalry, 1926,*" *CJ* 36, no. 146 (Jan. 1927): 107.

14. "The Happy Cavalryman," *CJ* 30, no. 127 (Apr. 1922): 197.

15. "Modern Defense Policies: Increased Importance of Cavalry," *CJ* 32, no. 133 (Oct. 1923): 450.

16. Constitution of the Cavalry Association, as quoted in "The Aim of the *Cavalry Journal,*" *CJ* 33, no. 136 (July 1924): 330.

17. Leon B. Kromer to John K. Herr, Mar. 7, 1938, NA, RG 177, Entry 39, 322.02.

18. "A Chief of Cavalry," *CJ* 23, no. 93 (Nov. 1912): 543–46; "A Chief of Cavalry," *CJ* 29, no. 119 (Apr. 1920): 83. The demand at this time was inspired by the effort of the French cavalry to get a chief as well, which puts the effort in the context of branch modernization based on copying French models and organization.

19. War Plans Division, Memorandum for the Adjutant General, Aug. 27, 1920, NA, RG 177, Entry 39, 322.02.

20. H. R. Crosby to the Inspector General, NA, RG 177, Entry 39, 322.02.

21. "The First Cavalry Division," *CJ* 34, no. 138 (Jan. 1925): 77.

22. Kojassa, Memorandum for Colonel Kent, July 5, 1938, NA, RG 177, Entry 39, 334.3. Henry, when he was chief of cavalry, privately negotiated an arrangement with

the commanding general of Eighth Corps Area, a personal friend, that would allow him to communicate directly with the division and its board. Henry to Edwin B. Winans, Mar. 24, 1931, NA, RG 177, Entry 39, 334.7. No other chief had such an arrangement.

23. Truscott noted several occasions when a "Riley Man" arrived at a unit in which he served and sought to change the command along lines learned at the school. Truscott, *Twilight of the U.S. Cavalry*, 53, 66, 67.

24. Truscott, *Twilight of the U.S. Cavalry*, 75, 76; Rufus S. Ramey, *He's in the Cavalry Now* (New York: McBride, 1944), 21–25; George H. Cameron, "The Cavalry School and Its New Functions," *CJ* 29, no. 119 (Apr. 1920): 7–9; Guy V. Henry, Jr. "The Cavalry School," *ME* 28, no. 158 (Mar./Apr. 1936): 103–4.

25. W. W. Grimes, "The Cavalry School, 1919–1929," *CJ* 38, no. 155 (Apr. 1929): 232.

26. The entering classes in September 1920 numbered nearly two hundred, while the classes before the world war totaled about fifty. "Notes for the Cavalry School," *CJ* 29, no. 121 (Oct. 1920): 316.

27. *Annual Report of the Commandant of the Cavalry School Fort Riley, Kansas, 1922* (Fort Leavenworth, KS: GSS, 1922), app. B, "Report of the Department of Tactics," 31.

28. R. S. Fleming, "Mission of the Cavalry School with Comments on Modern Cavalry and Cavalry Training," *CJ* 38, no. 154 (Jan. 1929): 43.

29. Truscott, *Twilight of the U.S. Cavalry*, 84; Robert A. Bush, "The Cavalry School," *CJ* 34, no. 139 (Apr. 1925): 202, 204.

30. Bush, "Cavalry School," 202.

31. "The Cavalry Board," *CJ* 29, no. 120 (July 1920): 122.

32. Bush, "Cavalry School," 204.

33. Clarence Lininger, "Some Trends at the Cavalry School," *CJ* 47, no. 207 (May/June 1938): 233.

34. "Cavalry School Notes," *CJ* 31, no. 129 (Oct. 1922): 433–34.

35. Truscott, *Twilight of the U.S. Cavalry*, 86, 87.

36. Ibid., 86.

37. "The Cavalry School," *CJ* 33, no. 135 (Apr. 1924): 240.

38. In his history of the U.S. Cavalry, Major General John Herr devotes far more space to discussing polo and other equestrian activities in the interwar period than to mechanization or any other development in the branch. The only reference he makes to himself is a picture of the 1923 American Military Polo Team that captured the World Polo Championship. Herr was a member of the team. John K. Herr and Edward S. Wallace, *The Story of the U.S. Cavalry, 1775–1942* (New York: Little Brown, 1953), 242, 244–48.

39. Truscott was also an outstanding polo player and notes the intensity of the interest in polo in the cavalry. At one point he was transferred from his regiment in Marfa, Texas, to First Cavalry Division headquarters at Fort Bliss, Texas, so he could play for its team in the national championships. Truscott frequently lists polo abilities among the qualities of officers he admired. Truscott, *Twilight of the U.S. Cavalry*, 74.

40. Mildrid H. Gillie, in her book regarding the role of Adna Chaffee in mechanizing the cavalry, claims that prior to taking on mechanization as a passion, he had considered himself a virtual polo professional within the cavalry. Gillie, *Forging the Thunderbolt:*

A History of the Development of the Armored Force (Harrisburg, PA: Military Service, 1947; reprint, Mechanicsburg, PA: Stackpole, 2006), 27. Steven Barry points out in a footnote: "The horse tradition still permeates the army to this day, especially at Fort Leavenworth and Fort Riley. Fort Leavenworth still conducts an annual fox hunt and maintains significant horse stables and show rings." Barry, *Battalion Commanders at War: U.S. Tactical Leadership in the Mediterranean Theater, 1942–1943* (Lawrence: University Press of Kansas, 2013), 206.

41. Noted in Willard A. Holbrook, "A Few Words to the Cavalry," *CJ* 29, no. 121 (Oct.1923): 249.

42. Hamilton Hawkins, "The Role of Cavalry," *CJ* 29, no. 121 (Oct. 1920): 265 (emphasis in the original).

43. Ibid.

44. TR 425-105, "The Employment of Cavalry," 1922 (draft), 3, NA, RG 177, Entry 39, 300.7.

45. "Employment of Cavalry," 1922 (draft), 2.

46. Ibid., 4.

47. Ibid., 6, 7.

48. Some officers even argued that mobility was merely the means by which the cavalry applied firepower and shock. Clarence Lininger, "Mobility, Firepower, and Shock," *CJ* 34, no. 139 (Apr. 1925): 179.

49. Hawkins, "Role of Cavalry," 260–65.

50. Ibid.

51. Karl S. Bradford, "Cavalry Combat," *CJ* 32, no. 133 (Oct. 1923): 392.

52. In a lecture at the Army War College in 1932, Henry still pointed to the use of cavalry as a shock weapon as a characteristic of European warfare rather than American. Henry, "Trend of Organization and Equipment of Cavalry in the Principal World Powers," 5–10.

53. Bradford, "Cavalry Combat," 385–95.

54. R. B. Trimble, "Modern Cavalry in Combined Mounted and Dismounted Action," *CJ* 44, no. 187 (Jan./Feb. 1939): 17.

55. Ibid.

56. Ibid.

57. George Williams, "Cavalry Reorganization," *CJ* 30, no. 123 (Apr. 1921): 158–61.

58. W. W. Gordon to Adjutant General, Aug. 7, 1929, NA, RG 177, Entry 39, 400.14.

59. Herbert B. Crosby, "Our New Cavalry Organization," Lecture, Sept. 19, 1928, U.S. Army War College Curricular Files, USAMHI.

60. Crosby to Adjutant General, Apr. 12, 1927, NA, RG 177, Entry 39, 322.02.

61. Crosby to Adjutant General, July 23, 1928, NA, RG 177, Entry 39, 322.02.

62. Adjutant General to the Chief of Cavalry, Apr. 23, 1928, NA, RG 177, Entry 39, 400.14.

63. Crosby to Adjutant General, Apr. 12, 1927; Douglas McCaskey to Adjutant General, Apr. 21, 1927; Robert L. Collins to the Chief of Cavalry, May 19, 1927, NA, RG 177, Entry 39, 322.02.

64. Pillow, Memorandum, Feb. 18, 1928, NA, RG 177, Entry 39, 400.14.

65. Except where otherwise noted, the material for the discussion here regarding the mechanized force is taken from Gillie, *Forging the Thunderbolt*, 19–47.

66. L. D. Gasser, Memorandum for the Chief of Staff, Feb. 20, 1931, NA, RG 177, Entry 40, 537.7.

67. Gasser, Memorandum for the Chief of Staff, Feb. 20, 1931.

68. Charles S. Lincoln to the Adjutant General, Oct. 1, 1928, NA, RG 177, Entry 40, 537.7.

69. Gasser, Memorandum for the Chief of Staff, Feb. 20, 1931.

70. The budget for 1928 had already been approved by Congress before the creation of the Experimental Mechanized Force was ordered. Charles L. Lincoln to the Adjutant General, Oct. [?], 1928; H. G. Wells, Memorandum for the Chief of Staff, Oct. 31, 1928; Adjutant General to James Parsons, Sept. 13, 1928, NA, RG 177, Entry 40, 537.3.

71. Pillow to Adjutant General, Jan. 7, 1929, NA, RG 177, Entry 39, 400.14.

72. Henry to the Chief of Staff, Mar. 24, 1931, NA, RG 407, Entry 39, 400.14.

73. "Extracts from the *Annual Report . . . 1932*," *CJ* 41, no. 174 (Nov./Dec. 1932): 30–32.

74. Henry to Chief of Staff, May 6, 1931, NA, RG 407, Entry 39, 400.14.

75. Ibid.

76. C. A. Summerall, Memorandum, July 29, 1929, NA, RG 407, Entry 39, 333.

77. Henry to the Chief of Staff, Mar. 24, 1931.

78. Ibid.

79. David E. Johnson claims that Major General Moseley, who was then deputy chief of staff, was a major force in the army's mechanization program and was likely the author of MacArthur's memorandum of May 1, 1931. Johnson, *Fast Tanks and Heavy Bombers*, 128.

80. "General Principles to Govern Mechanization and Motorization," in Douglas MacArthur to Adjutant General, May 1, 1931. It is unclear as to how and to whom this statement of General Principles was originally delivered. It is found in archives only as enclosures to later documents. See, for instance, Malin Craig to Various, Apr. 5, 1935, NA, RG 177, Entry 39, 322.0. It was copied into a press release given out on May 18, 1931 (NA, RG 177, Entry 39, 400.14).

81. Gillie, *Forging the Thunderbolt*, 41; MacArthur, "General Principles to Govern Mechanization and Motorization."

82. Barry, *Battalion Commanders at War*, 49. Also, David E. Johnson notes, "Major General Adna Chaffee designed the armored division to conduct traditional light cavalry missions." Johnson, *Fast Tanks and Heavy Bombers*, 222.

83. Aubrey Lippincott to Commander, Cavalry School, Oct. 10, 1931, NA, RG 177, Entry 39, 320.2. Johnson claims that the selection of Camp (later Fort) Knox as the base for the program of mechanizing cavalry was made because it was far removed from both the Office of the Chief of Cavalry in Washington and the Cavalry School at Fort Riley. Johnson, *Fast Tanks and Heavy Bombers*, 129.

84. On Henry's first visit with MacArthur as chief of staff, MacArthur pointed to cars parked in the street and said, "Henry, there is your Cavalry of the Future." Henry, "Brief Narrative," 65.

85. Henry Jr. to Floyd Hyndman, Apr. 22, 1933, NA, RG 177, Entry 39, 322.02.

86. The Chief of Cavalry's Office was responsible for developing the tables of organization for the regiment and for the mechanized brigade planned in the future. The development of these "TOs" provided opportunity for direct communications between Henry and Fort Knox. Memorandum for the Adjutant General, July 7, 1931; Memorandum for the Adjutant General, Jan. 6, 1932, NA, RG 177, Entry 39, 400.14; Henry to Commanding Officer, HQ Det. Mechanized Force, Jan. 15, 1932, NA, RG 407, 322.02; Memorandum for the Adjutant General, July 7, 1932, NA, RG 407, 400.14; E. M. Offley to Commandant, Cavalry School, Feb. 27, 1932; A. M. Miller, Memorandum for General Kromer, May 27, 1936, NA, RG 407, 322.02.

87. *Mechanized Cavalry* (Fort Riley, KS: Cavalry School, 1933), 3.

88. Ibid., 41, 47, 62.

89. J. R. Lindsey to Commanding General, Fifth Corps Area, Mar. 16, 1932, NA, RG 177, Entry 39, 322.02.

90. The idea, as formulated by MacArthur, provided for two kinds of cavalry units: "one, (horsed) in which the horse and mule may remain only where they cannot be replaced and the performance of difficult tactical missions, or for operations in difficult terrain where the horse and mule still give us the best mobility." MacArthur, "General Principles to Govern Mechanization and Motorization."

91. The Cavalry School adhered to the doctrine of two cavalries in its general statements. But in its text it devoted only two of eighty-five pages to combined operations. *Mechanized Cavalry*, 41, 42.

92. The *Cavalry Field Manual* remained organized on the principle of two cavalries. War Department, *Cavalry Field Manual*, 3 vols. (Washington, D.C., Government Printing Office, 1938).

93. Kromer to Assistant Chiefs of Staff, G-1 and G-3, Dec. 19, 1934; Aubrey Lippincott to Maj. C. P. Stearn, Dec. 18, 1934, NA, RG 177, Entry 39, 320.02.

94. Kromer to Assistant Chief of Staff, G-3, Feb. 27, 1935, NA, RG 177, Entry 39, 322.02.

95. Hughes, Memorandum for the Chief of Staff, Apr. 17, 1935, NA, RG 177, Entry 39, 322.02; Kromer to Assistant Chief of Staff, G-3, Feb. 27, 1935.

96. War Department, *Cavalry Field Manual*, 3:1.

97. Ibid., 3:67, 76, 78, 80, 81, 95, 96.

98. As R. W. Grow, a leader in the cavalry mechanization program worried, "The General Staff (and the Army) is drifting more and more toward a 'mechanized force' which is the first step in alienating a part of the cavalry and reducing the role of cavalry." Grow, Memorandum for Miller, Jan. 10, 1937, NA, RG 177, Entry 39, 322.02.

99. *FSR*, 13.

100. Henry to Chief of Cavalry, May 9, 1936, NA, RG 177, Entry 39, 322.02.

101. Robert W. Grow, "The Ten Lean Years: From the Mechanized Force 1930 to the Armored Force 1940," *Armor* (Jan/Feb. 1987): 27.

102. Henry indicated that he saw the rift between horse and mechanized cavalry growing in 1937. Henry to Chief of Cavalry, July 30, 1937, NA, RG 177, Entry 39, 334.3.

103. Kromer to President Cavalry Board, July 1, 1937, NA, RG 177, Entry 39, 334.3.

104. Daniel Van Voorhis to Chief of Cavalry, NA, RG 177, Entry 39, 334.3.

105. Miller, Memorandum to the Chief of Cavalry, Sept. 1, 1937, NA, RG 177, Entry 39, 334.3.

106. Herr first formulated his "not one man, not one horse" stand in a General Staff conference in which the Mechanized Board and Mechanized School were the major topics discussed. Herr, "Remarks re Conference with Assistant Chief of Staff, G-3," Oct. 10, 1938, NA, RG 177, Entry 39. 334.3.

107. Adjutant General to Commanding Generals of all Corps Areas, et al. Apr. 5, 1935, NA, RG 407, 537.

108. Hughes, Memorandum for the Chief of Staff, Apr. 17, 1935.

109. Malin Craig, Memorandum for the Deputy Chief of Staff, June 28, 1937, NA, RG 407, 537.3. Craig was heavily influenced by the Spanish Civil War and by the progress and direction of the mechanization program in Germany.

110. George B. Tyner, Memorandum for the Chief of Staff, Oct. 25, 1937, NA, RG 407, 537.3.

111. Kromer to Assistant Chief of Staff, G-3, Nov. 29, 1937, NA, RG 407, 537.3.

112. Herr, to Adjutant General, Apr. 13, 1938, NA RG 177, Entry 39, 334.3.

113. Lucian Truscott says that nearly all the instructors at Fort Riley and most of the students there were supportive of mechanization. Truscott, *Twilight of the U.S. Cavalry*, 103.

114. Hawkins referred to mechanization in 1938 as "Imagination Gone Wild" since it was based on "no foundation of knowledge." Hamilton S. Hawkins, "Imagination Gone Wild," *CJ* 47, no. 210 (Nov./Dec. 1938): 491. At the same time, Bruce Palmer Jr. referred to his father, Bruce Palmer, who was a leading mechanization advocate, as "a dreamer." "Conversations between General Bruce Palmer, Jr., and Lt. Col. James E. Shelton and Lt. Col. Edward P. Smith," Typescript USAMHI, 3. In their correspondence, supporters of mechanization tended to use evangelical terms such as "prophets," "conversion," and "gospel." This is noted in many places in Gillie, *Forging the Thunderbolt*.

115. "Cavalry Affairs before Congress," *CJ* 38, no. 212 (Mar./Apr. 1939): 130.

116. In talking about mechanized cavalry in late 1938, Herr declared: "It has not yet reached a position in which it can be relied upon to displace horse cavalry. For a considerable period of time it is bound to play an important but minor role while the horse cavalry plays the major role." Herr, Memorandum for the Chief of Staff, Oct. 17, 1938, NA, RG 177, Entry 39, 322.02.

117. Grow, "The Ten Lean Years" 21.

118. Hawkins pronounced the end of "complementarity" in 1939: "No large unit without a main or principal element in it which sets its pace and dictates its employment can be kept under control by its commander or operate with unity and effectiveness." Hawkins, "Imagination Gone Wild," 491.

119. One officer wrote: "Unquestionably the Cavalry service has fallen into a low estate in War Department circles within the last few years. Much of this was due to the presence in key positions of certain officers definitely hostile to cavalry, who were able to block the aims and ambitions of the Cavalry at every turn. Some of this hostility extended even to the form of attempting to create the impression that the principal role of Cavalry was reconnaissance rather than combat." Willis D. Crittenberger, Memorandum for the Chief of Cavalry, Aug. 4, 1938, Willis D. Crittenberger Papers, USAMHI.

120. Herr, "Remarks re Conference with Assistant Chief of Staff . . .," Oct. 10, 1938. As David Johnson notes, Herr had a new column written by horse-cavalry enthusiast Hamilton Hawkins, called "General Hawkins Notes," included in each issue of *Cavalry Journal*. Johnson, *Fast Tanks and Heavy Bombers*, 136.

121. The endgame of mechanization is best described in Johnson, *Fast Tanks and Heavy Bombers*, 138–44.

122. Grow, "The Ten Lean Years," 9.

123. Charles P. Summerall, "Cavalry in Modern Combat," *CJ* 39, no. 161 (Oct. 1930): 491–93.

124. Odom, *After the Trenches*, 146–47.

Conclusion

1. In his conclusion William O. Odom claims, "The army's decision to fund manpower over material fundamentally influenced its ability to modernize." Odom, *After the Trenches: The Transformation of the U.S. Army, 1918–1939* (College Station: Texas A&M University Press, 2008), 238. David E. Johnson claims, "The Army's decision not to invest in technology at the expense of personnel resulted in a protracted period in which technological development slowed to a glacial pace in all areas except aviation." Johnson, *Fast Tanks and Heavy Bombers: Innovation in the U.S. Army, 1917–1945* (Ithaca, NY: Cornell University Press, 1998), 114.

2. Paul Dickson, *The Rise of the G.I. Army, 1940–1941* (New York: Atlantic Monthly Press 2020), 16.

3. Ibid., 14–16.

4. Marshall was quoted as saying in regard to the ORC: "Just what we would have done in the first phase of our mobilization without [ROTC graduates] I do not know. I do know that our plans would have had to be greatly curtailed and the cessation of

hostilities on the European front would have been delayed accordingly." Quoted in Michael S. Neiberg, *Making Citizen-Soldiers: ROTC and the Ideology of American Military Service* (Cambridge, MA: Harvard University Press, 2000), 32.

5. John K. Mahon, *History of the Militia and the National Guard* (New York: Macmillan, 1983), 179–84.

6. Dickson, *Rise of the G.I. Army,* 14–16.

7. Ibid. 16.

8. Richard S. Faulkner, *The School of Hard Knocks: Combat Leadership in the American Expeditionary Forces* (College Station: Texas A&M University Press, 2012), 221.

9. Dickson, Rise of the G. I. Army, 16.

10. Brian McAllister Linn, *Guardians of Empire: The U.S. Army and the Pacific, 1902–1940* (Chapel Hill: University of North Carolina Press, 1997), 147.

11. *Report on the Organization of the Land Forces in 1912* (Washington, DC: Government Printing Office, 1912), NA, RG 165, 7280, 10.

BIBLIOGRAPHY

Archival Sources

Library of Congress, Washington, DC

Allen, Major General Henry T., Papers
Bliss, Major General Tasker H., Papers
Breckinridge, Henry S., Papers
Carter, Major General William II., Papers
Harbord, Lieutenant General James G. Harbord, Papers
Hines, Major General John L., Papers
McCoy, Major General Frank R., Papers
March, Major General Peyton C., Papers
Moseley, Major General George Van Horn, Papers
Palmer, Colonel John McAuley, Papers
Patton, Lieutenant General George C., Papers
Pershing, General John J., Papers
Scott, Major General Hugh L., Papers
Summerall, General Charles P., Papers
Wadsworth, James W., Papers
Wood, Major General Leonard, Diary and Papers

National Archives, Washington, DC

Record Group 165, War Department, General and Special Staff, Correspondence File
Record Group 177, Records of the Chiefs of Arms
Entry 9, Chief of Antiaircraft Artillery Records
Entry 34, Chief of Field Artillery Records
Entry 39, Chief of Cavalry Records
Entry 40, Chief of Infantry Records
Record Group 407, Office of the Adjutant General

Command and General Staff College, Fort Leavenworth, KS

Curricular Materials, 1920–1941

U.S. Army Military History Institute (USAMHI), Carlisle, PA

Crittenberger, Lieutenant General Willis D., Papers
Grow, Major General Robert W., Papers
Henry, Major General Guy V., Papers
Kromer, Major General Leon B., Papers
U.S. Army War College Curricular Files

Wisconsin State Historical Society, Madison

Haan, Major General William G., Papers

Official Annual Reports

United States Army

Assistant Secretary of War. *Annual Reports,* 1918–40.
Chief of Staff. *Annual Reports,* 1918–40.
Chief of the Militia Bureau (after 1933, National Guard Bureau), *Annual Reports,* 1919–40.
General Staff, Operations and Training Division, G-3. *Annual Reports,* 1922–38.
General Staff, War Plans Division, *Annual Reports,* 1920–23
Secretary of War. *Annual Reports,* 1918–40.

National Guard

National Guard Association, *Official Proceedings of the National Guard Association of the United State General Conference, 1919–1939*

Contemporary Service Journals

Army Ordnance, 1918–40
Cavalry Journal, 1900–1940
Chemical Warfare, 1920–40
Coast Artillery Journal, 1922–40
Field Artillery Journal, 1911–40
Infantry Journal, 1904–20
Journal of the Military Service Institute, 1900–1917
Journal of the United States Artillery, 1900–1922

Military Engineer, 1918–40
Reserve Officer, 1925–40

Newspapers

Army and Navy Journal, 1918–40
New York Times, 1920–40

Other Published Primary Sources

Baker, Ray S. *Woodrow Wilson: Life and Letters.* Garden City, NY: Doubleday Doran, 1937.

Bland, Larry, and Sharon Ritenour, eds. *The Papers of George Catlett Marshall.* Baltimore: Johns Hopkins University Press, 1981.

Eisenhower, Dwight D. *At Ease: Stories I Tell to Friends.* Garden City, NY: Doubleday, 1967.

March, Peyton. *The Nation at War.* Garden City, NY: Doubleday, 1927.

Snow, William J. *Signposts of Experience.* Fort Sill, OK: U.S. Field Artillery Association, 1941.

Spaulding, Oliver L. *The United States Army in War and Peace.* New York: Putnam 1937.

Truscott, Lucian K., Jr. *The Twilight of the U.S. Cavalry: Life in the Old Army, 1917–1942.* Lawrence: University Press of Kansas, 1989.

United States Army Cavalry School. *Cavalry Combat.* [Fort Riley, KS], 1937.

———. *Mechanized Cavalry.* [Fort Riley, KS: QMC Plant], 1932.

———. *Tanks.* Fort Riley, KS, 1927.

United States Army General Services School. *The Tactical Employment of Tanks in Battle.* Fort Leavenworth, KS: General Services School Press, 1923.

United States Congress. *Army Reorganization: Hearings before the Committee on Military Affairs, House of Representatives, 66th Congress, 1st Session.* Washington, DC: Government Printing Office, 1920.

United States Congress, House of Representatives. *Report to Accompany H.R. 5645: National Guard Bill.* Washington, DC: Government Printing Office, 1933.

United States Congress, Senate Military Affairs Subcommittee. *Hearings before the Sub-Committee on Army Reorganization, August 7–December 17, 1919.* Washington, DC: Government Printing Office, 1920.

United States War Department. General Staff. *FM100-5: Field Service Regulations.* Washington, DC: Government Printing Office, 1923.

———. *Infantry Field Manual.* Vol. 2, *Light Tanks.* Washington, DC: Government Printing Office, 1931.

Secondary Sources

Abrahamson, James L. *America Arms for a New Century: The Making of a Great Military Power*. New York: Free Press, 1981.

Addington, Larry H. "The U.S. Coast Artillery and the Problem of Artillery Organization, 1907–1954." *Military Affairs* 40, no. 1 (Feb. 1976): 1–6.

Ambrose, Stephen E. *Upton and the Army*. Baton Rouge: Louisiana State University Press, 1964.

Anders, Leslie. *Gentle Knight: The Life and Times of Major General Edwin Forrest Harding*. Kent, OH: Kent State University Press, 1985.

Astor, Gerald. *The Right to Fight: A History of African Americans in the Military*. Novato, CA: Presidio, 1998.

Ball, Harry P. *Of Responsible Command: A History of the U.S. Army War College*. Rev. ed. Carlisle Barracks, PA: Alumni Association of the U.S. Army War College, 1984.

Barry, Steven Thomas. *Battalion Commanders at War: U.S. Tactical Leadership in the Mediterranean Theater, 1942–1943*. Lawrence: University Press of Kansas, 2013.

Batchelor, John, and Ian Hogg. *Artillery*. New York: Scribner, 1958.

Beaver, Daniel R. *Newton Baker and the American War Effort, 1917–1919*. Lincoln: University of Nebraska Press, 1966.

Bernardo, Joseph C., and Eugene Bacon. *American Military Policy: Its Development since 1775*. Harrisburg, PA: Military Service Publishing, 1955.

Bigelow, Donald N. *William Conant Church and the Army and Navy Journal*. New York: Columbia University Press, 1952.

Bland, Larry I. "George C. Marshall and the Education of Army Leaders." *Military Review* 118, no. 3 (Oct. 1988): 27–37.

Boyton, Bernard L. "Army Reorganization 1920: The Legislative Story." *Mid America* 40, no. 4 (Apr. 1967): 115–28.

Brewer, Thomas L. "The Impact of Advanced Education on American Military Officers." *Armed Forces and Society* 2, no. 1 (Fall 1975): 63–88.

Buckley, Thomas H., and Edwin B. Strong Jr. *American Foreign and National Security Policies, 1914–1945*. Knoxville: University of Tennessee Press, 1987.

Butterworth, W. E. *Soldiers on Horseback: The Story of the United States Cavalry*. New York: W. W. Norton, 1967.

Carlton, John T., and John F. Slinkman. *The ROA Story*. Washington, DC: Reserve Officers Association of the United States, 1982.

Chambers, John W. *To Raise an Army: The Draft Comes to Modern America*. New York: Free Press, 1987.

Christie, J. Edward. *Steel Steeds Christie*. Manhattan, KS: Sunflower University Press, 1985.

Citino, Robert M. *Armored Forces: History and Sourcebook*. Westport, CT: Greenwood, 1994.

Clark, J. P. *Preparing for War: The Emergence of the Modern U.S. Army, 1815–1917.* Cambridge, MA: Harvard University Press, 2017.

Clemens, Jon. "Waking up for the Dream: The Crisis of Cavalry in the 1930s." *Armor* 99, no. 3 (May/June 1990): 20–23.

Clifford, John G. *The Citizen Soldiers: The Plattsburg Training Camp Movement, 1913–1970.* Lexington: University Press of Kentucky, 1972.

Cline, Ray S. *The Washington Command Post: Operations Division.* U.S. Military History of World War II Green Book. Washington, DC: Government Printing Office, 1951.

Coffman, Edward M. *The Hilt of the Sword: The Career of Peyton C. March.* Madison: University of Wisconsin Press, 1966.

———. *The Regulars: The American Army, 1898–1941.* Cambridge, MA: Belknap Press of Harvard University Press, 2004.

Conn, Stetson. "Changing Concepts of National Defense in the United States, 1937–1947." *Military Affairs* 28, no. 1 (Spring 1964): 1–7.

Cooney, Patrick. "U.S. Armor between the Wars." *Armor* 91, no. 2 (Mar./Apr. 1990): 18–22.

Cooper, Jerry. *The Rise of the National Guard: The Evolution of the American Militia, 1865–1920.* Lincoln: University of Nebraska Press, 1997.

Crossland, Richard B., and James T. Currie. *Twice the Citizen: A History of the United States Reserve, 1903–1983.* Washington, DC: Office of the Chief, Army Reserve, 1984.

Dastrup, Boyd L. *King of Battle: A Branch History of the U.S. Army's Field Artillery.* Fort Monroe, VA: U.S. Army Training and Doctrine Command, 1992.

———. "Travails of Peace and War: Field Artillery in the 1930s and 1940s." *Army History* 25 (Winter 1993): 33–41.

———. *The U.S. Army Command and General Staff College: A Centennial History.* Manhattan, KS: Sunflower University Press, 1982.

Derthick, Martha. *The National Guard in Politics.* Cambridge, MA: Harvard University Press, 1965.

D'Este, Carlo. *Patton: A Genius for War.* New York: HarperCollins, 1995.

Dickson, Paul. *The Rise of the G.I. Army, 1940–1941.* New York: Atlantic Monthly Press 2020.

Dupuy, Richard E. *The Military Heritage of America.* New York: McGraw-Hill, 1956.

———. *The National Guard: A Compact History.* Carmel, IN: Hawthorne, 1971.

Ekirch, Arthur A. *The Civilian and the Military.* New York: Oxford University Press, 1956.

Faulkner, Richard S. *The School of Hard Knocks: Combat Leadership in the American Expeditionary Forces.* College Station: Texas A&M University Press, 2012.

Finlayson, Kenneth. *An Uncertain Trumpet: The Evolution of U. S. Army Infantry Doctrine, 1919–1941.* Westport, CT: Greenwood, 2001.

Finnegan, John P. *Against the Specter of a Dragon: The Campaign for American Military Preparedness, 1914–1917.* Westport, CT: Greenwood, 1975.

Fletcher, Marvin. *The Peacetime Army, 1900–1941: A Research Guide.* Westport, CT: Greenwood, 1988.

Foner, Jack D. *Blacks in the Military in American History: A New Perspective.* Westport, CT: Prager, 1974.

Galloway, Eilene. *History of the United States Military Policy on Reserve Forces, 1775–1957.* Washington, DC: Government Printing Office, 1957.

Ganoe, William A. *The History of the United States Army.* New York: Appleton, 1974.

Gillie, Mildrid H. *Forging the Thunderbolt: A History of the Development of the Armored Force.* Harrisburg, PA: Military Service Publishing, 1947. Reprint, Mechanicsburg, PA: Stackpole, 2006.

Gole, Henry G. *The Road to Rainbow: Army Planning for Global War, 1934–1940.* Annapolis, MD: Naval Institute Press, 2003.

Griffith, Robert K., Jr. *Men Wanted for the U.S. Army: American Experience with an All-Volunteer Army between the World Wars.* Westport, CT: Greenwood, 1982.

Grotelueschen, Mark E. *The AEF Way of War: The American Army and Combat in World War I.* New York: Cambridge University Press, 2007.

Grow, Robert W. "The Ten Lean Years: From the Mechanized Force 1930 to the Armored Force 1940." *Armor* (Jan./Feb. 1987): 22–30; (Mar./Apr. 1987): 25–30; (May/June 1987): 21–28; (July/Aug. 1987): 23–29.

Gunsburg, Jeffrey A. "Samuel Dickenson Rockenbach: Father of the Tank Corps." *Virginia Cavalcade* (Summer 1976): 39–47.

Hacker, Barton C. "Imagination in Thrall: The Social Psychology of Military Mechanization, 1919–1939." *Parameters* 12, no. 1 (Spring 1982): 50–61.

Hagan, Kenneth J., and William P. Roberts. *Against All Enemies: Interpretations of American Military History from Colonial Times to the Present.* Westport, CT: Greenwood, 1986.

Hagedorn, Herman. *Leonard Wood: A Biography.* 2 vols. New York: Harper, 1931.

Hammond, Paul Y. *Organizing for Defense: The American Military Establishment in the Twentieth Century.* Princeton, NJ: Princeton University Press, 1961.

Hassler, Warren W. *With Sword and Shield: American Military Affairs, Colonial Times to the Present.* Ames: Iowa State University Press, 1982.

Hawkes, James H. "Antimilitarism at State Universities: The Campaign against Compulsry ROTC, 1920–1940." *Wisconsin Magazine of History* 49, no. 1 (Autumn,1965): 41–54.

Hechler, Kenneth. *History of the Armored Force.* Washington, DC: Historical Section, Army Ground Forces, 1946.

Hendrix, John T. "The Interwar Army and Mechanization: The American Approach." *Journal of Strategic Studies* 16, no. 1 (Mar. 1983): 75–108.

Herr, John K., and Edward S. Wallace, *The Story of the U.S. Cavalry, 1775–1942.* New York: Little Brown, 1953.

Hewes, James E., Jr. *From Root to McNamara: Army Organization and Administration, 1904–1963.* Washington, DC: Center for Military History, 1975.

Higham, Robin, ed. *A Guide to the Sources of United States Military History* New York: Archon, 1975.

Hill, Jim D. *The Minute Man in Peace and War: A History of the National Guard.* Mechanicsburg, PA: Stackpole, 1964.

Hoffmann, George F. "The Troubled History of the Christy Tank." *Army* (May 1986): 54–65.

———. "A Yankee Inventor and the Military Establishment: The Christie Tank Controversy." *Military Affairs* 39, no. 1 (Feb. 1975): 12–18.

Hoffmann, George F., and Donn A. Starry, eds. *Camp Colt to Desert Storm: The History of U.S. Armored Forces.* Lexington: University Press of Kentucky, 1999.

Hogg, Ian V. *A History of Artillery.* London: Hamlyn, 1974.

Holley, Irving B., Jr. *General John M. Palmer, Citizen Soldiers, and the Army of a Democracy.* Westport, CT: Greenwood, 1982.

House, Jonathan M. "John McAuley Palmer and the Reserve Components." *Parameters* 12, no. 3 (Sept. 1982): 19–26.

———. *Towards Combined Arms Warfare: A Survey of Tactics, Doctrine, and Organization in the Twentieth Century.* Fort Leavenworth, KS: U.S. Command and General Staff School, 1984.

Huntington, Samuel P. *The Soldier and the State: The Theory and Politics of Civil-Military Relations.* New York: Knopf, 1957.

Huzar, Elias. *The Purse and the Sword: Control of the Army by Congress through Military Appropriations, 1933–1950.* Ithaca, NY: Cornell University Press, 1950.

James, D. Clayton. *The Years of MacArthur.* Vol. 1, *1880–1941.* Boston: Houghton-Mifflin, 1970.

Janowitz, Morris. *The Professional Soldier.* New York: Free Press, 1969.

Johnson, David E. *Fast Tanks and Heavy Bombers: Innovation in the U.S. Army, 1917–1945.* Ithaca, NY: Cornell University Press, 1998.

Jones, Ralph E., George Rarey, and Robert J. Icks. *The Fighting Tanks since 1916.* Washington, DC: National Services Publishing, 1933.

Karsten, Peter, ed. *The Military in America.* New York: Free Press, 1980.

Kaufmann, J. E., and H. W. Kaufmann. *The Sleeping Giant: American Armed Forces between the Wars.* Westport, CT: Praeger, 1996.

Kemble, C. Robert. *The Image of the Army Officer in America: Background for Current Views.* Westport, CT: Greenwood, 1973.

Killigrew, John W. *The Impact of the Great Depression on the Army.* New York: Garland, 1960.

Kington, Donald M. *Forgotten Summers: The Story of the Citizens Military Training Camps, 1921–1940.* San Francisco: Two Decades, 1995.

Kinnell, Susan K. *Military History of the United States: An Annotated Bibliography.* Westport, CT: ABC-CLIO, 1986.

Kriedburg, Marvin A., and Merton G. Henry. *History of Military Mobilization in the United States Army, 1775–1945.* Washington, DC: Department of the Army, 1955.

Lane, Jack C. *America's Military Past: A Guide to Information Sources.* Farmington Hills, MI: Gale Research, 1980.

———. *Armed Progressive: Genera Leonard Wood.* Novato, CA: Presidio, 1978.

Lane, Winthrop D. *Military Training in Schools and Colleges in the United States: Facts and an Inpression.* New York: Committee on Military Training, 1926.

Lanning, M. L. *The African American Soldier from Crispus Attucks to Colin Powell.* New York: Birch Lane, 1997.

Lewis, Emanuel R. *Seacoast Fortifications of the United States: An Introductory History.* Washington, DC: Smithsonian Institution Press, 1970.

Linn, Brian McAllister. *The Echo of Battle: The Army's Way of War.* Cambridge, MA: Harvard University Press, 2007.

———. *Guardians of Empire: The U.S. Army and the Pacific, 1902–1940.* Chapel Hill: University of North Carolina Press, 1997.

Lowenthal, Mark, M. "Roosevelt and the Coming of the War: The Search for a United States Policy, 1937–1941." *Journal of Contemporary History* 16, no. 3 (Fall 1981): 413–40.

Lyons, Gene M., and John W. Masland. *Education and Military Leadership: A Study of the R.O.T.C.* Princeton, NJ: Princeton University Press, 1959.

———. "The Origins of ROTC." *Military Affairs* 23, no. 1 (Spring 1959): 1–12.

Macksey, Kenneth J. *Tank: A History of the Armoured Fighting Vehicles.* New York: Scribner, 1970.

———. *Tank Warfare: A History of Tanks in Battle.* New York: Stein and Day, 1972.

Mahon, John K. *History of the Militia and the National Guard.* New York: Macmillan, 1983.

Matheny, Michael R. *Carrying the War to the Enemy: American Operational Art to 1945.* Norman: University of Oklahoma Press, 2011.

Matloff, Maurice. *American Military History.* Washington, DC: Office of the Chief of Military History, U.S. Army, 1969.

McKenny, James E. "More Bang for the Buck in the Interwar Army: The 105mm Howitzer." *Military Affairs* 42, no. 4 (Winter 1978): 80–86.

Miller, Edward C. "Armor's First Struggle." *Armor* 94, no. 2 (Feb. 1985): 13–17.

Millett, Allan R., and Peter Maslowski. *For the Common Defense: A Military History of the United States of America.* New York: Free Press, 1984.

Millett, Allan R., and Williamson Murray, eds. *Military Effectiveness.* Boston: Unwin Hyman, 1988.

Millis, Walter. *Arms and Men.* New York: Putnam, 1956.

Mitchie, Peter S. *The Life and Letters of Emory Upton.* New York: Appleton, 1885. Reprint, New York: Arno, 1979.

Murray, Wiliamson, and Allen R. Millett. *Military Innovation in the Interwar Period.* Cambridge: Cambridge University Press, 1996.

Muth, Jorg. *Command Culture: Officer Education in the U.S. Army and the German Armed Forces, 1901–1940, and the Consequences for World War II.* Denton: University of North Texas, 2011.

Nalty, Bernard C. *Strength for the Fight: A History of Blacks in the Military.* New York: Free Press, 1986.

Nelson, Otto M. *National Security and the General Staff.* Fort Benning, GA: *Infantry Journal,* 1946.

Neiberg, Michael S. *Making Citizen-Soldiers: ROTC and the Ideology of American Military Service.* Cambridge, MA: Harvard University Press, 2000.

Nenninger, Timothy K. "Creating Officers: The Leavenworth Experience, 1920–1940." *Military Review* 69, no. 5 (Nov. 1989): 58–68.

———. "The Development of American Armor, 1917–1940." *Armor* 78, no. 1 (Jan./Feb. 1969): 46–51; 78, no. 2 (Mar./Apr. 1969). 34–38; 78, no. 3 (May/June 1969): 33–39; 78, no. 5 (Sept./Oct. 1969): 45–49.

———. "Leavenworth and Its Critics: The U.S. Army and General Staff School, 1920–1940." *Journal of Military History* 58, no. 2 (Apr. 1994): 199–232.

———. *The Leavenworth Schools and the Old Army: Education, Professionalism, and the Officer Corps of the U.S. Army, 1881–1918.* Westport, CT: Greenwood, 1978.

Odom, William O. *After the Trenches: The Transformation of the U.S. Army, 1918–1939.* College Station: Texas A&M University Press, 2008.

Orgill, Douglas *The Tank: Studies in the Development and Use of a Weapon.* London: Heineman, 1970.

Palmer, John M. *America in Arms: The Experience of the United States with Military Organization.* New Haven, CT: Yale University Press, 1941. Reprint, New York: Arno, 1979).

———. *An Army of the People: The Constitution of an Effective Force of Trained Citizens.* New York: Putnam, 1916.

Pappas, George S. *Prudens Futuri: The US Army War College, 1901–1967.* Carlisle Barracks, PA: Alumni Association of the U.S. Army War College, 1967.

Patton, Gerald W. *War and Peace: The Black Officer in the American Military, 1915–1941.* Westport, CT: Greenwood, 1981.

Paxson, Frederic L. *The Great Demobilization and Other Essays.* Madison: University of Wisconsin Press, 1941.

Peake, Louis A. "West Virginia's Best-Known Soldier since Stonewall Jackson, John L. Hines." *West Virginia History* 38 (Apr. 1977): 226–35.

Pearlman, Michael. *To Make Democracy Safe of America.* Champaign: University of Illinois Press, 1984.

Pearson, LeRoy. "Major General William G. Haan." *Michigan History* 9 (Jan. 1925): 3–16.

Pogue, Forrest C. *George C. Marshall: Education of a General, 1880–1939.* 4 vols. New York: Viking, 1962–87.

Pollard, James E. *Military Training in the Land-Grant Colleges and Universities.* Washington, DC: Association of State Universities and Land-Grant Colleges, 1962.

Ramey, Rufus. S. *He's in the Cavalry Now.* New York: Robert McBride, 1944.

Raugh, Harold E., Jr. "Pershing and Marshal: A Study in Mentorship." *Army* 38, no. 6 (June 1987): 52–63.

Riker, William H. *Soldiers of the States: The Role of the National Guard in American Democracy.* New York: Public Affairs, 1957.

Ross, Stephen T. *American War Plans, 1919–41.* New York: Garland, 1992.

Schaffer, Ronald. "The War Department's Defense of ROTC, 1920–1940." *Wisconsin Magazine of History* 53, no. 2 (Winter 1969–70): 108–20.

Schrier, Konrad F., Jr. "U.S. Army Tank Development, 1928–1940." *Armor* 99, no. 3 (May/June 1990): 24–29.

Segal, David. *Recruiting for Uncle Sam: Citizenship and Military Manpower.* Lawrence: University Press of Kansas, 1985.

Smythe, Donald. *Pershing: General of the Armies.* Bloomington: Indiana University Press, 1984.

Steffan, Randy. *The Horse Soldier, 1776–1943.* Norman: University of Oklahoma Press, 1978.

Stewart, Richard W. *American Military History.* Vol. 2: *The United States Army in a Global Era, 1917–2008.* Washington, DC: U.S. Army Center for Military History, 2016.

Sunderland, Riley. *History of the Field Artillery School.* Vol. 1, *1911–1942.* Fort Sill, OK: U.S. Field Artillery School, 1942.

Twichel, Heath. *Allen: The Biography of an Army Officer, 1859–1930.* New Brunswick, NJ: Rutgers University Press, 1974.

United States Army Command and General Staff College. *A Military History of the U.S. Army Command and General Staff College, 1881–1963.* Fort Leavenworth, KS: Command and General Staff College, 1964.

United States Field Artillery School. *History of the Development of Field Artillery Material.* Fort Sill, OK: Field Artillery School, 1941.

———. *Right of the Line: A History of American Field Artillery.* Fort Sill, OK: Field Artillery School, 1977.

Upton, Emory. *The Armies of Asia and Europe.* 1878. Reprint, Westport, CT: Greenwood, 1968.

———. *The Military Policy of the United States.* 1904. Reprint, Westport, CT: Greenwood, 1968.

Van Creveld, Martin. "The Training of Officers: From Military Professionalism to Irrelevance," *Military History Quarterly* 2, no. 3 (Spring 1990): 64–72.

Vandiver, Frank E. *Black Jack: The Life and Times of John J. Pershing.* College Station: Texas A&M University Press, 1977.

Vigman, Fred K., "The Theoretical Evaluation of Artillery after World War I." *Military Affairs* 16, no. 3 (Fall 1952): 115–18.

Vogel, Victor. *Soldiers of the Old Army*. College Station: Texas A&M University, 1990.

Wakefield, Wanda E. *Playing for War: Sports and the American Military, 1898–1945*. Albany: State University of New York Press, 1997.

Washburn, Charles G. *The Life of John W. Weeks*. Boston: Houghton Mifflin, 1928.

Watson, Mark S. *Chief of Staff: Prewar Plans and Preparations*. US Military History of World War II Green Book. Washington, DC: Government Printing Office, 1950.

Weigley, Russell F. *The American Way of War: A History of United States Military Strategy and Policy*. New York: Macmillan, 1973.

———. *History of the United States Army*. 1967. Reprint, Bloomington: Indiana University Press, 1984.

———. *Towards an American Army: Military Thought from Washington to Marshall*. New York: Columbia University Press, 1962.

Whisker, James B. *The Citizen Soldier and United States Army Policy*. Great Harrington, MA: North River, 1979.

Willeford, Charles. *Something about a Soldier*. New York: Random House, 1986.

Wilson, Dale E. *Treat 'em Rough: The Birth of American Armor, 1917–1920*. Novato, CA: Presidio, 1989.

Dissertations

Hamburger, Kenneth E. "The Technology, Doctrine, and Politics of U.S. Coast Defense, 1880–1945." PhD diss., Duke University, 1986.

Hirshauer, Victor B. "The History of the Army Reserve Officers Training Corps, 1916–1973." PhD diss., Johns Hopkins University, 1975.

Pohl, James W. "The General Staff and American Military Policy: The Formative Years, 1898–1917." PhD diss., University of Texas, 1967.

CPSIA information can be obtained
at www.ICGtesting.com
Printed in the USA
BVHW051135240722
642728BV00001B/1/J